Sea Battles

The Battle of Trafalgar

Sea Battles
A thousand years of naval conflict
Salamis to Tsu-Shima 480 BC - 1905

John Richard Hale

Sea Battles
A thousand years of naval conflict
Salamis to Tsu-Shima 480 BC - 1905
by John Richard Hale

First published under the title
Famous Sea Fights

Leonaur is an imprint
of Oakpast Ltd

Copyright in this form © 2009 Oakpast Ltd

ISBN: 978-1-84677-970-1 (hardcover)
ISBN: 978-1-84677-969-5 (softcover)

http://www.leonaur.com

Publisher's Notes

In the interests of authenticity, the spellings, grammar and place names used have been retained from the original editions.

The opinions of the authors represent a view of events in which he was a participant related from his own perspective, as such the text is relevant as an historical document.

The views expressed in this book are not necessarily those of the publisher.

Contents

Introduction	7
Salamis B.C. 480	9
Actium B.C. 31	32
The Battle of Svold Island A.D. 1000	47
Sluys 1340	62
Lepanto 1571	75
The Great Armada 1588	117
The Battle off the Gunfleet 1666	154
The Battle of the Saints' Passage 1782	170
Trafalgar 1805	186
The Coming of Steam and Armoured Navies	219
Lissa 1866	248
The Battle of the Yalu 1894	270
Santiago De Cuba 1898	294
Tsu-Shima 1905	315

Introduction

Three hundred years ago Francis Bacon wrote, amongst otherwise words:

To be Master of the Sea is an Abridgement of Monarchy.... The Bataille of Actium decided the Empire of the World. The Bataille of Lepanto arrested the Greatnesse of the Turke. There be many Examples where Sea-Fights have been Finall to the Warre. But this much is certaine; that hee that commands the Sea is at great liberty, and may take as much and as little of the Warre as he will. Whereas those, that be strongest by land, are many times neverthelesse in great Straights. Surely, at this Day, with us of Europe, the Vantage of Strength at Sea (which is one of the Principall Dowries of this Kingdome of Greate Brittaine) is Great; Both because Most of the Kingdomes of Europe are not merely Inland, but girt with the Sea most part of their Compasse; and because the Wealth of both Indies seemes in great Part but an Accessary to the Command of the Seas.[1]

The three centuries that have gone by since this was written have afforded ample confirmation of the view here set forth, as to the importance of "Battailes by Sea" and the supreme value of the "Command of the Sea." Not only "we of Europe," but our kindred in America and our allies in Far Eastern Asia have now their proudly cherished memories of decisive naval victory.

---
1. Bacon's Essay on *The Greatness of Kingdoms*, first published in 1597. The extract is from the edition of 1625.

I propose to tell in non-technical and popular language the story of some of the most remarkable episodes in the history of sea power. I shall begin with the first sea-fight of which we have a detailed history—the Battle of Salamis (B.C. 480), the victory by which Themistocles the Athenian proved the soundness of his maxim that "he who commands the sea commands all." I shall end with the last and greatest of naval engagements, the Battle of Tsu-shima, an event that reversed the long experience of victory won by West over East, which began with Salamis more than two thousand years ago. I shall have to tell of British triumphs on the sea from Sluys to Trafalgar; but I shall take instances from the history of other countries also, for it is well that we should remember that the skill, enterprise, and courage of admirals and seamen is no exclusive possession of our own people.

I shall incidentally describe the gradual evolution of the warship from the wooden, oar-driven galleys that fought in the Straits of Salamis to the steel-built, steam-propelled giants that met in battle in the Straits of Tsu-shima. I shall have something to say of old seafaring ways, and much to tell of the brave deeds done by men of many nations. These true stories of the sea will, I trust, have not only the interest that belongs to all records of courage, danger, and adventure, but also some practical lessons of their own, for they may help to keep alive that intelligent popular interest in sea power which is the best guarantee that the interests of our own navy—the best safeguard of the Empire—will not be neglected, no matter what Government is in power, or what political views may happen for the moment to be in the ascendant.

J.R.H.

Chapter 1

Salamis B.C. 480

The world has lost all record of the greatest of its inventors—the pioneers who in far-off ages devised the simple appliances with which men tilled the ground, did their domestic work, and fought their battles for thousands of years. He who hung up the first weaver's beam and shaped the first rude shuttle was a more wonderful inventor than Arkwright. The maker of the first bow and arrow was a more enterprising pioneer than our inventors of machine-guns. And greater than the builders of *Dreadnoughts* were those who "with hearts girt round with oak and triple brass" were the first to trust their frail *barques* to "the cruel sea." No doubt the hollowed tree trunk, and the coracle of osiers and skins, had long before this made their trial trips on river and lake. Then came the first ventures in the shallow sea-margins, and at last a primitive naval architect built up planked bulwarks round his hollowed tree trunk, and stiffened them with ribs of bent branches, and the first ship was launched.

This evolution of the ship must have been in progress independently in more places than one. We are most concerned with its development in that eastern end of the land-locked Mediterranean, which is the meeting-place of so many races, and around which so much of what is most momentous in the world's history has happened. There seems good reason for believing that among the pioneers in early naval construction were the men of that marvellous people of old Egypt to whom the world's civilization owes so much. They had doubtless learned their work on their own Nile before they pushed out by the channels of the Delta to the waters of the "Great Sea." They had invented the sail, though it was centuries before any one learned to do more than scud before the wind. It took long experience of the sea to discover that one could fix one's sail at an oblique angle with the mid-line of the ship, and play off rudder against sail to lay a course with the wind on the quarter or even abeam and not dead astern.

But there was as important an invention as the sail—that of the oar. We are so familiar with it, that we do not realize all it means. Yet it is a notable fact that whole races of men who navigate river, lake, and sea, successfully and boldly, never hit upon the principle of the oar till they were taught it by Europeans, and could of themselves get no further than the paddle. The oar, with its leverage, its capacity for making the very weight of the crew become a motive power, became in more senses than one the great instrument of progress on the sea. It gave the ship a power of manœuvring independently of the wind, the same power that is the essence of advantage in steam propulsion. The centuries during which the sailing ship was the chief reliance of navigation and commerce were, after all, an episode between the long ages when the oar-driven galley was the typical ship, and the present age of steam beginning less than a hundred years ago.

Sails were an occasional help to the early navigator. Our songs of the sea call them the "white wings" of the ship. For the Greek poet Æschylus, the wings of the ship were the long oars. The trader creeping along the coast or working from island to island helping himself when the wind served with his sail, and having only a small crew, could not afford much oar-power, though he had often to trust to it. But for the fighting ship, oar-power and speed were as important as mechanical horse-power is for the warships of the twentieth century. So the war galley was built longer than the trader, to make room for as many oars as possible on either side. In the Mediterranean in those early days, as with the Vikings of later centuries, the "Long Ship" meant the ship of war.

It is strange to reflect that all through human history war has been a greater incentive to shipbuilding progress than peaceful commerce. For those early navigators the prizes to be won by fighting and raiding were greater than any that the more prosaic paths of trade could offer. The fleets that issued from the Delta of the Nile were piratical squadrons, that were the terrors of the Mediterranean coasts. The Greek, too, like the Norseman, began his career on the sea with piracy. The Athenian historian tells of days when it was no offence to ask a seafaring man, "Are you a pirate, sir?"

The first Admirals of the Eastern Mediterranean had undoubtedly more likeness to Captain Kidd and "Blackbeard" than to Nelson and Collingwood. Later came the time when organized Governments in the Greek cities and on the Phœnician coast kept fleets on the land-locked sea to deal with piracy and protect peaceful commerce. But the prizes that allured the corsair were so tempting, that piracy revived again and again, and even in the late days of the Roman Republic the Consul Pompey had to conduct a maritime war on a large scale to clear the sea of the pirates.

Of the early naval wars of the Mediterranean—battles of more or less piratical fleets, or of the war galleys of coast and island states—we have no clear record, or no vestige of a record. Egyptians, Phœnicians, Cretans, men of the rich island state of which we have only recently found the remains in buried palaces, Greeks of the Asiatic mainland, and their Eastern neighbours, Greeks of the islands and the Peninsula, Illyrians of the labyrinth of creek and island that fringes the Adriatic, Sicilians and Carthaginians, all had their adventures and battles on the sea, in the dim beginnings of history.

Homer has his catalogue of ships set forth in stately verse, telling how the Greek chieftains led 120,000 warriors embarked on 1100 galleys to the siege of Troy. But no hostile fleet met them, if indeed the great armament ever sailed, as to which historians and critics dispute. One must pass on for centuries after Homer's day to find reliable and detailed records of early naval war. The first great battle on the sea, of which we can tell the story, was the fight in the Straits of Salamis, when Greek and Persian strove for the mastery of the near East.

King Darius had found that his hold on the Greek cities of Asia Minor was insecure so long as they could look for armed help to their kindred beyond the Archipelago, and he had sent his satraps to raid the Greek mainland. That first invasion ended disastrously at Marathon. His son, Xerxes, took up the quarrel and devoted years to the preparation not of a raid upon Europe, but of an invasion in which the whole power of his vast empire was to be put forth by sea and land.

It was fortunate for Greece that the man who then counted for most in the politics of Athens was one who recognized the all-importance of sea-power, though it is likely that at the outset all he had in mind was that the possession of an efficient fleet would enable his city to exert its influence on the islands and among the coast cities to the exclusion of the military power of its rival Sparta. When it was proposed that the product of the silver mines of Laurium should be distributed among the Athenian citizens, it was Themistocles who persuaded his fellow-countrymen that a better investment for the public wealth would be found in the building and equipment of a fleet.

He used as one of his arguments the probability that the Persian King would, sooner or later, try to avenge the defeat of Marathon. A no less effective argument was the necessity of protecting their growing commerce. Athens looked upon the sea, and that sea at once divided and united the scattered Greek communities who lived on the coasts and islands of the Archipelago. It was the possession of the fleet thus acquired that enabled Themistocles and Athens to play a decisive part in the crisis of the struggle with Asia.

It was in the spring of B.C. 480 that the march from Asia Minor began. The vast multitude gathered from every land in Western Asia, from the shores of the Mediterranean to the Persian Gulf and the wild mountain plateaux of the Indian border, was too numerous to be transported in any fleet that even the Great King could assemble. For seven days and nights it poured across the floating bridge that swayed with the current of the Dardanelles, a bridge that was a wonder of early military engineering, and the making of which would tax the resources of the best army of today.

Then it marched by the coast-line through what is now Roumelia and Thessaly. It ate up the supplies of the lands through which it passed. If it was to escape famine it must keep in touch with the ships that crossed and recrossed the narrow seas, bringing heavy cargoes of food and forage from the ports of Asia, and escorted by squadrons of long war galleys.

Every Greek city had been warned of the impending danger. Even those who remembered Marathon, the day when a few thousand spearmen had routed an Asiatic horde outnumbering them tenfold, realized that any force that now could be put in the field would be overwhelmed by this human tide of a million fighting men. But there was one soldier-statesman who saw the way to safety, and grasped the central fact of the situation. This was Themistocles the Athenian, the chief man of that city, against which the first fury of the attack would be directed. No doubt it was he who inspired the prophetess of Delphi with her mysterious message that "the Athenians must make for themselves wooden walls," and he supplied the explanation of the enigma.

The Persian must be met not on the land, but in "wooden walls" upon the sea. Victory upon that element would mean the destruction of the huge army on land. The greater its numbers the more helpless would be its position. It could not live upon "the country"; there must be a continual stream of sea-borne supplies arriving from Asia, and this would be interrupted and cease altogether once the Greeks were masters of the sea.

The Athens of the time was not the wonderful city that arose in later years, embellished by the masterpieces of some of the greatest architects and artists the world has ever known. The houses huddled round the foot of the citadel hill—the Acropolis—which was crowned with rudely built primitive temples. But the people whose home it was were startled by the proposal of Themistocles that their city should be abandoned to the enemy without one blow struck in its defence. Not Athens only, but every village and farm in the surrounding country was to be deserted. Men, women, and children, horses and cattle, were all to be conveyed across the narrow strait to the island of Salamis, which was to be the temporary refuge of the citizens of Athens and of the country-folk of Attica.

Would they ever return to their ruined homes and devastated lands, where they would find houses burned, and vines and olives cut down? Could they even hope to maintain themselves in Salamis? Would it not be better to fight in defence of their homes even against desperate odds and meet their fate at once, instead of only deferring the evil day? It was no easy task for the man of the moment to persuade his fellow-countrymen to adopt his own far-sighted plans. Even when most of them had accepted his leadership and were obeying his orders, a handful of desperate men refused to go. They took refuge on the hill of the Acropolis, and acting upon the literal meaning of the oracle toiled with axe and hammer, building up wooden barriers before the gates of the old citadel.

Everywhere else the city and the country round were soon deserted. The people streamed down to the shore and were ferried over to Salamis, where huts of straw and branches rose up in wide extended camps to shelter the crowds that could find no place in the island villages. In every wood on either shore trees were being felled. In every creek shipwrights were busy night and day building new ships or refitting old. To every Greek seaport messages had been sent, begging them to send to the Straits of Salamis as many ships, oarsmen, and fighting men as they could muster.

Slowly the Persian army moved southward through Thessaly. A handful of Spartans, under Leonidas, had been sent forward to delay the Persian advance. They held the Pass of Thermopylæ, between the eastern shoulder of Mount Æta and the sea. It was a hopeless position. To fight there at all with such an insignificant force was a mistake. But the Government of Sparta, slaves to tradition, could not grasp the idea of the plans proposed by the great Athenian. They were half persuaded to recall Leonidas, but hesitated to act until it was too late. The Spartan chief and his few hundred warriors died at their post in self-sacrificing obedience to the letter of their orders.

The Persians poured over the Pass and inundated the plains of Attica. The few Athenians who had persisted in defending the Acropolis of Athens made only a brief resistance against overwhelming numbers. They were all put to the sword and their fellow-countrymen in the island of Salamis saw far off the pall of smoke that hung over their city, where temples and houses alike were sacked and set on fire by the victors.

The winds and waves had already been fighting for the Greeks. The Persian war fleet of 1200 great ships had coasted southwards by the shores of Thessaly till they neared the group of islands off the northern point of Euboea. Their scouts reported a Greek fleet to be lying in the channel between the large island and the mainland. Night was coming on, and the Persians anchored in eight long lines off Cape Sepias. As the sun rose there came one of those sudden gales from the eastward that are still the terror of small craft in the Archipelago. A modern sailor would try to beat out to seaward and get as far as possible from the dangerous shore, but these old-world seamen dreaded the open sea.

They tried to ride out the gale, but anchors dragged and hundreds of ships were piled in shattered masses on the shore. Some were stranded in positions where they could be repaired and refloated as the weather cleared up; but by the evening of the third day, when at last the wind fell, only eight hundred galleys of the Persian armada were still in seaworthy fighting condition.

Here, as on other occasions, the very numbers of the Persian fleet proved a source of danger to it. The harbours that could give shelter to this multitude of ships were very few and far between, nor was it an easy matter to find that other refuge of the ancient navigator—a beach of easy slope and sufficiently wide extent to enable the ships to be dragged out of the water and placed high and dry beyond the reach of the angriest waves. The fact that ships were beached and hauled up the shore during bad weather, and in winter, limited their size, and in both the Persian and the Greek fleets there probably was not a ship much bigger than the barges we see on our canals, or as big as some of the largest sea-going barges.

The typical warship of the period of the Persian War was probably not more than eighty or a hundred feet long, narrow, and nearly flat-bottomed. At the bow and stern there was a strongly built deck. Between this poop and forecastle a lighter deck ran fore and aft, and under this were the stations of the rowers. The bow was strengthened with plates of iron or brass, and beams of oak, to enable it to be used as a ram, and the stern rose above the deck level and was carved into the head of some bird or beast. There was a light mast which could be rigged up when the wind served, and carried a cross-yard and a square sail. Mast and yard were taken down before going into action.

The Greeks called their war galleys *trieres*, the Romans *triremes*, and these names are generally explained as meaning that the ships were propelled by three banks or rows of oars placed one above the other on either side. The widely accepted theory of how they were worked is that the seats of the rowers were placed, not directly above each other, but that those who worked the lowest and shortest oars were close to the side of the ship, the men for the middle range of oars a little above them and further inboard, and the upper tier of rowers still higher and near the centre-line of the ship.

An endless amount of erudition and research has been expended on this question; but most of those who have dealt with it have been classical scholars possessing little or no practical acquaintance with seafaring conditions, and none of their proposed arrangements of three banks of oars looks at all likely to be workable and effective. A practical test of the theory was made by Napoleon III when his *History of Julius Cæsar* was being prepared. He had a *trireme* constructed and tried upon the Seine. There were three banks of oars, but though the fitting and arrangement was changed again and again under the joint advice of classical experts and practical seamen, no satisfactory method of working the superposed banks of oars could be devised.

The probability is that no such method of working was ever generally employed, and that the belief in the existence of old-world navies made up of ships with tier on tier of oars on either side is the outcome of a misunderstanding as to the meaning of a word. *Trieres* and *trireme* seems at first glance to mean triple-oared, in the sense of the oars being triplicated; but there are strong arguments for the view that it was not the oars but the oarsmen, who were arranged in "threes."

If this view is correct, the ancient warship was a galley with a single row of long oars on either side, and three men pulling together each heavy oar. We know that in the old navies of the Papal States and the Republics of Venice and Genoa in the Middle Ages and the days of the Renaissance, and in the royal galleys of the old French monarchy, there were no ships with superposed banks of oars, but there were galleys known as "*triremes*," "*quadriremes*," and "*pentaremes*," driven by long oars each worked by three, four, or five rowers. It is at least very likely that this was the method adopted in the warships of still earlier times.

A *trireme* of the days of the Persian War with fifty or sixty oars would thus have a crew of 150 or 180 rowers. Add to this some fifty or sixty fighting men and we have a total crew of over two hundred. In the Persian navies the rowers were mostly slaves, like the galley slaves of later times. They were chained to their oars, and kept in order or roused to exertion by the whip of their taskmasters. To train them to work together effectively required a long apprenticeship, and in rough water their work was especially difficult.

To miss the regular time of the stroke was dangerous, for the long oars projecting far inboard would knock down and injure the nearest rowers, unless all swung accurately together. The flat-bottomed galleys rolled badly in a heavy sea, and in rough weather rowing was fatiguing and even perilous work.

Some two hundred men in a small ship meant crowded quarters, and lack of room everywhere except on the fighting deck. But as the fleets hugged the shore, and generally lay up for the night, the crews could mostly land to cook, eat, and sleep. In the Persian ships belonging to many nations, and some of them to the Greek cities of Asia, Xerxes took the precaution of having at least thirty picked Persian warriors in each crew. Their presence was intended to secure the fidelity of the rest.

In the Greek fleet the rowers were partly slaves, partly freemen impressed or hired for the work. Then there were a few seamen, fishermen, or men who in the days of peace manned the local coasting craft. The chiefs of this navigating party were the *keleustes*, who presided over the rowers and gave the signal for each stroke, and the pilot, who was supposed to have a knowledge of the local waters and of wind and weather, and who acted as steersman, handling alone, or with the help of his assistants, the long stern oar that served as a rudder. The fighting men were not sailors, but soldiers embarked to fight afloat, and their military chief commanded the ship, with the help of the pilot. For more than two thousand years this division between the sailor and the fighting element in navies continued throughout the world. The fighting commander and the sailing-master were two different men, and the captain of a man-of-war was often a landsman.

In the Greek fleet which lay sheltered in the narrows, behind the long island of Eubœa while the Persians were battling with the tempest off Cape Sepias, the Admiral was the Spartan Eurybiades, a veteran general, who knew more about forming a phalanx of spearmen than directing the movements of a fleet. The military reputation of his race had secured for him the chief command, though of the whole fleet of between three and four hundred *triremes*, less than a third had been provided by Sparta and her allies, and half of the armada was formed of the well-equipped Athenian fleet, commanded by Themistocles in person. As the storm abated the fleets faced each other in the strait north of Eubœa.

In the Persian armada the best ships were five long galleys commanded by an Amazon queen, Artemisia of Halicarnassus, a Greek fighting against Greeks. She scored the first success, swooping down with her squadron on a Greek galley that had ventured to scout along the Persian front in the grey of the morning. Attacked by the five the ship was taken, and the victors celebrated their success by hanging the commander over the prow of his ship, cutting his throat and letting his blood flow into the sea, an offering to the gods of the deep. The cruel deed was something that inspired no particular sense of horror in those days of heathen war. It was probably not on account of this piece of barbarity, but out of their anger at being opposed by a woman, and a Greek woman, that the allied leaders of Greece set a price on the head of the Amazon queen; but no one ever succeeded in qualifying to claim it.

The Persians, hoping to gain an advantage from their superior numbers, now detached a squadron which was to coast along the eastern shores of Eubœa, enter the strait at its southern end, and fall on the rear of the Greeks, while the main body attacked them in front. Eurybiades and Themistocles had early intelligence of this movement, but were not alarmed by it. Shortly before sunset the Greeks bore down on the Persians, attacked them in the narrow waters where their numbers could not tell, sank some thirty ships by ramming them, and then drew off as the night came on.

It was a wild night. The Greeks had hardly regained their sheltered anchorage when the wind rose, lightning played round the mountain crests on either hand, the thunder rolled and the rain came down in torrents. The main Persian fleet, in a less sheltered position, found it difficult to avoid disaster, and the crews were horrified at seeing as the lightning lit up the sea masses of debris and swollen corpses of drowned men drifting amongst them as the currents brought the wreckage of the earlier storm floating down from beyond Cape Sepias. The hundred ships detached to round the south point of Eubœa were still slowly making their way along its rocky eastern coast. Caught in the midnight storm most of them drove ashore and were dashed to pieces.

In the morning the sea was still rough, but the Greeks came out of the strait, and, without committing themselves to a general action, fell upon the nearest ships, the squadron of Cilicia, and sank and captured several of them, retiring when the main fleet began to close upon them. On the third day the sea was calm and the Persians tried to force the narrows by a frontal attack. There was some hard fighting and loss on both sides, but the Greeks held their own. As the sun set the Persians rowed back towards their anchorage inside Cape Sepias.

When the sun rose again the Greek fleet had disappeared. Eurybiades and Themistocles had agreed in the night after the battle that the time was come to abandon the defence of the Eubœan Strait and retire to the waters of Salamis. The Persian army was now flooding the mainland with its myriads of fighting men, and was master of Attica. A fleet, depending so much on the land for supplies and for rest for its crews, could not maintain itself in the straits when the Persians held the mainland and were in a position to seize also the island of Eubœa.

Before sunrise the Greek ships were working their way in long procession through the Strait of Negropont. Early in the day they began to pass one by one the narrows at Chalcis, now spanned by a bridge. Then the strait widened, and there were none to bar their way to the open sea, and round Cape Sunium to their sheltered station in the straits behind the island of Salamis.

They had been reinforced on the way, and they now numbered 366 fighting ships. Those of Sparta and the Peloponnesus were 89, the Athenian fleet 180, while 97 more were supplied by the Greek islands, some of the ships from Melos and the Cyclades being *penteconters*, large vessels whose long oars were each manned by five rowers. Losses by storm and battle had reduced the Persian armada to some six hundred effective ships. The odds were serious, but not desperate.

But while the Persian fleet was directed by a single will, there were divided counsels among the Greeks. Eurybiades had most of the leaders on his side when he argued that Athens was hopelessly lost, and the best hope for Greece was to defend the Peloponnesus by holding the Isthmus of Corinth with what land forces could be assembled and removing the fleet to the waters of the neighbouring waters to co-operate in the defence. Themistocles, on the other hand, shrank from the idea of abandoning the refugees in the island of Salamis, and he regarded the adjacent straits as the best position in which the Greeks could give battle.

There, as in the channel of Eubœa, the narrow waters would do something to nullify the Persian advantage of numbers. For the Greeks, formed in several lines extending from shore to shore, could only be attacked by equal numbers. Only the leading ships of the attack would be in action at any given moment, and it would not matter how many hundred more were crowded behind them. With a column of spearmen on land the weight of the rearward ranks, formed in a serried phalanx, would force onward those in front. But with a column of ships formed in several successive lines in narrow waters any attempt of the rearward ships to press forward would mean confusion and disaster to themselves and those that formed the leading lines.

This would have been true even of ships under sail, but in battle the war galleys were oar-driven, and as the ships jammed together there would be entangled oars, and rowers flung from their benches with broken heads and arms. Better discipline, more thorough fighting-power on the Greek side, would mean that the leading ships of their fleet would deal effectually with their nearest adversaries, while the rearward ships would rest upon their oars and plunge into the *mêlée* only where disaster to a leading ship left an opening.

A doubtful story says that Themistocles, foreseeing that if the battle was long delayed the Spartan party would carry their point and withdraw to the isthmus, ran the risk of sending a message to King Xerxes, urging him to attack at once, hinting at a defection of the Athenian fleet, and telling him that if he acted without delay the Greeks were at his mercy, and that they were so terrified that they were thinking chiefly of how they might escape. Herodotus tells of a council of war of the Persian leaders at which the fighting Queen Artemisia stood alone in advising delay. She told the King that in overrunning northern Greece he had done enough for one campaign.

Let him settle down for winter quarters in Attica and he would see the Greek armament, already divided by jealousies and quarrels, break up and disperse. He could then prepare quietly for the conquest of the Peloponnesus in the spring. But Xerxes was more flattered by the opinion of the satraps who told him that he had only to stretch out his hands to destroy the Greek fleet and make himself undisputed master of the sea. And, just as Themistocles was despairing of being able to keep the fleet at Salamis, news came that the Persians had decided to attack.

The news was brought by Aristides, the son of Lysimachus, who had been unjustly exiled from Athens some years before, but now in the moment of his country's danger ran the blockade of the Persians in a ship of Ægina, and came to throw in his lot with his fellow-citizens. For the Greeks to set out for the isthmus under these circumstances would be to risk having to meet superior numbers in the open sea. All now agreed that the fate of Greece was to be decided in the waters of Salamis.

Xerxes looked forward to the coming struggle with assured hope of victory, and prepared to enjoy the spectacle of the disaster that was about to fall upon his enemies.

On the green slope of Mount Ægaleos, which commanded a full view of Salamis and the straits, the silken tents of the King and his Court were erected, a camp that was like a palace. Purple-dyed hangings, gilded tent poles with pomegranates of pure gold at the top of each, carpets bright with colour, carved furniture inlaid with ivory, all made up a display of luxurious pomp. Before the royal tents a golden throne had been erected. Fan-bearers took their post on either side, nobles who held the office of sword-bearers and cup-bearers waited at the steps of the throne.

On either side and on the slope below the ranks of the "Immortal Guard" were formed, ten thousand veterans, with armour and equipments gleaming with silver and gold. Along the shore from the white marble cliffs of Sunium by the port of Phalerum and far up the winding coast-line of the straits, hundreds of thousands more of this army of many nations stood in battle array. They were to witness the destruction of the Great King's enemies, and to take an active part in it when, as all expected, disabled Greek galleys would be driven ashore, and their crews would ask in vain for quarter. They were to share, too, in the irruption into Salamis once the fleet was master of the straits, and when the people of Athens, no longer protected by the sea, would be at the mercy of the Asiatic warriors.

Amid the blare of trumpets the King took his seat upon his throne, and watched his great armada sweeping towards the straits like a floating city. In those hundreds of long, low-sided ships thousands of slaves strained at the banks of heavy oars, encouraged by the shouts of the picked warriors who crowded the decks, and if their energies flagged, stimulated to new exertions by the whip of their taskmasters.

From every point of vantage in Salamis, women, old men, children, all who could not fight, looked out upon the sea, watching with heart-rending anxiety the signs of the approaching struggle. Death or slavery and untold misery would be their fate if numbers should prevail in the battle. In our days, in the hours before such a decisive struggle a people watches the newspapers, and waits for tidings of the fight in a turmoil of mingled hopes and fears. But whatever may be the result the individual, who is thus a spectator at a distance, runs no personal risks. It was otherwise in those days of merciless heathen warfare, and here all would see for themselves the changing fortunes of the fight on which their own fate depended.

The Greek fleet had been formed in two divisions of unequal strength. The smaller anchored in the western opening of the straits, furthest from the advance of the enemy's armada, and was detailed to prevent any attack through the narrows on the Greek rear. The main body, three hundred strong, was moored in successive lines, just inside the opening of the straits to the eastward. The best ships, the most trusted leaders, the picked warriors were in the foremost line.

On them the result of the day would chiefly depend, and here the man who had planned it all, commanded an Athenian war galley in the centre of the array. In this fact we see another striking difference between past and present. The modern specialization of offices and capacities which divides between different individuals the functions of political leader, general, and admiral was yet centuries distant in the future. Themistocles, who had advised the policy of naval war, was to be the foremost leader in the battle, and though purely naval tactics were to have some part in it, it was to be to a great extent a land battle fought out on floating platforms, so that one who had learned the art of war on land could act as an admiral on the sea.

Sixty thousand men-rowers and warriors were crowded on board the Greek fleet. At least twice as many must have been borne on the decks and rowers' benches of the Persian armada. Midway in the opening of the straits the Persians had occupied the rocky island of Psytalia. Its ledges and its summit glittered with arms, and beside it some light craft had taken post to assist friendly vessels in distress. Past the islet the great fleet swept in four successive divisions driven by the measured stroke of tens of thousands of oars.

On the left of the leading line was the Phœnician fleet led by the tributary kings of Tyre and Sidon, a formidable squadron, for these war galleys were manned by real seamen, bold sailors who knew not only the ways of the land-locked Mediterranean, but had ventured into the outer ocean. On the right were the ships of the Greek cities of Ionia, the long galleys of Ephesus, Miletus, Samos, and Samothrace. Here Greek would meet Greek in deadly strife. The rowers shouted as they bent to the long oars.

The warriors grouped in the prow with spear and javelin in hand sang the war songs of many nations. Along the bulwarks of the ships of Asia crouched the Persian and Babylonian archers, the best bowmen of the ancient world, with the arrow resting ready on the string. As the left of the leading line reached the opening of the strait the rowers reduced their speed, while on the other flank the stroke became more rapid. The long line was wheeling round the point of Salamis, and came in full sight of the Greek fleet ranged in battle array across the narrows.

The Athenian ships formed the right and centre of its leading line, the fleet of the Peloponnesus under the veteran Eurybiades was on the left. The rowers were resting on their oars, or just using them enough to keep the ships in position. As the Persians came sweeping into the straits the Greeks began to chant the Pæan, their battle hymn. The crash of the encounter between the two navies was now imminent.

For a few moments it seemed that already the Persians were assured of victory, for, seeing the enormous mass of the ships of Asia crowding the strait from shore to shore, and stretching far away on the open sea outside it, not a few of the European leaders lost heart for a while. The rowers began to backwater, and many of the ships of the first line retired stern foremost into the narrows. The rest followed their example, each one fearing to lose his place in the line, and be exposed in isolation to the attack of a crowd of enemies. It was perilously like the beginning of a panic that would soon end in disaster if it were not checked.

But it was soon over. The last of the retiring Greek ships was a galley of Pallene in Macedonia, commanded by a good soldier, Arminias. He was one of those who was doing his best to check the panic. Resolved that whoever else gave way he would sink rather than take to flight, he turned the prow of his *trireme* against the approaching enemy, and evading the ram of a Persian ship ran alongside of her. The intermingled oars broke like matchwood, and the two ships grappled. The battle had begun.

Attacked on the other side by another of the ships of Asia, Arminias was in deadly peril. The sight of their comrade's courage and of his danger stopped the retirement of the Greeks.

Their rowers were now straining every nerve to come to the rescue of the isolated *trireme*, and from shore to shore the two fleets met with loud outcry and the jarring crash of scores of voluntary or involuntary collisions.

All order was soon lost. The strait of Salamis was now the scene of a vast *mêlée*, hundreds of ships crowding together in the narrow pass between the island and the mainland. Themistocles in the centre with the picked ships of Athens was forcing his way, wedge-like, between the Phœnician and Ionian squadrons into the dense mass of the Persian centre. The bronze beaks ground their way into hostile timbers, oars were swept away, rowers thrown in confusion from their benches stunned and with broken limbs.

Ships sank and drowning men struggled for life; the Asiatic archers shot their arrows at close quarters, the spearmen hurled their javelins; but it was not by missile weapons the fight was to be decided. Where the stroke of the ram failed, the ships were jammed together in the press, and men fought hand to hand on forecastles and upper decks. Here it was that the Greeks, trained athletes, chosen men in the prime of life, protected by their armour and relying on the thrust of the long and heavy spear, had the advantage over the Asiatics. Only their own countrymen of the Ionian squadron could make any stand against them, and the Ionians had to face the spears of Sparta, in the hands of warriors all eager to avenge the slaughter of Thermopylæ.

Some of these Ionian Greeks, fighting under the Persian standard, won local successes here and there in the *mêlée*. They captured or sank several of the Spartan *triremes*. One of the ships of Samothrace performed an exploit like that of Paul Jones, when with his own ship sinking under the feet of his crew he boarded and captured the *Serapis*.

A Greek *trireme* had rammed the Samothracian ship, tearing open her side; but as she went down her Persian and Ionian crew scrambled on board their assailant and drove the Greeks into the sea at the spear-point. It was noted that few of the Persian crews were swimmers. When their ships sank they were drowned. The Greeks were able to save themselves in such a disaster. They threw away shield, helmet, and spear, and swam to another ship or to the island shore.

This fact would seem to indicate that with the exception of those who manned the Ionian and Phœnician squadrons the crews of the Persian fleet were much less at home on the sea than the Greeks. And we know from the result of many battles, from Marathon to the victories of Alexander, that on land the Greek was a better fighting man than the Asiatic. The soldiers of the "Great King," inferior in fighting-power even on the land, would therefore find themselves doubly handicapped by having to fight on the narrow platforms floating on an unfamiliar element, and the sight of ships being sunk and their crews drowned would tend to produce panic among them. So the Greek wedge forced itself further and further into the mass of hostile ships, and in the narrow waters numbers could not tell. The Greeks were never at any given moment engaged with a superior force in actual hand-to-hand conflict, and they had sufficient ships behind them to make good any local losses. Such a battle could have only one result.

All order had been lost in the Persian fleet at an early stage of the fight. The rearward squadrons had pressed into the strait, and finding that in the crowded waters they were endangering each other without being able to take any effective part in the battle they began to draw off, and the foremost ships, pressed back by the Greek attack, began to follow them towards the open water. The whole mingled mass of the battle was drifting eastward. The movement left the island of Psytalia unprotected by the Asiatic fleet, and Aristides, the Athenian, who had been watching the fight from the shore of Salamis, embarked a force of spearmen on some light vessels, ferried them across to Psytalia and attacked its Persian garrison.

They made a poor show of resistance, and to a man they were speared or flung over the rocks into the sea. The poet Æschylus, who was fighting as a soldier on one of the Athenian *triremes*, told afterwards, not in pity, but rejoicing at the destruction of his country's enemies, how the cries of the massacred garrison of Psytalia were heard above the din of the battle and increased the growing panic of the Persians.

Even those who had fought best in the Asiatic armada were now losing heart and taking to flight. Queen Artemisia, with her five galleys of Halicarnassus, had fought in the front line among the ships of the Ionian squadron. She was now working her way out of the *mêlée*, and in the confusion rammed and sank a Persian warship. Xerxes, watching the fight from his throne on the hillside, thought it was a Greek ship that the Amazon had destroyed and exclaimed: "This woman is playing the man while my men are acting like women!"

Two Persian ships in flight from the pursuing Greeks drove ashore at the base of Mount Ægaleos. Xerxes, in his anger at the disaster to his fleet, ordered the troops stationed on the beach to behead every officer and man of their crews, and the sentence was at once executed. The closing scene of the battle was, indeed, a time of unmitigated horrors, for while this massacre of the defeated crews was being carried out by the Persian guardsmen, the victorious Greeks were slaying all the fugitives who fell into their hands. The Admiral of the Persian fleet, Ariabignes, brother of Xerxes, was among the dead.

The pursuit was not continued far beyond the straits. The Greeks hesitated to venture into open waters where numbers might tell against them if the Persians rallied, and they drew back to their morning anchorage. The remnant of the Persian fleet anchored off the coast near Phalerum, the port of Athens, or took refuge in the small harbour. They were rejoined by a detachment which had been sent to round the south side of Salamis to attack the western entrance of the straits, but which for some reason had never been engaged during the day.

The victorious Greeks did not realize the full extent of their triumph. They expected to be attacked again next morning, and hoped to repeat the manœuvre which had been so far successful, of engaging the enemy in the narrows with each flank protected by the shore, and no room for a superior force to form in the actual line of fighting contact. But though they did not yet realize the fact, they had won a decisive victory. Xerxes had been so impressed by the failure of his great armada to force the narrows of Salamis that he had changed all his plans.

In the night after the battle he held a council of war. It was decided that the attack should not be renewed, for there was no prospect of a second attempt giving better results. Artemisia was directed to convey Prince Artaxerxes, the heir of the Empire, back to Asia. Xerxes himself would lead back to the bridge of the Hellespont the main body of his immense army, for to attempt to maintain it in Greece during the winter would have meant famine in its camps. The fleet was to sail at once for the northern Archipelago, and limit its operations to guarding the bridge of the Hellespont and protecting the convoys for the army. When the winter came it would have to be laid up; but by that time it was hoped Xerxes and the main body would be safe in Asia. Mardonius, the most trusted of his *satraps*, was to occupy northern Greece with a picked force of 300,000 men, with which he was to attempt the conquest of the Peloponnesus next year.

The Persian fleet sailed from the roadstead of Phalerum during that same night. How far the crews were demoralized by the defeat of the previous day is shown by the fact that there was something of a panic as the white cliffs of Sunium glimmered through the darkness in the moonlight and were mistaken for the sails of hostile Greek warships menacing the line of retreat. The Persians stood far out to sea to avoid these imaginary enemies. When the day broke Themistocles and Eurybiades could hardly credit the report that all the ships of Asia had disappeared from their anchorage of the evening before.

The Athenian admiral urged immediate pursuit, the Spartan general hesitated and at last gave a reluctant consent. The fleet sailed as far as the island of Andros, but found no trace of the enemy. In vain Themistocles urged that it should go further, and if it failed to find the enemy's fleet, at least show itself in the harbours of Asia and try to rouse Ionia to revolt. Eurybiades declared that enough had been accomplished, and refused to risk a voyage across the Archipelago in the late autumn. So the victorious fleet returned to Salamis, and thence the various contingents dispersed to be laid up for the winter in sheltered harbours and on level beaches, where a stockade could be erected and a guard left to protect the ships till the fine weather of next spring allowed them to be launched again.

When Xerxes reached the Hellespont with his army, after having lost heavily by disease and famine in his weary march through Thessaly, Macedonia, and Thrace, he found that the long bridge with which he had linked together Europe and Asia had been swept away by a storm. But the remnant of his fleet was there waiting to ferry across the strait what was left of his army, now diminished by many hundreds of thousands.

The next year witnessed the destruction both of the army left under Mardonius in northern Greece and of the remainder of the Persian fleet that had fought at Salamis. Pausanias, with a hundred thousand Greeks, routed the Persian army at Platæa. A fleet of 110 *triremes*, under the admirals Leotychides and Xantippus, sailed across the Archipelago in search of the Persian fleet. They found it in the waters of Samos, but the enemy retired towards the mainland without giving battle.

The Asiatics were disheartened and divided. The Ionians were suspected of disaffection. The Phœnicians were anxious only to return in safety to their own country and resume their peaceful trading, and as soon as they were out of sight of the Greeks, they deserted the Persian fleet, and sailed southwards, bound for Tyre and Sidon.

What was left of the fleet anchored under the headland of Mycale. There was no sign of a Greek pursuit. Rumour reported that the Athenian and Spartan admirals were intent only on securing possession of the islands, and would not venture on any enterprise against the coast of Asia. Perhaps it was because he still feared to risk another engagement on the sea, that the Persian admiral found a pretext for laying up his ships. He declared that they were so foul with weeds and barnacles that, as a prelude to any further operations, they must be beached and cleaned. They were therefore hauled ashore under the headland, and a stockade was erected round them, the fleet thus becoming a fortified camp guarded by its crews.

And then the dreaded Greek fleet appeared. Its hundred *triremes* could disembark some twenty thousand men, for arms were provided even for the rowers. A landing from low-sided ships of light draught was an easy matter. They were driven in a long line towards the shore. As they grounded, the warriors sprang into the water and waded to land. The rowers left their oars, grasped spear or sword, and followed them. The stockade was stormed; the ships inside it, dry with the heat of the Asiatic sun, and with seams oozing with tar, were set on fire and were soon burning fiercely. As the flames died down and the pall of smoke drifted far over the promontory of Mycale, a mass of charred timbers was all that was left of the great armada of Asia, and the victorious Greeks sailed homewards with the news that the full fruits of Salamis had been garnered.

CHAPTER 2

Actium B.C. 31

Actium was one of the decisive battles of the world—the event that fixed the destinies of the Roman Empire for centuries to come, made Octavian its dictator, and enabled him, while keeping the mere forms of Republican life, to inaugurate the imperial system of absolute rule, and reign as the first of the Roman Emperors, under the name and title of Augustus.

It brought to a close the series of civil wars which followed the murder of his grand-uncle, Julius Cæsar. The *triumvirs*, Mark Antony, Octavian, and Lepidus, had avenged the assassination by a wholesale proscription of their political opponents, all of whom indiscriminately they charged with the guilt of the deed; and had defeated Brutus and Cassius on the plains of Philippi. They had parcelled out the Empire among them, and then quarrelled over the spoil.

Octavian, the dictator of the West, had expelled Lepidus from the African provinces that had been assigned to him as his territory. Antony was now his only remaining rival. Cæsar's veteran lieutenant held the Eastern provinces of the Empire. During the years he had spent in the East he had become half Orientalized, under the influence of the famous Queen of Egypt, Cleopatra, for whose sake he had dismissed his wife Octavia, the sister of Octavian, in order that the Egyptian might take her place. He had appeared beside her in Alexandria wearing the insignia of the Egyptian god Osiris, while Cleopatra wore those of Isis. Coins and medals were struck bearing their effigies as joint rulers of the East, and the loyalty of Rome and the West to Octavian was confirmed by the sense of indignation which every patriotic Roman felt at the news that Antony spoke openly of making Alexandria and not Rome the centre of the Empire, and of founding with the Egyptian Queen a new dynasty that would rule East and West from the Nile.

The question to be decided in the civil war was therefore not merely whether Octavian or Antony was to be the ruler of the Roman world, but whether Eastern or Western influences were to predominate in shaping its destinies. Antony was preparing to carry the war into Italy, and assembled on the western shores of Greece an army made up of the Roman legions of the eastern provinces and large contingents of Oriental allies.

During the winter of B.C. 32–31, he had his head-quarters at Patræ (now Patras), on the Gulf of Corinth, and his army, scattered in detachments among the coast towns, was kept supplied with grain by ships from Alexandria. Antony's war fleet, strengthened by squadrons of Phœnician and Egyptian galleys, lay safely in the land-locked Ambracian Gulf (now the Gulf of Arta), approached by a winding strait that could easily be defended.

But Octavian had determined to preserve Italy from the horrors of war, by transporting an army across the Adriatic in the coming summer and deciding the conflict on the shores of Greece. An army of many legions was already in cantonments on the eastern coast of Italy, or prepared to concentrate there in the spring. His fleet crowded the ports of Tarentum (Taranto) and Brundusium (Brindisi), and minor detachments were wintering in the smaller harbours of southern Italy. Most of his ships were smaller than those to which they were to be opposed. It was reported that Antony had a considerable number of huge *quinqueremes*, and even larger ships of war, anchored in the Ambracian Gulf.

The ships of the Western Empire were mostly *triremes*; but there was the advantage that while Antony's fleet was largely manned by hastily recruited landsmen, Octavian had crews made up of experienced sailors. Many of them were of the race of the Liburni, men of the island-fringed coast of Dalmatia, to this day among the best sailors of the Adriatic, and his admiral was the celebrated Marcus Vipsanius Agrippa, who had to his credit more [1] than one naval success in the civil wars, amongst them a victory won off the headland of Mylæ, in the same waters that had been the scene of the triumph of Duilius.

Early in the spring, while the main body of Octavian's fleet concentrated at Brundusium, and the army that was to cross the Adriatic gathered around the harbour, Agrippa with a strong squadron put to sea, seized the port of Methone in the Peloponnesus, and using this place as his base of operations captured numbers of the Egyptian transports that were conveying supplies to the enemy's camps. Antony ought to have replied to this challenge by putting to sea with his combined fleet, forcing Agrippa to concentrate the Western armament to meet him, and deciding by a pitched battle who was to have the command of the sea in the Adriatic.

But Cæsar's old lieutenant, once as energetic and enterprising a soldier as his master, had now become indolent and irresolute. He was used to idling away weeks and months with Cleopatra and his semi-Oriental Court. Instead of venturing on a vigorous offensive campaign he left the initiative to his opponent, and with a nominally more powerful fleet at his disposal he passively abandoned the command of the sea to Agrippa and Octavian.

The Egypto-Roman army was ordered to concentrate on the southern shores of the Ambracian Gulf. A division of the fleet was moored in the winding strait at its entrance, but directed to act only on the defensive. Inside the Gulf the rest of the fleet lay, the largest ships at anchor, the smaller hauled up on the shore.

The crews had been brought up to full strength by enlisting mule-drivers, field-labourers, and other inexperienced landsmen, and would have been better for training at sea; but except for some drills on the landlocked waters they were left in

---

[1] Men of the same race of sailors and fishermen largely manned the victorious fleet of Tegethoff at Lissa, nineteen centuries later. See Chapter 11.

idleness, and sickness soon broke out among them and thinned their numbers. The ships thus inefficiently manned presented a formidable array. There were some five hundred in all, including, however, a number of large merchantmen hastily fitted for war service. Just as modern men-of-war are provided with steel nets hanging on booms as a defence against torpedoes, so it would seem that some at least of Antony's ships had been fitted with a clumsy device for defending them against attack by ramming.

Below the level of the oars, balks of timber were propped out from their sides at the water-line, and it was hoped that these barricades would break the full force of an enemy's "beak." But the invention had the drawback of diminishing the speed of the ship, and making quick turning more difficult, and thus it increased the very danger it was intended to avert.

Another feature of the larger ships, some of them the biggest that had yet been built for the line of battle, the *Dreadnoughts* of their day, was that wooden castles or towers had been erected on their upper decks, and on these structures were mounted various specimens of a rude primitive substitute for artillery, *ballistæ*, catapults, and the like, engines for discharging by mechanical means huge darts or heavy stones. These same towers were also to be the places from which the Eastern bowmen, the best archers of the ancient world, would shower their arrows on a hostile fleet.

But locked up in the bottle-necked Ambracian Gulf the great fleet, with its tower-crowned array of floating giants, had as little effect on the opening phase of the campaign as if its units had been so many castles on the shore. Agrippa soon felt that there was no serious risk of any attempt being made by Antony to interrupt the long and delicate operation of ferrying over an army of a hundred thousand men and some twelve thousand cavalry from Italy to the opposite shore of the Adriatic. He took the precaution of watching the outlet of the Ambracian Gulf with his swiftest ships.

The narrow entrance, while making it difficult to force a way into the Gulf, had the disadvantage of all such positions, that a large fleet would take a considerable time to issue from it into the open sea, and it was therefore comparatively easy to blockade and observe it. If Antony showed any sign of coming out, there would be time to bring up the whole fleet of Octavian to meet him in the open.

It was thus that Octavian was able securely to embark his army in successive divisions, and land it without interruption at the port of Toryne on the eastern coast of the Adriatic. Having assembled there, it marched southwards along the coast till it reached the hills on the northern shore of the Ambracian Gulf, and the two armies and fleets were in presence of each other.

The legions of Octavian encamped on a rising ground a few miles north of the entrance of the Gulf, and above a narrow neck of land which divided one of its inlets from the open sea. The coast is here hollowed into a wide bay, in which the main body of Agrippa's fleet was anchored, while a detached squadron observed the opening of the straits. The camp was surrounded by entrenchments, and connected with the station of the fleet by a road protected by lines of earthworks and palisades, for it was the custom of the Romans to make as much use of pick and spade as of sword and spear in their campaigns. On the site of the camp Octavian afterwards founded Nicopolis, "the City of Victory," as the memorial of his triumph.

From the camp on the hill there was a wide view over the Ambracian Gulf, a sheet of water some thirty miles long and ten wide, surrounded by an amphitheatre of hills sloping to flat, and in many places marshy, shores. On the wide waters the fleet of Antony lay moored, line behind line, a forest of masts and yards. In the narrows of the entrance some of his largest ships were anchored. Many of the ships of Phœnicia and Egypt displayed an Eastern profusion of colour in their painted upper works, their gilded bows, and their bright flags and streamers. Near the southern shore lay the state galley of Cleopatra, a floating palace, with its silken sails, gilded bulwarks, and oars bound and plated with silver.

A line of earthworks and forts across the neck of the northern point, garrisoned by the best of Antony's Roman veterans, defended one side of the narrows. The other side was a low-lying, triangular stretch of land, dry, sandy ground. The Greeks knew it as the *Akte*, just as the Italian sailors still call it the *Punta*, both words having the same meaning, "the Point." At its northern extremity on a rocky platform there rose a temple of Apollo, known as the "Aktion," the "sanctuary of the point," a place of pilgrimage for the fisher and sailor folk of the neighbourhood. Its name, Latinized into *Actium*, became famous as that of the naval battle.

On the level ground by the temple was the camp of the army of Antony and Cleopatra, a city of tents and reed-built huts, within its midst the gay pavilions of the Court. It was a mixed gathering of many nations—Roman legions commanded by veterans of the wars of Cæsar; Egyptian battalions in the quaint war dress we see on the painted walls of tombs by the Nile, and the semi-barbarous levies of the tributary kings of Eastern Asia. There were widespread dissension and mutual suspicion among the allies. Not a few of the Romans were chafing at their leader's subservience to a "Barbarian" queen.

Many of the Eastern kinglets were considering whether they could not make a better bargain with Octavian. The cavalry of both armies skirmished among the hills on the land side of the Gulf, and prisoners made by Octavian's troops readily took service with them. Then one of the Asiatic kings, instead of fighting, joined the hostile cavalry with his barbaric horsemen, and night after night Roman deserters stole into the camp of Octavian on the northern height.

An attempt led by Antony in person against the Roman entrenchments was beaten off. A detachment of the fleet tried to elude the vigilance of Agrippa and slip out to sea, but had to retire before superior numbers. Then both parties watched each other, while at the head-quarters of Antony councils of war were held to debate upon a plan of campaign. The situation was becoming difficult. For Octavian contented himself with holding his fortified camp with his infantry, drawing his supplies freely from oversea, while his cavalry prevented anything reaching Antony's lines from the land side, and Agrippa's fleet blockading the Gulf and sweeping the sea, made it impossible to bring corn from Egypt. Provisions were running short, and sickness was rife. A move of some kind must be made.

The veteran Canidius, who commanded the army under Antony, had like most of the Romans little faith in the efficiency of the fleet. He proposed to Antony that it should be abandoned, and that the army should march eastward into Macedonia, and, with an unexhausted country to supply it, await the pursuit of ten legions of Octavian in a favourable position. But Antony, influenced by Cleopatra, refused to desert the fleet, which was the one possible hope of reaching Egypt again, and rejecting an attack on the Roman entrenchments as a hopeless enterprise, he decided at last that all the treasure of Court and army should be embarked on the ships, and an effort made to break through the blockading squadrons.

While the preparations were being made, the Romans renewed their entreaties that their leader would rather stake his fortunes on a battle on land. One day a veteran centurion of his guard, who bore the honourable scars of many campaigns, addressing him with tears in his eyes, said to Antony: "Imperator, why distrust these wounds, this sword? Why put your hopes on wretched logs of wood? Let Phœnicians and Egyptians fight on the sea, but let us have land on which we know how to conquer or die." It is the appeal that Shakespeare puts into the mouth of one of Antony's soldiers:—

> O noble emperor, do not fight by sea;
> Trust not to rotten planks. Do you misdoubt
> This sword and these my wounds? Let the Egyptians
> And the Phœnicians go a-ducking; we
> Have used to conquer standing on the earth,
> And fighting foot to foot.[2]

The sight of the Egypto-Roman fleet crowding down to the

---

2. *Antony and Cleopatra*, Act 3, scene 7.

narrows with their sails bent on their yards showed that they meant to risk putting to sea, and Octavian embarked on Agrippa's fleet, with picked reinforcements from the legions. For four days the wind blew strongly from the south-west and the blockaded fleet waited for better weather. On the fifth day the wind had fallen, the sea was smooth and the sun shone brightly. The floating castles of Antony's van division worked out of the straits, and after them in long procession came the rest of the Roman, Phœnician, and Egyptian galleys.

From the hills to the northward of the straits, from the low-lying headland of Actium to the south, two armies, each of a hundred thousand men, watched the spectacle, and waited anxiously for the sight of the coming battle.

The Western fleet had steered to a position off the entrance formed in two divisions, the one led by Agrippa, the other by Octavian. Agrippa, whose experience and record of naval victory gave him the executive command, had no intention of risking his small ships in the narrows, where they would have been opposed by an equal number of heavier ships, more numerously manned, and would lose whatever advantage their superior handiness and seaworthiness gave them, through having no room to manœuvre. He kept his fleet of four hundred *triremes* sufficiently far from the shore to avoid the shelving shallows that fringe it near the entrance to the straits, and to have ample sea-room.

For some time the fleets remained in presence of each other, both hesitating to begin the attack. Antony knew that his slower and heavier ships would have the best chance acting inshore and on the defensive, and Agrippa was, on the other hand, anxious not to engage until he could lure them out seaward, where his light craft would have all the gain of rapid manœuvring.

It was not till near noon that at last the Western fleet closed with the Allies. The ships that first encountered were nearly all Roman vessels, for the Egyptian and Asiatic squadrons were not in the front line of Antony's fleet, and the brunt of the attack fell upon the sluggish giants that had been so elaborately fortified

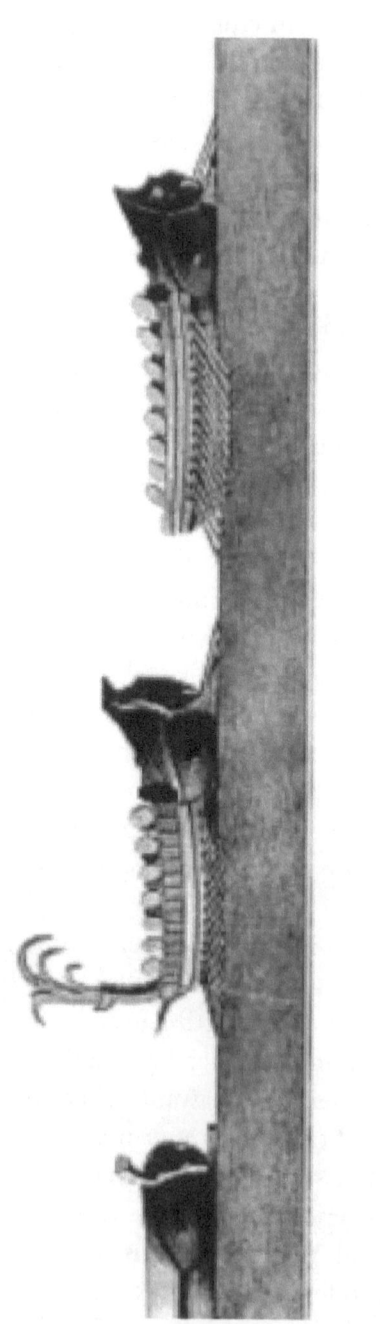

ROMAN WARSHIPS – AFTER THE PAINTINGS FOUND AT POMPEI

with booms in the water and towers and breastworks on their decks. As the attacking ships came into range, arrows, javelins, and stones flew hurtling through the air from the line of floating castles, missiles that did not, however, inflict much loss, for the men on the decks of the attacking fleet crouched behind bulwarks or covered themselves with their oblong shields, and their bowmen made some show of reply to the heavier discharge of engines of war on Antony's ships and to the more rapid shooting of the Asiatic archers. The days were still far off when sea fights would be decided by "fire," in the sense of the discharge of projectiles.

Could the tall ships have rammed the smaller and lower galleys of Octavian and Agrippa they would certainly have sent them to the bottom—a sunken ship for each blow of the brazen beak. But attempts at ramming were soon found by Antony's captains to be both useless and dangerous. It was not merely that their lighter and nimbler opponents easily avoided the onset. The well-trained crews evaded every attempt to run them down or grapple them, chose their own distance as they hovered round their huge adversaries, and presently as they gained confidence from impunity, began successfully to practise the manœuvre of eluding the ram, and using their own bows, not for a blow against the hull of the heavier ship, but to sweep away and shatter her long oars, that were too heavy to be saved by drawing them in or unshipping them. Successful attack on the oars was equivalent to disabling an adversary's engines in a modern seafight. And when a ship was thus crippled, her opponents could choose their own time to concentrate several of their ships for a joint attempt to take her by boarding.

The unwieldy ships of Antony's first line, with their halftrained and untrained crews, must have formed a straggling irregular line with large intervals as they stood out to sea, and it was this that gave Octavian's fleet the opportunity for the worrying tactics they adopted. Had the Egyptian and Phœnician ships come to the support of the leading line, their more sailorlike crews might have helped to turn the scale against Octavian.

But while the fight was yet undecided and before the Egyptian squadron had taken any part in it, a breeze sprang up from the land, blowing from the north-east. Then, to the dismay of Antony's veterans who watched the battle from the headland of Actium, it was seen that the Egyptians were unfurling their sails from the long yards. The signal had been given from Cleopatra's stately vessel, which as the battle began had rowed out to a position in the midst of the Egyptian squadron, and now shook out her purple sails to the breeze, silken fabrics of fiery red, that seemed at first glance like a battle-signal. But in battle sails were never used and ships trusted entirely to the oar, so to set the sails meant plainly that the fight was to be abandoned.

Driven by her silver-tipped oars, helped now with the land breeze that swelled her sails, Cleopatra's galley passed astern of the fighting-line on its extreme left, and sixty of the warships of Alexandria followed their queen. Those who watched from the land must have hoped against hope that this was a novel manœuvre, to use the breeze to aid the squadron of their allies to shoot out from behind the main body, gain the flank of the enemy, and then suddenly let the sails flap idly, furl or drop them, and sweep down with full speed of oars on the rear of the attack, with Cleopatra leading like Artemisia at Salamis.

But the "serpent of old Nile" had no such ideas. She was in full flight for Alexandria, with her warships escorting her and conveying the wealth that had been embarked when it was decided to put to sea. Was her flight an act of treachery, or the result of panic-stricken alarm at the sight of the battle? But even her enemies never accused her of any lack of personal courage, and there are many indications that it had been arranged before the fleet came out, that, as soon as an opportunity offered, Cleopatra with a sufficient escort should make for Egypt, where several legions were in garrison, and where even if the army now camped beside the Ambracian Gulf could not be extricated from its difficulties, another army might be formed to prolong the war.

But the withdrawal of the sixty ships threw the odds of battle heavily against the rest of Antony's fleet. And matters were made worse by its leader suddenly allowing his infatuation for the Queen of Egypt to sweep away all sense of his duty to his comrades and followers and his honour as a commander. As he saw Cleopatra's sails curving round his line and making for the open sea, he hastily left his flagship, boarded a small and swift galley, and sped after the Egyptians.

Agrippa was too good a leader to weaken his attack on the main body of the enemy by any attempt to interrupt the flight of the Egyptian squadron. When he saw the galley of Antony following it, he guessed who was on board, and detached a few of his *triremes* in pursuit. Antony was saved from capture only by the rearward ships of the fugitive squadron turning back to engage and delay the pursuers. In this rearguard fight two of the Egyptian warships were captured by Agrippa's cruisers. But meanwhile Antony's galley had run alongside of the royal flagship of the Egyptian fleet, and he had been welcomed on board by Cleopatra.

By this time, however, he had begun to realize the consequences of his flight. Half an hour ago he had stood on the deck of a fighting ship, where comrades who had made his cause their own were doing brave battle against his enemies. Now, while the fight still raged far away astern, he found himself on the deck of a pleasure yacht, glittering with gold and silver, silk and ivory, and with women and slaves forming a circle round the Queen, who greeted him as he trod the carpeted deck. He made only a brief acknowledgment of her welcome, and then turned away and strode forward to the bow, where he sat alone, huddled together, brooding on thoughts of failure and disgrace, while the royal galley and its escort of warships sped southward with oar and sail, and the din of battle died away in the distance, and all sight of it was lost beyond the horizon.

The withdrawal of the Egyptians was a palpable discouragement to all the fleet, but not all were aware that their leader, Antony, had shared Cleopatra's flight. Some of those who realized what had happened gave up all further effort for victory, and leaving the line drove ashore on the sandy beach of Actium, and abandoning their ships joined the spectators from the camp. Others made their way by the strait into the great land-locked haven of the Gulf. But most of the fleet still kept up the fight. The great ships that drifted helplessly, with broken oars, among the agile galleys of Agrippa's Liburnian sailors, or that grounded in the shallows nearer the shore, were, even in their helplessness as ships, formidable floating forts that it was difficult to sink and dangerous to storm.

More than one attempt to board was repulsed with loss, the high bulwarks and towers giving an advantage to the large fighting contingents that Antony had embarked. Some of them had drifted together, and were lashed side to side, so that their crews could mutually aid each other, and their archers bring a cross fire on the assailants of their wooden towers. Some ships had been sunk on both sides, and a few of the towered warships of the Eastern fleet had been captured by Agrippa, but at the cost of much loss of life.

To complete the destruction of the Antonian fleet, and secure his victory, Agrippa now adopted means that could not have been suddenly improvised, and must therefore have been prepared in advance, perhaps at the earlier period, when he was considering the chances of forcing a way into the Gulf. Fire was the new weapon, arrows wreathed with oiled and blazing tow were shot at the towers and bulwarks of the enemy. Rafts laden with combustibles were set on fire, and towed or pushed down upon the drifting sea-castles. Ship after ship burst into flame. As the fire spread some tried vainly to master it; others, at an early stage, abandoned their ships, or surrendered.

As the resistance of the defeated armada gradually slackened, and about four o'clock came to an end, it was found that a number of ships had taken refuge in the narrows and the Gulf; others were aground on the point; a few had been sunk, some more had surrendered, but numbers were drifting on the sea, wrapped in smoke and flame. Some of these sank as the fire reached the water's edge, and the waves lapped into the hollow hull, or the weight of half-consumed upper works capsized them. Others drifted ashore in the shallows, and reddened sea and land with the glare of their destruction far into the night.

For the men who had fought, the victory, complete as it was, had an element of disappointment. They had hoped to secure as a prize the treasures of Cleopatra, but these had been spirited away on the Egyptian fleet. But for the commanders, Octavian and his able lieutenant, there was nothing to regret. The battle had once more decided the issue between East and West, and had given Octavian such advantages that it would be his own fault if he were not soon master of the Roman World.

Within a few days the remnant of the defeated fleet had been surrendered or burned at its anchors. The army of Canidius, after a half-hearted attempt at an inland march, and after being further weakened by desertions, declared for Octavian, and joined his standards.

Cleopatra had entered the port of Alexandria with a pretence of returning in triumph from a naval victory. Laurel wreaths hung on spars and bulwarks, flags flew, trumpets sounded, and she received the enthusiastic greetings of Greeks and Egyptians as she landed. But the truth could not be long concealed, and under the blight of defeat, linked with stories of leaders deserting comrades and allies, Antony and Cleopatra failed to rally any determined support to their side when the conqueror of Actium came to threaten Egypt itself. Both ended their lives with their own hands, Cleopatra only resorting to this act of desperation when, after breaking with Antony, she failed to enslave Octavian with her charms, and foresaw that she would appear among the prisoners at his coming triumph in Rome.

2 September, B.C. 31—the day of Actium—is the date which most historians select to mark the end of the Roman Republic and the beginning of the Empire. The victor Octavian had already taken the name of his grand-uncle, Cæsar. He now adopted the title of Augustus, and accepted from army and senate the permanent rank of *Imperator*, inaugurating a system of absolutism that kept some of the forms of the old Republic as a thin disguise for the change to Imperialism.

On the height where he had camped before the battle, Nicopolis, the City of Victory, was erected. The ground where his tent had stood was the marble-paved forum, adorned with the brazen beaks of conquered warships. The temple of Apollo, on the point of Actium, was rebuilt on more ambitious lines, and on the level expanse of sandy ground behind it, every September, for some two hundred years, the "Actian games" were held to celebrate the decisive victory.

Augustus did not forget that to the fleet he had owed his success in the civil war, and naval stations were organized and squadrons of warships kept in commission even in the long days of peace that followed his victory. They served to keep the Mediterranean free from the plague of piracy, and to secure the growing oversea commerce of the Empire which had made the Mediterranean a vast Roman lake.

CHAPTER 3

The Battle of Svold Island A.D. 1000

In the story of the battles of Salamis and Actium we have seen what naval warfare was like in Greek and Roman times. It would be easy to add other examples, but they would be only repetitions of much the same story, for during the centuries of the Roman power there was no marked change in naval architecture or the tactics of warfare on the sea.

We pass, then, over a thousand years to a record of naval war waged in the beginning of the Middle Ages by northern races—people who had, independently of Greek or Roman, evolved somewhat similar types of ships, but who were better sailors, though for all that they still used the ship not so much as an engine of war as the floating platform on which warriors might meet in hand-to-hand conflict. Norseman, Dane, and Swede were all of kindred blood. The land-locked Baltic, the deep fiords of the Scandinavian Peninsula, the straits and inlets of the archipelago that fringes its North Sea coast, were the waters on which they learned such skill in seamanship that they soon launched out upon the open sea, and made daring voyages, not only to the Orkneys and the Hebrides, and the Atlantic seaboard of Ireland, but the Faroes, and to still more distant Iceland and Greenland, and then southward to "Vineland," the mainland of America, long after rediscovered by the navigators of the fifteenth century.

There is a considerable intermixture of Norse blood in the peoples of Great Britain and Ireland, and perhaps from this sea-loving race comes some of the spirit of adventure that has helped so much to build up our own naval power. When Nelson destroyed and captured the Danish fleet at Copenhagen, the Danes consoled themselves by saying that only a leader of their own blood could have conquered them, and that Nelson's name showed he came of the Viking line.

A chronicler tells how Charlemagne in his old age once came to a village on the North Sea shore, and camped beside it. Looking to seaward he saw far out some long low ships, with gaily painted oars, dragon-shaped bows, and sails made of brightly coloured lengths of stuff sewn together and adorned with embroidery along the yard. Tears came to his eyes as he said: "These sea-dragons will tear asunder the empire I have made."

They were Viking cruisers, on their way to plunder some coast town; and the old Emperor's prophecy was verified when the Norman, who was a civilized Norseman, became for a while the conquering race of Europe. Even before the death of Charlemagne the Norse and Danish sea-kings were raiding, plundering, and burning along the coasts of his Empire. Two hundred years of our own history is made up of the story of their incursions.

England and Ireland bore the first brunt of their onset, when they found the ways of the sea. But they ravaged all the western coasts of Europe, and even showed themselves in the Mediterranean. From the end of the eighth till the beginning of the eleventh century they were the terror of the western world, and early in that dark and stormy period their raids had grown into great expeditions; they landed armies that marched far inland, and they carved out principalities for themselves.

Western Europe had a brief respite at times when the Vikings fought amongst themselves. In early days there were frequent struggles for supremacy in Norway, between local kinglets and ambitious chiefs. Fighting was in the blood of the Northmen. Two sea-roving squadrons would sometimes challenge each other to battle for the mere sake of a fight. As Norway coalesced into a single kingdom, and as the first teachers of Christianity induced the kings to suppress piracy, there was more of peace and order on the Northern Seas. But in this transition period there was more than one struggle between the Scandinavian kingdoms, Norway, Sweden, and Denmark. One of the most famous battles of these northern wars of the sea-kings was fought in this period, when the old wild days of sea-roving were drawing to an end, and its picturesque story may well be told as that of a typical Norse battle, for its hero, King Olaf Tryggveson, was the ideal of a northern sea-king.

Olaf was a descendant of the race of Harold Haarfager, "Fair-haired Harold," the warrior who had united the kingdom of Norway, and made himself its chief king at the close of the ninth century. But Olaf came of a branch of the royal house that civil war had reduced to desperate straits. He was born when his mother, Astrid, was a fugitive in a lonely island of the Baltic. As a boy he was sold into slavery in Russia. There, one day, in the marketplace of an Esthonian town, he was recognized by a relative, Sigurd, the brother of Astrid, and was freed from bondage and trained to arms as a page at the Court of the Norse adventurers who ruled the land.

The "Saga" tells how Olaf, the son of Tryggva, grew to be tall of stature, and strong of limb, and skilled in every art of land and sea, of peace and war. None swifter than he on the snow-shoes in winter, no bolder swimmer when the summer had cleared the ice from the waters. He could throw darts with both hands, he could toss up two swords, catching them like a juggler, and keeping one always in the air. He could climb rocks and peaks like a mountain goat. He could row and sail, and had been known to display his daring skill as an athlete by running along the moving oars outside the ship. He could ride a horse, and fight, mounted or on foot, with axe or sword, with spear or bow.

In early manhood he came back to Norway to avenge the death of his father Tryggva, and then took to sea-roving, for piracy was still the Norseman's trade. He raided the shores of the Continent from Friesland to Northern France, but most of his piratical voyages were to the shores of our own islands, and many a seaboard town in England, Wales, Scotland, and Ireland saw Olaf's plundering squadron of swift ships. Five was the number of them with which he visited the Orkneys.

The Viking warships were small vessels. The ship dug out of the great grave mound at Sandefjord, in Norway, and now shown at Christiania, is seventy-seven feet long, with a beam of seventeen amidships, and a depth of just under six feet. Her draught of water would be only four feet, and she would lie very low in the water, but her lines are those of a good sea boat. She had one mast, forty feet high, to carry a crossyard and a square sail, and she had thirty-two oars, sixteen on each side. It says something for the seamanship of the Northmen that it was with ships like this they sailed the Atlantic waves off the west coast of Ireland, and made their way by the North Sea and the verge of the Arctic to the Faroes, Iceland, Greenland, and the mysterious "Vineland."[1]

Raiding in the Irish Sea, Olaf Tryggveson made a stay in a harbour of the Scilly Islands, and there he became a convert to Christianity. On the same voyage he married the Countess Gyde, sister of his namesake, Olaf Kvaran, the Danish King of Dublin. It was while he was staying in Ireland with the Dublin Danes that he heard news from Norway that opened larger ambitions to him. The land was divided among many chiefs, and the most powerful of them was hated as an oppressor by the people, who, he was told, would gladly welcome as their king

---

1. Some interesting light was thrown upon the voyages of the Norsemen by a practical experiment made in 1893. A Viking ship was built on the precise lines and dimensions of the ancient ship dug out of the mound of Gokstadt in 1880, 77 feet long with a beam of 17 feet, and was rigged with one mast and a square mainsail and jib foresail. As a prelude to her being shown at the Chicago Exhibition she was successfully taken across the Atlantic under sail and without an escorting ship. She left Bergen on May 1st, 1893, and arrived at Newport, Rhode Island, U.S.A., on June 13th. She was commanded by Captain Magnus Andersen, who in 1886 had performed the feat of crossing the Atlantic in an open boat. Andersen had a crew of eleven men in the Viking ship. He reported that she had met with some bad weather and proved an excellent sea boat. Her average speed was nine knots, but with a fair wind she did eleven. In the following year the ship was accidentally sunk in the Chicago river, and raised and broken up.

a leader as famed as Olaf Tryggveson, and representing the line of Harold the Fair-haired. Helped by the Danes of Ireland, he sailed back to Norway, to win its crown for himself, and to cast down the worship of Thor and Odin, and make the land part of Christendom.

In the first enterprise he was quickly successful, and in 995 he was recognized as King of Norway at Trondhjem. During the five years that he reigned he devoted much of his energy to the second part of his mission, and made among his countrymen many real converts, and found still more ready to accept external conformity. Sometimes he would argue, exhort, appeal to the reason and the goodwill of chiefs and people. But often the old Viking spirit of his pagan days would master him, and he would hack down with his battleaxe the emblems and the altars of Thor and Odin, and challenge the old gods to avenge the insult if they had the power, and then tell the startled onlookers that if they were to be loyal to him and live in peace they must accept the new and better creed.

The open sea and the deep fiords running far into the hills were the best highways of his kingdom, and Olaf spared no effort to maintain a good fighting fleet, the best ships of which lay anchored before his great hall at Trondhjem when he was at home. When he went out to war his path was by the sea. He hunted down the pirates and destroyed their strongholds in the northern fiords, with none the less zeal because these places were also the last refuge of the old paganism and its Berserker magicians.

He had built for his own use a ship called the *Crane* (*Tranen*), longer than ships were usually made at the time, and also of narrower beam. Her additional length enabled more oars to be used, and her sharp bow, carved into a bird's head, and her graceful lines made her the fastest ship in the fiords when a good crew of rowers was swinging to the oars. A good rowing-boat is generally a bad sailer, but Olaf had made the *Crane* swift enough under canvas, or to speak more accurately, when her sails of brightly dyed wool were spread. She was given high bulwarks, and must have had more than the usual four-foot draught of water, for she carried plenty of heavy stone ballast to stiffen her under sail.

With the *Crane* as his flagship, Olaf sailed northward to attack the Viking Raud, pirate and magician, who held out for the old gods and the old wild ways. Raud had another exceptionally large ship, the longest in Norway, and till the *Crane* was built the swiftest also. The bow, carved into a dragon's head and covered with brazen scales, gave Raud's ship the name of the *Serpent* (*Ormen*).

As Olaf sailed northward Raud and his allies met him in a skirmish at sea, but soon gave way to superior numbers, and Raud, when he steered the *Serpent* into the recesses of Salten Fiord, thought he had shaken off pursuit, especially as the weather had broken, and wild winds, stormy seas, and driving mists and rain squalls might well make the fiord inaccessible to Olaf's fleet. Raud sat late feasting and drinking, and in the early morning he still lay in a drunken sleep when the *Crane* slipped into the fiord despite mist and storm, and Olaf seized the dragon ship and made Raud a prisoner almost without striking a blow.

When the King returned to Trondhjem he had the two finest ships of the north, the *Crane* and the *Serpent*, the latter the largest, the former the swiftest vessel that had yet been launched on the northern seas. Proud of such weapons, he wondered if he could not build a warship longer than the *Serpent* and swifter than the *Crane*, and he consulted his best shipbuilder, Thorberg Haarklover, *i.e.* the "Hair-splitter," so named from his deftness with the sharp adze, the shipwright's characteristic tool in the days of wooden walls. Thorberg was given a free hand, and promised to build a ship that would be famous for centuries.

This was the *Lang Ormen*, or *Long Serpent*, a *Dreadnought* of those old Viking days. She was 150 feet long, and her sides rose high out of the water, but she had also a deep draught. The bow, strengthened with a cut-water of steel, was fashioned like the head of a huge dragon, the stern carved into a dragon's tail, and bow and stern were covered with scales of gold. She had sixty oars, and her crew was made up of no less than six hundred picked men, among them warriors whose names live in history.

For a while Olaf, with his great ships, reigned victoriously over Norway, defeating more than one effort of the old pagan Vikings to shake his power. One of these defeated rivals, Erik Jarl (Earl Erik), took refuge in Sweden, gathered there a number of adherents who had like himself fled from Norway to avoid Olaf's strong-handed methods of reform and conversion, and with them sailed the Baltic, plundering its coasts in the old Viking fashion. King Svend of Denmark was jealous of the power of Norway, welcomed Erik at his Court, and gave him his daughter's hand. Svend's queen, Sigrid, was a Swedish princess, and Erik set to work to form a triple league against Norway of which the three branches would be his own following of Norwegian malcontents and the Swedes and Danes.

Olaf had spent the summer of the year 1000, with a fleet of sixty ships, in the South-Eastern Baltic. Autumn was coming, and the King was preparing to return home before the wintry weather began, when news arrived that hastened his departure. It was brought by one of his *jarls*, Earl Sigvald, who came with eleven ships, manned by his clansmen, and reported that the rebel Erik had been joined by the kings of Sweden and Denmark, and the three fleets of the allies were preparing to fall upon Olaf on his homeward voyage. But Sigvald assured the King that if he would allow him to pilot the Norwegian fleet he would take it safely through channels deep enough for even the *Long Serpent*, and elude the hostile armada, which outnumbered Olaf's fleet three to one.

Sigvald, however, was a traitor. He had promised to lead Olaf into waters where the allied fleets would be waiting to attack him. And he knew they would be anchored inside the island of Rügen, near the islet of Svold.

So Olaf, trusting to his false friend, sailed westward from Wendland to his last battle. The "Saga" tells how on a bright morning, Erik Jarl and the two kings watched from Svold the approach of the Norwegian ships, and at first doubted if Olaf was with them, but when they saw the *Long Serpent* towering above the rest they doubted no longer, and gave orders for their 180 ships to clear for action, agreeing that Norway should be divided among them and the *Long Serpent* should be the prize of whoever first set foot on her deck, so sure were they that numbers would give them victory even against a champion of the seas like Olaf Tryggveson.

The swift *Crane* and the *Short Serpent*, taken from Raud of Salten Fiord, had sailed ahead of the fleet. They saw the ships of the allies crowding out of the channel between Svold and the mainland, and turned back to give the alarm. Thorkild, the half-brother of Olaf, who commanded the *Short Serpent*, urged the King to bear out to sea and avoid a fight with such desperate odds. But Olaf's blood was up. Like the *triremes* of the Mediterranean, the *Serpents*, *Dragons*, and *Cranes* of the northern seas used only the oars in battle, and the King gave the order which meant fighting. "Down with the sails!" he said. "Who talks of running away? I never fled yet and never will. My life is in God's hands, but flight would be shame forever."

The battle that followed is the most famous in Viking story. We know it chiefly through poetic records. But there is no doubt the "Saga" preserves for us much of the living tradition of the time, and if its writers yielded to the temptation of decorating their narrative with picturesque detail, it must be remembered that they told the tale of Olaf's last sea-fight to men who knew from experience what Northern war was like, so they give us what we chiefly want, a lifelike picture of a Viking battle.

Just as Shakespeare tells how at Shrewsbury "the King had many marching in his coats," and to this day in an Abyssinian army several nobles are dressed and armed like the King to divert personal attack from him, so, as he stood on the after-deck of the *Long Serpent*, Olaf had beside him one of his best warriors, Kolbiorn Slatter, a man like himself in height and build, and wearing the same splendid armour, with gilded shield and helmet and crimson cloak. Round them were grouped the picked fighting men of the bodyguard, the "Shield-burg," so called because it was their duty to form a breastwork of their shields and ward off arrows and javelins from the King. On the poop also were the King's trumpeters bearing the "war horns"—long horns of the wild ox, which now sounded the signal for battle. The droning call was taken up by ship after ship, as the shouting sailors sent down sails and yards on deck. The ships closed on each other side by side, and drew in their oars, forming in close line abreast, and then under bare masts the long array of war galleys, with their high bows carved into heads of beasts and birds and dragons, drifted with the current towards the hostile fleet.

The sailors were lashing the ships together as they moved. Manœuvring appears to have had small part in most Viking fights. The fleet became one great floating fortress, and as the ships met bow to bow the best warriors fought hand to hand on the forecastle decks.

The writer of the "Saga" tells how in the centre of the fleet the *Long Serpent* lay, with the *Crane* and the *Short Serpent* to port and starboard. The sterns of the three ships were in line, and so the bow of the *Long Serpent* projected far in front of the rest. As the sailors secured the ships in position, Ulf the Red-haired, who commanded on the forecastle of the *Long Serpent*, went aft and called out to the King that if the *Serpent* lay so far ahead he and his men would have tough work in the bow. "Are you afraid?" asked the King. "We are no more afraid forward than you are aft," replied Ulf, with a flash of anger. The King lost his temper and threatened Ulf with an arrow on his bowstring. "Put down your bow," said Ulf. "If you shoot me you wound your own hand," and then he went back to his post on the forecastle deck.

The allied fleet was now formed in line and bearing down on the Norwegians. Sigvald Jarl, who had lured the King into this ambush, hung back with his eleven ships, and Olaf with his sixty had to meet a threefold force. King Svend, with the Danish fleet, formed the enemy's centre. To his right Olaf's namesake, King Olaf Svensker, led the Swedish ships. On the left was Erik, with the rebel heathen Jarls of Norway. Olaf watched the enemy's

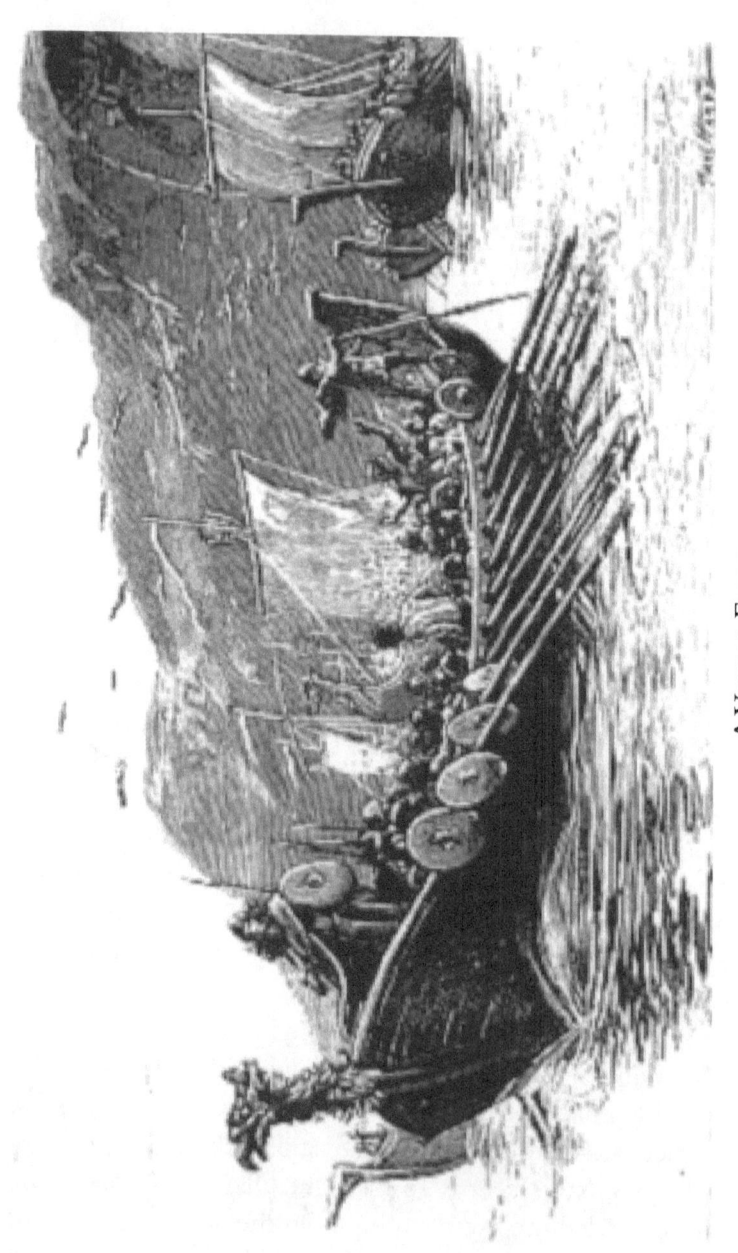

A Viking Fleet

approach and talked to Kolbiorn and the men of the Shieldburg. He did not reckon that the Danes or the Swedes would give much trouble, he said; the Danes were soft fellows, and the Swedes would be better "at home pickling fish" than risking themselves in fight with Norsemen, but Erik's attack would be dangerous. "These are Norwegians like ourselves. It will be hard against hard."

Perhaps we have here a touch of flattery for his countrymen from the poet of the "Saga," a Norseman telling the tale to men of his own race. However this may be, the words put into Olaf's mouth were true so far as the rebel Jarls were concerned, even if they did injustice to Dane and Swede.

Erik Jarl seems to have had some inventive talent and some idea of naval tactics. His ship was called the *Iron Beard*, because her bows bristled with sharpened spikes of iron. She was to be herself a weapon, not merely a means of bringing fighting men to close quarters for a hand-to-hand struggle. It is remarkable that, though it proved useful at the battle of Svold, the armed bow found no regular place in Viking warfare. The *Iron Beard* also anticipated modern methods in another way. Her bulwarks were covered with iron-plating.

It cannot have been of any serious thickness, for a Viking ship had not enough displacement to spare for carrying heavy armour; but the thin plates were strong enough to be a defence against arrows and spears, and as these would not penetrate a thick wooden bulwark it seems likely that the plating was fixed on a rail running along each side, thus giving a higher protection than the bulwark itself. Erik's ship was thus a primitive ironclad ram.

Though Olaf had spoken lightly of the Danes, it was King Svend's squadron that began the fight, rowing forward in advance of the rest and falling on the right and right centre of Olaf's fleet. The Swedes at first hung back. Svend himself on the left of the Danish attack steered straight for the projecting bows of the *Long Serpent*. Red-haired Ulf grappled the Danish King's ship, boarded her, and after a fierce fight in which the Norwegian battleaxes did deadly work, cleared her from end to end. King Svend saved his life by clambering on board of another ship. Olaf and his men from the high stern of the *Long Serpent* shot their arrows with telling effect into the Danish ships.

All along the centre the Norwegians held their own, and gradually the Danes began to give way. It was then only the Swedes worked their ships into the *mêlée* that raged in front of the line of Norwegian bows. To have swept round the line and attacked in flank and rear, while the Danes still grappled it in front, would have been a more effective method of attack, but the opponents thought only of meeting front to front like fighting bulls. It may be too that Olaf's fleet had so drifted that there was not much room to pass between its right wing on the land.

But however this may be, there was plenty of sea room on the left, and here Erik Jarl, in the *Iron Beard*, led the attack and used his advantage to the full. Part of his squadron fell upon the Norwegian front; but the *Iron Beard* and several of her consorts swung round the end of the line, and concentrated their attack on the outside ship. Erik had grasped a cardinal principle of naval tactics, the importance of trying to crush a part of the hostile line by bringing a local superiority of force to bear upon it.

It was "hard against hard"—Viking against Viking—but the Norwegians in the end ship were hopelessly outnumbered. They fought furiously and sold their lives dearly; but soon the armed bow of the *Iron Beard* drove between their ship and the next, the lashings were cut, and the Norwegian drifted out of the line, with her deck heaped with dead. Erik let her drift and attacked the next ship in the same way. He was eating up Olaf's left wing ship by ship, while the Danes and Swedes kept the centre and right busy.

It was the bloodiest fight that the North had ever seen, a fight to the death, for though there was now small hope of victory, the Norse battle madness was strong in Olaf and his men. As the day wore on the right held its own; but one by one every ship on the left had been cleared by Erik and the Jarls, and now the battle raged round the three great ships in the centre, the *Crane* and the two *Serpents*. Erik came up and drove the bow of the *Iron Beard* into the *Long Serpent's* bulwarks. The rebel Jarl stood on the forecastle behind the bristling spikes, his blood-stained battleaxe in hand and his Shield-burg standing close around him.

They had now hard work to ward off the arrows that came whistling from the *Long Serpent*, for at such close quarters Erik had been recognized, and more than one archer shot at him. The "Saga" tells how young Einar Tamberskelver, the best of the bowmen of Norway, so strong that he could send a blunt arrow through a bull's hide, had posted himself in the rigging of the *Long Serpent* and made the rebel Jarl his mark. His arrows rattled on the shields of Erik's guard. One of them grazed his helmet, whistled over the *Iron Beard's* deck and buried itself in her rudder-head. Crouching in the bow of the *Iron Beard* behind her armour plates was a Finnish archer, and the Finlanders were such good bowmen that men said sorcery aided their skill.

Erik told him to shoot the man in the *Serpent's* rigging. The Finn, to show his marksmanship, aimed at Einar's bowstring and cut it with his arrow. The bow released from the string sprang open and broke with a loud report. "What is that sound?" asked Olaf.

Einar sprang down from the rigging and answered, "It is the sound of the sceptre of Norway falling from your grasp." It was noticed that Olaf's hand was bleeding, "his gauntlet was full of blood," but he had given no sign when he was wounded. Arrows, javelins, and stones were falling in showers on the decks of the *Crane* and the *Serpents*, for the Danes and Swedes worsted in the close fight had drawn off a little, and were helping Erik's attack by thus fighting at a safer distance.

Erik now boarded the *Long Serpent* amidships, but was beaten back. He brought up more of his ships and gathered a larger boarding-party. The Danish and Swedish arrows had thinned the ranks of Ulf's men in the *Long Serpent's* bows. When Erik led a second storming-party on board, Danes and Swedes too came clambering over the bow, and the *Long Serpent* attacked on all sides was cleared to the poop. Here Olaf fought with Kolbiorn, Einar and the men of the Shield-burg around him. He was somewhat disabled by his wounded hand, but he still used his battle-axe with deadly effect. The attacking party were not quite sure which of the tall men in gilded armour was the King, but at such close quarters some of them soon recognized him, and Erik called to his men not to kill Olaf, but to make him prisoner. Olaf knew well that if his life was spared for a while it would be only to put him to death finally with the cruelty the heathen Vikings delighted in inflicting on their enemies.

As his men fell round him and his party was driven further and further astern, he must have seen that, outnumbered as his men were, and with himself wounded, he would soon be overmastered and made prisoner. There was just one chance of escape for the best swimmer in Norway. Holding up his shield he stepped on the bulwark, threw the shield at his enemies, and dived overboard. Kolbiorn tried to dive with him, but was seized and dragged back to the ship. When Erik found he was not the King he spared his life.

The few who remained of the Shield-burg sprang overboard. Some were killed by men who were waiting in boats to dispose of the fugitives, others escaped by diving and swimming, and reached Danish and Swedish ships where they asked for, and were given, quarter. Einar, the archer, was one of those thus saved, and he is heard of later in the Danish wars of England.

Olaf was never seen again. Sigvald's ships, after having watched the fight from afar, were rowing up to the victorious fleets, and for a long time there was a rumour that King Olaf had slipped out of his coat of mail as he swam under water, and then rose and eluded Erik's boats, and reached one of Sigvald's ships, where he was hidden. The tale ran that he had been taken back to Wendland, where he was waiting to reappear some day in Norway and claim his own. But years went on and there were no tidings of King Olaf Tryggveson. He had been drowned in his armour under the stern of the *Long Serpent*.

King Olaf is still, after nine centuries, one of the popular heroes of the Norwegian people. He had a twofold fame, as the ideal of a sea-king, as the ruler who tried in his own wild untaught way to win the land of the Fiords to Christendom. Another Olaf, who completed this last work a few years later, and who, like Olaf Tryggveson, reigned over Norway in right of his prowess and his descent from Harold the Fair-haired, is remembered as St. Olaf, saint and martyr; but no exploit of either king lives in popular tradition so brightly as the story of Olaf Tryggveson's death-battle at Svold. "My life is in God's hands," he had said, "but flight would be shame forever." His fight against desperate odds and ending in defeat and death won him fame for ever.

CHAPTER 4

Sluys 1340

The gold "nobles" of the coinage of King Edward III show in conventional fashion the King standing in the waist of a ship with a high bow and poop, the red-cross banner of St. George at the stern and the lions of England and the lilies of France emblazoned on his shield. The device typifies his claim to the sovereignty of the narrow seas between England and the Continent, the prize won for him by the fleet that conquered at Sluys.

Sluys is often spoken of as the sea-fight that inaugurated the long victorious career of the British Navy. It would be more correct to say that it was the battle which, by giving King Edward the command of the Channel, made his successful invasion of France possible, and secured for England the possession of Calais. Holding both Dover and Calais the English for two centuries were masters of the narrow sea-gate through which all the trade between northern Europe and the rest of the world had to pass. They had the power of bringing severe pressure to bear upon the German cities of the Hansa League, the traders of the Low Countries, the merchants of Spain, Genoa, and Venice, by their control of this all-important waterway. Hence the claim upheld till the seventeenth century that the King of England was "Sovereign of the Seas," and that in the Channel and the North Sea every foreign ship had to lower her sails and salute any English "King's ship" that she met.

Sluys, which had such far-reaching consequences, was not

the first of English naval victories. Alfred the Great maintained in the latter part of his reign a fleet of small ships to guard the coasts against the Norse and Danish pirates, and this won him the name of founder of the British Navy. But for centuries after there was no attempt at forming or keeping up a regular naval establishment. Alfred's navy must have been dispersed under his weaker successors, for the Northmen never found any serious obstacles to their raids.

Harold had no navy, and the result was that in a single twelve-month England was twice invaded, first by Harold Hadrada and Tostig, who were beaten at Stamford Bridge, and then by William the Norman, who conquered at Hastings. But even the Conqueror had no fighting fleet. His ships were used merely to ferry his army across the Channel, and he made no attempt to use them against the Northmen who harried the east coast. The record of victory begins with the reign of King John, when in 1213 William Longsword, his half-brother, with a fleet gathered from the shipping of Dover and the south-eastern ports, destroyed a French fleet that had assembled on the coast of the Netherlands to transport an invading army to England.

Damme (*i.e.* "the dams or embankments to keep out the sea") was then a fortified port. It is now a Dutch village, some miles from the coast, in the midst of green meadows won from the sea, with roads shaded by avenues of trees, and only the traffic of its canal to remind it that it once had a harbour.

Four years later Hubert de Burgh, Governor of Dover Castle, defeated another attempted raid on England by improvising a fleet and attacking the French squadron in the Straits. De Burgh got to windward of the French, then sailed down on them, grappled and boarded them. There was an incident which happily we do not hear of again in naval warfare. As the English scrambled on board of the French ships they threw quicklime in the eyes of their opponents.

It was, no doubt, an ugly trick of piratical fighting, for in those days when there was no police of the seas there was a certain amount of piracy and smuggling carried on by the men of

Dover and the Cinque Ports. Just as for lack of police protection highway robbery was a danger of travel by road, so till organized naval power developed there was a good deal of piracy in the European seas, and peaceful traders sailed in large fleets for mutual protection, just as travellers on land took care to have companions for a journey. The Channel was also enlivened by occasional fights for fishing-grounds between fleets of fishing-craft, and the quicklime trick of Hubert de Burgh's battle was probably one of the methods of this irregular warfare.

Edward I had a navy which did useful service by coasting northward, as his armies marched into Scotland, and securing for them regular supplies and reinforcements by sea. Under his weak successor the sea was neglected, and it was the third Edward who used the navy effectually to secure that his quarrel with France should be fought out, not on English ground, but on the Continent, and thus became the founder of the sea power of England.

There was no Royal Navy in the modern sense of the term. When the King went to war his fleet was recruited from three different sources. The warship was a merchantman, on board of which a number of fighting-men, knights, men-at-arms, archers and billmen were embarked. These were more numerous than the crew of sailors which navigated the ship, for the largest vessels of the time were not of more than two to three hundred tons, and as oars were not used in the rough seas of the Channel and there was only one mast with a single square sail, and perhaps a jib-foresail, the necessary hands for sailing her were few.

There was a dual command, the knight or noble who led the fighting-men being no sailor, and having a pilot under him who commanded the sailors and navigated the ship. This dual arrangement (which we have seen at work in the fleets of more ancient days) left its traces in our Navy up to the middle of the nineteenth century, when ships of the Royal Navy still had, besides the captain, a "sailing master" among their officers.

The King owned a small number of ships, which he maintained just as he kept a number of knights in his pay to form his personal retinue on land. During peace he hired these ships out to merchants, and when he called them back for war service he took the crews that navigated them into his pay, and sent his fighting-men on board. But the King's ships were the least numerous element in the war fleet. Merchantmen were impressed for service from London and the other maritime towns and cities, the feudal levy providing the fighting complement.

A third element in the fleet was obtained from the Cinque Ports. There were really seven, not five, of them—Dover, Hythe, Hastings, Winchelsea, Rye, Romney, and Sandwich. Under their charter they enjoyed valuable privileges, in return for which they were bound to provide, when the King called upon them, fifty-seven ships and twelve hundred men and boys for fifteen days at their own expense, and as long after as the King paid the necessary charges. The naming of so short a term of service shows that maritime operations were expected not to last long. It was, indeed, a difficult matter to keep a medieval fleet at sea, and the conditions that produced this state of things lasted far into the modern period.

Small ships crowded with fighting-men had no room for any large store of provisions and water. When the first scanty supply was exhausted, unless they were in close touch with a friendly port, they had to be accompanied by a crowd of storeships, and as the best merchantmen would naturally have been impressed for the actual fighting, these would be small, inferior, and less seaworthy ships, and the fleet would have to pay as much attention to guarding its convoy as to operating against an enemy. No wonder that as a rule the most that could be attempted was a short voyage and a single stroke.

It was in 1340 that King Edward III challenged the title of Philip of Valois to the crown of France, and by claiming it for himself began "the Hundred Years' War." Both sides to the quarrel began to collect fleets and armies, and both realized that the first struggle would be on the sea. It would be thus decided whether the war was to be fought out on French or on English ground.

The French King collected ships from his ports and strengthened his fleet by hiring a number of large warships from Genoa, then one of the great maritime republics of the Mediterranean. The Genoese sailors knew the northern seas, for there were always some of their ships in the great trading fleet that passed up the Channel each spring, bringing the produce of the Mediterranean countries and the East to the northern ports of Europe, and returned in the late summer laden with the merchandise of the Hansa traders.

Early in the year King Philip had assembled a hundred and ninety ships, large and small, French and Genoese, off the little town of Sluys on the coast of Flanders. The fleet lay in the estuary of the river Eede. Like Damme, Sluys has now become an inland village. Its name means "the sluice," and, like Damme, reminds us how the people of the Netherlands have for centuries been winning their land from the sea by their great system of dams to keep the sea-water back, and sluices to carry the river-water to the sea. The estuary of the Eede where the French fleet anchored is now pasture land traversed by a canal, and the embankments that keep the sea from the meadow lands lie some miles to the westward of the place where King Edward won his great naval victory.

Had the French acted at once, there was nothing to prevent them from opening the war by invading England. Perhaps they did not know how slowly the English fleet was assembling.

In the late spring when the French armament was nearly complete, King Edward had only forty ships ready. They lay in the estuaries of the Orwell and the Stour, inside Harwich, long a place of importance for English naval wars in the North Sea. Gradually, week after week, other ships came in from the Thames, and the northern seaports, from Southampton and the Cinque Ports, and even from Bristol, creeping slowly along the coasts from harbour to harbour. All this time the French might have swept the seas and destroyed the English in detail; but they waited for more ships and more men, and the time of opportunity went by.

At last in the beginning of June the English King had two hundred ships assembled, from decked vessels down to open sailing-boats. An army crowded on board of them, knights and nobles in shining armour, *burghers* and peasants in steel caps and leather jerkins, armed with the long-bow or the combined pike and long battleaxe known as the "bill." The King's ship flew the newly adopted royal standard in which the golden lions on a red field, the arms of England, were quartered with the golden lilies of France on a field of blue, and another banner displaying the device that is still the flag of the Royal Navy, the Red Cross of St. George on a field of white, the banner adopted by Richard Cœur de Lion in his Crusade.

The other ships flew the banners of the barons and knights who commanded them, and on the royal ship and those of the chief commanders there were trumpeters whose martial notes were to give the signal for battle. As a knight of the Middle Ages despised the idea of fighting on foot, and there might be a landing in Flanders, some of the barons had provided for all eventualities by taking with them their heavy war horses, uncomfortably stabled in the holds of the larger ships.

The fleet sailed southward along the coast, keeping the land in sight. The two hundred ships of varying rates of speed and handiness could not move in the ordered lines of a modern naval armament, but streamed along in an irregular procession, closing up when they anchored for the night. From the North Foreland, with a favourable wind behind them, they put out into the open sea, and steering eastward were out of sight of land for a few hours, a more venturous voyage for these coasting craft than the crossing of the Atlantic is for us today. It must have been a trying experience for knight and yeoman, and they must have felt that a great peril was past when the tops of church towers and windmills showed above the horizon, and then the low shore fringed with sandhills and the green dykes came in sight.

Coasting along the shore north-eastwards, the fleet reached a point to the north-west of Bruges, not far from where the watering-place of Blankenberg now stands. It had been ascertained from fishermen and coast-folk that the French fleet was still at Sluys, and it was decided to proceed no further without reconnoitring the enemy. The larger ships anchored, the smaller were beached. The fighting-men landed and camped on the shore to recover from the distresses of their voyage, during which they would have been cramped up in narrow quarters.

Instead of, like a modern admiral, sending some of his lighter and swifter ships to take a look at the enemy, King Edward arranged a cavalry reconnaissance, a simpler matter for his knightly following. Some of the horses were got ashore, and a party of knights mounted and rode over the sandhills towards Sluys. They reached a point where, without being observed by the enemy, they could get a good view of the hostile fleet, and they brought back news that made the King decide to attack next day.

The French fleet was commanded by two knights, the Sieur de Kiriet and the Sieur de Bahuchet. Kiriet's name suggests that he came of the Breton race that has given so many good sailors and naval officers to France, so perhaps he knew something of the sea. Associated with the two French commanders there was an experienced fighting admiral, a veteran of the wars of the Mediterranean, Barbavera, who commanded the Genoese ships. Though they had a slight superiority of numbers and more large ships than the English, Kiriet and Bahuchet were, as one might expect from their prolonged inactivity, very wanting in enterprise now that the crisis had come.

They were preparing to fight on the defensive. It was in vain that the experienced commander Barbavera urged that they should weigh anchor and fight the English in the open sea, where numbers and weight would give them an advantage that would be lost in the narrow waters of the Eede estuary. They persisted in awaiting the attack.

The French fleet was anchored along the south shore of the river-mouth, sterns to the land, its left towards the river-mouth, its right towards the town of Sluys. The vessel on the extreme left was an English ship of large size, the *Great Cristopher*, captured in the Channel in the first days of the war. The ships were grouped in three divisions—left, centre, and right. Kiriet and Bahuchet adopted the same plan of battle that King Olaf had used at Svold. The ships in each of the three divisions were lashed together side by side, so that they could only be boarded by the high narrow bows, and there was an addition to the Norse plan, for inboard across the bows barricades had been erected formed of oars, spars, and planking, fastened across the forecastle decks.

Behind these barriers archers and Genoese cross-bowmen were posted. There was a second line of archers in the fighting-tops, for since the times of Norse warfare the masts had become heavier, and now supported above the crossyard a kind of crow's nest where two or three bowmen could be stationed, with shields hung round them as a parapet.

The fleet thus was converted into a series of three long, narrow floating forts. It was an intelligible plan of defence for a weak fleet against a strong one, but a hopeless plan for an armament strong enough to have met its opponents on the open sea, ship to ship. At Svold, Erik Jarl had shown that such an array could be destroyed piecemeal if assailed on an exposed flank, and at Sluys the left, where the *Great Cristopher* lay to seaward, positively invited such an attack.

King Edward saw his advantage as soon as his knights came back from their adventurous ride and told him what they had seen, and he arranged his plans accordingly. His great ships were to lead the attack, and concentrate their efforts on the left of the French line. The rest were to pass inside them and engage the enemy in front, on the left, and centre. The enemy had by tying up his ships made it impossible to come to the rescue of the left, even if the narrow waters of the estuary would have allowed him to deploy his force into line.

The English would have, and could not fail to keep, a local superiority from the very outset on the left of the enemy, and once it came to close quarters they would clear the French and Genoese decks from end to end of the line, taking ship after ship. While the attack developed the English archers would prepare the way for it by thinning the ranks of their enemies on the ships in the centre and then on the right.

At dawn on 24 June—the day of battle—the wind was blowing fair into the mouth of the Eede, but the tide was ebbing, and the attack could not be driven home till it turned, and gave deep water everywhere between the banks of the inlet. King Edward used the interval to array his fleet and get it into position for the dash into the river. His ships stood out to sea on the starboard tack, a brave sight with the midsummer sun shining on the white sails, the hundreds of banners glowing with red, blue, white, and gold, the painted shields hanging on poop and bulwark. On the raised bows and sterns of the larger ships barons and knights and men-at-arms stood arrayed in complete armour. The archers were ranged along the bulwarks, or looked out from the crow's-nest-tops over the swelling sails.

Old Barbavera must have longed to cut lashings, slip cables, drift out on the tide, and meet the English in the open, but he was in a minority of one against two. And now the tide was dead slack and began to turn, and King Edward's trumpets gave the expected signal for action. As their notes rang over the sea the shouting sailors squared the yards and the fleet began to scud before the wind for the river-mouth, where beyond the green dykes that kept the entrance free a forest of masts bristled along the bank towards Sluys.

The English came in with wind and tide helping them, several ships abreast, the rest following each as quickly as she might, like a great flock of sea-birds streaming towards the shore. There could be no long ranging fire to prelude the close attack. At some sixty yards, when men could see each other's faces across the gap, the English archers drew their bows, and the cloth-yard arrows began to fly, their first target the *Great Cristopher* on the flank of the line. Bolts from cross-bows came whizzing back in reply. But, as at Crecy soon after, the long-bow with its rapid discharge of arrows proved its superiority over the slower mechanical weapon of the Genoese cross-bowmen.

But no time was lost in mere shooting. Two English ships crashed into the bows and the port side of the *Cristopher*, and with the cry of "St. George for England!" a score of knights vied with each other for the honour of being first on board of the enemy. The other ships of the English van swung round bow to bow with the next of the French line, grappled and fought to board them. King Edward himself climbed over the bows of a French ship, risking his life as freely as the youngest of his esquires. Then for a while on the French left it was a question of which could best handle the long, heavy swords, made not for deft fencing work, but for sheer hard hacking at helmet and breastplate.

Behind this fight on the flank, ship after ship slipped into the river, but at first attacked only the left division closely, those that had pushed furthest in opening with arrow fire on the centre and leaving the right to look helplessly on. The English archers soon cleared the enemy's tops of their bowmen, and then from the English masts shot coolly into the throng on the hostile decks, their comrades at the bulwarks shooting over the heads of those engaged in the bows. The English arrows inflicted severe loss on the enemy, but the real business was done by the close attack of the boarding-parties, that cleared ship after ship from the left inwards, each ship attacked in turn having to meet the knights and men-at-arms from several of the English vessels.

But the French fought with determined courage, and hour after hour went by as the attack slowly worked its way along the line. The slaughter was terrible, for in a sea-fight, as in the storming of a city wall, no quarter was asked or given. The crews of the captured ships were cut down as they fought, or driven over the stern into the water, where, for the most part, their heavy armour drowned them.

It was past noon, and the tide was turning when the left and centre, the squadrons of Kiriet and Bahuchet, were all captured. Then the attack raged round the nearest vessels on the right, tall ships of the Genoese. Most of these, too, were taken, but as the tide ran out King Edward feared his large ships would ground in the upper waters of the estuary, and the signal was given to break off the attack, an order welcome even to the weary victors.

Barbavera, with a few ships, got clear of the beaten right wing and lay up near Sluys, while the English plundered and burned some of their prizes and took the best of them out to sea on the ebbing tide. In the night the Genoese admiral slipped out to sea, and got safely away. The French fleet had been utterly destroyed, and the Genoese sailors had no intention of further risking themselves in King Philip's quarrel. They thought only of returning as soon as might be to the Mediterranean.

King Edward went on to Ghent, after landing his fighting-men, and sending his fleet to bring further forces from England. Henceforth for many a long year he might regard the Channel as a safe highway for men and supplies for the war in France.

The victory of the English had cost them a relatively trifling loss. The French losses are said to have been nearly 30,000 men. Strange to say, among the English dead were four ladies who had embarked on the King's ship to join the Queen's Court at Ghent. How they were killed is not stated. Probably they were courageous dames whose curiosity led them to watch the fight from the tall poop of the flagship as they would have watched a tournament from the galleries of the lists, and there the crossbow bolts of the Genoese found them.

There is an old story that men feared to tell King Philip the news of the disaster, and the Court jester broke the tidings with a casual remark that the French must be braver than the English, for they jumped into the sea by scores, while the islanders stuck to their ships. The defeat at sea prepared the way for other defeats by land, and in these campaigns there appeared a new weapon of war—rudely fashioned cannon of short range and slow, inaccurate fire—the precursors of heavier artillery that was to change the whole character of naval warfare.

It was the coming of the cannon that inaugurated the modern period. But before telling of battles in which artillery played the chief part, we must tell of a decisive battle that was a link between old and new. Lepanto—the battle that broke the Turkish power in the Mediterranean—saw, like the sea-fights of later days, artillery in action, and at the same time oar-driven galleys

Mediterranean Craft of the Sixteenth Century

A Galley

A Carrack or Frigate

fighting with the tactics that had been employed at Salamis and Actium, and knights in armour storming the enemy's ships like Erik Jarl at Svold and King Edward at Sluys.

CHAPTER 5

Lepanto 1571

The Turk has long been known as the "sick man of Europe," and the story of the Ottoman Empire for a hundred years has been a tale of gradual dismemberment. Thus it is no easy matter for us to realize that for centuries the Ottoman power was the terror of the civilized world.

It was in 1358 that the Ottomans seized Gallipoli, on the Dardanelles, and thus obtained their first footing in Europe. They soon made themselves masters of Philippopolis and Adrianople. A crusading army, gathered to drive the Asiatic horde from Europe, was cut to pieces by the Sultan Bajazet at Nicopolis in 1396. On the day after the battle ten thousand Christian prisoners were massacred before the Sultan, the slaughter going on from daybreak till late in the afternoon. The Turk had become the terror of Europe.

Constantinople was taken by Mahomet II in 1453, and the Greek Empire came to an inglorious end. Then for more than a century Austrians, Hungarians, and Poles formed a barrier to the advance of the Asiatic power into Central Europe.

But the Turks during this century became a maritime power. They had conquered the Crimea and were masters of the Black Sea. They had overrun Greece and most of the islands of the Archipelago. They had threatened Venice with their fleets, and had for a while a foothold in Southern Italy. They took Rhodes from the Knights of St. John, annexed Syria and Egypt, and the Sultan of Constantinople was acknowledged as the Khalifa of Islam, the representative of the Prophet by the Mohammedan states of North Africa—Tripoli, Tunis, and Morocco. In 1526 the victory of Mohacs made the Turks masters of Hungary. They had driven a wedge deep into Europe, and there was danger that their fleets would soon hold the command of the Mediterranean.

These fleets were composed chiefly of large galleys—lineal descendants (so to say) of the ancient *triremes*. There was a row of long oars on either side, but sail power had so far developed that there were also one, two, even three tall masts, each crossed by a long yard that carried a triangular lateen sail. The base of the triangle lay along the yard, and the apex was the lower corner of the triangular sail, which could be hauled over to either side of the ship, one end of the yard being hauled down on the other side. The sail thus lay at an angle with the line of the keel, with one point of the yard high above the masthead, and by carrying the sheet tackle of the point of the sail across the ship, and reversing the position of the yard, the galley was put on one tack or the other.

Forward, pointing ahead, was a battery of two or more guns, and there was sometimes a second but lighter battery astern, to be used when the galley was escaping from a ship of superior force. Turks, in the Eastern Mediterranean, Moors in the West, recruited their crews of rowers by capturing Christian ships and raiding Christian villages, to carry off captives who could be trained to the oar. This piracy, plundering, and slave-hunting went on in the Mediterranean up to the first years of the nineteenth century, when, after the Turks themselves had long abandoned it, the sea rovers of the Barbary States in the western waters of the inland sea still kept it up, and European nations paid blackmail to the Beys of Tripoli, Tunis, and Algiers to secure immunity for their ships and sailors.

In the fifteenth and sixteenth centuries no part of the Mediterranean was free from the raids of the Moslem pirates. Such was the peril of the sea that ships used to carry two sets of sails, one white for use by day, the other black, in order to conceal their movements in the darkness. Thousands of Christian slaves were always wearing out their miserable lives in the galleys and prisons of the Mohammedan ports. Isolated expeditions were sometimes made by this or that Christian power for their deliverance. Two religious orders were founded to collect alms for their ransom, to minister to them in their captivity, and to negotiate for their deliverance. But all this was only a mitigation of the evil, and year after year there went on the enslavement of Europeans, men for the galleys, women for the harems.

One would have thought that all Europe would have banded itself together to drive back the Turk from the Danube and sweep the *corsairs* from the Mediterranean. To their honour be it said that successive Popes endeavoured to arouse the old crusading spirit, and band civilized and Christian Europe together for an enterprise that was to the advantage of all, and the neglect of which was a lasting disgrace. But their efforts were long defeated by the mutual quarrels and jealousies and the selfish policy of the European powers. Venice and Genoa long preferred to maintain peace with the Sultans, in order to have the undisturbed monopoly of the Eastern trade. France was too often the ally of the Turk, thanks to her traditional rivalry with the House of Austria, the rulers of the German Empire. The pressure of Turkish armies on the Eastern frontiers of the Empire made it impossible for the Emperors to use their full strength on the Rhine or in North Italy.

Again and again Rome uttered the cry of alarm, and the warning passed unheeded. But at last it was listened to, when a new outburst of aggressive activity on the part of the Turks for a while roused the maritime nations of the Mediterranean from their lethargy, and then a glorious page was added to the story of naval warfare.

In the year 1566 Suleiman the Magnificent died. He had conquered at Mohacs and besieged Vienna, enlarged the boundaries of the Ottoman Empire on land, and made its fleets the terror of the Mediterranean; but the year before he died his *pashas* had failed disastrously in their attempt on Malta, and his successor, Selim II (whom Ottoman historians surname "the Drunkard"), was reported to be a half-imbecile wretch, devoid of either intelligence or enterprise. So Europe breathed more freely. But while the "Drunkard" idled in his *seraglio* by the Golden Horn, the old statesmen, generals, and admirals, whom Suleiman had formed, were still living, and Europe had lulled itself with false hopes of peace.

For the sake of their Eastern trade interests the Venetians had as far as possible stood neutral in the wars between Turk and Christian, and had long been in undisturbed possession of Cyprus. For eighty years they had held it under a treaty that recognized certain rights of the Sultan to the island as a dependency of Egypt. They had stood neutral while Suleiman took Rhodes and besieged Malta, though on either occasion the intervention of the Venetian fleet would have been a serious blow to the Ottoman power. The Venetian Senate was therefore disagreeably surprised when an envoy from Constantinople demanded the evacuation of Cyprus, and announced that the Sultan intended to exercise his full rights as sovereign of the island. The armaments of the Republic were at a low ebb, but *Doge* and Senate rejected the Ottoman demand, and defied the menace of war that accompanied it.

The neutrality of Venice had been the chief obstacle to the efforts of Pius V to form a league of the maritime powers of Southern Europe against the common enemy of Christendom. When, therefore, the Venetian ambassadors applied to the Vatican for help, the Pope put the limited resources of his own states at their disposal, and exerted his influence to procure for them help from other countries. Pius saw the possibility of at last forming a league against the Turk, and was statesman enough to perceive that a more effective blow would be struck against them by attacking them on the sea than by gathering a crusading army on the Theiss and the Danube.

His own galleys were prepared for service under the orders of Prince Colonna, and a subsidy was sent to Venice from the papal treasury to aid in the equipment of the Venetian fleet. The papal envoys appealed to the Genoese Republic, the Knights of Malta, and the Kings of France and Spain to reinforce the fleets of Rome and Venice. But France and Spain were more interested in their own local ambitions and jealousies, and even Philip II gave at first very limited help. With endless difficulty a fleet of galleys was at last assembled, Maltese, Genoese, Roman, Venetian, united under the command of Colonna. By the time the Christian armament was ready a larger Turkish fleet had appeared in the waters of Cyprus and landed an army, which, under its protection, began the siege of Nicosia. After long delays Colonna's fleet reached Suda Bay in Crete, and joined a squadron of Venetian galleys kept for guardship duties in Cretan waters.

Though Colonna was in nominal command, the fleet was really controlled by a committee of the chiefs of its various squadrons. There were endless councils of war, and it is a trite saying that "councils of war do not fight." Prudent caution is oftener the outcome of such debates than daring enterprises. There was a time, in the first days of September, when, if the Suda fleet had gone boldly to the relief of Nicosia, it might have raised the siege, for the Venetian garrison was making such a vigorous defence that in order to press the siege the Turkish pashas had stripped their fleet of thousands of fighting-men to employ them in the trenches. But the golden opportunity passed by, and when at last Colonna took his galleys across to the coast of Asia Minor, Nicosia had fallen, and the Turks had begun the siege of the other Cypriote fortress, Famagusta.

Again there were divided counsels and pitiful irresolution. The commanders of the various contingents were brave men, veterans of the Mediterranean wars. But the coalition lacked one determined leader who could dominate the rest, decide upon a definite plan of action, and put it into energetic execution. Time was wasted till the bad weather began. Then the various squadrons made their way to the ports where they were to pass the winter. A squadron of the Venetians remained in the Cretan ports. The rest dispersed to the harbours of Italy and the Ionian islands.

The aged pontiff heard with bitter disappointment that nothing had been accomplished. The news might well have made even a younger man lose heart. But with undaunted courage he devoted himself to forming a more powerful combination for the great effort of the coming summer.

It was all-important to secure the alliance of the King of Spain, who was also ruler of Naples and Sicily. But it was only after long negotiations and smoothing away of endless jealousies between Spain and Venice, that at last the treaty of the "Holy League" was signed by the Republic of Venice, the King of Spain, and the Pope, Pius V undertaking to bring in help from the minor Princes and Republics of Italy and the Knights of Malta.

It was proposed that there should be a fleet of three hundred ships, of which two hundred were to be galleys and a hundred *navi*, that is full-rigged sailing-ships. It was the first time that the sailing-ship had been given so important a place in naval projects in the Mediterranean, and this shows the change that was rapidly coming into naval methods. The allies were jointly to raise a force of 50,000 fighting-men, including 500 gunners.

Once the treaty was arranged preparations were pushed forward, but again there were wearisome delays. It was easy enough to build galleys. The arsenal of Venice had once laid a keel at sunrise and launched the galley before sunset. But to recruit the thousands of oarsmen was a longer business. It was not till well into the summer of 1571 that the armada of the Holy League began to assemble at the appointed rendezvous, Messina. Meanwhile, the Turks were pressing the siege of Famagusta, blockading it by land and sea, and sapping slowly up to its walls. The heroic commandant of the place, Antonio Bragadino, a worthy son of Venice, made an active defence, retarding by frequent sorties the progress of the enemy's siege works.

By the month of June the Turks had lost nearly 30,000 men, including those who fell victims to the fever that raged in their camps. Bragadino's garrison had been thinned by the enemy's fire, by sickness, and by semi-starvation, and at the same time the magazines of ammunition were nearly empty. Behind the yawning breaches of the rampart an inner line of improvised defences had been erected, and the citadel was still intact. If he had had a little more flour and gunpowder, Bragadino would have held out as stubbornly as ever. But with starving men, empty magazines, and no sign of relief, he had to accept the inevitable. He sent a flag of truce to Mustapha Pasha, the Ottoman general, and relying on the impression made by his stubborn defence, asked for generous terms.

Mustapha professed a chivalrous admiration for the heroism of the Venetians. It was agreed that the garrison should march out with the honours of war, and be transported under a flag of truce to Crete and there set at liberty. The Ottoman general pledged himself to protect the people of Famagusta, and secure for them the free exercise of their religion.

The war-worn soldiers marched out. Bragadino, with the Venetian nobles, were received at Mustapha's tent with every mark of honour. But no sooner had the officers been separated from their men, and these divided into small parties, than all were made prisoners, bound, and robbed of all their personal property. The Turks had often shown remorseless cruelty after victory, but they generally observed the terms of a capitulation honourably. Mustapha's conduct was an unexampled case of treachery and barbarity.

The Venetian soldiers were sent on board the Turkish galleys and chained to their oars as slaves. Bragadino saw his officers beheaded before the *Pasha's* tent. He might have saved his life by becoming a renegade, but he was incapable of such apostasy and treason. The barbarian, in whose power he was, invented new torments for his victim. Bragadino had his ears and nose cut off, and thus mutilated he was paraded round the Turkish army, and then rowed in a boat through the fleet, and everywhere greeted with insult and mockery. Then Mustapha sentenced his prisoner to be flayed alive. The torture had hardly begun when he expired, dying the death of a hero and a martyr. Mustapha sent to Selim the Drunkard as trophies of the conquest of Cyprus the heads of the Venetian nobles and the skin of Bragadino stuffed with straw. The news of the fall of Famagusta and the horrors that followed it did not reach the allied fleet till long after it had sailed from Messina.

But even during the period of preparation there were tidings that might well have inspired the leaders of the League with a new energy. The danger from the East was pressing. In the spring the Ottoman fleet in the waters of Cyprus had been reinforced with new galleys from the arsenal of Constantinople, and a squadron of Algerine *corsairs* under the renegade Pasha Ulugh Ali, one of the best of the Turkish admirals. Thus strengthened, the fleet numbered some two hundred and fifty sail. Even before Famagusta fell Mustapha detached powerful squadrons which harried the Greek *archipelago*, and then rounding the capes of the Morea, made prizes of peaceful traders and raided villages along the western shores of Greece and in the Ionian islands.

During the period of the Turkish power Europe was saved again and again from grave danger, because the Ottoman Sultans and the Pashas of Barbary never seem to have grasped the main principles of maritime warfare. They had no wide views. Most of the men who commanded for them on the sea had the spirit of pirates and buccaneers rather than of admirals. They put to sea to harry the trade of the Christian states and to raid their coast villages, and so secure prizes, plunder, and slaves. They frittered away their strength on these minor enterprises. Again and again occasions offered, when to concentrate their naval forces for a series of campaigns that would sweep the Christian fleets one by one from the sea would have made them masters of the Mediterranean, placed its commerce and its coasts at their mercy, and opened the way for a career of conquest, but they allowed these opportunities to escape.

The peril that menaced European civilization in 1571 was that at last the Moslem powers of the Mediterranean were actually combining their sea forces for a great effort of maritime conquest. Their operations were still delayed by their traditional disposition to indulge in plundering raids, or to wait for the fall of a blockaded fortress, instead of making the destruction of the opposing sea power their first object. If the *pashas* of Selim's fleets had really understood their business, they might have destroyed the Christian squadrons in detail before they could effect their concentration in the waters of Messina. But the Turkish admirals let the opportunity escape them during the long months when the "Holy League" was being formed and its fleets made ready for action.

That the danger was met by the organization of a united effort to break the Moslem power on the sea was entirely due to the clear-sighted initiative and the persistent energy of the aged Pius V. He had fully realized that the naval campaign of 1570 had been paralysed by the Christian fleet being directed, not by one vigorous will, but by the cautious decisions of a permanent council of war. He insisted on the armament of 1571 being under the direction of one chief, and exercising his right as chief of the League, Pius V had to select the commander of its forces; he named as captain-general of the Christian armada Don Juan of Austria.

Don Juan was then a young soldier, twenty-four years of age. He was the son of the Emperor Charles V and his mistress, Barbara Blomberg of Ratisbon. His boyhood had been passed, unknown and unacknowledged by his father, in a peasant household in Castille. As a youth he had been adopted by a noble family of Valladolid. Then Philip II had acknowledged him as his half-brother, and given him the rank of a Spanish Prince. He studied at Alcala, having for his friends and companions Alexander Farnese, the "Great Captain" of future years, and the unfortunate Don Carlos. Don Juan's rank gave him early the opportunity of displaying in high command his marked genius for war.

He was employed in expeditions in the Mediterranean, and directed the suppression of the Moorish revolt in Granada in 1570. He was then named "Capitan-General del Mar"—High Admiral of the Spanish fleets. Young as he was when Pius V appointed him commander-in-chief of the forces of the Holy League, his services by land and sea, as well as his princely rank, gave him the necessary prestige to enable him to command even older generals like Marco Antonio Colonna, the leader of the papal and Italian forces, and the veteran Sebastian Veniero, who directed those of Venice.

During the period of concentration it was Veniero who had the most difficult problem to solve. The Venetian fleet had separated into two divisions at the close of the campaign of 1570. The weaker wintered in the harbours of Crete. The stronger detachment passed the winter at Corfu, in the Ionian islands. In the early summer of 1571 Veniero took command at Corfu, and occupied himself with preparing the fleet for sea, and reinforcing it with new galleys from the arsenal of Venice, and newly raised drafts of sailors, rowers, and fighting-men. Before his preparations were complete, the vanguard of the Turkish armada, continually reinforced from the East, appeared on the western coasts of Greece.

To attack them with the force he had at hand would be to court destruction. Ulugh Ali, who commanded the vanguard of the enemy, was perhaps the best-hated of the Moslem admirals. A Calabrese fisherman, he had been captured as a young man by one of the Barbary *corsairs*, and spent some miserable years chained as a galley-slave at an oar. At last his endurance broke down, and he escaped from his misery by becoming a Mohammedan. Under his new name he rose rapidly to command, enriched himself by successful piracy, and before long won himself the rank of a *Pasha* and a vice-royalty in North Africa. But, happily for Europe at large, though unfortunately for many a village along the shores of Greece and Illyria, Ulugh Ali as admiral of the Turkish fleets remained still a pirate, with the fixed idea that a plundering cruise was better than a naval campaign. Had the renegade been more admiral than pirate, he had an opportunity of changing the course of history in that early summer of 1571.

His fleet cruising off the coasts of Epirus held a central strategic position in relation to the still dispersed Christian fleets. The papal contingents on the western shores of Italy and the Spanish fleets in the ports of the Two Sicilies, or coasting from

Spain by the Gulf of Lyons and the Italian shores, were, it is true, beyond his immediate reach, but he could easily lop off one important branch of the triple League by cutting off the Venetians. The squadron from Crete must pass him to the southward; the more important contingent from Corfu must pass between him and Southern Italy in narrow seas where he could hardly fail to bring it to action, and if it fought, the chances were he would overwhelm it. Or he might attack it at Corfu, or drive it from the island back upon Venice. If he had good luck he might hope to be in time even after this to strike a blow also at the Cretan squadron.

But he thought only of plundering and burning along the coasts, carrying off crowds of prisoners, some of whom were at once added to his crews of chained rowers. Veniero at Corfu had to steel his heart against entreaties to come to the rescue of the mainland coast population. He could not save them, and he dared not destroy his fleet in a hopeless effort. He must seize the opportunity while the Turks were occupied with their raids to sail unopposed to Messina. He decided even to risk the loss of Corfu. He was acting on the sound principle that in war all minor objects must be sacrificed to the chief end of the campaign. But he could not be sure that in obeying his original orders, and taking his fleet to Messina, he was not in another way risking his position, perhaps his life. He was leaving to the Turks the temporary command of the Adriatic.

After he left Corfu they carried fire and sword along the Illyrian coast. There was a panic in Venice, and the city of the lagoons made hasty preparations for defence. But Veniero's action was soon justified. The news that the Christian armada was assembled at Messina alarmed Ulugh Ali into abandoning any further enterprises in the Adriatic, and his squadrons withdrew to join the concentration of the Turkish fleets at the entrance of the Gulf of Corinth.

It was not till 23 August that the Spanish Prince arrived at Messina, took command of the assembled fleets, and proceeded at once to organize his forces, and issued his sailing and battle orders.

Nearly three hundred ships crowded the harbour of Messina. There were three fleets, the Italian squadrons under the papal admiral Colonna, the Venetian fleet, and the fleet of Philip II formed of the ships of Spain and Naples. The main force of the three fleets was made up of galleys. But there were also six *galleasses* and some seventy frigates, the former depending chiefly, the latter entirely, on sail power for propulsion. The frigate was, in the following century and almost up to our time, what the cruiser is in the armoured navies of today.

But in the Mediterranean fleets of the fifteenth century the *frigata* represented only an early type, out of which the frigate of later days was developed. She was a small sailing-ship, sometimes a mere yacht, armed only with a few light guns. The frigates were used to convey stores, the swifter among them being often employed as dispatch boats. Depending entirely on the wind, it was not always easy for them to accompany a fleet of galleys. Don Juan gave up the idea of making them part of his fighting fleet. It was still the period of the oar-driven man-of-war, though the day of sails was close at hand.

The six *galleasses* represented a new type, a link between the oared ships of the past and the sailing fleets of the immediate future. They were heavy three-masted ships, with rounded bows, and their upper works built with an inward curve, so that the width across the bulwarks amidships was less than that of the gundeck below. The frames of warships were built on these lines till after Nelson's days. This "tumble home" of the sides, as it was called, was adopted to bring the weight of the broadside guns nearer the centre line of the ship, and so lessen the leverage and strain on her framework.

The guns had first been fired over the bulwarks, but at a very early date port-holes were adopted for them. The *galleass* had a high forecastle and poop, each with its battery of guns, pointing ahead, astern, and on each side. Other guns were mounted on the broadsides in the waist of the ship; and to command the main-deck, in case an enemy's boarders got possession of it, lighter guns were mounted on swivels at the back of the forecastle and on the forepart of the poop. Compared to the low, crowded galley, the *galleass* was a roomy and much more seaworthy ship. She was generally a slow sailer, but in order to enable her to make some progress, even in calms or against a head wind, and so work with a fleet of galleys, she had a rowers' deck, under her main or gundeck, and on each side twelve or fifteen oars of enormous length, each worked by several men.

She had the drawbacks of most compromises. She could not sail as well as the frigate, and her speed with the oar was much less than that of the galley. But the gain was that she could be used as a floating battery, carrying many more guns than the few pieces mounted in the galley's bows. The *galleass's* guns were high above the water, and the galleys dreaded their plunging fire. Each of Don Juan's six *galleasses* carried some thirty guns of various calibres, and to defend their high sides against an attack by boarders, their fighting-men were chiefly *arquebusiers*.

In order to fuse the triple fleet of the Allies into one armada, and to avoid the risk of international jealousies, Don Juan proceeded to form his galleys into five squadrons, each made up of ships selected from the three fleets, so that none of these divisions could claim to act only for Rome, or Spain, or Venice.

The organization of the Christian armada may be thus summed up in tabular form:—

Division	Commander	Galleys	Sailing-Ships
Vanguard	Juan de Cardona	7	
7			
Main line of battle			
Left Wing	Argostino Barbarigo	53	Frigates 70
Centre	Don Juan de Austria	62	—
Right Wing	Giovanni Andrea Doria	50	76
Reserve	Alvoro de Bazon, Marquis of Santa Cruz	30	These frigates sailed during the voyage as a separate squad under Don Cesar d'Aavalos. They were employed as store-ships and tenders.

Galleys of the Knights of Malta in action with Turkish Galleys

Total   202+76 s/s = 278 ships in all

It is interesting to note that instead of choosing one of the large sailing-vessels as his flagship, Don Juan displayed his flag, the standard of the League, from the masthead of the largest of the Spanish galleys, the *Reale*, a splendid ship built for the Viceroy of Catalonia three years before. She had sixty oars, a battery of guns pointing forward through a breastwork in the bow, and another gun on her high poop, pointing over her stern, which was adorned with elaborate wood carvings, the work of Vasquez of Seville, one of the most famous sculptors of the day. She had a crew of 300 rowers and 400 fighting-men.

In the battle-line two other great galleys were to lie to right and left of the *Reale*, on her starboard, the flagship of Colonna, the papal admiral, and to port that of Veniero the Venetian, flying the lion banner of St. Mark. Next to these were the galleys of the Princes of Parma and Urbino. On the extreme right of the centre was the post of the flagship of the Knights of Malta, commanded by the Grand Master Giustiniani. All the galleys of the central squadron flew blue pennons as their distinguishing flag.

The vanguard and the right flew green triangular flags. When the line was formed Cardona and his seven galleys were to take post on the left or inner flank of the right division. Doria, the Genoese admiral, was on the extreme right.

The left flew yellow pennons. Its admiral was the Venetian Barbarigo, a veteran of many a hard-fought campaign.

Santa Cruz, the admiral of the reserve squadron, was posted in the middle of his line, flying his flag on board the *Capitana* or flagship of the Neapolitan squadron. All the flagships had as a distinctive mark a long red pennon at the foremast-head.

Twenty-eight thousand fighting-men were embarked on the fleet. The Italian soldiers were the most numerous, then came the Spaniards. There were about 2000 of other nationalities, chiefly Germans. The Venetian galleys were rather short of fighting-men, and to remedy this weakness Veniero, though with some reluctance, consented to receive on board of them detachments of Don Juan's Spanish infantry.

On almost every ship there were serving a number of young gentlemen volunteers. To give a list of their names and of the commanders of *galleasses* and galleys and detachments of troops embarked would be to draw up a roll of the historic names of Italy and Spain. Lepanto might well be described as not only the closing battle of crusading days, but the last battle of the age of chivalry. And, strange to say, on board of one of Colonna's galleys, acting as second in command of its fighting-men, there was a young Spaniard who was to "laugh Europe out of its chivalry"—Don Miguel Cervantes de Saavedra, author of *Don Quixote* some thirty years later.

At the end of the first week of September the fleet was ready for sea, but the start was delayed by bad weather. For several days a storm raged in the Straits of Messina, accompanied by thunder and lightning and torrents of rain. At length, on the 14th, the sky cleared and the sea went down. Next day Don Juan sent off the squadron of frigates under the command of Don Cesar d'Avalos, with orders to proceed to Taranto and await the main body of the fleet there.

At sunrise on the 16th the great fleet left Messina. The *Reale* led the way; the tall *galleasses* were towed out by the galleys. It took some hours for the whole armada to clear the harbour, then, on the admiral's signal, they set their sails, and with wind and oar steered south-westward across the straits. The first day's voyage was only a few miles. Don Juan was taking the opportunity of reviewing his fleet, and testing his arrangements for its formation. Each captain had his written orders giving his position when under way and in the line of battle. It was in this formation the fleet anchored along the Italian coast beyond Reggio, on a front of five miles.

Next day the fleet rounded Cape Spartivento, the toe of Italy, and after an attempt to continue the voyage on the 19th was forced by bad weather to put back and anchor under shelter of the land for some twenty-four hours.

As the weather improved, Don Juan decided not to coast round the Gulf by Taranto, but to lay his course from Cape Colonna for Cape Santa Maria (the heel of Italy), and then across the opening of the Adriatic to Corfu. A frigate was sent to inform D'Avalos of the change of plans, and the armada, helped by a favouring wind, stood out to sea and for a while lost sight of land.

It was known that the Turkish fleet had concentrated in or near the opening of the Gulf of Corinth. It might also have put to sea, and Don Juan took precautions in view of a possible encounter during his voyage. Cardona, with his seven swift galleys of the vanguard, was directed to keep twenty miles ahead during the daytime, closing in to a distance of only eight miles at sunset, and increasing the interval again at dawn. The three squadrons of the main body appear to have been formed each in line ahead, the leading ships, those of the admirals, at the head of each squadron, with such lateral intervals between the columns that line of battle could be formed, by the ships coming up to right and left of their flagships. Santa Cruz with the reserve acted as a rearguard, and was to assist any vessel that might be in difficulties. The rear ship of each squadron was to display a large lantern at the mast-head after dark. The admiral's ship was distinguished by three large lanterns.

Forty galleys were detached to bring reinforcements of infantry from Taranto and Gallipoli. Four swift galleys under the command of Gil d'Andrada were sent on in advance to obtain information of the Ottoman fleet.

From Cape Santa Maria the course was set for the Ionian Islands. On the morning of 24 September, through the driving rain that accompanied a heavy thunderstorm, the look-outs of the vanguard could distinguish the chain of islands north of Corfu, the islets of Merlera, Fano, and Samothraki, which with the reefs that almost connect them form a natural breakwater. The wind and sea were rising, and the fleet anchored inside the shelter of the islands and reefs. It was not until 26 September that it reached at length the harbour of Corfu. It had taken ten days to complete a passage that the tourist from Messina to Corfu now covers in a single day.

At Corfu the commandant of the fortress had terrible tales to tell of Ulugh Ali's raid on the island, and the horrors that the Turks had perpetrated in the villages, which now presented a scene of ruin and desolation. Gil d'Andrada rejoined the fleet there. He had not seen the Turkish armament, but he had obtained news of it from coasters and fishermen. He estimated from these reports that it was inferior in numbers to the Christian fleet, and he had learned that, as if conscious of its weakness, it had taken shelter well up the Gulf of Corinth, in the Bay of Lepanto. The bay lies eastward of the point where the gulf contracts into a narrow strait between the "Castles of Roumelia" and "the Morea," then held by the Turks. The defences were of such strength that at the time the strait was popularly known as "the Little Dardanelles."[1] It was thought that it would be hopeless for the allied fleet to attempt to force the passage.

Four days were spent in the waters of Corfu, and 4000 troops of the garrison were embarked. Gil d'Andrada's four galleys had again been sent away to reconnoitre the enemy. On 30 September the weather was fine and the wind favourable, so Don Juan led his fleet from Corfu to the Bay of Gomenizza, thirty miles to the south-east, on the coast of Albania. The *galeasses* guarded the entrance of the bay; the galleys were moored inside it, bow on to the shore, with their guns thus directed towards it. Working parties were landed under their protection to obtain supplies of wood and water. On 2 October some Spaniards engaged in the work were surprised and made prisoners by Turkish irregulars, Albanian horsemen, who carried them off to the headquarters of Ali Pasha, the Turkish *generalissimo*, at Lepanto.

Gil d'Andrada rejoined at Gomenizza with news that the Turkish fleet was not more than 200 strong; that pestilence had broken out among its fighting-men, and that many of the galleys were undermanned. This encouraged Don Juan to attempt an

---

1. Admiral Jurien de la Gravière in his study of the campaign of Lepanto remarks that many a fortified strait has owed its inviolability only to its exaggerated reputation for the strength of its defences, and adds that in the Greek war of independence a French sailing *corvette*, the *Echo*, easily fought its way into the gulf past the batteries, and repassed them again when coming out a few days later.

attack upon it as it lay in the gulf.

But Ali Pasha had also received reports that led him to underrate the strength of the Christian armada, and so induced him to put out to sea in search of it. Twice he had reconnoitred the allied fleet. Before Don Juan arrived at Messina, Ulugh Ali had sent one of his *corsairs*, Kara Khodja, to cruise in Sicilian waters. The corsair painted every part of his ship a dead black, and one dark night, under black sails, he slipped into Messina harbour. The utter daring of his enterprise assisted him. Gliding like a ghost about the roadstead, unmarked and unchallenged, he counted galleys, galleasses, and frigates, and brought back an under-estimate of the allied strength, only because the fleet was not yet all assembled.

He repeated his exploit while the fleet lay in the waters of Corfu. He could not approach so closely as at Messina, but what he saw led him to believe it was no stronger than when he first reconnoitred it. When Ali Pasha questioned the prisoners taken at Gomenizza, using torture to make them answer him, he thought their admissions confirmed Kara Khodja's reports. So he decided to come out of Lepanto and attack the allied armada.

Thus each fleet believed the other to be inferior in strength, and consequently desired an early engagement. The Turkish fleet was made up of 210 galleys and 64 *galliots* and smaller craft, 274 sail in all, and its commander, Ali Pasha, was one of the veteran admirals of Suleiman's victorious days; 25,000 soldiers had been embarked under the Seraskier, or General, Pertev Pasha. Ali had organized his fleet in four divisions, centre, right wing, left wing, and reserve. All the ships had oars as well as sails, and though Ali had no huge floating batteries, like the six *galleasses* of Don Juan's fleet, the Turkish admiral could match the Christians with galley for galley, and have a surplus of 8 galleys and 66 smaller craft.

Of these the 44 *galliots* were almost as useful as the galleys. Unlike the latter, which had two and often three masts, the *galliot* had only one, and was smaller in size. But the Turkish *galliots*, mostly belonging to the piratical states of North Africa, were as large as many of the Christian galleys of the second class; they could sail well, and they were manned by crews of fighting-men that had a long record of piratical warfare.

The organization of Ali's fleet was:—

Division	Galleys	*Galliots*	Smaller Crafts	Totals
Main line of battle				
Right Wing	54	2	—	56
Centre	87	8	—	95
Left Wing	61	32	—	93
Reserve	8	2	20	30
Totals	210	44	20	274

The fifty galleys of the right wing were ships from Egypt, the ports of Asia Minor, and the arsenal of Constantinople, united under the command of Mohammed Chuluk Bey, Governor of Alexandria, known among the Christian sailors of the Mediterranean as Mohammed Scirocco. The centre, commanded by Ali in person, was made up of galleys from Rhodes and the Greek islands, and from Constantinople and Gallipoli, and the Tripolitan squadron under Djaffir Agha, Governor of Tripoli. The left under Ulugh Ali, the Viceroy of Algiers, included ships from Constantinople, Asia Minor, Syria, and the ports of North-west Africa. The reserve, chiefly composed of small craft, was under the command of Murad Dragut of Constantinople.

There were a good many Greek and Calabrese renegades among the captains of the galleys, but the Syrians and the mixed Arab race of Alexandria had learned the ways of the sea; some even of the Turks were good sailors, and the men of Tripoli, Tunis, and Algiers had made the sea their element. The thousands of rowers, who provided the propelling power of the galleys, were for the most part Christian slaves, chained to their heavy oars, by which they slept when the fleet anchored, living a life of weary labour, often half starved, always badly clothed, so that they suffered from cold and wet.

Death was the immediate penalty of any show of insubordination, and the whip of their taskmasters kept them to their work. There were men of all classes among them, sailors taken from prizes, passengers who had the bad luck to be on board captured ships, fishermen and tillers of the soil carried off in coast raids. They were short-lived, for their masters did not spare them, and considered it a more economic policy to work the rowers to the utmost and replace them by other captures when they broke down.

The oarsmen of the allied fleet had also a hard lot, but not as bad as that of Ali Pasha's galley-slaves, because in the Christian fleet there was a considerable proportion of men hired for the campaign. But there was also a servile element, Turks taken prisoner in previous campaigns and chained to the oar in reprisal for the treatment of Christian captives by Ottoman commanders, and a considerable number of what we should now call convicts sentenced to hard labour, a rough lot of murderers, brigands, thieves, and the like.

It must be remembered that in most European countries the sentence for such offences would have been death. The convict galley-slaves of Don Juan's fleet were encouraged by the prospect of winning either complete pardon or a remission of part of their sentences if there was a victory, and to enable them to co-operate in winning it, they were told that they would be freed from their chains and armed when the day of battle came.

The 25,000 fighting-men of Ali Pasha's fleet were chiefly militia. There were only a few thousand of the formidable Janissaries. And among the small arms of the Turkish fleet there were more bows and arrows than muskets. Don Juan had, on the other hand, a considerable number of *arquebusiers* on his ships. He had the further advantage that while even the largest of the Turkish galleys had only low bulwarks, the galleys of the allied fleet were provided with *pavesades*, large bucklers and shields, to be fitted along the bulwarks when clearing for action, and also permanent cross barriers to prevent a raking fire fore and aft.

When Ali left the roadstead of Lepanto, and brought his fleet out from behind the batteries of the "Little Dardanelles," he believed he had such a marked superiority over the allied fleet that victory was a certainty, and he expected to find Don Juan either at Gomenizza or in the waters of the Ionian Islands. Pertev Pasha and several of the admirals had opposed Ali's decision, and had urged him either to remain at Lepanto, or run out of the gulf, round the Morea, and wait in the eastern seas for the campaign of next year. Their reason for this advice was that many of the fighting-men were new levies unused to the sea. But Ali's self-confidence made him reject this prudent counsel.

On 2 October, Don Juan had made up his mind to leave Gomenizza, enter the Gulf of Corinth, and risk an attack on the passage of the Little Dardanelles. Accordingly in the afternoon he gave orders that the fleet should prepare to sail at sunrise next day. During the long delay in the island waters belated news came that Famagusta had fallen on 18 August, and with the news there was a terrible story of the horrors that had followed the broken capitulation. The news was now six weeks old, and this meant that the whole of the enemy's fleet might be concentrated in the Gulf of Corinth, but after the disasters of Cyprus an attempt must be made to win a victory against all or any odds.

At sunrise the armada streamed out of the Bay of Gomenizza, and sped southwards with oar and sail. The Gulf of Arta was passed, and the admirals were reminded not of the far-off battle that saw the flight of the Egyptian Queen and the epoch-making victory of Augustus Cæsar, but of a sea-fight in the same waters only a few years ago that had ended in dire disaster to the Christian arms. Then through the hours of darkness the fleet worked its way past the rock-bound shores of Santa Maura, whose cliffs glimmered in the moonlight. The roar of the breakers at their base warned the pilots to give them good sea room. In the grey of the morning the peaks and ridges of Ithaca and Cephalonia rose out of the haze upon the sea, and soon after sunrise the fleet was moving through the narrow strait between the islands.

In the strait there were shelter and smooth water, but the wind was rising, backing from north-west to west, and raising a sea outside Cephalonia that sent a heavy swell sweeping round its southern point and into the opening of the narrows. As the leading ships reached the mouth of the strait Don Juan did not like the look of the weather, and decided to anchor in the Bay of Phiscardo, a large opening in the Cephalonian shore just inside the strait.

For two days the fleet lay weather-bound in the bay. During one of these days of storm Kara Khodja, the Algerine, tried again to reconnoitre the fleet, but was driven off by the guardships at the entrance of the strait.

On 6 October the wind shifted to the east and the sea began to go down. Don Juan refused to wait any longer. The fleet put to sea, under bare masts, and, rowing hard against the wind and through rough water, it worked its way slowly across to the sheltered waters on the mainland coast between it and the islands of Curzolari. Here the fleet anchored for the night, just outside the opening of the Gulf of Corinth. Not twenty miles away up the gulf lay the Turkish fleet, for Ali had brought it out of the Bay of Lepanto, and anchored in the Bay of Calydon.

When the sun rose on the 7th, the wind was still contrary, blowing from the south-east. But at dawn the ships were under way, and moving slowly in long procession between the mainland and the islands that fringe the coast. There was a certain amount of straggling. It was difficult to keep the divisions closed up, and the tall *galleasses* especially felt the effect of the head wind, and some of the galleys had to assist them by towing.

As the ships of the vanguard began to clear the channel between Oxia Island and Cape Scropha, and the wide expanse of water at the entrance of the Gulf of Corinth opened before them, the look-outs reported several ships hull down on the horizon to the eastward, the sun shining on their white sails, that showed like flecks of cloud on the sea-line.

The signal was sent back, "Enemy in sight," for the number of sails told it must be a fleet, and could be none other than that of Ali Pasha. The allied squadrons began to clear for action, and Don Juan displayed for the first time the consecrated ban-

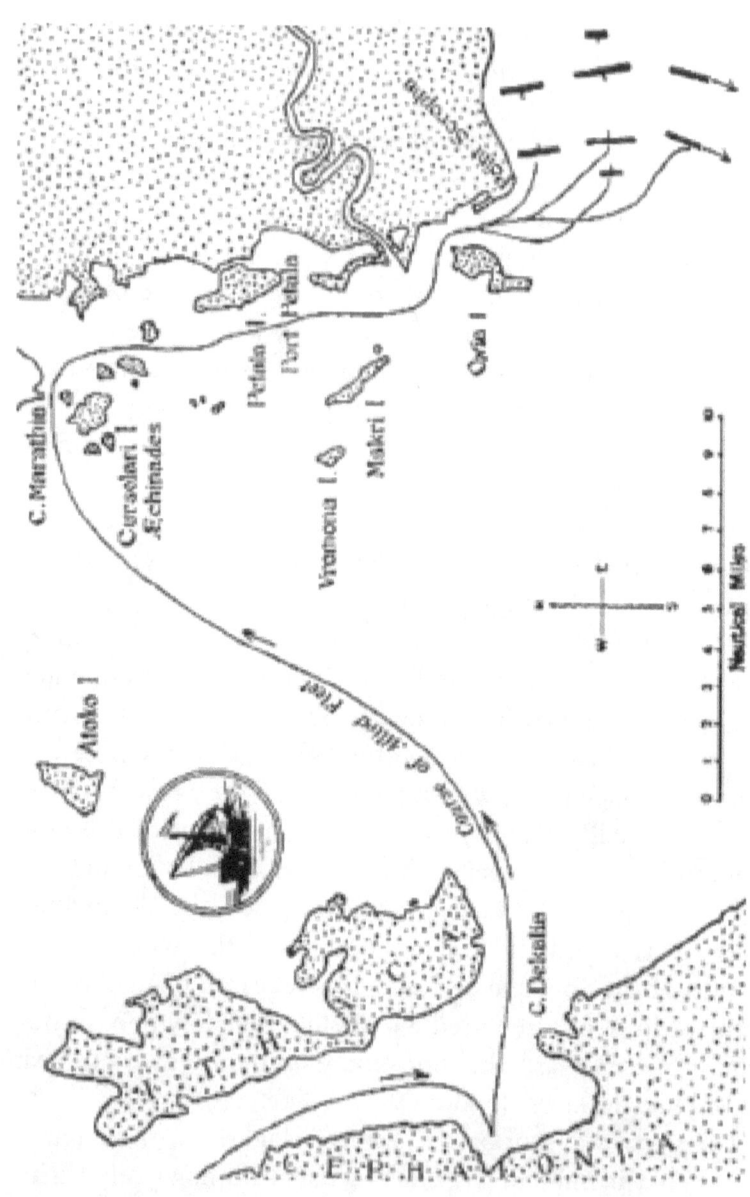

Lepanto – Course of Allied Fleet from Ithaca Channel to scene of Battle

ner sent him by Pius V, a large square flag embroidered with the crucifix and the figures of Saints Peter and Paul.

It was an anxious time for the Christian admiral. His fleet, now straggling for miles along the coast, had to close up, issue from the channel, round Cape Scropha, and form in battle array in the open water to the eastward. If the Turks, who had the wind to help them, came up before this complex operation was completed, he risked being beaten in detail.

While the fleet was still working its way through the channel, Don Juan had sent one of the Roman pilots, Cecco Pisani forward in a swift galley to reconnoitre. Pisani landed on Oxia, climbed one of its crags, and from this lofty outlook counted 250 sail in the enemy's fleet, which was coming out along the north shore of the gulf, the three main squadrons abreast, the reserve astern of them. Returning to the *Reale*,[2] the pilot gave a guarded report to Don Juan, fearing to discourage the young commander now that battle was inevitable, but to his own admiral, the veteran Colonna, he spoke freely. "*Signor*," he said, "you must put out all your claws, for it will be a hard fight."

Then the wind suddenly fell and the sea became calm as a lake. The Turks were seen to be furling their now useless sails. The rapidity with which the manœuvre was simultaneously executed by hundreds of ships excited the admiration of the Christians. It showed the enemy had well-disciplined and practised crews. But at the same time the fact that at a crisis, when every moment gained was priceless, the Turks had lost the fair wind, convinced the allies that Heaven was aiding them, and gave them confidence in the promises of their chaplains, greycowled Franciscans and black-robed Dominicans, who were telling them that the prayers of Christendom would assure them a victory.

Their young chief, Don Juan, left the *Reale* and embarked in a swift brigantine, in which he rowed along the forming line of the fleet. Clad in complete armour he stood in the bow holding up a crucifix, and as he passed each galley he called on officers

---

2. The flagship.

and men to spare no effort in the holy cause for which they were about to fight. Then he returned to his post on the poop of the *Reale*, which was in the centre of the line, with several other large galleys grouped around her. As each ship was pulled into her fighting position, the Christian galley-slaves were freed from the oar and given weapons with which to fight for the common cause and their own freedom.

It was intended that the galleys of the left, centre, and right should form one long line, with the six *galleasses* well out in front of them, two before each division. These were to break the force of the Turkish onset with their cannon. But when the long line of the enemy's galleys came rushing to the onset, Don Juan's battle array was still incomplete. Barbarigo's flagship was on the extreme left under the land. His division had formed upon this mark, "dressing by the left," as a soldier would say. The tall *galleasses* of two gallant brothers, the Venetians Ambrogio and Antonio Bragadino, kinsmen of the hero of Famagusta, lay well out in front of the left division.

All the ships had their sails furled and the long yards hauled fore and aft. Don Juan had formed up the centre division, two more *galleasses* out in front, the *Reale* in the middle of the line, the galleys of Veniero and Colonna to right and left, and two selected galleys lying astern, covering the intervals between them and the flagship. Only a few oars were being used to keep the ships in their stations. So far so good, but the rest of the allied fleet was still coming up. The reserve was only issuing from the channel behind Cape Scropha, and Doria was leading the right division into line, with his two *galleasses* working up astern, where their artillery would be useless. Thus when the battle began not much more than half of the Christian armada was actually in line. But for the sudden calm the position would have been even worse.

It was almost noon when the battle began. The first shots were fired by the four *galleasses*, as the long line of Ottoman galleys came sweeping on into range of their guns. Heavy cannon, such as they carried, were still something of a novelty in

LEPANTO
1. ALLIES FORMING LINE OF BATTLE –
TURKS ADVANCING TO ATTACK

naval war, and the Turks had a dread of these tall floating castles that bristled with guns, from which fire, smoke, and iron were now hurled against them. One of the first shots crashed into the deck of Ali Pasha's flagship, scattering destruction as it came. The Turkish line swayed and lost its even array. Some ships hesitated, others crowded together in order to pass clear of the *galleasses*. Daring captains, who ventured to approach with an idea of boarding them, shrank back under the storm of musketry that burst from their lofty bulwarks. The Turkish fleet surged past the *galleasses*, broken into confused masses of ships, with wide intervals between each squadron, as a stream is divided by the piles of a bridge.

This disarray of the Turkish attack diminished the fire their bow-guns could bring to bear on the Christian line, for the leading galleys masked the batteries of those that followed. Along the allied left and centre, lying in even array bows to the attack, the guns roared out in a heavy cannonade. But then as the Ottoman bows came rushing through the smoke, and the fleets closed on each other, the guns of the galleys were silent. For a few moments the fight had been like a modern battle, with hundreds of guns thundering over the sea. Now it was a fight like Salamis or Actium, except for the sharp reports of musketry in the *mêlée* and the cannon of the *galleasses* making the Turkish galleys their mark when they could fire into the mass without danger to their friends.

The first to meet in close conflict were Barbarigo's division on the allied left and Mohammed Scirocco's squadron, which was opposed to it on the Turkish right. The Egyptian Pasha brought his own galley into action on the extreme flank bow to bow with the Venetian flagship, and some of the lighter Turkish galleys, by working through the shallows between Barbarigo and the land, were able to fall on the rear of the extreme left of the line, while the larger galleys pressed the attack in front. The Venetian flagship was rushed by a boarding-party of *Janissaries*, and her decks cleared as far as the mainmast. Barbarigo, fighting with his visor open, was mortally wounded with an arrow in his face, and was carried below.

But his nephew Contarini restored the fight, and with the help of reinforcements from the next galley drove the boarders from the decks of the flagship. Contarini was mortally wounded in the midst of his success. But two of his comrades, Nani and Porcia, led a rush of Venetians and Spaniards on to Mohammed Scirocco's flagship, whose decks were swept by the fire of the *arquebusiers* before the charge of swords and pikes burst over her bows. The onset was irresistible. The Turks were cut down, stabbed, hurled overboard, Mohammed himself being killed in the *mêlée*.

By the time the great galley of Alexandria was thus captured the landward wings of the two fleets were mingled together in a confused fight, in which there was little left of the original order. There was more trace of a line on the allied or Christian side. The Turks had not broken through them, but they had swung round, somewhat forcing Mohammed's galleys towards the shore. When the standard of the Egyptian admiral was hauled down by the victorious Venetians, and the rowers suddenly ceased to be slaves and fraternized with the conquerors, some of the captains on the Turkish right lost heart, drove their galleys aground in the shallows and deserted them for the shore, where they hoped to find refuge among friends. On Don Juan's left, though the fighting continued in a fierce *mêlée* of ships locked together, and with crews doing wild work with loud *arquebuse* and clashing sword, the battle was practically won.

Meanwhile there had been close and deadly fighting in the centre. The main squadron of the Turks had, like their right division, suffered from the fire of the advanced *galleasses*. Several shots had struck the huge galley that flew the flag of the Capitan-Pasha, Ali, a white pennon sent from Mecca, embroidered in gold with verses of the Koran. Ali steered straight for the centre of the Christian line, where the group of large galleys, the *Reale* with the embroidered standard of the Holy League, Colonna's ship with its ensign of the Papal Keys, and Veniero's with the Lion-flag of St. Mark, told him he was striking at the heart of

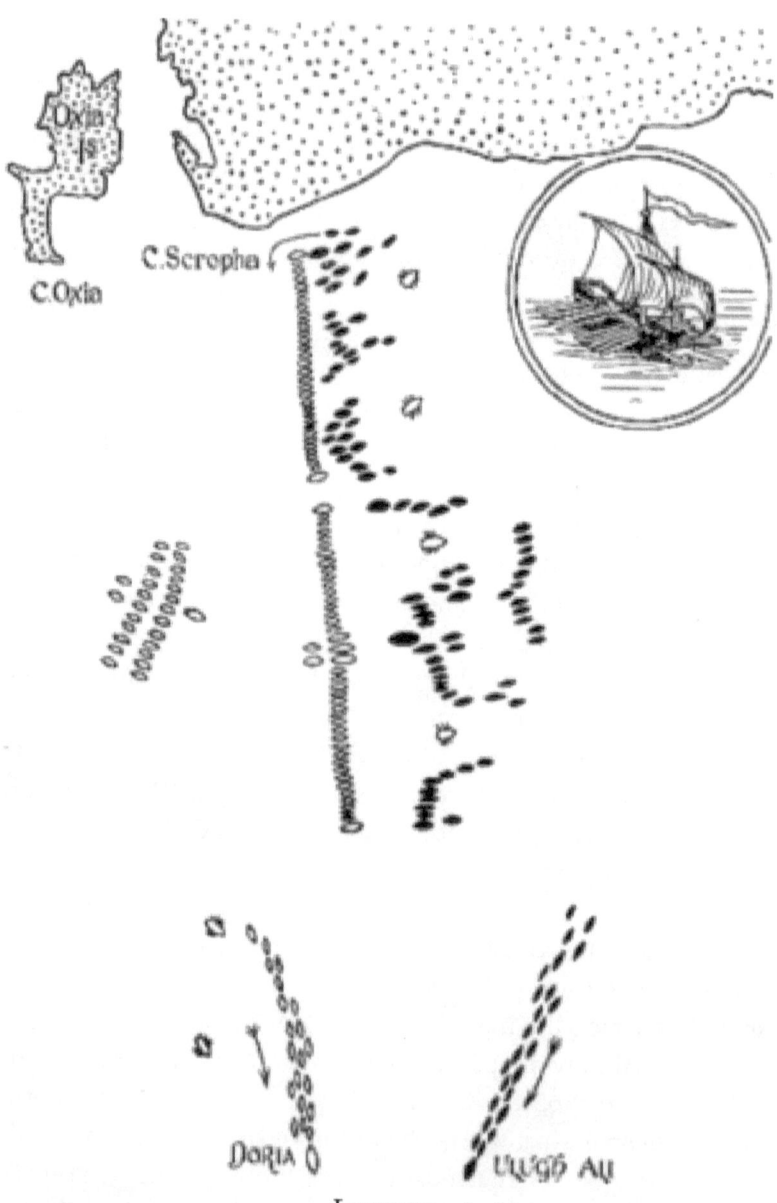

Lepanto
2. Beginning of the Battle (Noon, Oct. 7 1571)

the confederacy. He chose Don Juan's *Reale* for his adversary, relying on the Seraskier Pertev Pasha, and the Pasha of Mitylene on his left and right, to support him by attacking the other two flagships.

Ali held the fire of his bow-guns till he was within a short musket-shot of his enemy, and then fired at point-blank. One of his cannon-balls crashed through the bow barrier of the *Reale*, and raked the rowers' benches, killing several oarsmen. As the guns of the *Reale* thundered out their reply, the bow of the Turkish flagship, towering over the forecastle of Don Juan's vessel, came through the smoke-cloud and struck the Spanish ship stern to stern with a grinding crash and a splintering of timber, throwing down many of the crew. The Turkish bow dug deep into the Spanish ship, and in the confusion of the collision it was thought for a moment she was sinking, but a forward bulkhead kept her afloat.

Ali's ship rebounded from the shock, then glided alongside the *Reale* with much mutual smashing of oars. The two ships grappled, and the hand-to-hand fight began. At the same time Pertev Pasha grappled Veniero's flagship, and another Turkish galley, commanded by Ali's two sons, forced its way through the line and engaged the two galleys that lay astern of the flagship. Then the Pasha of Mitylene closed upon Colonna's ship, and all along the centre the galleys came dashing together. The crash of broken oars, the rattling explosions of *arquebuses* and grenades, the war-notes of the Christian trumpets and the Turkish drums, the clash of swords, the shouts and yells of the combatants, rose in a deafening din. Froissart wrote in an earlier day that sea-fights were always murderous.

This last great battle of the medieval navies had the character of its predecessors. In this fight at close quarters on the narrow space afforded by the galleys' decks there was no question of surrender on either side, no thought but of which could strike the hardest and kill the most. Nor could men, striving hand to hand in the confusion of the floating *mêlée*, know anything of what was being done beyond their limited range of view, so that even the admirals became for the moment only leaders of small groups of fighting-men. On the poop and forecastle of the *Reale* were gathered men whose names recalled all that was greatest in the annals of Spanish chivalry, veterans who had fought the Moor and voyaged the western ocean, and young cavaliers eager to show themselves worthy sons of the lines of Guzman and Mendoza, Benavides and Salazar. Don Juan, arrayed in complete steel, stood by the flagstaff of the consecrated standard.

Along the bulwarks four hundred Castilian *arquebusiers* in corselet and head-piece represented the pick of the yet unconquered Spanish infantry. The three hundred rowers had left the oars, and, armed with pike and sword, were ready to second them, when the musketry ceased and the storming of the Turkish galleys began. From Ali's ship a hundred archers and three hundred musketeers of the *Janissary* corps replied to the fire of the Spaniards. The range was a few feet. Men were firing in each other's faces, and at such close quarters the *arquebuse* with its heavy ball was a more death-dealing weapon than the modern rifle. Such slaughter could not last, and the *caballeros* were eager to end it by closing on the Turks with cold steel.

Twice they dashed through the smoke over Ali's bulwarks, and for a while gained a footing on the deck of the enemy's flagship. Twice they were driven back by the reinforcements that Ali drew from the crews of galleys that had crowded to his aid. Then the Turks came clambering over the bows of the *Reale*, and nearly cleared the forecastle. Don Bernardino de Cardenas brought up a reserve from the waist of the ship and attacked the Turkish boarders in the bows. He was struck by a musket-ball. It dinted his steel helmet, but failed to penetrate. Cardenas fell, stunned by the shock of the blow, and died next day, "though he showed no sign of a wound."

Don Juan himself was going forward sword in hand to assist in the fight in the bows of the *Reale*, and Ali was hurrying up reinforcements to the attack. It was a critical moment. But Colonna just then struck a decisive blow. He had boarded and stormed the ship that attacked him, a long galley commanded by

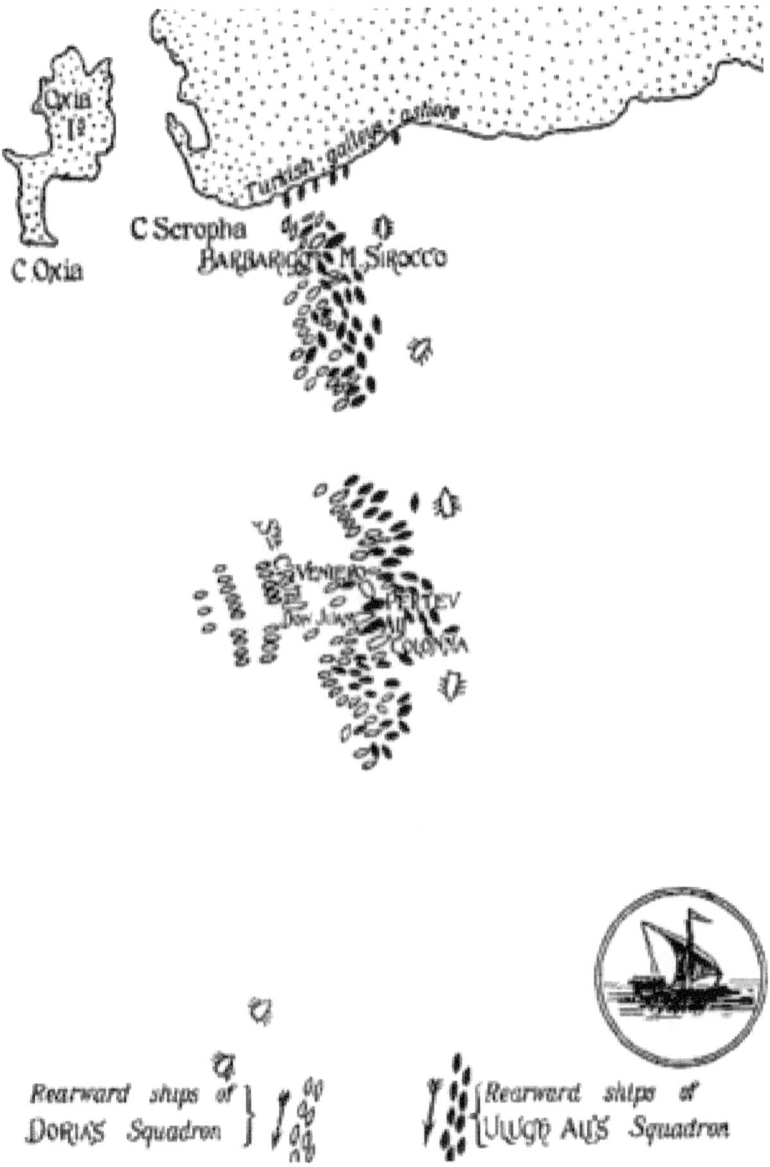

LEPANTO
3. THE *MÊLÉE* (ABOUT 12.30 P.M.)

the Bey of Negropont. Having thus disposed of his immediate adversary, he saw the peril of the *Reale*. Manning all his oars, he drove the bow of his flagship deep into the stern of Ali's ship, swept her decks with a volley of musketry, and sent a storming-party on to her poop. The diversion saved the *Reale*. The Spaniards hustled the Turks over her bows at point of pike, and Ali, attacked on two sides, had now to fight on the defensive.

On the other side of the *Reale* Veniero's flagship was making a splendid fight. It is the details of those old battles that bring home to us the changes of three centuries. A modern admiral stands sheltered in his conning tower, amid voice tubes and electrical transmitters. Veniero, a veteran of seventy years, stood by the poop-rail of his galley, thinking less of commanding than of doing his own share of the killing. Balls and arrows whistled around him, along the bulwarks amidships his men were fighting hand to hand with the Seraskier's galley that lay lashed alongside. There were no orders to give for the moment, so he occupied himself with firing a blunderbuss into the crowd on the Turkish deck, and handing it to a servant to reload with half a dozen balls, and then firing again and again.

Here, too, in the main squadron were fighting the galleys of Spinola of Genoa, of the young Duke of Urbino, of the Prince of Parma, of Bonelli, the nephew of Pius V, of Sforza of Milan, and Gonzaga of Solferino, and the young heirs of the Roman houses of Colonna and Orsini. Venice had not all the glory of Lepanto. All Italy still remembers that every noble family, every famous city, from the Alps to Sicily, had its part in the battle.

Colonna's timely aid to the *Reale* was the turning-point of the fight in the centre. Led by Vasquez Coronada and Gil d'Andrada, the Spanish infantry poured into Ali's ship, and winning their way foot by foot cleared her decks. Not one of her four hundred fighting-men survived. Ali himself was one of the last to fall. One account says that when all was lost he cut his throat with his dagger, another that he was shot down at close quarters. His head was cut off, placed on a pike, and carried to Don Juan with the captured standard of Mecca. The chivalrous young admiral turned with disgust from the sight of the blood-dripping head, and ordered it to be thrown into the sea.

The battle had lasted an hour and a half. Don Juan saw in the capture of the enemy's flagship the assurance of victory. Like all great commanders, he knew the value of moral effect. He hoisted the consecrated banner of the League at the tall masthead of the conquered galley, and bade his trumpeters blow a flourish and his men shout victory. In the confusion and uproar of the *mêlée* not many of the ships would see what was happening round the *Reale*, but this demonstration would attract the attention of friends and foes in the centre of the fight. It was just one of the moments when, both parties becoming exhausted by the prolonged struggle, success would belong to the side that could put forth even for a while the more vigorous effort, and the sight of the papal standard fluttering from the Turkish mast, instead of the banner of Mecca, inspired this effort on the part of the Christians, and depressed and discouraged their adversaries.

Pertev Pasha had lost heavily under the fire of the Venetian flagship, and had failed in an effort to board her. He cut his galley adrift. Veniero let her go, and turned to attack other enemies. Pertev's ship drifted down on two Christian galleys, and was promptly boarded and taken. The *Seraskier* slipped on board of a small craft he was towing astern, reached another ship, and, giving up all hope of victory, fled with her from the fight. Veniero had meanwhile rammed and sunk two other galleys. He was wounded with a bullet in the leg, but he had the wound bandaged and remained on deck. The old man gave Venice good reason to be proud of her admiral.

Along the left and centre of the Christian armada there was now victory. Admirals and captains were busy storming or sinking such of the enemy's ships as still maintained the fight. On the left Barbarigo had been mortally wounded, and the losses had been heavy, but the success was so pronounced that large numbers of men had been landed to hunt down the Turkish fugitives on the shore. In the centre there was still some hard fighting. Here it was that Miguel Cervantes, leading the stormers to the capture of a Turkish galley, received three wounds, one of which cost him his left hand.

When the battle began at noon, first on the allied left, then in the centre, Doria, the Genoese admiral who commanded the right, was not yet in position. His orders were to mark with his flagship the extreme right of the line of battle so that the rest of his division could form on this point. But it was soon seen that he was keeping away, steering southward into the open sea, with his division trailing after him in a long line, the galleasses that should have been out in front coming slowly up behind the squadron. Ulugh Ali with the left wing of the Turkish fleet had also altered his course, and was steering on a parallel line to that taken by the Genoese. Some of the Christian captains who watched these movements from the right centre thought that Doria was deserting the armada, and even that he was in flight, pursued by Ulugh Ali.

Doria afterwards explained that, as he steered out from behind the centre to take up his position in the battle line, he saw that Ulugh Ali, instead of forming on Ali Pasha's flank, was working out to seaward, and he therefore believed that the Algerine was trying to get upon the flank of the allied line, in order to envelop it and attack from both front and rear, so as to crush the extreme right with a local superiority of force. His plan was, therefore, to confine himself to observing Ulugh Ali's movements, steering on a parallel course in the hope of eventually closing and meeting him fairly ship to ship.

Doria was an old sailor, perhaps the most experienced leader in the fleet, except the veteran Veniero. If he had been less of a tactician, perhaps he would have come into action sooner. And it is strange that, while playing for position against Ulugh Ali, he did not realize that if, instead of continually increasing his own distance from the centre, he had at any moment turned back towards it, he could thus force the Algerine admiral either to close with him or leave him free to overwhelm the Turkish main squadron by enveloping its left.

It was Ulugh Ali, not Doria, who turned back and ventured

on a stroke like this. The Algerine had, after all, outmanœuvred the over-clever Genoese. The course taken by the two squadrons had, with the drift of the current, placed Ulugh Ali's rearmost ships actually somewhat nearer the seaward flank of the main fighting lines than Doria's galleys, which his squadron also outnumbered. A signal ran down the long line of the Turkish left, and while some of the galleys turned and bore down on Doria's division, the rest swung round and, before Doria had quite realized what was happening, Ulugh Ali, with the heaviest ships of his division, was rushing towards the fight in the centre.

The brunt of the Algerine's onset fell upon a dozen galleys on Don Juan's right flank. The furthest out, the flagship of the Knights of Malta, was attacked by seven of the enemy's vessels. Next to her lay the papal galley *Fiorenza*, the Piedmontese *Margarita di Savoia*, and seven or eight Venetian ships. All these were enveloped in the Turkish attack which engaged the line in front, flank and rear. There were no enemies the Algerines hated so fiercely as the Knights of Malta, but, even though they had the flagship of the Order at such a fearful disadvantage, they did not venture to close with it until they had overwhelmed the knights and their crew with a murderous fire of bullets and arrows at close quarters.

Then they boarded the ship and disposed of the few surviving defenders. The commander, Giustiniani, wounded by five arrows, and a Sicilian and a Spanish knight alone survived, and these only because they were left for dead among the heaps of slain that encumbered the deck. Ulugh Ali secured as a trophy of his success the standard of the Knights. In the same way the *Fiorenza* and the *San Giovanni* of the papal squadron, and the Piedmontese ship, were rushed in rapid succession. On the *Fiorenza* the only survivors were her captain, Tomasso de Medici, and sixteen men, all wounded; the captain of the *San Giovanni* was killed with most of his men, and the captain of the Savoyard ship survived an equally terrible slaughter, after receiving no less than eleven wounds.

But Ulugh Ali was not to be allowed to "eat up" the line

ship by ship. Reinforcements were now arriving in rapid succession. First Santa Cruz, with the reserve, dashed into the fight, and though twice wounded with shot from a Turkish *arquebuse*, drove his flagship into the midst of the Algerines. Don Juan cut adrift a captured ship he had just taken in tow, and with twelve galleys hastened to assist the reserve in restoring the fight.

Doria, leaving part of his division to encounter the galleys Ulugh Ali had detached against it, led the rest into the *mêlée*. Colonna and Veniero were supporting Don Juan. The local advantage of numbers, which Ulugh Ali at first possessed, soon disappeared, but for more than an hour the fight continued with heavy loss on both sides. Then the Algerine admiral struggled out of the *mêlée*, and with fourteen ships fled north-westward, steering for Cape Oxia and the wide channel between Ithaca and the mainland. Santa Cruz and Doria pursued for a while, but a wind sprang up from the south-east, and the fugitives set their long lateen sails. Under sail and oar a *corsair* could generally defy pursuit.

The pursuers gave up the chase and returned to where Don Juan and the other admirals were securing their prizes, clearing the decks of dead, collecting the wounded, and hurriedly repairing damages. It was now after four o'clock, and less than three hours of daylight remained for these operations. Besides the handful that had escaped with Ulugh Ali, a few galleys had got away into the Gulf of Corinth, making for Lepanto, but the great Turkish armada had been destroyed, and the victorious armament was mistress of the Mediterranean.

The success had been dearly bought. On both sides the losses in the hard-fought battle had been terrible. The allies had about 7500 men killed or drowned, two-thirds of these fighting-men, the rest rowers. The nobles and knights had exposed themselves freely in the *mêlée*, and Spain, Malta, Venice, and the Italian cities had each and all their roll of heroic dead. The list of the Venetians begins with the names of seventeen captains of ships, including the admiral Barbarigo, besides twelve other chiefs of great houses who fought under the standard of St. Mark in com-

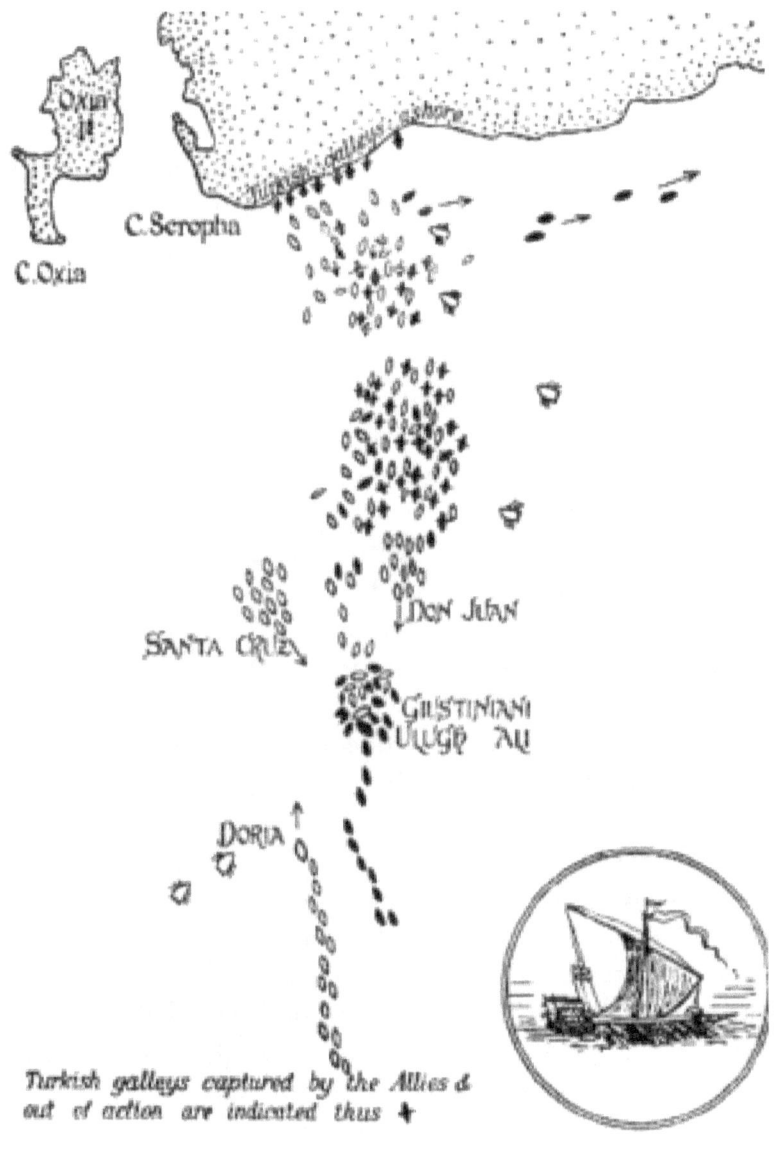

LEPANTO
4. ULUGH ALI'S COUNTER-ATTACK (ABOUT 2.30P.M.)

mand of companies of fighting-men. No less than sixty of the Knights of St. John "gave their lives that day for the cause of Christ," to quote the annalist of the Order.

Several others were wounded, and of these the Prior Giustiniani and his captain, Naro, of Syracuse, died soon after. One of the knights killed in the battle was a Frenchman, Raymond de Loubière, a Provençal. Another Frenchman, the veteran De Romegas, fought beside Don Juan on the *Reale*, and to his counsel and aid the commander-in-chief attributed much of his success in the campaign. The long lists of the Spanish, Neapolitan, Roman, and Genoese nobles who fell at Lepanto include many historic names.

The losses of the defeated Moslems were still heavier. The lowest estimate makes the number of the dead 20,000, the highest 30,000. Ali Pasha and most of his captains were killed. Ali's two sons and several of his best officers were among the prisoners. Fifteen Turkish galleys were sunk or burned, no less than 190 ships were the prizes of the victors. A few galleys had escaped by the Little Dardanelles to Lepanto. A dozen more had found refuge with Ulugh Ali in the fortified harbour of Santa Maura. The Algerine eventually reached Constantinople, and laid at the feet of Sultan Selim the standard of the Knights of Malta, which he had secured when he was in temporary possession of Giustiniani's flagship.

Don Juan's best trophies of victory were the 12,000 Christian slaves found on board the captured galleys. They were men of all nations, and some of them had for years toiled at the oar. Freed from their bondage, they carried throughout all Christendom the news of the victory and the fame of their deliverer.

Hardly three hours of daylight remained when the battle ended, and the Christian admirals reluctantly abandoned the pursuit of Ulugh Ali. The breeze that had aided the Algerine in his flight was rapidly increasing to a gale, and the sea was rising fast. The Christian fleet, encumbered with nearly two hundred prizes, and crippled by the loss of thousands of oars shattered in the fight, was in serious danger in the exposed waters that had been the scene of the battle. By strenuous and well-directed efforts the crews of oarsmen were hurriedly reorganized. Happily the wind was favourable for a run through the Oxia Channel to the Bay of Petala. The prizes were taken in tow. Sails were set. Weary men tugged at the oar, knights and nobles taking their places among them. As the October night deepened into darkness, amid driving rain and roaring wind-squalls, the fleet anchored in the sheltered bay.

The gale that swept the Adriatic was a warning that the season for active operations was drawing to a close, and the admirals reluctantly decided that no more could be done till next spring. The swiftest ships were sent off to carry the good news of Lepanto to Rome and Messina, Venice and Genoa, Naples and Barcelona. The fleet returned in triumph to Messina, and entered the port trailing the captured Turkish standards in the water astern of the ships that had taken them, while pealing bells and saluting cannon greeted the victors.

Lepanto worthily closed the long history of the oar-driven navies. The *galleasses*, with their tall masts and great sails, and their bristling batteries of cannon, which lay in front of Don Juan's battle line, represented the new type of ship that was soon to alter the whole aspect of naval war. So quickly came the change that men who had fought at Lepanto were present, only seventeen years later, at another world-famed battle that was fought under sail, the defeat of King Philip's "Grand Armada" in the Narrow Seas of the North.

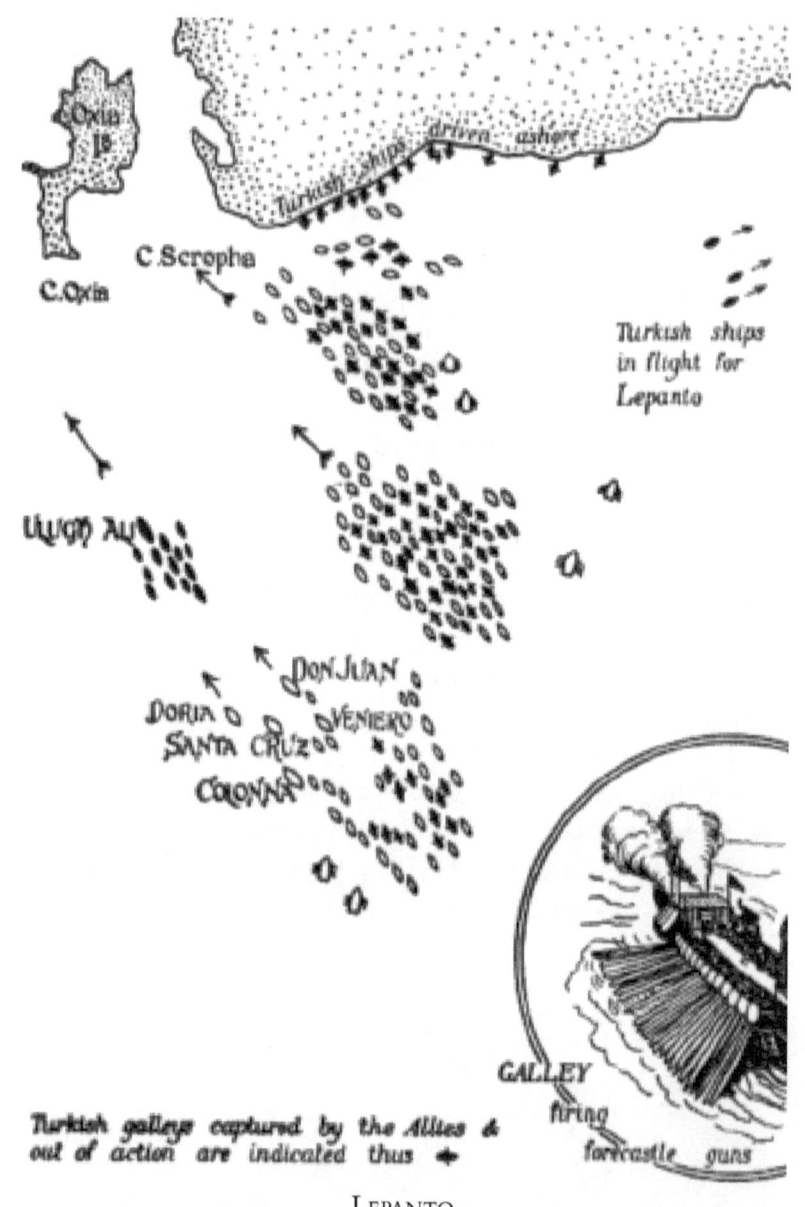

LEPANTO
FLIGHT OF ULUGH ALI - ALLIED FLEET FORMING UP WITH CAPTURED PRIZES AT CLOSE OF BATTLE (ABOUT 4P.M.)

CHAPTER 6

The Great Armada 1588

Attend, all ye who list to hear
Our glorious England's praise.
I sing of the thrice famous deeds
She wrought in ancient days,
When that great fleet 'Invincible'
Against her bore in vain
The richest spoils of Mexico,
The bravest hearts of Spain.

Thus Macaulay begins his stirring ballad of the Armada. The lines have helped to perpetuate a popular error—one of the many connected with the story as it is generally told in our English histories. It somehow became the fashion at a very early date to speak of the defeat of the so-called "Invincible Armada" of Spain. But the Spaniards never gave their fleet such a name. In the contemporary histories and in Spanish official documents it is more modestly and truthfully spoken of as the "Gran Armada"—"the great armed force." And, by the way, our very use of the word "armada" is based on popular ignorance of the Spanish language, and on the impression produced in England by the attempt of Philip II to make himself master of the narrow seas, and invade our islands. An "armada" is not necessarily a fleet. It is an armed force, an "army" either marching on land or embarked for service on the sea, in which case fleet and fighting-men are included in the word.

Philip II was King not of Spain only, but also of Portugal and of the Two Sicilies, ruler of other European lands and "Lord of the Indies," the Sovereign of a widespread maritime Empire in Asia, Africa, and America, that had been won by a hundred years of enterprise on the part of sailors and soldiers like Columbus and Vasco da Gama, Cortes, Pizarro, and Albuquerque.

The tradition of Spanish victory on the sea was a proud one, and as we have seen Spain had borne a leading part in the latest of decisive naval victories, when the Turkish power in the Mediterranean was shattered at Lepanto; King Philip might therefore reasonably look forward to success for his great fleet, and if it could once secure the mastery of the Channel, the invasion of England might be regarded as no very perilous enterprise. For the Spanish infantry were the best soldiers of the day, and the Duke of Parma, who was to command the land operations, was one of the best and most experienced leaders in Europe.

Looking back on the events of the wonderful year of the Armada, we must try to divest ourselves of the ideas of today, and see things as the men of the time saw them. Philip counted on divisions among the people of England. The event proved that he was mistaken, but he had reasonable grounds for the view he took. A hundred years later another fleet conveyed a foreign army across the narrow seas from the Netherlands to change effectively the course of English affairs. It found a divided people, and the invading army was welcomed by a party strong enough to effect a Revolution that was a new starting-point in English history. Nor must we suppose that the policy of Philip II was directed entirely by religious views. If kings were easily swayed by such motives, there would have not been such difficulty about organizing a League against the Turk.

Professor Laughton, in his introduction to the *State Papers relating to the Defeat of the Armada*, puts the matter so clearly that it is worth while quoting his words at some length:—

> It is not strange that the action of the fleet was for long misunderstood, and that the failure of the Spaniards should have been represented—as it often is even now—as due to a Heaven-sent storm. '*Flavit Deus et dissipati sunt*' was

accepted as at once a true and pious explanation of the whole thing. It was, too, a flattering and economical belief. We were, it has been argued, a nation peculiarly dear to the Almighty, and He showed His favour by raising a storm to overwhelm our enemy, when the odds against us were most terrible. From the religious point of view such a representation is childish; from the historical it is false. False, because the Spanish fleet, after being hounded up Channel, had sustained a crushing defeat from the English, a defeat in which they lost many ships and thousands of men before they fled to the north.... Childish, because in affairs of State Providence works by recognized means, and gives the victory, not by disturbing the course of nature and nature's laws, but by giving the favoured nation wise and prudent commanders, skilful and able warriors; by teaching their hands to war and their fingers to fight. But, in fact, much of the nonsense that has been talked grew out of the attempt, not unsuccessfully made, to represent the war as religious; to describe it as a species of crusade instigated by the Pope, in order to bring heretical England once more into the fold of the true Church. In reality nothing can be more inaccurate. It is, indeed, quite certain that religious bitterness was imported into the quarrel; but the war had its origin in two perfectly clear and wholly mundane causes.

Professor Laughton then goes on to explain what these causes were:

(1) the attempts of Drake and Hawkins to break the Spanish monopoly of trade in the West Indies by armed expeditions, which included the capture of Spanish ships and the sacking of Spanish trading posts. The Spaniards regarded Drake and Hawkins as smugglers and pirates, and in vain asked Elizabeth to disavow and make amends for their acts.

(2) The countenance and assistance which had been given

by the English to the King's rebellious subjects in the Low Countries."

The King was glad enough to put forward religious reasons as the motives for his enterprise in the hope of thus enlisting new allies on his side, but, like so many other wars, the conflict between Spain and England, which began in 1585, arose largely from rivalry in trade.

The Marquis of Santa Cruz, the same who had commanded the allied reserve at Lepanto, was then the most famous and the most trusted of King Philip's admirals. Santa Cruz urged upon him the advisability of attempting an invasion of England itself, as the only effective means of cutting off the support given by Elizabeth to the revolt of the Netherlands, and checking at their source the raids on the West Indies. In March, 1586, he submitted to his master an elaborate plan for the operation. Santa Cruz's scheme was an ambitious project for concentrating the whole force of the Spanish Empire in an attack on England. Some 500 ships, great and small, were to be assembled in the ports of the Spanish peninsula, and 85,000 men embarked on them.

Philip II thought the scheme too vast, and, above all, too costly. He substituted for it another plan, which was more economical. Santa Cruz was to assemble in the Atlantic ports of the Peninsula a fleet of more modest proportions, just strong enough to secure command of the Channel. This done, he was to cover the transportation across the narrow seas of the Spanish army that was already operating in the Netherlands, under the Duke of Parma. The army of the Netherlands would be reinforced with all the fighting-men that could be spared from the fleet. This was in its essential points the plan of campaign of the "Gran' Armada" of 1588.

It was intended that the attempt should be made in the summer of 1587. It was delayed for a twelvemonth by a daring enterprise of Francis Drake, a memorable enterprise, because in proposing it he laid down the true principle for the defence of England against invasion. His policy was that of Edward III at Sluys, his principle that it was better to keep the enemy occupied on his own coasts rather than await him on those of England. On 2 April, 1587, Drake sailed for Spain with only thirty ships, and surprised and burned the half-armed transports and storeships collected at Cadiz for fitting out the Armada. His dashing enterprise had made its departure for that year impossible.

Before the preparations for the next summer's campaign were completed the Marquis of Santa Cruz died, and Spain lost her best and most experienced admiral. King Philip put in his place a great noble, Guzman, Duke of Medina-Sidonia, who pleaded in vain to be excused, frankly declaring to his sovereign that he felt unfit for such high command, as he had scant knowledge of war and no experience of the sea. It is supposed that the King persisted in the nomination because Medina-Sidonia's hereditary rank would place him above the jealousies of the subordinate commanders, and he hoped to supply for the Marquis's inexperience by sending veteran sailors and soldiers with him as his staff-officers and divisional commanders.

By the middle of May, 1588, the Armada was at last ready to sail from the Tagus. In England there had been the wildest reports as to its numbers and strength. These exaggerations were repeated by the popular historians of the fighting in the Channel, and have become almost a national tradition. The Spanish galleons were said to be floating monsters, more like castles than ships; the fleet was so numerous that it hid the sea, and looked like a moving town; it "seemed as if room would scarce be found on the ocean for so vast an armament."

The glory of the English victory was great enough to need no exaggeration to enhance it. But in sober fact there was no such enormous disparity, as is generally imagined, between the opposing forces. Large and small, there were 130 ships in the Armada. The detailed catalogue of them, from the list sent by Medina-Sidonia to Philip II, has been reprinted by Captain Duro in his *Armada Invencibile,* and by Professor Laughton in his *State Papers relating to the Armada.* From these sources I take a summarized table giving the statistics of the Armada, and then add some particulars as to various squadrons, ships, and commanders:—

Divisions	Ships	Tons	Guns	Soldiers	Sailors	Total Men
Armada of Portugal	12	7737	347	3330	1293	4623
" " Biscay	14	6567	238	1937	863	2800
" " Castille	16	8714	384	2458	1719	4171
" " Andalusia	11	8762	240	2327	780	3105
" " Guipuzcoa	14	6991	247	1992	616	2608
" " the Levant	10	7705	280	2780	767	3523
Squadron of "urcas" (hulks or storeships)	23	10271	384	3121	608	3729
"Patasses" and "zabras" (small craft)	22	1121	91	479	574	1093
Neapolitan galleasses	4	—	200	773	468	1341
Galleys	4	—	20	—	362	362
	130	57868	2431	19295	8050	27365
Rowers (in galleasses and galleys)						2088
Grand total, soldiers, sailors and rowers						29453

The first point to note about the Armada is that it was almost entirely a fleet of sailing-ships. The new period of naval war had begun. There had been hundreds of galleys at Lepanto, seventeen years earlier, but there were only four in the Armada, and none of these reached the Channel. The long, low, oar-driven warship, that for two thousand years had done so much fighting in the Mediterranean, proved useless in the long waves of the Atlantic.[1] The only oared ships that really took part in the campaign were the four *galleasses*, and in these the oar was only auxiliary to the spread of sail on their three full-rigged masts. The *galleasse* has been described in the story of Lepanto. It was an intermediate or transition type of ship. It seems to have so impressed the English onlookers that the four *galleasses* are given quite an unmerited importance in some of the popular narratives of the war.

But the day of sails had come, and the really effective strength of the Armada lay in the tall galleons of the six "armadas" or squadrons of Portugal, the Spanish provinces, and the Levantine traders. The galleon was a large sailing-ship, but even as to the size of the galleons the popular tradition of history is full of exaggeration. Built primarily for commerce, not for war, they carried fewer guns than the *galleasses*, though many of them were of heavier tonnage. In those days every large trader carried a certain number of guns for her protection, but such guns were mostly of small calibre and short range.

The largest galleons were in the armada of the Levant. The flagship, *La Regazona*, commanded by Martin de Bertendona, was the biggest ship in the whole fleet, a great vessel of 1249 tons. But she only mounted 30 guns, mostly light pieces. Compare this with the armament of the *galleasses*, and one sees the difference between ships built for war and galleons that were primarily traders. The largest of the four *galleasses* was only of 264 tons, the smallest 169, but each of the four mounted 50

---

1. Galleys were used in the land-locked Mediterranean and Baltic up to the first years of the nineteenth century, but the only sailors who ever ventured to take galleys into the wild weather of the Atlantic were the Norse Vikings.

The "Great Armada" entering the Channel

guns. In all the six armadas of galleons there were only seven ships of over a thousand tons. There were fourteen more of over 800, and a considerable number of under 500 tons. But the galleon looked larger than she really was. Such ships had high bulwarks and towering fore and stern castles, and they appear to have been over-rigged with huge masts and heavy yards.

A galleon under full sail must have been a splendid sight, the bows and stern and the tall "castles" tricked out with carving, gold and colour. Great lanterns were fixed on the poop. The sails were not dull stretches of canvas, but bright with colour, for woven into or embroidered on them there were huge coats-of-arms, or brilliantly coloured crosses, and even pictures of the saints with gilded haloes. From the mastheads fluttered pennons thirty or forty feet long, and flagstaffs displayed not only the broad standard of the Lions and Castles of Spain, but also the banners of nobles and knights who were serving on board.

But the tall ship, with her proud display of gold and colour, was more splendid than formidable, and the Elizabethan seamen had soon realized the fact. Built originally for the more equable weather of the trade-wind region in the South Atlantic, she was not so well fitted for the wilder seas and changing winds of the North. She was essentially an unhandy ship. In bad weather she rolled heavily, and her heavy masts and spars and high upper works strained the whole structure, so that she was soon leaking badly. With the wind abeam and blowing hard, her tall sides and towering castles were like sails that could not be reefed, a resisting surface that complicated all manœuvres. The guns that looked out from her port-holes were mostly small cannon, many of them mere three and four-pounders, of short range and little effect. So small was the dependence the Spaniards placed upon them that they carried only the scantiest supply of ammunition.

The fighting method of the galleon was to bear close down upon her opponent, run her aboard, if possible, pour down a heavy fire of musketry from the high bulwarks and castles, so as to bring a plunging shower of bullets on the enemy's decks, and then board, and let pike and sword do their work as they had done at Lepanto. These were, after all, the methods of the soldier, the tactics of the war-galley. It was the merit of Howard, Hawkins, Drake, and the other great captains, who commanded against the Armada, that they fought as seamen, using their more handy and better handled ships to choose their own position and range, refusing to let the Spaniards close, and bringing a more powerful, longer-ranging, and better served artillery to bear with destructive effect on the easy targets supplied by the tall galleons. It is worth noting that while there were more soldiers than seamen in the Armada, there were more seamen than soldiers in the fleet that met it in the narrow seas.

If the Armada had a commander whose only merit was personal courage, the admirals of the various squadrons were all men of long experience in war, both by land and sea. Martinez de Recalde, the second in command and admiral of the armada of Biscay, was a veteran seaman. Diego Flores de Valdes, the admiral of Castille, was an enterprising and skilful leader, and if his advice had been taken at the outset there might have been a disaster for England. Pedro de Valdes, the admiral of Andalusia, had sailed the northern seas, and Medina-Sidonia was told he might rely on his local knowledge. Moncada, the admiral of the galleasses, was a "first-rate fighting-man," and De Leyva, the general of the troops embarked, who had taken command of the *Rata Coronada*, a great galleon of 800 tons in the Levant armada, showed that he was sailor as well as soldier.

The Duke of Parma, who commanded the army that was to be embarked from the Netherlands, was counted the best general of the day, and his 30,000 Spanish regular infantry were the most formidable body of troops then in Europe. His orders from the King were to build or collect a flotilla of flat-bottomed barges to ferry his army across the straits under the protection of the Armada, and for months thousands of shipwrights had been at work in fishing ports and creeks, canals and rivers along the coast between Calais and Ostend. The Dutch rebels held Flushing and the mouth of the Scheldt, and they had a small but efficient fleet ready to do good service as the ally of England—a fact often overlooked in our popular stories of the Armada. Parma had proposed that he should attempt to reduce Flushing and obtain command of the Scheldt, as a preliminary to the enterprise against England.

The Armada could then run for the Scheldt, and make Antwerp its base of operations. But Philip was impatient of further delays. Though the best of the Spanish admirals were against him, the King insisted that the Armada need only run up Channel and obtain temporary command of the straits to enable Parma to embark his army in the flotilla even from an open beach. In the King's mind the necessity of destroying the hostile sea power as a prelude to any scheme of invasion was disregarded or was not understood.

On 30 May, in fine weather, the Armada at last sailed from Lisbon. The reports sent back to Philip II by Medina-Sidonia, as the fleet passed Cape Finisterre and stood out into the Bay of Biscay, told that all was well. But a few days later a storm from the Atlantic swept the sea, and partly dispersed the Armada. The storeships held on till they sighted the Scilly Islands, and then, finding they had parted from the fleet, turned back. Into the northern ports of Spain came scattered ships that had lost spars and sails, some of them leaking so badly that only hard labour at the pumps kept them afloat. Medina-Sidonia, with the main body, made for Corunna, where he ordered the stragglers to reassemble. On 19 June he wrote to the King reporting his arrival.

Then he sent letters betraying so much discouragement and irresolution that one wonders he was not promptly relieved of his command. He proposed that the whole enterprise should be abandoned and some means found for arranging terms of peace. He reported that the fleet had suffered badly in the storm; that there was much sickness on board; that large quantities of provisions had gone bad, and must be replaced; and that the ships were short of water. Instead of dismissing him from the command, the King wrote to his admiral ordering and encouraging him to renew the attempt. The ships were refitted and provisioned, and drafts of men collected to replace the invalided soldiers and sailors. Early in July the Armada was again ready for sea.

The news that King Philip's Great Armada had been beaten back by the wild Biscay gales reached England when the whole country was in a fever of preparation for resistance. A commission of noblemen and gentlemen had been appointed "to sett doune such meanes as are fittest to putt the forces of the Realme in order to withstand any invasion." The Lord-Lieutenants of the counties were directed to be ready to call out the local levies, which formed a roughly armed, and mostly untrained, militia. Garrisons were organized in the seaports, formed of more reliable and better equipped men, and a small force was collected at Tilbury to oppose a landing in the Thames estuary. Faggots and brushwood were piled on hill-tops from Land's End to Berwick to send the news of the Spaniards' arrival through England by a chain of beacon fires.

The best of the Queen's advisers, men like the Lord Admiral Howard of Effingham, and such experienced seamen as Hawkins, Drake, and Fenner, realized, and succeeded in persuading the Council, that it was on the sea, and not on the land, that England must be protected from invasion. Their letters in the Armada State Papers are full of practical lessons even for the present time. While insisting that the main effort must be concentrated on the fleet, they did not disregard the advisability of subsidiary preparations on land, in case of accidents. But Howard insisted that a few well-trained men were worth fourfold their number of irregular levies, and wrote to the Council:—

> I pray your Lordships to pardon me that I may put you in remembrance to move her Majesty that she may have an especial care to draw ten or twelve thousand men about her own person, that may not be men unpractised. For this she may well assure herself that 10,000 men, that be practised and trained together under a good governor and expert leaders, shall do her Majesty more service than any 40,000 which shall come from any other parts of the

realm. For, my Lords, we have here 6000 men in the fleet, which we shall be able, out of our company, to land upon any great occasion, which being as they have been trained here under captains and men of experience, and each man knowing his charge and they their captains, I had rather have them to do any exploit than any 16,000 men out of any part of the realm.

The fleet, from which Howard of Effingham was ready to land these trained men if necessary, was even more numerous than the Armada itself, though the average size of the ships was smaller. On the list there appear the names of no fewer than 197 ships, ranging in size from the *Triumph* of 1100 tons (Frobisher's ship) down to small coasting craft.

The flagship, the *Ark*, or *Ark Royal*, was a vessel of 800 tons. Contemporary prints show that she had a high poop and forecastle, but not on the exaggerated scale of the Spanish galleons; and that she had four masts, and was pierced with three tiers of port-holes for guns, besides gun-ports in the stern. She had a crew of 270 mariners, 34 gunners, and 126 soldiers.

Contrary to the system on which the Armada was manned, the seamen in every ship of the English fleet exceeded the soldiers in number. The *Ark* carried no less than 44 guns, namely, 4 "cannon" (60-pounders), 4 "*demi*-cannon" (30-pounders) 12 "*culverins*" (long 18-pounders), 12 "*demi-culverins*" (long 9-pounders), 6 "*sakers*" (6-pounders), and six smaller pieces, some of them mounted inboard for resisting boarders at close quarters.[2] This was an armament equalled by few of the Spanish ships, and the fact is that the English ships as a rule were better armed than

---

2. These old wooden ships had a much longer life than the steel battleship of today, which becomes obsolete and is broken up after twenty years. The *Ark*, launched in 1587 (and built at the cost of £5000=£50,000 in the money of today), was refitted and renamed the *Anne Royal* (after James I's queen) in 1608; was the flagship of the Cadiz expedition of 1625, and was broken up in 1636. Hawkins's ship, the *Victory*, was launched in 1561; she sailed as the *Resolution* in Blake's fleet under the Commonwealth; was renamed the *Royal Prince* at the Restoration, and was burned in 1666 during Charles II's Dutch war. She was then over a hundred years old and still fit "to lie in the line of battle."

the Spaniards.

But few of Howard's fleet were of heavy tonnage. There were only two ships of over 1000 tons; one of 900; two of 800; three of 600; five or six of 500, and all the rest less than 400 tons, many of them less than 100. But though the English ships were smaller than the Spaniards, they were better at sailing and manœuvring, thoroughly handy craft, manned by sailors who knew how to make them do their best, and who were quite at home in the rough northern seas.

The main body of the fleet under Howard of Effingham assembled at Plymouth. Detached squadrons under Lord Henry Seymour and Sir W. Winter watched the Straits of Dover. Some of the captains thought Plymouth had been unwisely chosen as the station of the main fleet, pointing out that a south or southwest wind, which would be a fair wind for the Spaniards, would be a very foul one for ships working out of the long inlet of Plymouth Harbour.

In June, Howard had news that the Armada was not only at sea, but far on its voyage. Merchantmen ran for shelter to Plymouth, and told how they had met at least two squadrons of large ships with great red crosses on their foresails off Land's End, and in the entrance of the Channel. One ship had been chased and fired on by a Spaniard. Then all trace of the enemy was lost. There was no news of him in the Channel or on the Irish coasts. The weather had been bad, and it was rightly conjectured that the squadrons sighted off Land's End were only detachments of the Armada scattered by the storm, and that the great fleet had put back to Spain, probably to Corunna. This was soon confirmed by reports from France.

For a while there was an impression that the danger was over. Drake, Hawkins, and other captains urged that now was the time to take the English fleet to the Spanish coast and destroy the crippled and discouraged Armada in its harbours. But the Queen and her Council hesitated to adopt so bold a policy, and only a few ships were sent out to watch for the enemy in the Bay of Biscay. These returned driven before a strong south wind, and then fugitives from the Channel brought news that there was a crowd of ships off the Lizard, and Howard in a short note reported that he had gone out to engage them. The Armada had come in earnest at last.

After refitting at Corunna, Medina-Sidonia had sailed on 22 July with fine weather and a fair south wind. Progress was not rapid, for the great fleet's speed was that of its slowest ships. On the 26th, when the Armada was well out to sea off the headlands of Brittany, the morning was dull and cloudy, and towards noon the wind went round to the northward and increased to half a gale, raising a heavy sea. The course was changed to the eastward, and the ships were kept under shortened sail. The four galleys, unable to face the rising storm, ran for shelter towards the French coast, and never rejoined. They went southwards before the wind. One was wrecked near Bayonne. The three others reached Spain.

All next day the gale blew heavily. The Armada, scattered over a wide extent of sea, beat slowly to windward, working away from the dangerous French coast. Many ships temporarily parted company. It looked as if there would be another failure. But on Thursday the 28th (to quote the Spanish admiral's diary) "the day dawned clear and bright, the wind and sea more quiet than the day before. Forty ships were counted to be missing." The admiral sent out three *pinnaces* to look for them, and next day, Friday, 29 July (19 July, O.S.), had news that all but one of them were with Pedro de Valdes off the Lizard. This was the crowd of ships reported that same day to Howard at Plymouth.

The missing ship, the *Santa Ana*, the flagship of Biscay, rejoined later. In the evening Medina-Sidonia saw the coast of England, and notes that it was "said to be the Lizard." On the Saturday the admiral writes that "at dawn the Armada was near with the land, so as we were seen therefrom, whereupon they

---

3. Macaulay, writing his ballad of the Armada before the full English and Spanish records of the time were available, represents the news as being brought to Plymouth by a merchantman that had seen "Castille's black fleet lie heaving many a mile" out by the Channel Islands, where the Armada was never sighted. The "tall *Pinta*" chased her for hours. There was no such ship in the Armada.(Cont. Nxt pge)

made fire and smokes."³ The crew of a captured fishing-boat later in the day told him they had seen the English fleet coming out of Plymouth, and in the evening Medina-Sidonia's diary tells that "many ships were seen, but because of the mist and rain we were unable to count them."

A council of war had been held on board his flagship, the *San Martin*. The wind was south-west, the very wind to carry the Armada into Plymouth, and dead against the English fleet coming out. De Leyva proposed that the opportunity should be taken to attack the English in Plymouth Sound. Once in the narrow waters the Spaniards could run them aboard and have the advantage of their superior numbers of fighting-men in a hand-to-hand conflict on the decks. The soldier's advice was good, but the sailors were against him. They argued that the fleet must enter Plymouth Sound in line ahead at the risk of being destroyed in detail, as the shoals at the entrance (those on which the breakwater of today stands) left only two narrow channels. De Leyva's bold plan was rejected, and it was decided that the Armada should proceed up Channel.

Next day the fighting began. The wind had shifted to the north-west, a good enough wind for working up Channel on the port tack. English contemporary accounts say the Armada was formed in a half-moon, a centre and two wings slightly thrown forward. Howard had as yet only brought part of his fleet out of Plymouth, but though greatly outnumbered by the Spaniards, he had his best ships and his most enterprising captains with him, and nothing daunted by the grand array of the Armada, he began a series of harassing attacks upon it.

It was Sunday morning, 31 July, according to the Spanish reckoning, the 21st according to the Old Style still used in England. It

---

Macaulay took the name of one of Columbus's caravels to adorn his ballad. Instead of the enemy seeing "fire and smokes" at dawn, he describes with more picturesque effect, how, in the night—
From the deep the Spaniards saw
Along each southern shire,
Cape after cape in endless range,
Those twinkling points of fire.

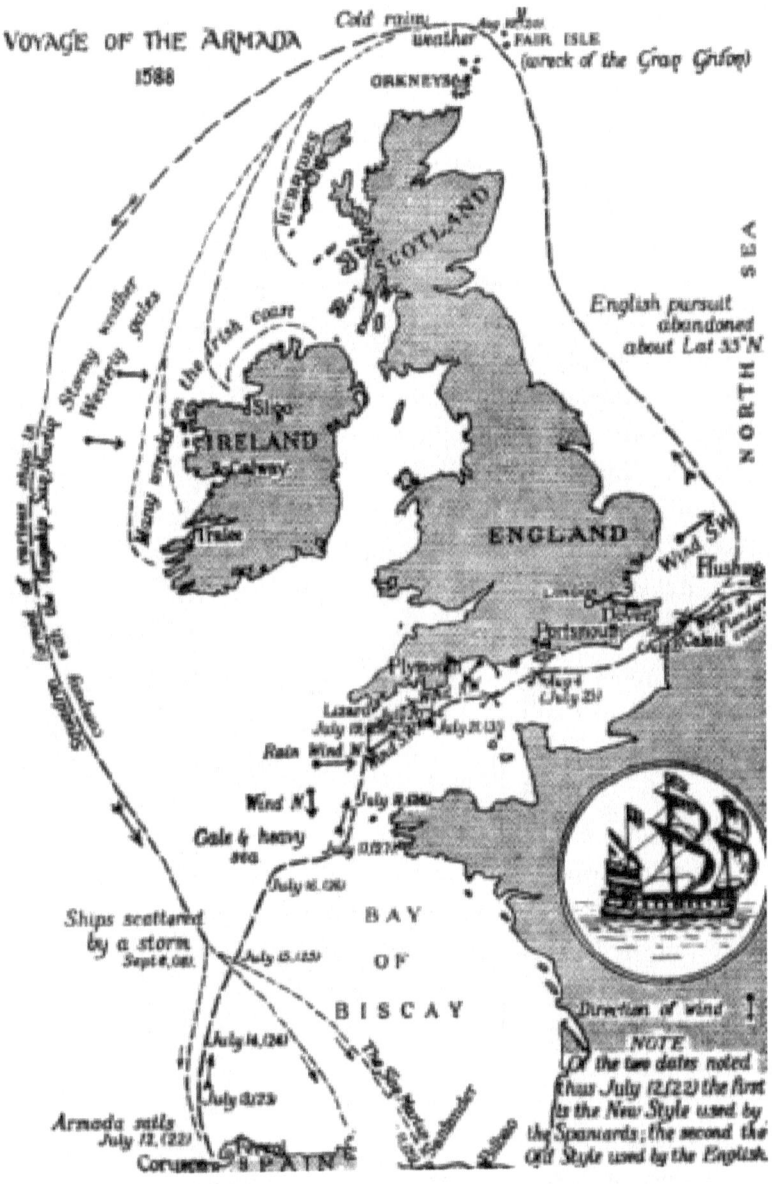

VOYAGE OF THE ARMADA 1588

was a sunny day, with just enough wind to help the nimble, seaworthy English ships in their guerrilla tactics. Howard's policy was to take full advantage of the three factors that were on his side in the solution of the problem, better seamanship in his crews, better gunnery, and handier ships. To close with and grapple in the fashion of earlier naval battles would have been to risk being crushed by superior numbers. His policy was to hang upon the flank or rear of the Armada, close in and try to cripple one or more ships by artillery fire, slip away if the enemy turned upon him, come on again as they gave up the attempt to close, and he was ready all the time to swoop down upon and capture any ship that might be detached from her consorts.

At the time arm-chair critics on shore found fault with what they considered the half-hearted conduct of the admiral, and the Queen's Council inquired why it was that none of the Spanish ships had been boarded. Sir Walter Raleigh, who, as Professor Laughton notes, "must have often talked with Howard, and Drake, and Hawkins, while the business was fresh in their memories," thus explains and defends the admiral's conduct:—[4]

> Certainly, he that will happily perform a fight at sea must believe that there is more belonging to a good man of war upon the waters than great daring, and must know that there is a great deal of difference between fighting loose or at large and grappling. To clap ships together without consideration belongs rather to a madman than to a man of war; for by such an ignorant bravery was Peter Strozzi lost at the Azores, when he fought against the Marquis of Santa Cruz.
>
> In like sort had the Lord Charles Howard, Admiral of England, been lost in the year 1588, if he had not been better advised than a great many malignant fools were, that found fault with his demeanour. The Spaniards had an army aboard them, and he had none; they had more ships than he had, and of higher building and charging; so

---

4. *Historie of the World*, edit. 1736, 2, 565, quoted by Professor Laughton, *State Papers relating to the Defeat of the Spanish Armada*, vol. 1, Introduction, p. 66.

that, had he entangled himself with those great and powerful vessels, he had greatly endangered this kingdom of England. For twenty men upon the defences are equal to a hundred that board and enter; whereas then, contrariwise, the Spaniards had a hundred for twenty of ours, to defend themselves withal. But our admiral knew his advantage and held it; which had he not done, he had not been worthy to have held his head.

The shift of the wind to the north-west had given the English the weather gage. They could run down before it on the enemy, and beat back against it in a way that was impossible for the clumsy galleons. Thus Howard and his captains could choose their own position and range during the fighting. It began by a *pinnace*, appropriately named the *Defiance*, firing a shot at the nearest Spaniards, a challenge to battle. Medina-Sidonia held his course and took no notice of it. Howard's squadron now swept past his left, and then engaged his rear ships.

The admiral himself in the *Ark* steered for De Leyva's tall galleon, the *Rata Coronada,* perhaps taking her to be the flagship of the whole Armada. The two ships were soon in action, the English gunners firing at the Spaniard's great hull, and De Leyva's men aiming at the masts and yards of the *Ark* in the hope of bringing down her spars and sails, crippling and then boarding her. The better gunnery was on the English side. They fired three shots to the Spaniards' one, and every shot told on the huge target. And shots in the hull meant much loss of life and limb in the crowded decks.

As Recalde with the rear division shortened sail, and turned to the help of De Leyva, the *Ark* and her consorts bore away, only to return again to the attack, bringing their guns into action against Recalde's huge galleon, the *Santa Ana*, and Pedro Valdes's ship, the *Rosario, Capitana,* or flagship of the Biscayan armada. These two had become separated from the main body with a few of her ships that now formed a kind of rearguard. Frobisher in the *Triumph* and Hawkins in the *Victory* were prominent in the attack. On the Spanish side several of the flagships joined in this rearguard fight.

The admirals showed a chivalrous disposition to come to close quarters, and thus Howard was engaged with some of the largest and best commanded ships of the enemy. Oquendo, the admiral of Guipuzcoa, in his 1200-ton galleon, called, like that of Recalde, the *Santa Ana*, had soon to draw out of the fight, with his ship on fire and badly damaged, not by the English cannon, but by a powder explosion on his main gundeck.[5] One only wonders that such accidents were not frequent on both sides, for the powder was ladled into the guns from open gunpowder kegs, and matches were kept burning beside each gun.

The "fighting loose and at large" went on for about three hours. Recalde's ship was badly hulled, and also had her rigging cut up and one of her masts damaged. Pedro Valdes's flagship, the *Rosario*, was twice in collision with a consort, with disastrous results. Her bowsprit was carried away, and her foremast went over the side, the strain on the rigging bringing down the main topmast with it. When the English drew off just before sundown, Valdes was busy cutting away the wreckage. Medina-Sidonia shortened sail to enable the rearward ships to rejoin, and then held his course up Channel.

Valdes sent a request to him that a ship should be detailed to tow the disabled *Rosario*, which otherwise could not keep up with the fleet. It is generally stated that Medina-Sidonia took no notice of the message, and abandoned Valdes to his fate, but in his narrative the Duke reports to King Philip that he personally endeavoured to assist the disabled *Rosario*, and succeeded in removing the wounded from her, only failing to save her "owing to the heavy sea and the darkness of the weather."

The English do not seem to have been troubled by the weather, and it cannot have been very bad, or the wounded could not have been taken by boats from Oquendo's ship. Evidently no great effort was made to succour the *Rosario*, and the ships detailed for the work did not like to lie in isolation so

---

5. "Her two decks and her poop were blown up: in which was the paymaster of this Armada with part of the King's Treasure."—Medina-Sidonia's narrative.

near the English during the night. The impression in the Armada certainly was that the gallant Valdes had been shamefully abandoned by the admiral.

Before sunset a council of war had been held by Howard on board the *Ark*. It was decided to follow up the Armada through the short summer night. To Drake in the *Revenge* was assigned the task of keeping touch with them and guiding the pursuit by displaying a large stern lantern on his ship.

After dark Howard lost sight of the lantern, and then thought he had picked it up again, but at daylight he found that he must have steered by a light in the Armada, for as the day broke he lay with only a few ships perilously near the main body of the enemy. Drake explained that in the darkness he had thought that some ships of the enemy were turning back, and had followed them. He had certainly failed in his important duty, and there was a suspicion that the veteran buccaneer was really manoeuvring to make sure of a prize, for at sunrise his ship, the *Revenge*, lay near the crippled *Rosario*, which had been deserted by her consorts. He summoned Valdes to surrender, and the Spaniard, with his ship helpless and menaced by the main English fleet, hauled down his flag. The huge galleon was towed into Weymouth, the first prize of the campaign.

Howard had drawn off from the enemy, helped to secure the *Rosario*, and rallied his own fleet, which had straggled during the night. This day, Monday, 1 August (or 22 July, Old Style), there was no fighting, the Armada working slowly up Channel, followed by the English out of cannon-range. Medina-Sidonia formed a rearguard of forty galleons and three *galleasses*, "in all 43 of the best ships of the Armada to confront the enemy, so that there should be no hindrance to our joining with the Duke of Parma; and the Duke with the rest of the Armada should go in the van, so that the whole fleet was divided into only two squadrons, Don Alonso de Leyva taking the rear under his charge."

At 11 a.m. Oquendo's ship was reported to be sinking. Her crew and "the King's money" were taken out of her, and the *Santa Ana*, largest but one of King Philip's galleons, disappeared under the grey-green waves of the Channel. In two days the Armada had lost two of its divisional flagships.

Howard had been reinforced during the day from the Western Channel ports. After the free expenditure of powder and shot the previous day, his magazines were half empty, and he husbanded his ammunition and followed up the Spaniards out of fighting range, writing to Portsmouth to have all ships there ready to join him. "We mean so to course the enemy," he added, "that they shall have no leisure to land."

Seymour reported to the Council from Dover that the Armada was well up Channel, and he feared they might seize the Isle of Wight. He asked for "powder and shot" for his squadron—"whereof we have want in our fleet, and which I have divers times given knowledge thereof." All the English commanders felt this want of ammunition and supplies. The Queen's parsimony was endangering the country.

On the Tuesday morning, 2 August (23 July, Old Style), the Armada was off Portland. In the night the wind had gone round to the north-east, and as the sun rose Howard's fleet was seen to be between the Spaniards and the land and to leeward of them. Medina-Sidonia was no sailor, but his veteran commanders saw the chance the shift of the wind had given them. The Armada turned from its course up Channel, and on the starboard tack stood towards the English fleet, hoping in Spanish phrase to catch the enemy "between the sword and the wall."

It was an anxious moment for Howard and his captains when the Armada came sweeping down on them, the *galleasses* in front pushing ahead with sail and oar, behind the long lines of galleons with the wind in the painted sails of their towering masts. It looked as if the Spaniards would soon be locked in close fight with the English squadron, with every advantage on the side of King Philip's floating castles. Led by the *Ark*, the English ships began to beat out to seaward with scant room for the manœuvre.

But just as the close fight seemed inevitable and the tall *Regazona* had almost run the *Ark* aboard, and while both ships were wrapped in a fog of powder smoke, the wind suddenly shifted again, backing to the northward. Howard was now working out well from the land, and every moment improved the position.

There was a heavy cannonade on both sides, but as the range lengthened, the advantage was with the better gunners of the English ships. The *galleasses*, led by the great *Florencia*, tried, with the help of their long oars, to fall on the English rear, the galleons tacked and made one more attempt "to come to hand-stroke," but, writes Sidonia, "all to little effect, the enemy avoiding our attack by the lightness of their vessels." Good seamanship told. Howard's ships were soon in a position to resume the "fighting loose" tactics of the first battle, and the Spaniards knew that at this game they were the losers. So the Armada bore away, resuming its course up Channel, and the cannonade died down into dropping long shots, and then ceased, for Howard had no ammunition to spare.

On the Wednesday the two fleets crept slowly up Channel, the English some six miles astern of the Armada. Once they closed up, and a few shots were exchanged with the *galleasses* in Recalde's rearguard. But Howard did not want to fight. He was only "putting on a brag countenance," for he was woefully short of ammunition, and writing urgently for much-needed supplies. The wind had fallen, and in the afternoon some of the galleons were drifting along, heeled over by shifting guns and stores to enable the carpenters slung over the sides to plug shot-holes near the waterline.

On Thursday the fleets were off the Isle of Wight, and it was almost a calm, with occasional flaws of wind to help them on their way. Welcome reinforcements from Portsmouth joined Howard, and he received some ammunition. Soon after sunrise there was a sharp fight. The *Santa Ana* and a Portuguese galleon had fallen astern of the Armada, and Hawkins, in the *Victory*, supported by several other ships, attacked them. He had done considerable damage to the *Santa An*a, and already reckoned her a prize, when the ever-ready De Leyva, with the great *Rata* and the *galleasses*, came to the rescue, and Hawkins reluctantly drew off. Howard, with the *Ark*, and his nephew, Lord Thomas Howard, in the *Golden Lion*, had come up to cover the retirement of Hawkins. They became involved in a fight with the Spanish rearguard, and the *Ark* was damaged, according to one account, by a collision, but it seems more likely that her steering gear was temporarily put out of order by a chance shot. She fell behind her consorts, and lowered boats to tow her out of action. For the moment the wind was helping the Spaniards, and, led by Medina-Sidonia himself, several galleons turned to attack the *Ark*. But the wind freshened and changed suddenly, and the English ships escaped from their dangerous position, and so the fight ended.

On the Friday it was almost a dead calm. It was a bright summer day, and from the hills of the Isle of Wight there was a wondrous spectacle of the two fleets drifting idly over miles of sea, with the sails flapping against the masts. On board the *Ark*, now repaired and again fit for action, there was a stately ceremony, the admiral, in the Queen's name, conferring knighthood on Hawkins, Frobisher and several other of the captains who had taken a leading part in the fighting. It was decided not to engage the enemy again till the fleets had reached the Straits of Dover. Shortness of ammunition was the reason for this decision.

Medina-Sidonia was anxious on the same score. He sent off a pilot-boat to the Duke of Parma, asking him to send him a supply of "four, six, and ten-pound shot," "because much of his ammunition had been wasted in the several fights." The mention of such small weights shows with what light artillery most of the galleons were armed. He also asked Parma to send forty light craft to join the Armada, "to the end he might be able with them to close with the enemy, because our ships being very heavy in comparison with the lightness of those of the enemy, it was impossible to come to hand-stroke with them."

At sunset the wind freshened, and at daybreak on Saturday the English were seen following up closely, but there was no fighting, "the Armada sailing with a fair wind and the rear close up, and in very good order." At 10 a.m. the French coast near

Boulogne was in sight. At four in the afternoon the Armada was off Calais, and at five orders were given to anchor in Calais roads, "seven leagues from Dunkirk," or between Calais and Gravelines. The Spaniards noticed that some thirty-six ships had joined Howard's fleet, which anchored about a league away. The new arrivals were Seymour's and Winter's squadrons from Dover and the Downs.

Medina-Sidonia now believed that he had all but accomplished his task. English writers say that the enemy were disappointed and discouraged when they anchored off Calais, but there is no proof of this in contemporary Spanish accounts. Medina-Sidonia thought it a success that he had got into touch with the Viceroy of the Netherlands. He had sent off a messenger to his head-quarters at Dunkirk, asking him to embark his army at once, and declaring his readiness to convoy it across Channel.

But Medina-Sidonia was in a fool's paradise. His ignorance of war was the ultimate source of his satisfaction with the outlook. Better men, like Leyva and Recalde, realized that until the enemy's fleet was not merely eluded, but effectively beaten, there could be no invasion of England. The French Governor of Calais told the admiral that a change in the weather might make his position very unpleasant, and Medina-Sidonia urged Parma to act at once by telling him "that he could not tarry without endangering the whole fleet."

But Parma was neither ready nor anxious for any prompt action. The fleet of the Netherlanders, some fifty sail, was blockading most of the places along the coast where he had prepared his flat-bottomed boats. He knew better than to embark the force he had in hand at Dunkirk till Howard's fleet was disposed of.

But Howard was determined not to leave the Armada undisturbed in its exposed anchorage. He had no sooner been joined by Seymour and Winter than he hurriedly prepared eight small craft in his own fleet to be used as fireships, by turning over to them all the inflammable lumber he could collect from the other vessels, and removing their guns, ammunition, and stores.

Medina-Sidonia had spent the Sunday writing pressing letters to the Prince of Parma, and obtaining fresh water and other supplies from Calais. When the long summer twilight ended the Armada was still riding at anchor, the irregular lines of dark hulls stretching for miles, with lanterns flickering at yard-arm or poop, and guard-boats rowing about the outskirts of the floating city. At midnight there was a cry of alarm passed from ship to ship. The tide was running strong from the westward through the Straits, and sweeping along on its current came eight dark masses, each defined in the night by a red flicker of fire that rose higher and spread wider as the English fireships came nearer and nearer.

Three years before, when Parma was besieging Antwerp, the revolted Netherlanders had attacked the bridge he had thrown across the river below the city by sending drifting down upon it a ship laden with powder barrels, with a burning fuse and powder-train to fire them, and blocks of stone heaped over them to increase the force of the explosion. The awful destruction caused by this floating volcano made the Spaniards long after fearful of the attempt being repeated elsewhere, and Medina-Sidonia tells in his diary that when Howard's fireships came drifting through the summer night off Gravelines, he and his captains thought that they were likely to be *maquinas de minas,* "contrivances of mines," like the terrible floating mine of Antwerp.

With this suspicion, all idea of grappling them was abandoned. As they drew nearer there was something like a panic in the Armada. The admiral signalled to weigh anchor and make sail, but few of the ships waited for the tedious operation of getting the heavy anchors up to the cat-heads by slow hand labour on windlass or capstan. In most of the galleons the carpenter's broad axe hacked through the cables and left the anchors deep in Channel mud. Sails were hurriedly shaken out, and like a startled flock of sheep the crowd of ships hurried away to the eastward along the coast in wild disorder.

Moncada, the admiral of the *galleasses,* in the San Lorenzo, collided with the galleon *San Juan de Sicilia,* and the great *gal-*

leass dismasted and with shattered oars drifted on a back eddy of the tide towards Calais bar. The fireships went aground here and there, and burned harmlessly to the water's edge. Medina-Sidonia, seeing the danger was over, fired a gun as a signal for the fleet to anchor, but most of the ships had cut their cables, and had no spare anchors available on deck, and they drifted along the coast, some of them as far as Dunkirk. The sunrise on the Monday morning showed the great fleet widely scattered, only a few of the best ships being with the admiral. Moncada's flagship had been left by the falling tide hard aground on Calais bar.

The English attacked the stranded *galleass* in *pinnaces* and boats, Howard with some of the larger ships standing by "to give the men comfort and countenance." Some of the Spaniards escaped to the shore. The rest, headed by Moncada, made a brave stand against the boarders, who swarmed up her sides, led by one Richard Tomson, of Ramsgate. Moncada was killed, and the ship taken. The English pillaged her, but the hulk was abandoned and seized later by the French Governor of Calais.

During this fight on the bar Medina-Sidonia had reassembled about half his fleet, which he formed in a great crescent off Gravelines. The wind was from the west, and numbers of galleons were away to leeward. Some of them were in dire peril of driving ashore. Howard saw his advantage, and the whole English fleet bore down on the Spanish crescent. It was the nearest thing to a pitched battle in the whole Armada campaign. The English came on with wind and tide helping them and, with the confidence that was the outcome of their growing sense of superiority, ventured to close quarters with the tall Spaniards, while taking care never to give them the chance of grappling and boarding. As the fight went on the Spaniards worked slowly towards the north-east edging off the land, for their deep draught and the fate of Moncada's *galleass* made them anxious about the Flanders shoals.

Howard and Hawkins led the English centre, Drake and Frobisher the right, Seymour and Winter the left. Not a shot was fired till they were at musket range, and then the English guns roared out in a well-sustained cannonade in which every shot told. It was the first of modern naval battles, the fights decided by gunfire, not by hand-to-hand conflict on the decks. The Spaniards answered back with their lighter and more slowly served artillery, and with a crackle of musketry fire. Before noon the Spanish cannon were mostly silent, for sheer lack of ammunition, and the galleons defended themselves only with musket and *arquebuse*, while striving in vain to close and grapple with their enemies. Spars and rigging were badly cut up, shots between wind and water were letting the sea into the huge hulls.

Just as the English thought the *San Juan de Sicilia* had been put out of action and would be their prize, the galleon heeled over and went to the bottom. Soon the fight was only sustained by the rearward ships, the rest trying to extricate themselves from the *mêlée*, not for any lack of courage, but because all their ammunition was gone, their decks were encumbered with wreckage from aloft, and the men were toiling at the pumps to keep them afloat.

The English at last drew off from their persistent attacks on the rearward ships, only because after a hot cannonade of seven hours they were running short of ammunition; so they used the advantage of position and better seamanship and seaworthiness to break off from the battle, Howard hanging out the "council flag" from the *Ark*, as a signal to his leading captains to come on board and discuss the situation with him.

Medina-Sidonia, in his diary of the day, says nothing of the sinking of the *San Juan de Sicilia*, but he goes on to tell how the *San Felipe* and the *San Mateo* were seen drifting helplessly towards the shoals of the Zealand coast; how efforts were made to take off their crews, but these failed, "for the sea was so high that nothing could be done, nor could the damage be repaired which the flagship had suffered from great shot, whereby she was in danger of being lost."

This talk of rough seas shows that, brave though he undoubtedly was in battle, the Duke had the landsman's exaggerated alarm at the choppy waves of the Channel, and regarded as a gale and a storm what a sailor would call fine weather with a bit of a breeze. None of the English commanders thought that there was a high sea that summer afternoon.

In the night it blew somewhat harder from the north-west, and as the early dawn came it was seen that the Armada was in a perilous position. The galleons, many of them with badly damaged spars and rigging, many more without anchors at their cat-heads ready to bring them up, were being forced nearer and nearer to the low sandy shores that were marked only by the white foam of the breakers, and the leadsmen were giving warning that the keels were already dangerously near to the shelving bottom along the outlying fringe of shoals.

The English ships, with plenty of sea-room, looked on without closing in to attack. Little ammunition was left, and Howard and his captains were not going to waste good powder and shot on ships that seemed doomed to hopeless destruction. Some of Medina-Sidonia's captains proposed that he should show the white flag and obtain the help of the English to tow the endangered vessels off the lee shore, but he refused to hear of such base surrender, and told them he was prepared for death. He tells in his journal of the day how a sudden change of the wind saved the fleet:—

> The enemy held aloof, seeing that our Armada must be lost. The pilots on board the flagship—men of experience of that coast—told the Duke at this time that it was not possible to save a single ship of the Armada; for that with the wind as it was in the north-west, they must all needs go on the banks of Zeeland; that God alone could prevent it. Being in this peril and without any remedy, God was pleased to change the wind to west-south-west, whereby the fleet stood towards the north without hurt to any ship.

The deliverance was not quite as complete as the Duke supposed. Far astern the great *San Mateo* had grounded on the shoals "between Ostend and Sluys." Next day three English ships came to take her, but the Spaniards, notwithstanding their helpless plight, made a desperate fight for two hours before they surrendered. Don Diego de Pimentel was in command, with several nobles among his officers and volunteers. These were spared, for the sake of the ransom they might fetch, but no quarter was given to the common crowd. William Borlas, one of the captors, wrote to Secretary Walsingham:

> I was the means that the best sort were saved; and the rest were cast overboard and slain at the entry.[6]

These Elizabethan sea-fighters were as cruel as they were brave.

Other ships drifted ashore or found their way into ports along the low coast to the north-eastward, but all these were taken by Prince Maurice of Nassau, admiral of the United Provinces, who with some thirty sail gleaned up the wreckage of the Armada, though he had taken no part in the fighting, only blockading Parma's flotillas as his share of the service.

Meanwhile, saved by the shift of the wind, the main body of the Armada was speeding into the North Sea, led by Medina-Sidonia in the leaky *San Martin*. Howard and the English fleet held a parallel course, shepherding the enemy without closing in to fire a single shot. Howard was again, to use the phrase of the time, "putting on a brag countenance," for he was in no condition for serious fighting, even against such crippled opponents. The magazines of the English fleet were all but empty, its "cannon, *demi*-cannon, sakers, and falconets" doomed to useless silence, food and water short in supply, and much sickness among the tired crews, who were complaining that they were badly fed and that the beer was undrinkable.

In the evening Medina-Sidonia held a council of war on board the *San Martin*. Soldiers and sailors, veterans of many wars, and the chief pilots of the fleet sat round his cabin table, and there was anxious debate. No one could say how long it would be before Parma's army was ready; ammunition and provisions

---

6. "Entry" = boarding the ship.

were short, men falling sick, ships badly damaged, though only a dozen had been actually lost. The wind was increasing from the south-south-west, and the pilots urged that the best course was to run up the North Sea, round the north of Scotland, reach the open Atlantic, and so return to Spain without further fighting.

Some of the best of the officers, men who had been throughout in the thick of the fighting, protested against this course, to which their admiral was evidently inclined. *Recalde, Oquendo,* and *Leyva* spoke for the brave minority. Most of the great fleet was still safe, and Recalde begged the Duke to lie off and on till the wind blew fair for the Channel again, and then risk another fight. Leyva supported him, and said that though his own ship, the *Rata Coronada,* had been sorely battered, was leaking like a sieve, and had only thirty cartridges in her magazine, he would rather take her into action again and sink fighting than see the Armada run away northward like a pack of cowards. But what seemed the easiest course prevailed. Medina-Sidonia saved his conscience as a soldier by summing up the resolution of the council as a decision to sail northward, but turn back and fight if the wind and weather became favourable.

So in the following days the Armada sped northward before the south-west wind, which sometimes blew hard and raised a sea that increased the distress of the Spaniards. Howard followed with the English fleet, just keeping the Armada in sight. If the Spanish admiral shortened sail to collect his rearward stragglers, Howard followed his example, making no attempt even to close and cut off the nearest ships. He was still reluctantly compelled by empty magazines and half-empty lockers to be content merely "to put on a brag countenance." His shortness of supplies forced him at last to lose touch of the enemy. Off the Firth of Forth he abandoned the pursuit.

When the English ships returned to their ports the captains were not at all sure what had become of the Armada. Some thought it might have gone to the harbours of Norway and Denmark to winter and refit there, and renew the attempt next spring. One sees in the letters of Secretary Walsingham the uncertainty that prevailed among the Queen's counsellors, and some disappointment that the victory was not more complete, though this was the result of himself and his colleagues leaving Howard so ill supplied. On the same day (8 August, Old Style) Walsingham writes to Lord Burghley:

> It is hard now to resolve what advice to give Her Majesty for disarming, until it shall be known what is become of the Spanish fleet"; and to the Lord Chancellor: "I am sorry the Lord Admiral was forced to leave the prosecution of the enemy through the wants he sustained. Our half-doings doth breed dishonour and leaveth the disease uncured.

Meanwhile, the Armada had held its course to the northward, sometimes sighted far off from a Scottish headland. On 20 August (10th, Old Style), twelve days after the battle off Gravelines, it was passing between the Orkneys and Shetlands, heading for the Atlantic, helped by a change of wind which now blew from the east, filling the great sails, but chilling the southern sailors and soldiers to the bone. Though it was summer, the cold was like that of winter, and the bitter weather grew even worse as the galleons sailed on into the North Atlantic. The great ships straggled for miles over grey foam-flecked seas, under dull cloud-packed skies that sent down showers of sleety rain.

Men huddled below in the crowded gundecks, and in fore and stern castles, and there were days when only the pilots kept the deck, while gangs of men took their turn at the never-resting pumps. There were semi-starvation and fever in every ship. The chaplains were busy giving the last consolations of religion to dying men, and each day read the burial service over a row of canvas-shrouded dead, and "committed them to the deep."

The Armada no longer held together. Small groups formed haphazard squadrons, keeping each other company, but many ships were isolated and ploughed their way alone over the dreary sea. Many, despite hard work at the pumps, settled lower and lower in the water each day, and at last sank in the ocean, their fate unknown and unrecorded till, as the months went by and there was no news of them, they were counted as hopelessly lost. Of others the fate is known.

In his sailing instructions Medina-Sidonia had been warned that he should take "great heed lest you fall upon the island of Ireland for fear of the harm that may happen to you on that coast," where, as a sixteenth-century sailor wrote, "the ocean sea raiseth such a billow as can hardly be endured by the greatest ships." There was heavy weather in the "ocean sea" that August and September, but even so the galleons that steered well to the westward before shaping their course for Spain, and kept plenty of sea-room by never sighting the "island of Ireland," succeeded in getting home, except where they were already so badly damaged and so leaky that they could not keep afloat. But along the coasts of Scotland and Ireland there was a succession of disasters for those who clung to, or were driven into, the landward waters.

The first mishap occurred when the Armada was rounding the north of Scotland. The *Gran Grifon*, the flagship of Juan Lopez de Medina, admiral of the *urcas* or storeships, drove on the rocks of Fair Isle, the solitary cliff-bound island in the channel between the Orkneys and Shetlands. Here such few as escaped the waves lived for some six weeks in "great hunger and cold." Then a fishing-boat took them to Anstruther in Fifeshire, where they surrendered to the *bailies*. Lopez de Medina was among this handful of survivors. Melville, the Presbyterian minister of Anstruther, describes him as "a very reverend man of big stature and grave and stout countenance, grey haired and very humble like," as he asked quarter for himself and his comrades in misfortune.[7]

Other distressed ships fled from the Atlantic storms for shelter inside the Hebrides. Three entered the Sound of Mull, where one was wrecked near Lochaline, and a second off Salen. The

---

7. In some histories of the Armada and in more than one standard book of reference Lopez de Medina is confused with Medina-Sidonia, and it is stated that it was the flagship of the whole Armada that was lost on Fair Isle.

third, the great *galleass Florencia*, went down in Tobermory Bay. The local fishermen still tell the traditional story of her arrival and shipwreck. She lies in deep water, half-buried in the sand of the bottom, and enterprising divers are now busy with modern scientific appliances trying to recover the "pieces of eight" in her war-chest, and the silver plate which, according to a dispatch of Walsingham's, was the dinner-service of the "Grandee of Spain" who commanded her.

But it was on the shores of the "island of Ireland" that the most tragic disasters of the Armada took place. Its wrecks strewed the north and west coasts. Fitzwilliam, the "Deputy" or the Viceroy, in Dublin, and Bingham, the Governor of Connaught, had taken precautions to prevent the Spaniards finding shelter, water, and food in the ports by reinforcing the western garrisons. Bingham feared the Irish might be friendly to the Spaniards, and industriously spread among the coast population tales that if they landed the foreigners would massacre the old and carry the young away into slavery. The people of the ports, who had long traded with Spain, knew better, but some of the rude fisher-folk of the west coast perhaps believed the slander.

Where shipwrecked crews fell into the hands of Bingham's men no mercy was shown them. He marched four hundred prisoners into Galway, and his troops massacred them in cold blood, and then he reported that, "having made a clean despatch of them both within the town, and in the country abroad, he rested Sunday all day, giving praise and thanks to God for Her Majesty's most happy success in that action, and our deliverance from such dangerous enemies."

One of the *urcas* came into Tralee Bay in an almost sinking condition, with her crew reduced to twenty-three men, ill and half starved and unable to work the ship. Sir Edward Denny, the Governor of Tralee Castle, was absent. The Spaniards surrendered to Lady Denny and her garrison. The men begged for their lives, and some said they had friends in Waterford who would pay ransom for them; but the lady had them all put to the sword, because "there was no safe keeping for them."

In all, some twenty-five galleons were dashed to pieces under the giant cliff walls of the Irish coast, or on outlying skerries and rocky headlands. In a few cases the Irish coast folk helped the survivors, but too often they were as cruel as the English, and killed and plundered them. Sir George Carew wrote to the Queen, rejoicing that there was now "blood between the Irish and the King of Spain." The Government troops marched along the coasts hunting for Spaniards. The Lord-Deputy Fitzwilliam accompanied one of these parties, and told how in Sligo Bay he saw miles of wreckage, "timber enough to build five of the greatest ships that ever I saw, besides mighty great boats, cables, and other cordage, and some such masts for bigness and length, as I never saw any two could make the like."

Fitzwilliam fairly revelled in the destruction of the Spaniards. He wrote to Secretary Walsingham:

> Since it hath pleased God by His hand upon the rocks to drown the greater and better sort of them, I will, with His favour, be His soldier for the despatching of those rags which yet remain.

At last he got tired of this miserable kind of "soldiering," and proclaimed mercy for all Spaniards in Ireland who surrendered before 15 January, 1589. Numbers of ragged and starving men surrendered. Others had already been smuggled over to Scotland, still an independent country, where they were well treated and given transport to Spain.

The gallant Alonso de Leyva, after escaping from the wreck of his good ship the *Rata Coronada* in Blacksod Bay, was steering for Scotland in one of the *galleasses* that had rescued him and his comrades, when the ship was driven by a storm against the wild cliffs of Dunluce Castle, near the Giant's Causeway. The *galleass* was shattered to matchwood, and Leyva perished with all on board save five who swam ashore.

In the last days of September the surviving ships of the Armada came straggling into the northern ports of Spain with starving, fever-stricken crews. Medina-Sidonia had kept some fifty sail together till 18 September. He had resigned all active duties of command to his lieutenants, Flores and Bobadilla, for he was ill and broken in spirit. His hair had whitened, and he looked like an old man, as he sat all day in the "great cabin" of the *San Martin*, with his head in his hands.

A Biscay gale scattered the remnant of the Armada, and on 21 September the *San Martin* appeared alone off Santander. The wind had fallen; her sails hung loose from the yards, and the long swell that followed the gale was driving the ship towards the rocks outside the port. Some boats went out and towed her in. Most of the crew were sick. Nearly two hundred had been buried at sea.

Recalde and Oquendo brought their ships home, but landed broken with the hardships of the terrible voyage, and only survived it a few weeks. Every ship that arrived told of the many buried at sea, and landed scores of dying and fever and scurvy-stricken men, so that all the northern ports were like great hospitals. When the last galleon had struggled into harbour, fifty-five great ships were still missing. The best of the leaders were dead. Not more than a third of the sailors and soldiers survived. It was a disaster from which Spain as a naval power never really recovered. For fifty years to come the Spanish infantry still upheld their claim to be invincible on the battlefield, but the tall galleon had ceased to be the mistress of the seas.

The campaign of the Armada is remarkable not only for inaugurating the modern period of naval war, the era of the sail and the gun, but also because, though it ended in disaster for one side and success for the other, there was from first to last in the long series of engagements in the narrow seas no battle "fought to a finish."

In all the fighting the English showed that they had grasped the essential ideas of the new warfare, and proved themselves better sailors and better gunners, but the number of the ships they took or destroyed was insignificant. Howard was so crippled by parsimonious mismanagement on the part of his Government that he had to be content with "half-doings," instead of decisive results. But there was worse mismanagement on the Spanish side, and this led first to failure, then to disaster.

The story of the Armada is full of useful lessons, but for England its message for all time is that her true defence against invasion lies not in armies, but upon the sea. The Elizabethan captains knew well that if once Parma's veterans landed in Kent or Essex, the half-trained levies gathered by the beacon fires could do little to stop their onward march. So they took care to make the narrow seas an impassable barrier to the enemy by harrying the covering fleet and making it hopeless for Parma even to think of sending his transports to sea. The lesson is worth remembering even now.

CHAPTER 7

The Battle off the Gunfleet 1666

The decline of Spain as a great power was largely due to the unsuccessful attempt to coerce the Dutch people. Out of the struggle arose the Republic of the United Provinces, and Holland, won from the sea, and almost an amphibious state, became in a few years a great naval power. A hardy race of sailors was trained in the fisheries of the North Sea. Settlements were established in the Far East, and fleets of Dutch East Indiamen broke the Spanish monopoly of Asiatic trade. It was to obtain a depot and watering-place for their East Indiamen that the Dutch founded Cape Town, with far-reaching results on the future development of South Africa.

A Dutch fleet had assisted in defeating the Armada, but the rise of this naval power on the eastern shores of the narrow seas made rivalry with England on the waters inevitable. In the seventeenth century there was a series of hard-fought naval wars between England and the United Provinces.

Under the two first Stuart Kings of England there were quarrels with the Dutch that nearly led to war. The Dutch colonists and traders in the Far Eastern seas had used high-handed measures to prevent English competition. Nearer home there were disputes as to the right claimed by the King's ships to make any foreign ship lower her flag and salute the English ensign. But it was not till the days of the Commonwealth that the first war broke out. It was a conflict between two republics. Its immediate cause was Cromwell's Navigation Act, which deprived the

Dutch of a considerable part of their carrying trade. The first fight took place before the formal declaration of war, and was the result of a Dutch captain refusing the customary salute to a Commonwealth ship.

In this, as in the later conflicts with Holland, while England was still able to live on its own products, the Dutch were in the position in which we are now, for the command of the sea was vital to their daily life. Their whole wealth depended on their great fishing fleets in the North Sea; their Indiamen which brought the produce of the East to Northern Europe through the Straits of Dover; and the carrying trade, in which they were the carriers of the goods of all Central Europe, which the Rhine and their canals brought into their ports. The mere prolongation of a naval war meant endless loss to the merchants and shipowners of Holland.

The development of ocean-borne commerce had led to great improvements in shipbuilding in the three-quarters of a century since the days of the Armada, and the fleets that met in the Channel and the North Sea during Cromwell's Dutch war were far more powerful than those of Medina-Sidonia and Howard. The nucleus of the English fleet had been formed by the permanent establishment created by Charles I, but the ships for which he had levied the "Ship Money" were used against him in the Civil War, for the seafaring population and the people of the ports mostly sided with the Parliament.

The operations against Rupert in the Mediterranean, the war with the Algerines, and the expeditions to the West Indies had helped to form for the Commonwealth a body of experienced officers and seamen, and in Blake, Cromwell had at least one admiral of the first rank. The fleets on both sides sometimes numbered as many as a hundred sail. The guns mounted in broadside tiers had come to be recognized as the weapons that must decide a sea-fight, and in this first Dutch war we see on both sides attempts to use tactical formations that would give the best scope to gun power.

Though a battle was always likely to develop into an irregular *mêlée*, in which the boldest exchanged broadsides and the shirkers hung back, there were attempts to fight in regular lines, the ships giving each other mutual support. Want of traditional experience, marked differences in the speed and manœuvring power of ships, and the rudimentary character of the signalling, made it difficult to keep the line, but it was early recognized as an ideal to be aimed at.

The old oar-driven galleys, with their heavy batteries in the bows and all the guns pointing ahead, went into battle, as at Lepanto, in line abreast. The broadside battleship would thus have her guns pointed at her consorts. The line abreast was used only to bear down on the enemy. The fighting formation was the line ahead. This was adopted at first as a fleet running down from windward closed upon its enemy.

Unless they were actually running away, the other side would be sailing in line ahead with the wind abeam. It was soon realized that in this formation an admiral had his fleet under better control, and gradually the normal formation for fleets became line ahead, and hostile fleets either fought running on parallel courses on the same tack, or passed and repassed each other on opposite tacks. But this was the result of a long evolution, and the typically formal battles fought out by rule in the "close-hauled line ahead" belong to the eighteenth century.

The first Dutch war ended with Blake's victory off the Kentish Knock. The second war, in the days of Charles II, is best remembered in England in connection with a national disgrace, the Dutch raid on Chatham and the blockade of the Thames. This disaster was the result of a piece of almost incomprehensible folly on the part of the King and his advisers. But it came shortly after a great naval victory, the story of which is by most forgotten. It is worth telling again, if only to show that the disaster in the Thames was not the fault of the British navy, and that even under Charles II there were glorious days for our fleet. It is also interesting as a typical naval battle of the seventeenth century.

Hostilities began in 1664 without a formal declaration of

The "Sovereign of the Seas" launched 1637.
A typical warship of the 17th Century

war, the conflict opening with aggressions and reprisals in the colonial sphere of action. English fleets seized Dutch trading ships on the African coast and Dutch islands in the West Indies. In North America the Dutch settlement of New Amsterdam, at the mouth of the Hudson, was occupied, annexed, and renamed New York in honour of His Highness the Duke of York, the brother of the King. England drifted into the war as the result of conflicts in the colonies, and was in a state of dangerous unreadiness for the struggle on the sea.

"God knows how little fit we are for it," wrote Pepys, who as Secretary of the Navy knew the whole position. There was the utmost difficulty in obtaining men for the ships that were being got ready for sea. The pressgangs brought in poor creatures whom the captains described as a useless rabble. There were hundreds of desertions. Happily the Dutch preparations were also backward, and England had thus some breathing time.

In June the two fleets, under the Duke of York and the Dutch Admiral Opdam, each numbering nearly a hundred sail, were in the North Sea, and on the 3rd they met in battle, some thirty-five miles south-east of Lowestoft. Opdam was driven back to the Texel with the loss of several ships. The Duke of York had behaved with courage and spirit during the fight, and was covered with splashes of the blood of officers killed beside him on the quarter-deck, where he himself was slightly wounded. But he showed slackness and irresolution in the pursuit, and failed to reap the full results of his victory.

During the rest of the summer there were more or less successful enterprises against Dutch trade; but the plague in London, in the ports and dockyards, and even in the fleet itself, seriously interfered with the prosecution of the war. As usual at that time, the winter months were practically a time of truce. In the spring of 1666 both parties were ready for another North Sea campaign.

The Dutch had fitted out more than eighty ships under Admiral De Ruyter, and the English fleet was put under the command of Monk, Duke of Albemarle, with Prince Rupert, the fiery cavalry leader of the Civil War, as his right-hand man. Both were soldiers who had had some sea experience. It was still the time when it was an ordinary event for a courtier to command a battleship, with a sailor to translate his orders into sea language and look after the navigation for him. Pepys tells how he heard Monk's wife, the Duchess of Albemarle (perhaps echoing what her husband had said in private), "cry mightily out against the having of gentlemen captains, with feathers and ribbons, and wish the King would send her husband to sea with the old plain sea-captains that he served with formerly."

Monk and Rupert went to join the fleet that was assembling at the Nore on 23 April. It was not ready for sea till near the end of May. On 1 June, when part of the fleet was detached under Rupert to watch the Straits of Dover, Monk met De Ruyter (who was in superior force) off the Essex coast and began a battle that lasted for four days. The news of the first day's fighting set London rejoicing, but soon there came disappointing reports of failure.

The four days' battle had ended in defeat. Outnumbered as he was, Monk had made a splendid fight on the first two days, hoping from hour to hour for Rupert's arrival. On the third day, the Sunday, he had to retire towards the Thames, covering his retreat with a rearguard of sixteen of his best ships. Several of these touched on the Galloper Sand, and Ascue's ship, the *Prince*, ran hard aground on the bank. Ascue struck his flag, and the Dutch burned his ship, abandoning an effort to carry her off because at last Rupert's squadron was in sight. On the fourth day a confused *mêlée* of hard fighting off the Thames mouth ended in Monk retiring into the river. He had lost twenty ships and some three thousand men; but he had fought so well that the Dutch bought their victory dearly, and, after attempting for a few days to blockade the Thames, had to return to Holland to refit and make good their losses.

Amid the general discouragement at the failure of the fleet there was an outburst of mutual accusations of misconduct among the captains, and even some bitter attacks on Monk, the

"General at Sea." Fault was found with the dividing of the fleet on a false report; with Monk's haste to attack the Dutch when he was short of ships; and, finally, with his retreat before the enemy into the Thames. Monk, however, did not bear himself like a beaten man. He spoke of the long battle as, at the worst, an indecisive engagement, and said he had given the Dutch as many hard knocks as he had taken, and now knew how to defeat them. He had sufficient influence at Court to be able to retain his command, and so could look forward to trying his fortune again before long.

The work of refitting the fleet was taken in hand. At any cost, the danger of a blockade of the Thames must be averted, so the merchants of the City combined to help with money, and even some of the rich men of the Court loosed their purse-strings. A fine three-decker launched at Chatham was named the *Loyal London*, in compliment to the exertions of the City, and work was pushed on so rapidly that she was soon ready for commission. Many of the ships had been shorthanded in the four days' battle. The pressgangs were now set vigorously to work, and, though there was a constant drain of desertions to contend with, the numbers on board the ships at Chatham and in the lower Thames rose day by day.

At the end of June a new impetus was given to the preparations by the reappearance of De Ruyter's fleet. He had repaired damages more quickly than his opponents, and put to sea to blockade the Thames. It was on 29 June that the fishermen of Margate and Broadstairs saw a great crowd of strange sail off the North Foreland. It was the Dutch fleet of over a hundred ships, great and small, and commanded by De Ruyter, Van Tromp, and Jan Evertszoon. Some of the ships stood in close to Margate. The militia of the county was called out, and the alarm spread along the southern coast, for the rumour ran that the Dutch had come to cover a French invasion.

But no Frenchmen came, and the Hollanders themselves did not send even a boat's crew ashore. They were quite satisfied with stopping all the trade of London by their mere presence off the Thames, and they had the chance too of picking up homecoming ships that had not been duly warned. So, favoured by fine summer weather, the Dutch admirals cruised backwards and forwards in leisurely fashion between the North Foreland and the outer end of the Gunfleet Sand. They watched with their light craft all the channels that traverse the tangle of sandbanks and shallows in the estuary of the river; but their main fleet was generally somewhere off the Essex coast, for on that side of the estuary lay the channels then best known and most used, the Swin and the Black Deep.

The fleet which thus for some three weeks held possession of the very gateway to the Thames numbered seventy-three line-of-battle ships, twenty-six frigates, and some twenty light craft fitted to be used as fireships. By great exertions Monk and Rupert had got together in the lower Thames eighty-seven fighting-ships and a squadron of fireships. Some fifteen more frigates might have been added to the fleet, but it was thought better to leave them unmanned, and use their crews for strengthening those of the larger ships.

The fleet assembled at the Nore had full complements this time. The men were eager to meet the enemy, and numbers of young gallants from the Court had volunteered for service as supernumeraries. The *Loyal London,* fresh from the builders' hands at Chatham yard, with her crew of eight hundred men, was said to be "the best ship in the world, large or small." Pepys noted that it was the talk of competent men that this was "much the best fleet, for force of guns, greatness and number of ships, that ever England did see." England had certainly need of a good fleet, for she never met on the sea a more capable and determined enemy than the Dutch. In fact, the republic of the United Provinces was perhaps the only state that ever contended on anything like equal terms against England for the command of the sea.

When at last Monk and Rupert were ready to sail they had to wait for a favourable wind and tide, and, with the help of their pilots, solve a somewhat delicate problem. This problem was something like that which a general on land has to solve when it is a question of moving a large force through defiles of which the other end is watched by the enemy's main army. But it had special complications that the soldier would not have to take into account.

Monk's fleet sailing in line ahead, the only order in which it could traverse the narrow channels, would cover about nine miles from van to rear. There were then no accurate charts of the Thames estuary such as we now possess, and the pilots of the time believed the possible ways out for large ships to be fewer and more restricted than we know them to be at present. They advised Monk to take his fleet out from the Nore through the Warp and the West Swin, which form a continuous, fairly deep channel on the Essex side of the estuary along the outer edge of the Maplin Sands.

At the outer end of the Maplins a long, narrow sandbank, known as the Middle Ground, with only a few feet of water over it at low tide, divides the channel into two parallel branches, the East Swin and the Middle Deep. At the end of the Middle Ground these two channels and a third (known as the Barrow Deep) unite to form the broad King's Channel (also known as the East Swin), where there is plenty of sea room, and presently this again expands into the open sea.

In those old days of sailing-ships a fleet working its way out of the narrower channels inside the Middle Deep in presence of an enemy would court destruction if the whole of its fighting strength could not be brought out into the wide waters of the King's Channel on a single tide. If only part of it got out before the tide turned, the van might be destroyed during the long hours of waiting for the rearward ships to get out and join in.

On 19 July Monk brought his ships out to the Middle Ground, beside which they remained anchored in a long line till the 21st, waiting for a favourable wind and a full tide. The ebb flows fast through the narrows from west to east, and weighing shortly before high water on the 22nd, the fleet spread all sail to a fair wind, and led by the *Royal Charles* with Monk and Rupert on her quarter-deck, the long procession of heavy battleships worked out into King's Channel, soon helped by a racing ebb. Those who saw the sight said that no finer spectacle had ever been witnessed on the seas, and certainly England had never till then challenged battle with a more powerful fleet. Officers and men were in high spirits and confident of victory, Rupert as eager as when in his younger days he led his wild charges of cavaliers, Monk impatient with prudent counsels urged by timid pilots, and using sharp, strong language to encourage them to take risks which he as a landsman did not appreciate.

Not a ship touched ground. Some Dutch ships were sighted on the look-out off the edge of the Gunfleet, but they drew off when Captain Elliot, in the *Revenge*, led a squadron of nine ships-of-the-line and some fireships to attack them. De Ruyter, who had been waiting with his main fleet off the Naze, stood out to sea, having no intention of beginning a battle till there were long hours of daylight before him. As the sun went down the English fleet anchored in the seaward opening of the King's Channel, with the *Royal Charles* near the buoy that marked the outer end of the Gunfleet Sands, and on both sides men turned in with the expectation of hard fighting next morning.

At daybreak the English fleet weighed anchor. The Dutch fleet was seen some miles to seaward and more to the south, sailing in three divisions in line ahead. Evertszoon was in command of the van; De Ruyter of the centre; Van Tromp of the rear. There were more than a hundred sail. Monk stood towards them before a light breeze, challenging battle in the fashion of the time with much sounding of trumpets and beating of drums. But De Ruyter kept his distance, working to the southward outside the tangle of shallows in the Thames estuary.

All day the fleets drifted slowly, keeping out of gunshot range. Towards evening the wind fell to a sullen calm with a cloudy sky, and Monk and De Ruyter both anchored outside the Long Sand. After sunset there came a summer storm, vivid flashes of lightning, heavy thunder-peals, and wild, tempestuous gusts of wind. The anchors held, but Monk lost one of his best ships, the *Jersey*. She was struck by lightning, which brought down a mass of spars and rigging on her decks, and so crippled her that she had to leave the fleet at dawn.

The Dutch fleet had disappeared. De Ruyter had weighed anchor during the storm and run out to sea. Monk suspected that he had gone back to his old cruising ground off the Naze, and when the wind fell and the weather cleared up in the afternoon of the 24th he weighed and sailed for the end of the Gunfleet to look for the enemy in that neighbourhood. He found no trace of him, and anchored again off the Gunfleet that evening, getting under way again at two in the morning of the 25th.

De Ruyter's light craft had kept him informed of Monk's movements. The Dutch admiral had avoided battle, when it was first offered, because he hoped to manœuvre for the weather gage, but the failing wind before the storm had made it hopeless to attempt to work to windward of the English. At a council of war held on board De Ruyter's flagship on the evening of the 24th it was decided to accept battle next day, even if the Dutch had to fight to leeward. When the sun rose the two fleets were in sight, "eight leagues off the Naze," De Ruyter in his old position to seaward and southward of Monk.

The English "general at sea" had ninety-two battleships and seventeen fireships at his disposal. Following the custom of the time, the English was, like the Dutch fleet, organized in three divisions. The van, distinguished by white ensigns, was commanded by Sir Thomas Allen; the centre, or red division, flew the red ensign (now the flag of our merchant marine), and was under the personal command of Monk and Rupert; the rear, under Sir Jeremy Smith, flew the blue ensign.

Battles at sea were now beginning to be fought under formal rules which soon developed into a system of pedantic rigidity. It was a point of honour that van should encounter van; centre, centre; and rear, rear. The Dutch were moving slowly under shortened sail in line ahead to the south-east of the English. Monk formed his fleet in line abreast on the port tack. The orders were that as they closed with the enemy the ships were to bear up on to a course parallel to that of the Dutch and engage in line ahead, division to division and broadside to broadside.

Training cruises and fleet manœuvres were still things of a far-off future, and the ships of Monk's three divisions were all unequal in speed and handiness, so the manœuvre was not executed with the machine-like regularity of a modern fleet. The van and centre came into action fairly together, but the rearward ships straggled into position, and Tromp was able to give some of the first comers a severe hammering before their consorts came into action and relieved them of some of the brunt of his fire.

The first shots had been fired between nine and ten a.m. Till after two in the afternoon there was a close engagement, a steady, well-sustained cannonade, with no attempt at manœuvring on either side, the fleets drifting slowly before the light wind, wrapped in powder smoke, in the midst of which both sides made attempts to use their fireships against each other. The only success was secured by the Dutch, who set the *Resolution* ablaze. She drifted out of the line and burned to the water's edge after her crew had abandoned her. There was heavy loss of life in both fleets.

For want of anything but the most rudimentary system of signalling, admirals had little control of a fight once it was begun. Monk, in the *Royal Charles*, had to content himself with marking out De Ruyter's flagship, the *Seven Provinces*, as his immediate opponent, and fighting a prolonged duel with her. He walked his quarter-deck chewing tobacco, a habit he had acquired as a precaution against infection during the London plague. He spoke at the outset with undeserved contempt of his opponent. "Now," he said, "you shall see this fellow come and give me two broadsides and then run." But De Ruyter's broadsides thundered for hour after hour. However, the dogged persistency of the Dutch was met with persistent courage as steady as their own.

London listened anxiously to the far-off rumbling of the cannonade on the North Sea waters. Mr. Pepys went to Whitehall and found the Court "gone to chapel, it being St. James's Day." Then he tells how—

by and by, while they are at chapel and we waiting chapel being done, come people out of the park, telling us that the guns are heard plainly. And so everybody to the park, and by and by the chapel done, the King and Duke into the bowling-green and upon the leads, whither I went, and there the guns were plain to be heard; though it was pretty to hear how confident some would be in the loudness of the guns, which it was as much as ever I could do to hear them.

All the Eastern counties must have heard the cannon-thunder droning and rumbling like a far-off summer storm through the anxious hours of that July day. As the afternoon went on even Dutch endurance found it hard to stand up against the steadily sustained cannonade of Monk's centre and van divisions, and De Ruyter and Evertszoon began to make sail and work further out to sea, as if anxious to break off the fight. Monk, Rupert, and Allen, with the White and Red Divisions, followed them up closely, making, however, no attempt to board, but keeping up the fire of their batteries, and waiting for a chance to capture any crippled ship that might fall astern. Four of the enemy were thus taken. So the main bodies of both fleets worked out into the North Sea on parallel courses, making no great way, for the wind was falling.

The rear divisions, Tromp's and Jeremy Smith's ships, did not follow the general movement, for Tromp had never quite lost the advantage he had gained in the opening stage of the battle. He kept his ships under shortened sail, and hammered away doggedly at the Blue Division. This was the moment when Monk might well have either reinforced Smith, or turned with all his force on Tromp, and overwhelmed and destroyed his squadron. It was made up of twenty-five line-of-battle ships and six frigates, and its loss would have been a heavy blow to Holland.

But on sea as on land there was still little of the spirit of ordered combination. Just as Rupert at Marston Moor had destroyed the opposing wing of the Roundheads with a fierce charge of his cavaliers, and then pursued, without a thought of using his advantage to fall upon the outnumbered and exposed centre of the enemy, so now Monk and Rupert pressed upon De Ruyter and Evertszoon, though Tromp was at their mercy, and Smith was in serious peril. Thus the engagement broke into two separate battles as the summer evening drew on.

Darkness ended the fight, and in the night the wind fell almost to a calm. Sunrise on the 26th showed the fleets drifting in disorder on a smooth sea, with their heavy sails hanging loose from the yards, only filled now and then by disappointing flaws of wind. The crews were busy repairing damages and transferring the wounded to the lighter craft. All day the only shots fired were discharged by a couple of brass toy cannon mounted on a pleasure yacht which Rupert had brought with him.

Taking advantage of a mere ruffle of wind, so light that it could not move the big ships, the *Cavalier Prince* ran his yacht under the stern of the huge flagship of De Ruyter, and fired into him. The Dutchman had no guns bearing dead aft, and the *Prince* was able to worry him for a while, till there came one of those stronger gusts of wind that filled the sails of the *Seven Provinces*, and she swung round, showing a broadside that could blow the yacht out of the water. But before a gun could be fired the yacht, with all sails spread, was racing back to the English fleet, and Rupert returned to the *Royal Charles* as pleased as a schoolboy with his frolic.

During the night of the 26th the wind rose, and De Ruyter steered for the Scheldt, followed up by Monk's two divisions. The Dutch admiral covered his retreat with his best ships, and a running fight began at dawn. Even before the sun rose the sounds of a heavy cannonade had come through the darkness, telling that Tromp and Smith were hard at it again in their detached battle. Early in the day Monk abandoned the chase of the Dutch, and steered towards the sound of the cannonade. Soon the fleet came in distant sight of the battle.

Tromp with the "Zealand squadron" was making a dogged retreat, working to the south-east, close-hauled on the wind from the north-east. Monk tacked and made more than one attempt to place himself across the course of the Dutchmen, hoping to catch them between his fleet and Smith's Blue Division as between hammer and anvil. But Tromp slipped between his enemies and was before long in full sail for Holland, with the three English divisions combined in a stern chase. Monk said that if Smith had pressed Tromp closer early in the day, his retreat would have certainly been cut off. Smith and his friends protested that if the "general at sea" had laid his fleet on a better course, Tromp would have been taken. The honours of this last move in the game were with the Dutchman.

A substantial victory had been gained, though there were few trophies to show for it. The enemy had been met and forced by sheer hard knocks to abandon his station off the mouth of the Thames, and take refuge in his own ports. Monk was on the Dutch coast, picking up returning merchantmen as prizes, blockading the outgoing trade, and keeping the great fishing fleet in ruinous idleness. With the help of information supplied by a Dutch traitor, Monk reaped further advantage from his victory and inflicted heavy additional loss on the enemy.

On 8 August the fleet sailed into the roadstead behind the long island of Terschelling, one of the chain of islands at the mouth of the Zuyder Zee, and burned at their anchors a hundred and sixty Dutch merchantmen that had taken shelter there, including several great East Indiamen. Next day landing-parties burned and plundered the ranges of warehouses on the island, and destroyed the town of Terschelling. The loss to the Dutch traders was estimated at over a million sterling.

The victorious battle off the Thames in July, 1666, is practically forgotten, so far as the popular tradition of our naval successes goes. It has not even a name by which it might live in the memory of our people. But it practically broke the power of Holland and brought the war to an end. What men do remember, and what has banished from their minds the living tradition of the great North Sea battle, is the ugly fact that in the following year De Ruyter sailed unopposed into the Thames, and captured and burned in the Medway dismantled ships that had fought victoriously against him in the North Sea battle—the *Royal Charles* being among his prizes.

The fleets had, as usual at the time, been laid up for the winter. The money available for fitting them out in the following spring was diverted to other purposes and squandered by the King and the Court. Charles counted on having no need to commission a great fleet in the summer. He knew the Dutch were feeling the strain of the war and the destruction of their trade, and would soon have to patch up a peace, and he opened preliminary negotiations. Such negotiations must be prudently backed by an effective force on the war footing.

The King had practically disarmed as soon as there was a prospect of peace. But the Dutch had fitted out the fleet in view of possible contingencies, and De Witt and De Ruyter could not resist the temptation of revenging the defeat of 1666 and the sack of Terschelling by a raid on the Thames and Medway. It was the dishonesty and incapacity of the King and his parasite Court that laid England open to the shameful disaster that dimmed for all time the glory of Monk and Rupert's victory. But even after De Ruyter's exploits at Chatham the Dutch had no hope of continuing the war, and within a few weeks of the disaster peace was signed at Breda. The story of the Dutch raid is a lasting lesson on the necessity of an island power never for a moment relaxing the armed guard of the sea.

CHAPTER 8

The Battle of the Saints' Passage 1782

In the days when fleets in action relied upon the oar, all fighting was at close quarters, and, as we have seen in our study of typical battles of this period, naval engagements fought out at close quarters gave very definite results, the fleet that was defeated being practically destroyed.

When battles began to be fought under sail, with the gun as the chief weapon, a new method had to be evolved. The more the fire of broadside batteries was relied upon, the greater was the tendency to fight at short artillery range, without closing to hand-to-hand distance, and when the sailors and sea-fighters of the seventeenth century adopted line ahead as the normal formation for making the most of broadside fire, battles had a marked tendency to degenerate into inconclusive artillery duels.

In both the English and the French navies—the two powers that after the naval decline of Spain and Holland disputed the command of the sea—the tactics of the battle in line ahead soon crystallized into a pedantic system. For a hundred years the methods of English admirals were kept in rigid uniformity by a code of "Fighting Instructions for the Navy," drawn up under the direction of the Duke of York (afterwards James II), when he was still Lord High Admiral of England in his brother's reign. These instructions were a well-meant attempt to provide a "sealed pattern" for naval engagements. They contemplated set, formal battles with both fleets in line ahead, sailing on parallel courses, or passing and repassing each other on opposite tacks, exchanging broadsides as the guns bore.

The French adopted similar methods. If the English had any advantage in their tactics, it was in their ideas of gunnery. The French aimed at masts and rigging, in the hope of crippling an adversary in her sail power and forcing her to fall out of the moving line. The English believed in making the hull their target, aiming "between wind and water" to start dangerous leaks, or sending their shot into the crowded gun-decks to put the enemy's batteries out of action.

Under such methods battles became formal duels, in which, as often as not, there was no great result, and both sides claimed the victory. The story of many of the naval campaigns of the first three-quarters of the eighteenth century is weary reading. It was in the last quarter of the century that English admirals learned to fight again at close quarters, and to strike crushing blows at an enemy. The new period of energetic, decisive fighting began with a famous battle in West Indian waters in 1782, and culminated in the world-renowned victories of Nelson, who was a young captain on the North American station "when Rodney beat the Comte de Grasse" in the battle of the Saints' Passage.

Born when George I was King, Rodney was a veteran of many wars when he won his West Indian triumph. He had fought the French under Hawke, and was with Boscawen at the taking of Louisburg. In 1759 he bombarded Havre, and burned the transport flotilla collected at the mouth of the Seine for a raid on England. Three years later, as commander-in-chief on the Leeward Islands station, he captured Martinique, St. Lucia, and Grenada, and learned the ways of the West Indian seas.

Then came years of political disfavour, half-pay and financial embarrassment, until in an hour of darkness for England, with the American colonies in successful revolt and Frenchman and Spaniard besieging Gibraltar by land and sea, the veteran admiral was recalled to active service, and found and seized the great

Guns and carronades in use in the British Navy in the latter part of the 18th Century

opportunities of his life. Sailing south with a relieving fleet, he fell in with and captured a Spanish convoy off Finisterre, and then surprised and destroyed Lungara's Spanish squadron, taking seven ships out of eleven, and chasing the rest into Cadiz.

The appearance of his fleet before Gibraltar saved the fortress, and then in February, 1780, he sailed across the Atlantic to try conclusions with De Guichen, whose powerful fleet based on Martinique was threatening all the English possessions in the West Indies. So far numbers and opportunity had been on his side. He had now to depend more on skill than fortune, and meet a more equal opponent.

At his head-quarters at St. Lucia in April, 1780, Rodney heard that the French fleet under De Guichen had sailed from Martinique. On the 17th he fought an indecisive action with the enemy, an action notable for what Rodney attempted, not for what he accomplished. Twice again on later days Rodney met De Guichen, but none of the three battles did more than inflict mutual loss on the combatants, without producing any decisive result. The campaign was, like so many others in the West Indies, a struggle for the temporary possession of this or that port or island, De Guichen's whole strategy being based on the idea of avoiding the risks of a close engagement that might imperil his fleet, and trying to snatch local advantages when he could elude his enemy.

In 1781 Rodney was compelled by ill-health temporarily to give up the West Indian command and return to England. In the spring of 1782 he was again sent to the West Indies, at a moment when the situation of affairs was most menacing for British power beyond the Atlantic. Cornwallis had been forced to surrender at Yorktown, and the success of the revolted American colonies was now assured. The French fleet in the West Indies had been joined by reinforcements under the Comte de Grasse, who had gone out as commander-in-chief, taking with him a considerable military force that was to combine with an expedition from the Spanish American colonies, not for the capture of some small islands in the Antilles, but for the conquest of Jamaica, the centre of British power and British trade in the West Indian seas.

Kempenfeldt, a good sailor (now remembered chiefly as the admiral who "went down with twice three hundred men," when the *Royal George* sank at Spithead), dispersed and destroyed at the mouth of the Channel a large French convoy of supplies for De Grasse, and drove the squadron that protected it into Brest. With his task thus lightened, Rodney put to sea with four ships of the line, and after a stormy passage reached Barbadoes on 19 February, 1782. Sailing thence to Antigua, he formed a junction with and took command of the West Indian fleet, which Hood had commanded during his absence in England. From Antigua he took the fleet to St. Lucia, where he established his headquarters in Gros Islet Bay. St. Lucia was the favourite base of operations of our West Indian fleets in the old wars, and the scene of much desperate fighting by land and sea. The year before De Grasse had failed in an attempt to seize it.

The fleet of the Comte de Grasse was only some forty miles away to the northward. It lay at Martinique, in the bay of Fort Royal (now Fort de France). Though it has nothing to do with the fortunes of Rodney and De Grasse, it is interesting to note that in a convent school looking out on the bay there was just then a little schoolgirl named Josephine de la Pagerie, daughter of an artillery lieutenant in the garrison, who was to live to be Empress of the French, when France was the mistress of Europe.

During the month of March both fleets were busy preparing for sea. Rodney was reinforced from England, and a small squadron from Brest joined De Grasse. The reinforcements received during March had given Rodney the advantage of numbers. He had thirty-six sail of the line to oppose the thirty that were with De Grasse at Martinique. In the English fleet there were five great three-deckers, three of them carrying 98 and two of them 90 guns. There were twenty-one 74's, a 70-gun ship, and nine 64's. In the French fleet there was one of the largest war vessels then afloat, De Grasse's flagship, the *Ville de Paris*, of 104 guns. There were five ships of 80 guns, twenty of 74, one of 70, and three of 64.

This enumeration gives Rodney an advantage of six ships and more than two hundred guns. It is quite true that the ships of the same rating in the French service were generally larger than the English, but even apart from numbers, the latter had advantages in armament that were more important than any trifling difference in size. The English guns were mostly mounted on an improved system that gave a larger arc of training fore and aft, the practical result being that as ships passed each other the Frenchman was kept longer under fire than the Englishman.

Further, the English ships mounted, besides the guns counted in their armament, a number of carronades, mounted on the upper decks, short guns of large calibre, throwing a heavy shot when the fighting was carried on at close quarters, a weapon not yet introduced in the French navy. Thanks to these improvements in the armament of his ships, Rodney had an advantage in gun-power beyond the mere superiority in numbers of ships and guns. He had a further advantage in the fact that a larger number of his ships were copper-sheathed. This meant less fouling while the ships were waiting at their anchorage, and therefore better speed for the English when they put to sea.

De Grasse was encumbered with a large convoy of merchantmen and storeships, and many of his ships were overcrowded with the troops destined for the descent on Jamaica. It was expected that when he sailed it would be to form, in the first instance, a junction with the Spanish part of the expedition off San Domingo. Rodney kept his fleet at St. Lucia, ready to weigh anchor on the shortest notice, and a smart frigate, the *Andromache* (commanded by Captain Byron, grandfather of the poet), cruised off Martinique, watching the Frenchman.

At dawn on 8 April Byron saw that the French were coming out, and he hastened to St. Lucia under press of sail with the news. Off the port he flew the signal that told Rodney that De Grasse was at sea. Anchors came up and sails were shaken out, and Rodney set off in pursuit, knowing that De Grasse had a very few hours' start of him.

The few hours did not count for much, provided the English admiral could once get on the Frenchman's track. The danger of missing him could only arise from making at the outset a wrong judgment as to the course on which the enemy would sail. It was De Grasse's business to avoid a battle until he had safely taken his huge convoy to San Domingo and joined hands with his Spanish allies. Rodney judged that he would most likely follow the long curve of the chain of islands that fringe the Caribbean Sea, steering by Puerto Rico for San Domingo. In the night of the 8th the English fleet passed Martinique. Next morning it was off the west coast of Dominica, making good speed, and away to the northward a far-spreading crowd of sails showed that Rodney had guessed rightly. The French fleet and convoy were in sight.

Dominica is a mass of volcanic ridges, falling to the seaward in precipitous cliffs, rising landward tier above tier and shooting up into rocky spires that culminate in the towering peak of the Morne Diablotin, five thousand feet high. Under the shelter of this rugged island, while the prevailing trade wind blows steadily from the eastward, there are sudden calms, or irregular flaws of wind blowing now from one point, now from another, diverted by the irregular ridges of the high land. This April morning the sun had hardly risen when the wind fell, and the two fleets drifted slowly, with loose-hanging sails.

Near the north end of the island lay the convoy. A little to the southward De Grasse's thirty battleships straggled in a long line over some six miles of sunlit sea. Off the centre and south of the island Rodney's larger fleet was stretched out in line ahead. It was formed in three divisions. Hood, in the 90-gun *Barfleur*, commanded the van. Rodney, with his flag flying in a tall three-decker, the *Formidable*, of 98 guns, was in the centre. The rear was commanded by Rear-Admiral Samuel Drake, a namesake and descendant of that other Drake whose name had been the terror of the West Indian seas in Elizabethan days.

Suddenly there came a flaw of wind sweeping from the south

round the end of the island, so narrow that most of the English fleet hardly felt it. It filled the sails of Hood's ships in the van, and they steered for two French battleships that dropped astern of their consorts. One of the Frenchmen passed close under the tiers of guns in the leading English ship, but not a shot was fired at her as she swept by and rejoined her consorts. Rodney had not yet flown the signal for battle, and these were still the days when personal enterprise and decision were not encouraged among the captains of a fleet.

As the breeze filled the sails of the Frenchmen, Grasse signalled to the convoy to bear away before it to the north-westward, while he with his fighting-ships set his course for the channel between Dominica and Guadeloupe. He rightly judged that Rodney would follow the warships, and thus the convoy would have a good start. The channel towards which the French fleet was heading is known as the Saints' Passage, "not on the surmise that it leads to Heaven,"[1] but because along its northern waters stretches a line of rocky islets known to the French as "*les Iles des Saintes.*"

The nine ships of Hood forming the English van had gone far ahead of the rest of the fleet. If De Grasse had not had his mind so centred on the idea of avoiding a battle, there is little doubt that he might have brought an overwhelming force to bear on them. Luckily for Rodney, he contented himself with sending his second in command, Vaudreuil, to skirmish with them, passing and repassing Hood's division at long range and firing at masts and rigging in the hope of disabling them for further pursuit.

Hood returned the fire, doing as much damage as he suffered, and towards midday the rest of the English had worked up to him by taking advantage of every breath of wind that blew over the ridges of Dominica. Then the wind fell again, and all through the night and the following day (10 April) the fleets lay in sight of each other beyond even distant cannon shot, Vaudreuil's and Hood's crews busying themselves with repairing

---

1. Treves, *Cradle of the Deep*, p. 175.

rigging and replacing damaged spars.

During the 11th De Grasse tried to get his fleet through the Saints' Passage, working by short tacks to windward, and baffled and delayed by sudden calms. In the afternoon several of his ships were still to the westward of the strait, and Rodney, who had been getting gradually to the northward, despite the frequent failure of the wind under the lee of Dominica, was at last near enough seriously to threaten these laggards. In order to save them from being overwhelmed by the whole English fleet, De Grasse gave up the advantage of weary hours of hard work and came back before the wind out of the strait.

At sunset the two fleets lay to the westward of the Saints' Passage, and there was no probability that De Grasse would attempt to tack through it during the hours of darkness. In the night Rodney manœuvred to get to windward of the enemy, and at daylight on the 12th the two fleets were within striking distance, De Grasse to the leeward, his fleet in a straggling line over some nine miles of sea. Rodney had his opportunity of forcing on a decisive battle at last.

At some distance from the French line a partly dismasted line-of-battle ship, the *Zelé*, was seen in tow of a frigate. She had been in collision with the flagship during the night, and had been so badly damaged that De Grasse was sending her away to Guadeloupe. Rodney's ships had lost their order of battle somewhat in the darkness, and while he was reforming his line he detached a couple of ships to threaten the disabled *Zelé*. This had the effect he intended. It removed De Grasse's last hesitation about fighting.

The French line was soon seen bearing down on the port tack, the rearward ships crowding sail to close up. Rodney's battle line, in reversed order, led by Drake and the rear division, was already on a course that would bring the two fleets sweeping past each other, and the leading ship, the *Marlborough*, was steered so as to make the passage a close one. Rodney had hoisted the signal to engage the enemy to leeward. While the fleets were closing he sat in an armchair on his quarterdeck, for he was older than his sixty-four years, broken by long illness and only sustained by his dogged spirit.

One of his captains, Savage of the *Hercules*, also went into battle seated in an armchair beside the bulwarks of his ship. He was lame with gout and unable to stand or walk without help. When the firing began, and the ships were passing each other amid a thunder of broadsides and a hail of shot and bullets, Captain Savage gravely raised his cocked hat to salute each enemy as she ranged up abreast of the *Hercules*. What would those old sailors have thought of the naval commander of today peeping through the slits in the steel walls of a conning tower? But it is only fair to ask also what they would have thought of shells weighing half a ton bursting in fiery destruction.

The *Marlborough*, approaching on a converging course, came to close quarters with the *Brave*, the sixth ship in De Grasse's line, and then, shifting her helm to bring her course parallel to that of the enemy, exchanged broadsides with the Frenchman. Ship after ship came into action in the same way. The speed was nearer three than four knots, and the lines some six miles long, so it was more than an hour before the leading English battleship was abreast of and engaged with the rearmost Frenchman.

As ship passed ship there was a thunder of artillery, a rattle of small arms. Then a brief lull till the guns of two more opponents bore on each other. But in this cannonade the English had the advantage of the heavy blows struck by their large-bore carronades at close range, and the fact that their gun-mountings enabled them to keep a passing ship longer under fire than was possible for the French gunners. In De Grasse's ships, crowded with troops, the slaughter was terrible.

As the fight went on and the French ships came under the crushing fire of adversary after adversary, it was seen that it was only with difficulty the officers kept the men at the guns. In this first hour of the fight the French began to throw the dead overboard to clear their encumbered decks, and a strange horror was added to the scene, for shoals of sharks that had followed the fleets to pick up anything thrown overboard now swarmed around them, lashing the water into foam as they struggled for their human prey.

At length the leading English ship was abeam of the rearmost of De Grasse's fleet. Over some six miles of sea the two battle lines extended, every ship ablaze with fire-flashes from her guns and with the dense smoke-clouds drifting around the English vessels and wrapping them in the fog of war. If the battle was now to be fought out on the old traditional method, the fleets would clear each other, wear and tack and repass each other in opposite directions with a second exchange of fire. But now came the event that made the battle of the Saints' Passage epoch-making in naval history.

What precisely happened is wrapped in a fog of controversy as dense as the smoke-fog that enveloped Rodney's fleet at the decisive moment. One thing is certain. The old admiral suddenly changed all his plans, and executed a new manœuvre with the signal he himself was disobeying—the order to engage to leeward—still flying from his flagship. The act was the sudden seizing of an unexpected opportunity. But some of the merit of the new departure was due to Rodney's right-hand man, his "Captain of the Fleet,"

Sir Charles Douglas. Douglas was one of those whose minds had been influenced by new theories on naval war, which were just then in the air. In Britain a Scotch country gentleman, John Clerk, of Eldin, had been arguing for some time in pamphlets and manuscripts circulated among naval officers against the formal methods that led to indecisive results. His paper plans for destroying an enemy were no doubt open to the criticism that they would work out beautifully if the enemy stuck to the old-fashioned ways and attempted no counter-stroke.

But the essence of Clerk's theories was that parallel orders of battle meant only indecisive cannonading; that to crush an enemy one must break into his line, bring parts of it under a close fire, not on one side, but on both, and decide the fate of the ships thus cut off by superior numbers and superior gun power before the rest could come to their help. His plans might not work out with the mechanical exactitude described in his writings, but they would tend to produce the close *mêlée*, where the best men and the steadiest fire would win, and after such an encounter there would not be merely a few masts and spars shot away, and a few holes to be plugged, but the beaten side would be minus a number of ships sunk, burned, or taken, and condemned to hopeless inferiority for the rest of the campaign.

Clerk was not the only man who put forward these ideas. A French Jesuit professor of mathematics had worked out plans for securing local advantage of numbers in a sea-fight at close quarters; but while French naval officers laughed at naval battles worked out with a piece of chalk and a blackboard, British sailors were either themselves thinking out similar schemes or were beginning to think there might be something in the Scotch laird's diagrams.

It was at the critical moment when the two fleets lay side by side in parallel lines on opposite courses, wrapped in the battle-smoke, that Douglas, looking out through a gap in the war-cloud, saw that a sudden flaw of wind blowing steadily from the south-east was flattening the French sails against the masts and checking their speed. The same sudden change of wind was filling the English sails, and the masters were squaring the yards to it, while the Frenchmen to keep any way on their ships had to bring their bows partly round towards the English line. Between the *Glorieux*, the ship immediately opposed to Rodney's flagship, the *Formidable*, and the next Frenchman in the line, the *Diadème*, a wide gap was opening up. Douglas saw the chance offered to his admiral.

Half the English fleet was ahead of the *Formidable*, engaged with the rearward French ships. If the *Formidable* pushed through the gap, leading the rest of the line after her, the French rear would be cut off from the van and brought under a double fire at close quarters, and there would be a fair prospect of destroying it before De Grasse could come back to its support. He rushed to Rodney's side. Moments were precious. He urged his plan in the briefest words.

At first the old admiral rejected it. "No," he said, "I will not break my line."[2] Douglas insisted, and the two officers stepped to the opening in the bulwarks at the gangway and looked out. The *Formidable* was opposite the tempting gap in the French line. Rodney in a moment changed his mind, and told Douglas that he accepted his plan.

In the haste to carry it out the signal to fight to leeward of the French was forgotten and left flying. The *Formidable* turned her high bows into the gap, and swept through it with all her hundred guns and her carronades in action, pouring broadside after broadside right and left into the *Glorieux* and the *Diadème*. Six ships in succession swung round and followed in the wake of the flagship, which was now engaged with the French on the windward side. Shattered by successive blasts of well-directed fire, the *Diadème* was drifting a helpless wreck, and the rearward ships, with their way checked, were huddling in confusion behind her, English ships firing into them on both sides. Through another gap in the French line, ahead of De Grasse's giant *Ville de Paris*, other English ships made their way in the dense cloud of smoke, some of the captains hardly aware of what they were doing. The French van had meanwhile forged ahead, and then, as the wind suddenly fell to a dead calm, it was seen that De Grasse's fleet was broken into three isolated fragments.

To the southward lay the van ships under De Bougainville becalmed, with no enemy in range of them. The *Ville de Paris*, with several of her consorts of the French centre, formed another group, with the whole of the rearward English division exchanging fire with them at long range. The rear of the French, under Vaudreuil, and the ships of the centre cut off by Rodney's manœuvre were huddled together, with Hood's division and the ships that had followed the *Formidable* through the line

---

2. Rodney in at first refusing was upholding the strict letter of the "Fighting Instructions," which forbade breaking the line or changing the order of battle during an action. Instruction XVI laid it down that:—

"In all cases of fight with the enemy the commanders of His Majesty's ships are to keep the fleet in one line, and (as much as may be) to preserve that order of battle, which they have been directed to keep before the time of fight."

shepherding them. The loss of the wind had made it difficult or impossible to keep the broadsides bearing, and for an hour the action died down into a desultory cannonade.

When the breeze came again over the ridges of Dominica, De Bougainville's division, now far to leeward, made no attempt to succour De Grasse. Only one of his ships slowly beat up to the main battle. The French admiral tried to get away to the westward, but Hood clung doggedly to him, while Rodney and Drake completed the defeat of Vaudreuil and the French rear. The *Diadème* soon struck her colours. A frigate tried to tow the dismasted *Glorieux* out of the *mêlée*, but the captain of the *Glorieux*, De Kerlessi, saw that the effort would only end in the friendly frigate being also captured, and with his own hand he cut the tow-rope and hauled down his flag. Then the *César* struck her colours, and while the rearward ships were being thus disposed of, in the broken centre the *Hector* and the *Ardent* surrendered to Hood's division.

The English attack was now concentrated on the centre, and the battle raged fiercely round the French flagship, distinguished by her huge bulk and her towering masts. One by one these came down, trailing in a tangle of spars, sails, and rigging over her sides. Her crowded decks were a shambles of dead and dying, but still De Grasse fought on—for honour, not for victory. His van held aloof, his broken rear was in flight. Five of his ships had struck. Still he kept his guns in action till Hood in his flagship, the *Princesse*, ranged close up alongside of him and poured in a series of destructive broadsides. Then the French flag came down at last, and De Grasse went on board the *Princesse* and gave up his sword to the vice-admiral.

The sun was going down when the French flagship surrendered. The captured *César*, set on fire by her crew, was blazing from stem to stern. The other prizes had been secured. Rodney attempted no pursuit of the scattered French ships that were sailing away to the southward and the north-westward. Enough had been done, he said. It was now his business to refit his fleet and take it to Jamaica. He had shattered the French power in the

West Indian seas and made himself the master of the field of operations. A younger and more vigorous man would have perhaps marked down Vaudreuil's or Bougainville's fugitive divisions for utter destruction. But Rodney was content with the solid success he had obtained.

The losses of the French fleet had been very heavy. In their crowded decks the English fire had effected something like a massacre. On board the *Ville de Paris* more men had been killed and wounded than in the whole English fleet. Very few officers and men had escaped some kind of wound. Many of the ships that had got away were now very shorthanded, with leaking hulls, and spars and rigging badly cut up.

The effect of the victory was to enable England to obtain much better terms in the treaty that was signed next year. A disastrous war was closed by a brilliant success. But England owed to it more than this temporary advantage. It was a new beginning, the opening event of the period of splendid triumphs on the sea on the reputation of which we are still living. To quote the words of Rodney's latest biographer,[3]

> it marked the beginning of that fierce and headlong yet well-calculated style of sea-fighting which led to Trafalgar, and made England undisputed mistress of the sea.

---

[3]. David Hannay, *Rodney (English Men of Action)*, p. 213.

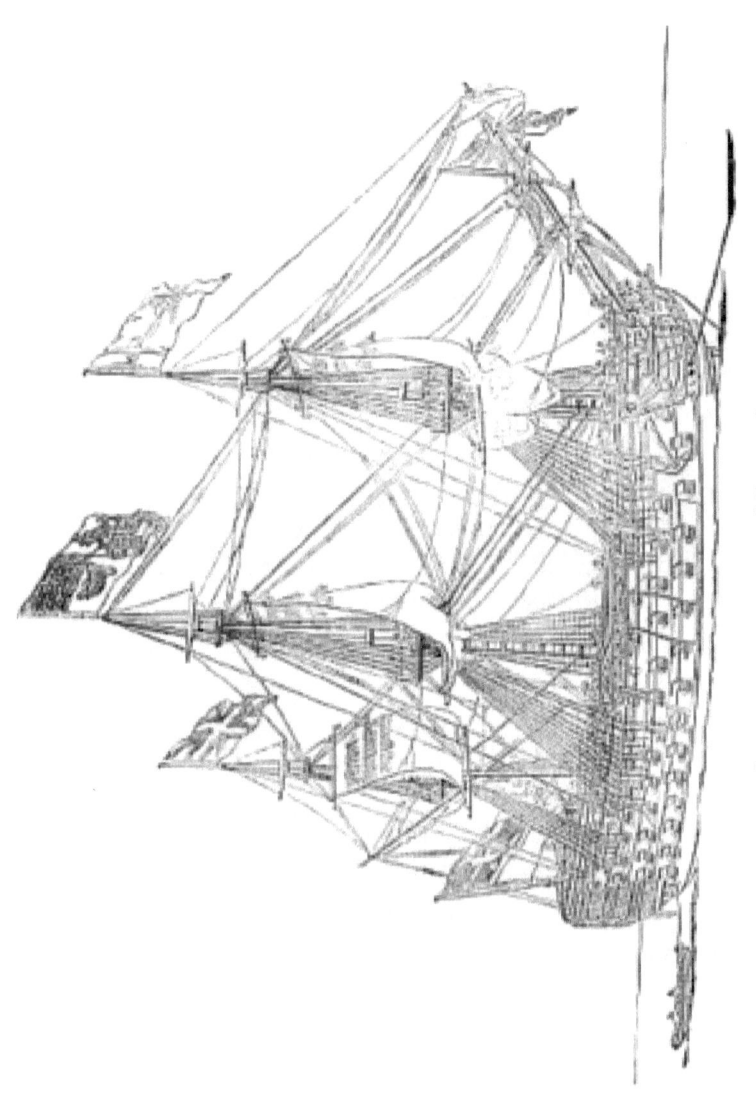

A THREE-DECKER OF NELSON'S TIME

CHAPTER 9

Trafalgar 1805

The closing years of the eighteenth century and the opening years of the nineteenth represent the most splendid period in the annals of the British Navy. Howe destroyed the French fleet in the Atlantic on "the glorious First of June, 1794," Nelson died in the midst of his greatest victory off Cape Trafalgar on 21 October, 1805. Little more than eleven years separated the two dates, and this brief period was crowded with triumphs for Britain on the sea. The "First of June," St. Vincent, Camperdown, the Nile, Copenhagen, and Trafalgar are the great names in the roll of victory; but "the meteor flag of England" flew victorious in a hundred fights on all the seas of the world.

Men who were officers young in the service on the day when Rodney broke at once the formal traditions of a century and the battle-line of the Comte de Grasse lived through and shared in the glories of this decade of victory. A new spirit had come into the navy. An English admiral would no longer think he had done his duty in merely bringing his well-ordered line into cannon-shot of an enemy's array and exchanging broadsides with him at half-cannon range. Nor was the occupation of a port or an island recognized as an adequate result for a naval campaign. The enemy's fighting-fleet was now the object aimed at. It was not merely to be brought to action, and more or less damaged by distant cannonading. The ideal battle was the close fight amid the enemy's broken line, and victory meant his destruction.

The spirit of the time was personified in its greatest sailor.

Nelson's battles were fought in grim earnest, taking risks boldly in order to secure great results. Trafalgar—the last of his battles, and the last great battle of the days of the sail—was also the final episode in the long struggle of Republican and Imperial France to snatch from England even for a while the command of the sea.

When Napoleon assembled the Grand Army at Boulogne, gave it the official title of the *"Armée d'Angleterre,"* and crowded every creek from Dunkirk to Havre with flat-bottomed boats for its transport across the Channel, he quite realized that the first condition of success for the scheme was that a French fleet should be in possession of the Channel at the moment his veterans embarked for their short voyage. He had twenty sail of the line, under Admiral Ganteaume, at Brest; twelve under Villeneuve at Toulon; a squadron of five at Rochefort under Admiral Missiessy; five more at Ferrol; and in this last port and at Cadiz and Cartagena there were other ships belonging to his Spanish allies. But every port was watched by English battleships and cruisers. The vigilant blockade had been kept up for two years, during which Nelson, who was watching Toulon, had hardly been an hour absent from his flagship, the *Victory*; and Collingwood, in the *Royal Sovereign,* did not anchor once in twenty-two months of alternate cruising and lying to.

Napoleon's mind was ceaselessly busy with plans for moving his fleets on the sea as he moved army corps on land, so as to elude, mislead, and out-manœuvre the English squadrons, and suddenly bring a concentrated French force of overwhelming strength into the narrow seas. The first move in these plans was usually assigned to the Toulon fleet. According to one project it was to give Nelson the slip, make for the Straits of Gibraltar, combine with the Cadiz fleet in driving off or crushing the blockading squadron before that port, sail north with the liberated vessels, fall on the blockading ships before Rochefort and Brest, and then sweep the Channel with the united squadrons. In other projects French fleets were to run the blockades simultaneously or in succession, raid the West Indies, draw off a part of the naval forces of England to the other side of the Atlantic, and then come swooping back upon the Channel.

In the plan finally adopted the first move was to be the escape of the Toulon fleet; the second, the threat against the West Indies. Its execution was entrusted to Villeneuve, because Napoleon, ever since the escape of his squadron from the disaster in Aboukir Bay, had regarded him as "a lucky man," and luck and chance must play a great part in such a project.

Nelson did not keep up a close and continuous blockade of Toulon with his fighting-fleet of battleships. He used Sardinia as his base of supplies, and there were times when all the heavier ships were in Sardinian waters, while his frigates watched Toulon. His previous experiences had led him to believe that if the French Mediterranean fleet came out it would be for another raid on Egypt, and this idea was confirmed by reports that Villeneuve was embarking not only troops, but large quantities of saddlery and muskets.

The story of the saddles seemed to indicate an expedition to a country where plenty of horses could be obtained to mount a body of cavalry—horses, too, that when they were bought or requisitioned would not have saddles that a European trooper was used to. Nelson did not want to keep the French shut up in Toulon. He was anxious to catch them in the open sea, and with his fleet on the coast of Sardinia and his frigates spread out in a fan to the northwards he counted on bringing Villeneuve to action if he attempted to reach the Levant.

In January, 1805, the frigates brought news that the French were out, and Nelson at once disposed his fleet to intercept their expected voyage to Egypt. He found no trace of them in the direction he expected, and he was greatly relieved on returning from a hurried rush eastward to learn that bad weather had driven Villeneuve back to his port. "These gentlemen," he said, "are not accustomed to the Gulf of Lyons gales, but we have buffeted them for twenty-one months without carrying away a spar."

On 30 March Villeneuve came out of Toulon again with eleven ships of the line. This time, thanks to Nelson's fixed idea about Egypt, he got a good start for the Atlantic. As soon as his frigates brought the news that the French were out, Nelson strung out his ships from the south point of Sardinia to Sicily and the African coast. He thus watched every possible avenue to the Eastern Mediterranean, ready to concentrate and attack the enemy as soon as he got touch of them anywhere. But not a French sail was sighted.

Villeneuve had run down past the Balearic Islands to Cartagena, where Admiral Salcedo was in command of a Spanish squadron. But the Spaniards were not ready for sea, and Villeneuve was anxious to be west of the Straits of Gibraltar as soon as possible, and could not wait for his dilatory allies. On 8 April he passed through the Straits. Then he steered for Cadiz, drove off Sir John Orde's blockading squadron of six sail, and entered the harbour on the 9th.

At Cadiz there were Admiral Gravina's Spanish fleet and a French battleship, the *Aigle*. Again the Spaniards were mostly unready for sea, but six of them and the *Aigle* joined Villeneuve when he sailed out into the Atlantic steering for the West Indies, now at the head of eighteen battleships and seven frigates.

Information was difficult to obtain and travelled slowly a hundred years ago. It was not till 11 April that Nelson learned that Villeneuve had passed through the Straits of Gibraltar eight days before. Then, while the French were running down into the trade wind that was to carry them westward, Nelson, still ignorant whether they were raiding the West Indies or Ireland, but anxious in either case to be in the Atlantic as soon as might be, had to work his way slowly towards the Straits against stormy head winds, and then wait wearily at anchor on the Moorish coast for a change of wind that would carry him into the ocean. He was suffering from disappointment, depression, and ill-health. It was not till 7 May that he passed the Straits. He had made up his mind that the French were probably bound for the West Indies, and he followed them. They had a long start, but he trusted to find them among the islands and make the West Indian seas once more famous for a great British victory.

On 4 June he reached Barbadoes, and began his search, only to miss the French, thanks to false information, and learn too late that they were returning to Europe. Villeneuve had paid only a flying visit to the West Indies, leaving Martinique on 5 June, the day after Nelson arrived at Barbadoes, and steering first north, then eastwards across the Atlantic. Nelson followed on 13 June, and reached Gibraltar without once sighting his enemy.

He had, however, taken the precaution of dispatching a fast sailing brig to England with the news that the French fleet was returning to Europe. This ship, the *Curieux*, actually got a glimpse of the enemy far off in mid ocean, and outsailed him to such good purpose that the Admiralty was able to order the squadrons blockading Brest and Rochefort to unite under the command of Sir Robert Calder and try to intercept Villeneuve on his way back.

Though inferior in numbers to the allied fleet, Calder brought it to action in thick, foggy weather on 22 July, some ninety miles off the Spanish Cape Finisterre. The battle, fought in semi-darkness, was a desultory, indecisive encounter, and though Calder cut off and took two Spanish ships of the line, the feeling in England, when the news arrived, was not one of satisfaction at his partial success, but of undeserved indignation at his having failed to force the fighting and destroy the enemy's fleet.

Villeneuve took his fleet into Vigo Bay. According to the plan of campaign, now that he had shaken off Nelson's pursuit, he should have sailed for the Channel, picking up the Brest and Rochefort squadrons on his way. Napoleon, at Boulogne, was ceaselessly drilling the Grand Army in rapid embarkation and disembarkation, and hoping each day for news of his admiral's dash into the Channel. But Villeneuve, who knew Keith had a squadron in the Channel, and had a vague dread of Nelson suddenly making his appearance, had a better appreciation of the small chance of the scheme giving any result than the imperious soldier-Emperor, who had come to believe that what he ordered must succeed.

From Vigo, Villeneuve wrote to the Minister of Marine, Decrès, that his fleet was hardly in condition for any active enterprise. It had met with trying weather in the Atlantic. His flagship, the *Bucentaure*, had been struck and damaged by lightning. All the ships needed a dockyard overhaul. There was sickness among the crews. He had to land hundreds of men and send them to hospital. He wanted recruits badly, and Vigo afforded only the scantiest resources for the refitting of the ships. He was already thinking of going back to Cadiz. He moved his fleet to Corunna, but there he found things in such a condition that he reported that he could not even find hospital room for the sick.

From Napoleon came pressing orders to push on to the Channel at all risks. On 11 August Villeneuve put to sea, picking up a combined French and Spanish squadron from the neighbouring port of Ferrol. He meant to sail to Brest, bring out the squadron there, and call up the ships at Rochefort by sending on a frigate in advance with orders for that port. (The frigate was captured on the way by a British cruiser.) He sent a dispatch overland to Napoleon to say that at last he was coming.

In the Bay of Biscay, two days out from Corunna, he was told by a Danish merchant-ship that there was a great fleet of British battleships close at hand to the northward. The news was false. A few hours before the captain of a British cruiser had stopped the Dane and purposely given him this false information, in the hope that it would reach the French and mislead them. Except a few scattered cruisers, there was nothing between Villeneuve and the ports of Brest and Rochefort—nothing that could stop his projected concentration.

Nelson had waited a few days at Gibraltar, where the news of Calder's fight had not arrived. He communicated with Collingwood, who was watching Cadiz with six ships, and then, conjecturing that the object of the French expedition might be Ireland, he sailed north and was off the Irish coast on 12 August, the day after Villeneuve left Corunna. Finding no trace of the enemy, he joined the squadron of Cornwallis off Ushant on 15 August, and then, broken in health and depressed at what seemed a huge failure, he went back to England to spend some time with Lady

Hamilton at Merton.

Villeneuve had hardly heard of the imaginary fleet when the wind, which had so far been fair, went round to the north. This decided the irresolute admiral. To the dismay of his captains he suddenly altered his course and ran before the wind southward to Cadiz, where he arrived on 22 August, contenting himself with watching the retirement of Collingwood's six ships and making no effort to envelop and cut them off with his enormously superior force. Collingwood promptly resumed the blockade when the French and Spanish anchored, and deluded Villeneuve into the belief that the blockade was in touch with a supporting fleet by keeping one of his ships well out in the offing, and frequently signalling through her to imaginary consorts below the horizon.

On the very day that Villeneuve anchored at Cadiz, Napoleon sent off from Boulogne this pressing dispatch to him at Brest:—

> Admiral, I trust you have arrived at Brest. Start at once. Do not lose a moment. Come into the Channel with our united squadrons, and England is ours. We are all ready. Everything is embarked. Come here for twenty-four hours and all is ended, and six centuries of shame and insult will be avenged.

When he heard that the admiral had lost heart and turned back he was furious. But he had already formed plans for an alternative enterprise. The English ministry had succeeded in forming a new coalition with Austria and Russia as a means of keeping the Emperor occupied on the Continent. On 27 August Napoleon issued his orders for the march of the Grand Army to the Danube, and on 1 September he started on the career of victory, the stages of which were to be Ulm, Austerlitz, Jena, and Friedland.

To Villeneuve he sent, through Decrès, bitter reproaches and new orders for a naval campaign in the Mediterranean. Decrès, writing to his old comrade, transmitted the new plan of campaign and softened down the Emperor's angry words. Villeneuve reported that he could not leave Cadiz for some time. He was doing all that was possible to refit his fleet and find full crews for the French and Spanish ships. For the latter men were provided by pressing landsmen into the service.

"It is pitiful," wrote a French officer, "to see such fine ships manned with a handful of seamen and a crowd of beggars and herdsmen." In the councils of war held at Cadiz there were fierce disputes between the French and Spanish officers, the latter accusing their allies of having abandoned to their fate the two ships lost in Calder's action. The jealousy between the two nations rose so high that several French sailors were stabbed at night in the streets.

The English Government knew nothing of the inefficient state and the endless difficulties of the great fleet concentrated at Cadiz, and regarded its presence there as a standing danger. Collingwood was reinforced, and it was decided to send Nelson out to join him, take over the command, blockade the enemy closely, and bring him to action if he ventured out.

Nelson sailed from Spithead on 15 September in his old flagship the *Victory*, accompanied by the *Euryalus*, Captain Blackwood, one of the swiftest and smartest frigates in the navy. Picking up the battleships *Thunderer* and *Ajax* on the way, he joined the fleet off Cadiz on 28 September.

Villeneuve had written to Decrès that none of the ships were in really good order, and that the Spanish vessels were "quite incapable of meeting the enemy." Only a portion of his fleet had had the slight training afforded by the Atlantic voyage. The rest had lain for years in harbour, and many of them had crews chiefly made up of recently enrolled landsmen. Many of the captains held that if there was to be a fight it would be useless to manœuvre or to attempt an artillery duel, and that the only chance of success lay in a hand-to-hand fight by boarding. But, then, to produce the position for boarding meant being able to manœuvre. Villeneuve was supported by most of the superior officers of the fleet in the opinion that he had better stay at

Cadiz; but from Napoleon there came reiterated orders for the fleet to enter the Mediterranean.

The last hesitation of the unfortunate admiral was ended by the news that Admiral Rosilly was coming from Paris to supersede him. If he did not attempt something, his career would end in disgrace. He held a final council of war, gave his last instructions to his officers, and then wrote to Decrès that he would obey the Emperor's orders, though he foresaw that they would probably lead to disaster.

Contrary winds from the westward delayed his sailing for some days after this decision. Reefs and local currents made it difficult to work a large fleet out of Cadiz without a fair wind. A smaller but better-trained fleet than that of Villeneuve had once taken three days to get out, and a portion of the fleet at sea and unsupported would be in deadly peril. On 17 October the wind began to work round to the eastward. Next day it fell almost to a calm, but it increased towards evening, and Villeneuve, after a conference with his Spanish colleague, Admiral Gravina, signalled that the ships were to weigh anchor at sunrise on the 19th.

Nelson had been watching Cadiz for three weeks, keeping his fleet well out at sea, with his frigates close in to the port, and a chain of ships acting as connecting links with them to pass on information by signalling with flags by day and lanterns by night. The system of signalling had been lately so improved that it was fairly rapid and reliable, and Nelson kept his fleet out of sight, and requested that the names of ships sent to reinforce him should not appear in the papers, as he hoped to delude Villeneuve into a false idea that he had a very inferior force before Cadiz. He feared that if the whole array of his fleet were visible from the look-out stations of the port the allies would remain safe at anchor.

During this period of waiting he had had more than one conference with his captains, and had read and explained to them a manuscript memorandum, dated 9 October, setting forth his plans for the expected battle. His plan of battle excited an enthusiasm among them, to which more than one of them afterwards bore testimony. They said that "the Nelson touch" was in it, and it is generally taken for granted that they saw in it something like a stroke of genius and a new departure in tactics. I hope it is not presumption on my part to suggest that their enthusiasm was partly the result of their seeing that their trusted leader was thoroughly himself again and, to use a familiar phrase, meant business, and they had a further motive for satisfaction in seeing how thoroughly he relied on them and how ready he was to give them a free hand in carrying out his general ideas.

The "Nelson touch" memorandum of 9 October and the whole plan of the battle have been, and still are, the subject of acute controversy, the various phases of which it would be far too long to discuss. It is strange that after the lapse of a hundred years and the publication of a vast mass of detailed evidence—British, French, and Spanish—there are still wide differences of opinion as to how the most famous naval battle in history was actually fought out. There is even much uncertainty as to the order in which the British ships came into action.

The memorandum shows that Nelson originally contemplated a formation in three lines, an advanced division to windward, a main division under his personal command, and a lee division under his second-in-command, Collingwood. The final grouping of the ships in the battle was in two divisions. In the following list of the British fleet the names of ships are arranged in the same order in which they appear in Collingwood's dispatch, written after the action:—

Windward Line

Ships.	Guns.	Commanders.
Victory	100	Vice-Admiral Lord Nelson. Captain Hardy.
Téméraire	098	" Harvey.
Neptune	098	" Fremantle.
Leviathan	074	" Bayntun.
Conqueror	074	" Pellew.

Ship	Guns	Commander
Britannia	100	Rear-Admiral Lord Northesk. Captain Bullen.
Agamemnon	064	" Sir E. Berry.
Ajax	064	Lieutenant Pilfold.
Orion	074	Captain Codrington.
Minotaur	074	" Mansfield.
Spartiate	074	" Sir F. Laforey.
Africa	064	" Digby.

LEEWARD LINE

Ships.	Guns.	Commanders.
Royal Sovereign	100	Vice-Admiral Collingwood. Captain Rotherham.
Belleisle	074	" Hargood.
Mars	074	" Duff.
Tonnant	080	" Tyler.
Bellerophon	074	" Cooke.
Colossus	074	" Morris.
Achille	074	" King.
Dreadnought	098	" Conn.
Polyphemus	064	" Redmill.
Revenge	074	" Moorsom.
Swiftsure	074	" Rutherford.
Defiance	074	" Durham.
Thunderer	074	Lieutenant Stockham.
Defence	074	Captain Hope.
Prince	098	" Grindall.

Besides one frigate of 38 guns, three of 36, and two brigs of 12 and 8 guns.

This was the fleet that lay off Cape Sta. Maria, some fifty miles from Cadiz, on Saturday, 19 October, 1805, and received from the frigates watching the port the message, passed on by connecting ships, that the enemy was at last coming out.

Villeneuve, like Nelson, had originally divided his fleet into three divisions. On the day of battle it fought in an order which was (as we shall see) partly the result of chance, arrayed in a long double line. He had deliberately mixed together in his array the French and Spanish units of his fleet, to avoid the dangers that might arise from mutual jealousies if they were drawn up in divisions apart. Instead of giving the list of his fleet according to the *ordre de bataille* drawn up in Cadiz harbour long before the event, it will be more convenient to arrange the list as they actually lay in line from van to rear on the day of battle.

The following, then, is the list of the allied Franco-Spanish fleet:

Ships.	Guns.	Commanders.
★ *Neptuno*	080	
Scipion	074	Captain Bellanger.
Intrépide	074	Commodore Infernet.
Formidable	080	Rear-Admiral Dumanoir le Pelley. Captain Letellier.
★ *Rayo*	100	Commodore Macdonel.
Duguay-Trouin	074	Captain Touffet.
Mont Blanc	074	Commodore La Villegris.
★ *San Francisco de Asis*	074	Captain de Flores.
★ *San Agustino*	074	" Cagigal.
Héros	074	" Poulain.
★ *Santisima Trinidad*	130	Rear-Admiral Cisneros. Commodore de Uriarte.
Bucentaure	080	Vice-Admiral Villeneuve. Captain Magendie.
Neptune	080	Commodore Maistral.
Redoutable	074	Captain Lucas.
★ *San Leandro*	064	" Quevedo.
★ *San Justo*	074	" Gaston.
Indomptable	080	Commodore Hubert.
★ *Santa Ana*	112	Vice-Admiral de Alava.
Fougueux	074	Captain Baudouin.
★ *Monarca*	074	" Argumosa.
Pluton	074	Commodore Cosmao Kerjulien.
† *Algéciras*	074	Rear-Admiral Magon.

* † *Bahama*	074	Captain Letourneur. Commodore Galiano.
† *Aigle*	074	Captain Gourrège.
† ‡ *Swiftsure*	074	" Villemadrin.
† *Argonaute*	074	" Epron.
* † *Montanez*	074	" Alcedo.
* † *Argonauta*	080	" Pareja.
† *Berwick*	074	Commodore Filhol-Camas.
† *San Juan Nepomuceno*	074	Commodore de Churucca.
† *Ildefonso*	074	Commodore de Vargas.
† *Achille*	074	Captain Deniéport.
† *Principe de Asturias*	112	Admiral Gravina. Rear-Admiral Escaño.

Besides five 40-gun frigates and two corvettes, one of 18, the other of 16 guns.

* Names of Spanish ships are distinguished by being marked with an asterisk.
† Ships of the "Squadron of Observation" originally intended to act independently under Gravina.
‡ Formerly British.

So far as mere figures can show it, the relative strength of the opposing fleets may be thus compared:—

LINE OF BATTLE

	Ships	Guns
British Fleet	27	148
Allied Fleet	33	3626

LIGHTER SHIPS

	Frigates	Guns	Brigs & Corvettes	Guns
British Fleet	4	146	2	20
Allied Fleet	5	200	2	30

But here once more—as so often happens in naval war—the

mere reckoning up of ships and guns does not give the true measure of fighting power. The British fleet was immeasurably superior in real efficiency, and the French and Spanish leaders knew this perfectly well.

The morning of 19 October was fine and clear with the wind from the shore. So clear was the day that the lookout in the foretop of the *Euryalus* could see the ripples on the beach. As the sun rose the enemy's ships were seen to be setting their topsails, and one by one they unmoored and towed down towards the harbour mouth. It was a long process working the ships singly out of harbour. Blackwood, of the *Euryalus*, stood close in, and from early morning till near 2 p.m. was sending his messages to the distant fleet.

Hoisted 7.20 a.m. transmitted to the Victory soon after 9 a.m.:

The enemy's ships are coming out.

11 a.m.:

Nineteen under sail. All the rest have top-yards hoisted except Spanish rear-admiral and one line-of-battle ship.

About 11.3:

Little wind in harbour. Two of the enemy are at anchor.

Noon:

Notwithstanding little wind, enemy persevere to get outward. The rest, except one line, ready, yards hoisted.

Just before 2 p.m.:

Enemy persevering to work outward. Seven of line already without and two frigates.

When the fleet began to show in force outside, Blackwood drew off to a distance of four miles from the shore and still watched them. He knew the *Euryalus* could outsail the fastest of the enemy if they tried to attack him. His business was to keep them under observation. He could see that for want of wind they were forced to work out ship after ship by towing them with rowing-boats. He knew they could not be all out till the Sunday morning, and he knew also that Nelson had acknowledged his messages and was beating up nearer and nearer to the port, though with the light winds he could only make slow progress. Unless the enemy scuttled back into the harbour a battle was inevitable.

On the Sunday morning (20 October) the wind freshened and enabled Villeneuve to bring out the last of his ships. They were hardly out when the wind changed and blew strong from the south-west, with squalls of rain. The French admiral signalled the order to tack to the southward under shortened sail. The fleet had been directed to sail in five parallel divisions, each in line ahead, but for want of training in the crews the ships lost station, and the formation was very irregular. At four in the afternoon the wind changed again to the north-west, but it was very light and the fleet moved slowly. To the westward all day the *Euryalus* and *Sirius* frigates were seen watching Villeneuve's progress, and just as darkness was closing in one of the French frigates signalled that there were twenty sail coming in from the Atlantic.

If there had been more wind, Villeneuve might have crowded all sail for the Straits, but he could only creep slowly along. Flashes and flares of light to seaward showed him the British were exchanging night signals in the darkness. He felt he was closely watched, and he was haunted by the memory of the disastrous night battle in Aboukir Bay. Though the wind had gone down the sea was rough, with a heavy swell rolling in from the westward, the well-known sign of an Atlantic storm that might break on the Spanish coast before many hours. The flickering signals of the British fleet seemed to come nearer as the darkness of the moonless autumn night deepened, and about nine a shadowy mass of sails was seen not far off. It was the *Euryalus* that had closed in with every light shaded to have a near look at the enemy.

There was an alarm that the British were about to attack, and

Villeneuve signalled to clear for action and form the prescribed double line of battle. The sharp drumbeats from the French ships, the lighting up of open ports, the burning of blue lights, showed Blackwood what was in progress. It was nearly two hours before the lines were formed, and there was much confusion, ships slipping into stations not assigned to them; and Gravina, who had been directed to keep twelve of the best ships as an independent reserve, or "squadron of observation," placing them in the line instead of forming independently. Then the fleet went about, reversing its order. Villeneuve had given up the idea of reaching the Straits without a battle, and was anxious to have the port of Cadiz under his lee when the crisis came.

Nelson's fleet, in two columns in line ahead, was drawing nearer and nearer to his enemy. Between the two fleets the *Euryalus* flitted like a ghost, observing and reporting every move of the allies, and sometimes coming quite near them. When the enemy reversed their order of sailing, Blackwood's ship was for a short time ahead of their double line, and saw the allied fleet looking like "a lighted street some six miles long."

After midnight the alarm in the Franco-Spanish fleet had passed off, and all the men who could be spared had turned in. At dawn on the Monday the French frigate *Hermione* reported the enemy in sight to windward, and at seven Villeneuve again gave the order to clear for action.

The sight of the allied fleet had called forth a great outburst of exultation on board of Nelson's ships. "As the day dawned," wrote one of his officers, "the horizon appeared covered with ships. The whole force of the enemy was discovered standing to the southward, distant about nine miles, between us and the coast near Trafalgar. I was awakened by the cheers of the crew and by their rushing up the hatchways to get a glimpse of the hostile fleet. The delight they manifested exceeded anything I ever witnessed."

Opposing fleets separated by only nine miles of sea would in our day be exchanging long-range fire after a very few minutes of rapid approach. It was to be nearly six hours before Nelson and Villeneuve came within fighting distance. The wind had become so slight that the British fleet was often moving at a speed of barely more than a knot over the grey-green ocean swells.

Still anxious to fight, with Cadiz as a refuge for disabled ships, Villeneuve presently signalled to his fleet to go about. After they altered their order of sailing and began to sail to the northward, moving very slowly with the wind abeam (close-hauled on the port tack), the course of the Victory was a little north of east, directed at first to a point about two and a half miles ahead of the leading ship of the enemy.

The *Royal Sovereign,* leading the leeward line on a parallel course, was about a mile to the southward. As the allied fleet was moving so as presently to cross the course of the British, the result would be that at the moment of contact the line led by the Victory would come in a little ahead of the enemy's centre, and the *Royal Sovereign* to the rearward of it. But the courses of the two fleets did not intersect at right angles. Many of the current plans of the battle, and, strange to say, the great model at the Royal United Service Institution (though constructed while many Trafalgar captains were still living), are misleading in representing the British advance as a perpendicular attack in closely formed line ahead.

In the heavy swell and the light wind the allied fleet had succeeded in forming only an irregular line when it went about. There were wide gaps, some of them covered by ships lying in a second line; and the fleet was not in a straight line from van to rear, but the van formed an obtuse angle with the rearward ships, the flat apex towards Cadiz, so that some of Nelson's officers thought the enemy had adopted a crescent-formed array. At the moment of contact Collingwood's division was advancing on a course that formed an acute angle of between forty and fifty degrees with the line and course of the French rear.

The result would be that the ships that followed the *Royal Sovereign* were brought opposite ship after ship of the French line and could fall upon them almost simultaneously by a slight alteration of the course. But the French van line lay at a greater angle to the windward attack, and here the British advance was much nearer the perpendicular.

Nelson had in his memorandum forbidden any time being wasted in forming a regular battle-line. The ships were to attack in the order and formation in which they sailed. If the enemy was to leeward (as was the case now), the leeward line, led by Collingwood, was to fall upon his rearward ships. Meanwhile, the windward line, led by the *Victory*, would cut through the enemy just in advance of the centre, and take care that the attack on the rear was not interfered with. Collingwood was given a free hand as to how he did his work.

Nelson reminded the captains that in the smoke and confusion of battle set plans were likely to go to pieces, and signals to be unseen, and he left a wide discretion to everyone, noting that no captain could do wrong if he laid his ship alongside of the nearest of the enemy. The actual battle was very unlike the diagram in the memorandum, which showed the British fleet steering a course parallel to the enemy up to the actual attack, and some of the captains thought that in the confusion of the fight Nelson and Collingwood had abandoned the plan. But if its letter was not realized, its spirit was acted upon. Nelson had said he intended to produce a *mêlée*, a close fight in which the better training and the more rapid and steady fire of the British would tell.

It was a novelty that the two admirals each led a line into the fight. The traditional position for a flagship was in the middle of the admiral's division, with a frigate near her to assist in showing and passing signals along the line. To the French officers it seemed a piece of daring rashness for the flagships to lead the lines, exposing themselves as they closed to the concentrated fire of several ships.

"This method of engaging battle," wrote Gicquel des Touches, an officer of the *Intrépide*, "was contrary to ordinary prudence, for the British ships, reaching us one by one, and at a very slow speed, seemed bound to be overpowered in detail by our superior forces; but Nelson knew his own fleet—and ours."

This was, indeed, the secret of it all. He knew the distant fire of the enemy would be all but harmless, and once broadside to broadside, he could depend on crushing his opponents.

This was why he did not trouble about forming a closely arrayed battle-line, but let his ships each make her best speed, disregarding the mere keeping of station and distance, so that though we speak of two lines, Collingwood's ships trailed out over miles of sea, and Nelson's seemed to the French to come on in an irregular crowd, the *Victory* in the leading place, having her two nearest consorts not far astern, but one on each quarter, and at times nearly abreast. Every stitch of canvas was spread, the narrow yards being lengthened out with the booms for the studding-sails. Blackwood had been called on board the *Victory* for a while during the advance.

Nelson asked him to witness his will, and then talked to him of the coming victory, saying he would not be satisfied with less than twenty prizes. He was cheerful and talked freely, but all the while he carefully watched the enemy's course and formation, and personally directed the course of his own ship. He meant, as he had said before, to keep the enemy uncertain to the last as to his attack, and as the distance shortened he headed for a while for the enemy's van before turning for the dash into his centre. Cheerful as he was, he did not expect to survive the fight. He disregarded the request of his friends to give the dangerous post at the head of the line to another ship, and though it was known that the enemy had soldiers on board, and there would be a heavy musketry fire at close quarters, he wore on his admiral's uniform a glittering array of stars and orders.

To the advancing fleet the five miles of the enemy's line presented a formidable spectacle. We have the impressions of one of the midshipmen of the *Neptune* in a letter written after the battle, and he tells how—

> It was a beautiful sight when their line was completed, their broadsides turned towards us, showing their iron teeth, and now and then trying the range of a shot to ascertain the distance, that they might, the moment we came within

point-blank (about 600 yards), open their fire upon our van ships—no doubt with the hope of dismasting some of our leading vessels before they could close and break their line. Some of the enemy's ships were painted like ourselves with double yellow streaks, some with a broad single red or yellow streak, others all black, and the noble *Santissima Trinidad* with four distinct lines of red, with a white ribbon between them, made her seem to be a superb man-of-war, which, indeed, she was.

The Spanish flagship was the largest ship afloat at the time, and she towered high above her consorts. It was not the first time Nelson had seen her in battle, for she was in the fleet that he and Jervis defeated twelve years before off Cape St. Vincent.

As the fleets closed the famous signal, *England expects that every man will do his duty!* flew from the *Victory*. At half-past eleven the *Royal Sovereign,* leading the lee line, was within a thousand yards of the enemy, making for a point a little to rearward of his centre, when the *Fougueux,* the ship for which she was heading, fired a first trial shot. Other ships opened fire in succession, and the centre began firing at the *Victory* and her consorts. Not a shot in reply was fired by the British till they were almost upon the allies. In the windward line the *Victory,* already under fire from eight ships of the allied van, began the battle by firing her forward guns on the port side as she turned to attack the French admiral's flagship, the 100-gun *Bucentaure.*

Just as the *Victory* opened fire, at ten minutes to twelve, Collingwood, in the *Royal Sovereign,* had dashed into the allied line. He passed between the French *Fougueux* and the *Santa Ana*, the flagship of the Spanish Rear-Admiral Alava, sending one broadside crashing into the stern of the flagship, and with the other raking the bows of the Frenchman. "What would not Nelson give to be here!" said Collingwood to his flag-captain. The hearty comradeship of the two admirals is shown by the fact that at that moment Nelson, pointing to the *Royal Sovereign's* masts towering out of the dense smoke-cloud, exclaimed, "See how that noble fellow, Collingwood, takes his ship into action!"

TRAFALGAR

Swinging round on the inside of the *Santa Ana*, Collingwood engaged her muzzle to muzzle. For a few minutes of fierce fighting he was alone in the midst of a ring of close fire, the Fougueux raking him astern, and two Spanish and one French ship firing into his starboard side. The pressure on him decreased as the other ships of his division, coming rapidly into action, closed with ship after ship of the allied rear. Further relief was afforded by Nelson's impetuous attack on the centre.

He was steering the *Victory* to pass astern of the *Bucentaure*. Captain Lucas, of the *Redoutable*, the next in the line, saw this, and resolved to protect his admiral. He closed up so that his bowsprit was almost over the flagship's stern, and the *Bucentaure*'s people called out to him not to run into them. The *Victory* then passed astern of the *Redoutable*, raking her with a terribly destructive broadside, and then ranged up alongside of her. Lucas had hoped to board the first ship he encountered. He grappled the English flagship, and while the soldiers in the French tops kept up a hot fire on the upper decks, the broadside guns were blazing muzzle to muzzle below, and a crowd of boarders made gallant but unsuccessful attempts to cross the gap between the two ships, the plucky Frenchmen being everywhere beaten back.

The *Redoutable's* way had been checked, and through the gap between her and the *Bucentaure* came the *Neptune* to engage the French flagship, while the famous "fighting *Téméraire*," which had raced the *Victory* into action, passed astern of the *Redoutable* and closed with the Spanish *San Justo*. Ship after ship of both the British divisions came up, though there were long gaps in the lines. The *Belleisle*, second of Collingwood's line, was three-quarters of a mile astern of the *Royal Sovereign* when the first shots were fired. It was nearly two hours before the rearmost English ships were engaged.

Meanwhile, the leading eight ships of the French van, commanded by Admiral Dumanoir, in the *Formidable*, after firing at the *Victory* and her immediate consorts, as they came into action, had held on their course, and were steadily drifting away from the battle. In vain Villeneuve signalled to them to engage the enemy. Dumanoir, in a lame explanation that he afterwards wrote, protested that he had no enemy within his reach, and that with the light wind he found it impossible to work back, though he used boats to tow his ships round. The effort appears to have been made only when he had gone so far that he was a mere helpless spectator of the fight, and his most severe condemnation lies in the fact that without his orders two of his captains eventually made their way back into the *mêlée* and, though it was too late to fight for victory, fought a desperate fight for the honour of the flag they flew.

Dumanoir's incompetent selfishness left the centre and rear to be crushed by equal numbers and far superior fighting power. But it was no easy victory. Outmatched as they were, Frenchmen and Spaniards fought with desperate courage and heroic determination. Trafalgar is remembered with pride by all the three nations whose flags flew over its cloud of battle-smoke.

There is no naval battle regarding which we possess so many detailed narratives of those who took part in it on both sides, and it would be easy to compile a long list of stirring incidents and heroic deeds. Though the battle lasted till about five o'clock, it had been practically decided in the first hour. In that space of time many of the enemy's ships had been disabled, two had been actually taken; and, on the other hand, England had suffered a loss that dimmed the brightness of the victory.

In the first stage of the fight Nelson's flagship was engaged with the *Redoutable* alone, the two ships locked together. Presently the *Téméraire* closed on the other side of the Frenchman, and the *Victory* found herself in action with a couple of the enemy that came drifting through the smoke on the other side of her, one of them being the giant *Santisima Trinidad*. Before the *Téméraire* engaged her, the Redoutable had been fearfully damaged by the steady fire of the *Victory*, and had also lost heavily in repeated attempts to board the English flagship.

Only a midshipman and four men succeeded in scrambling on board, and they were at once killed or made prisoners. Captain Lucas, of the *Redoutable*, in the report on the loss of his ship, told how out of a crew of 643 officers and men, sailors and soldiers, three hundred were killed, and more than two hundred badly wounded, including most of the officers; the ship was dismasted, stern-post damaged, and steering gear destroyed, and the stern on fire; she was leaking badly, and most of the pumps had been shot through; most of the lower-deck guns were dismounted, some by collision with the enemy's sides, some by his fire, and two guns had burst. Both sides of the ship were riddled, in several places two or more ports had been knocked into one, and the after-deck beams had come down, making a huge gap in the upper-deck. The *Redoutable*, already in a desperate condition, became a sinking wreck when the *Téméraire* added her fire to that of the flagship.

But the *Victory* had not inflicted this loss herself unscathed. One of her masts had gone over the side, and there had been heavy loss on her upper decks and in her batteries. The wheel was shot away. Several men had been killed and wounded on the quarter-deck, where Nelson was walking up and down talking to Captain Hardy. One shot strewed the deck with the bodies of eight marines. Another smashed through a boat, and passed between Nelson and Hardy, bruising the latter's foot, and taking away a shoe-buckle. All the while there came a crackle of musketry from a party of sharpshooters in the mizen-top of the *Redoutable*, only some sixty feet away, and Nelson's decorations must have made him a tempting target, even if the marksmen did not know who he was.

At twenty minutes past one he was hit in the left shoulder, the bullet plunging downwards and backwards into his body. He fell on his face, and Hardy, turning, saw some of the men picking him up. "They have done for me at last, Hardy," he said. "I hope not," said the captain. And Nelson replied: "Yes, my backbone is shot through." But he showed no agitation, and as the men carried him below he covered his decorations with a handkerchief, lest the crew should notice them and realize that they had lost their chief, and he gave Hardy an order to see that tiller-lines were rigged on the rudder-head, to replace the shattered wheel.

His flag was kept flying, and till the action ended the fleet was not aware of his loss, and looked to the Victory for signals as far as the smoke allowed. He had not been ten minutes among the wounded on the lowest deck when the cheers of the crew, following on a sudden lull in the firing, told him that the *Redoutable* had struck her colours.

Twenty minutes later the *Fougueux*, the second prize of the day, was secured. She had come into action with the *Téméraire* while the latter was still engaged with the *Redoutable*. On the surrender of the latter the *Téméraire* was able to concentrate her fire on the *Fougueux*. Mast after mast came down, and the sea was pouring into two huge holes on the water-line when the shattered ship drifted foul of the *Téméraire*, and was grappled by her. Lieutenant Kennedy dashed on board of the Frenchman, at the head of a rush of boarders, cleared her upper decks, hauled down her flag, and took possession of the dismasted ship.

Between two and three o'clock no less than nine ships were taken, five Spanish and four French. Villeneuve's flagship, the *Bucentaure*, was one of these. She struck a few minutes after two o'clock. At the opening of the battle she had fired four broadsides at the approaching *Victory*. Nelson gave her one shattering broadside in reply at close quarters, as he passed on to attack the *Redoutable*. As this ship's way was stopped, and a space opened between her and the French flagship, Captain Fremantle brought his three-decker, the *Neptune*, under the *Bucentaure's* stern, raking her as he passed through the line and ranged up beside her.

Then Pellew brought the *Conqueror* into action beside her on the other side, and as chance allowed her guns to bear the *Victory* was at times able to join in the attack. French accounts of the battle tell of the terrible destruction caused on board the *Bucentaure* by this concentrated fire. More than two hundred were *hors de combat*, most of them killed. Almost every officer and man on the quarter-deck was hit, Villeneuve himself being slightly wounded. The men could hardly stand to the guns, and at last their fire was masked by mast after mast coming down with yards, rigging and sails hanging over the gun muzzles.

Villeneuve declared his intention of transferring his flag to another ship, but was told that every boat had been knocked to splinters, and his attendant frigate, which might have helped him in this emergency, had been driven out of the *mêlée*. As the last of the masts went over the side at two o'clock, the *Conqueror* ceased firing, and hailed the *Bucentaure* with a summons to surrender. Five minutes later her flag, hoisted on an improvised staff, was taken down, and Captain Atcherley, of the *Conqueror's* marines, went on board the French flagship, and received the surrender of Admiral Villeneuve, his staff-officer Captain Prigny, Captain Magendie, commanding the ship, and General de Contamine, the officer in command of the 4000 French troops embarked on the fleet.

Next in the line ahead of the *Bucentaure* lay the giant *Santisima Trinidad*, carrying the flag of Rear-Admiral Cisneros. As the fleets closed, she had exchanged fire with her four tiers of guns with several of the British ships. When the *mêlée* began she came drifting down into the thick of the fight. For a while she was engaged with the *Victory* in the dense fog of smoke, where so many ships were tearing each other to pieces in the centre. The high-placed guns of the *Trinidad's* upper tier cut up the *Victory's* rigging and sent down one of her masts.

The English flagship was delivered from the attack of her powerful antagonist by the *Trinidad* drifting clear of her. By this time Fremantle was attacking her with the *Neptune*, supported by the *Colossus*. At half-past one a third ship joined in the close attack on the towering *Trinidad*, which every captain who got anywhere near her was anxious to make his prize. This new ally was the battleship Africa. During the night she had run out to the northward of the British fleet. Nelson had signalled to her early in the day to rejoin as soon as possible, but her captain, Digby, needed no pressing. He was crowding sail to join in the battle.

He ran down past Dumanoir's ships of the van squadron, putting a good many shots into them, but receiving no damage from their ill-aimed fire. Then he steered into the thick of the fight, taking for his guide the tall masts of the *Trinidad*. At 1.30 he opened fire on her. At 1.58 all the masts of the *Trinidad* came down together, the enormous mass of spars, rigging, and sails going over her side into the water as she rolled to the swell. She had already lost some four hundred men killed and wounded (Admiral Cisneros was among the latter).

Many of her guns had been silenced, and the fall of the masts masked a whole broadside. She now ceased firing and surrendered. In the log of the Africa it is noted that Lieutenant Smith was sent with a party to take possession of her. He does not seem to have succeeded in getting on board, for the *Trinidad* drifted with silent guns for at least two hours after, with no prize crew on board. It was at the end of the battle that the *Prince* sent a party to board her and took her in tow.

Another flagship, the three-decker *Santa Ana*, carrying the flag of Rear-Admiral Alava, became the prize of the *Royal Sovereign*. Collingwood had opened the fight by breaking the line astern of her. His raking broadside as he swept past her had put scores of her crew out of action. When he laid his ship alongside of her to leeward, it was evident from the very first that she could not meet the English ship on anything like equal terms.

In a quarter of an hour his flag-captain, Rotherham, grasped Collingwood's hand, saying: "I congratulate you, sir. Her fire is slackening, and she must soon strike." But the *Santa Ana* fought to the last, till only a single gun, now here, now there, answered the steady, pounding fire of the *Royal Sovereign's* broadside. At 2.30 her colours came down. Collingwood told his lieutenant to send the Spanish admiral on board his own ship, but word was sent back that Alava was too badly wounded to be moved. More than four hundred of the *Santa Ana's* crew had been killed and wounded.

The *Tonnant*, third ship in Collingwood's line, and one of the prizes taken in the Battle of the Nile, captured another flagship, that of the gallant Rear-Admiral Magon, the *Algéciras*. As the *Tonnant* went through the allied line, after exchanging fire with the *Fougueux* and the *Monarca*, the *Algéciras* raked her astern, killing some forty men. The *Tonnant* then swung round and engaged the *Algéciras*, and was crossing her bows when Magon, trying to run his ship alongside her, to board, entangled his bowsprit in the main rigging of the English ship.

She was thus held fast with only a few forward guns bearing, while most of the broadside of the *Tonnant* was raking her. From the foretop of the *Algéciras* a party of marksmen fired down on the English decks and wounded Captain Tyler badly. Admiral Magon, in person, tried to lead a strong body of boarders over his bows into the English ship. Mortally wounded, he was carried aft, and of his men only one set foot on the *Tonnant*. This man was at once stabbed with a pike, and would have been killed if an officer had not rescued him.

The ships lay so close that the flashes of the *Tonnant's* guns set fire to the bows of the *Algéciras*, and the flames spread to both ships. A couple of British sailors dragged the fire-hose over the hammock-nettings, and while the guns were still in action they worked to keep down and extinguish the flames. One by one the masts of the *Algéciras* went into the sea, carrying the unfortunate soldiers in the tops with them. In a little more than half an hour she lost 436 men, including most of her officers. Her position was hopeless, and at last she struck her colours. The prize crew that boarded her found Magon lying dead on the deck, with his captain, badly wounded, beside him.

The *Bellerophon* (famous for her fight at the Nile, adding to her record of hard fighting today, and destined to be the ship that was to receive the conqueror of Europe as a prisoner) followed the *Tonnant* into action, and found herself engaged with the Spanish *Monarca* on one side, and the French *Aigle* on the other. She came in collision with the *Aigle*, and their yards locked together. The *Bellerophon's* rigging was cut to pieces; two of her masts were carried away, and numbers of her crew were struck down, her captain being wounded early in the day.

A little after half-past one the *Aigle* drifted clear, and was engaged by, and in half an hour forced to strike to, the *Defiance*.

Meanwhile the *Bellerophon* was hard at work with two Spanish ships, the *Monarca* and the *Bahama,* and so effectually battered them that at three o'clock the former was a prize, and the other surrendered half an hour later.

The *Tonnant,* after her capture of Magon's ship, shared in the victory over another brave opponent, Commodore Churucca, and his ship, the *San Juan Nepomuceno.* Churucca was the youngest flag-officer in the Spanish navy. He had won a European reputation by explorations in the Pacific and on the South American coasts. Keen in his profession, recklessly courageous, deeply religious, he was an ideal hero of the Spanish navy, in which he is still remembered as *"El Gran Churucca,"* the "great Churucca," who "died like the Cid." He had no illusions, but told his friends he was going to defeat and death, and he knew that when he left Cadiz he was bidding a last farewell to the young wife he had lately married.

"The French admiral does not know his business," he said to his first lieutenant, as he watched the van division holding its course, while the two English lines rushed to the attack. As the English closed with the Spanish rear, Churucca's ship came into close action with the *Defiance,* and was then attacked in succession by the *Dreadnought* and the *Tonnant.* The *San Juan* fought till half her men were *hors de combat,* several guns dismounted, and two of the masts down.

As long as Churucca lived the unequal fight was maintained. For a while he seemed to have a charmed life, as he passed from point to point, encouraging his men. He was returning to his quarter-deck, when a ball shattered one of his legs. "It is nothing—keep on firing," he said, and at first he refused to leave the deck, lying on the planking, with the shattered limb roughly bandaged. He sent for his second in command, and was told he had just been killed.

Another officer, though wounded, took over the active command when at last Churucca, nearly dead from loss of blood, was carried below. He gave a last message for his wife, sent a final order that the ship should be fought till she sank, and then said he must think only of God and the other world. As he expired the *San Juan* gave up the hopeless fight. The three ships all claimed her as their prize, but it was the *Dreadnought* that took possession.

The French *Swiftsure*, once English, was won back by the Colossus, after a fight in which the *Orion* helped for a while. With her capture one-third of the enemy's whole force, including several flagships, was in English hands. The victory was won; it was now only a question of making it more and more complete.

Shortly after three o'clock the Spanish 80-gun ship *Argonauta* struck to the *Belleisle*, which had been aided in her attack by the English *Swiftsure*. A few minutes later the Leviathan took another big Spaniard, the *San Agustino*, carrying her with a rush of boarders. It was about four o'clock that, after an hour of hard fighting, the *San Ildefonso* hauled down her colours to the *Defence*. About this time the French *Achille* was seen to be ablaze and ceased firing. In the earlier stages of the fight she had been engaged successively with the *Polyphemus, Defiance,* and *Swiftsure*.

Her captain and several of her officers and nearly 400 men had been killed and wounded when she was brought to close action by the *Prince*. Her fore-rigging caught fire, and the mast coming down across the decks started a blaze in several places, and the men, driven from the upper deck by the English fire, had to abandon their attempts to save their ship. She was well alight when at last she struck her colours, and the Prince, aided by the little brig *Pickle*, set to work to save the survivors of her crew. She blew up after the battle. The *Berwick* was another ship taken before four o'clock, but I cannot trace the details of her capture.

While the battle still raged fiercely, Admiral Dumanoir, in the Formidable, was steering away to the north-westward, followed by the *Mont Blanc, Duguay-Trouin,* and *Scipion*. But two ships of his division, the *Neptuno* and the *Intrépide*, had disregarded his orders, and turned back to join in the fight, working the ships' heads round by towing them with boats. The *Intrépide* led. Her captain, Infernet, was a rough Provençal sailor, who had fought his way from the forecastle to the quarter-deck. Indignant at Dumanoir's conduct, he had early in the battle given orders to steer for the thickest of it. "*Lou capo sur lou Bucentaure!*" ("Head her for the Bucentaure!") he shouted in his native *patois*.

He arrived too late to fight for victory, but he fought for the honour of his flag. After engaging several British ships, Infernet struck to the *Orion*. An officer of the *Conqueror* (which had taken part in the fight with the *Intrépide*) wrote:

> Her captain surrendered after one of the most gallant defences I ever witnessed. His name was Infernet, and it deserves to be recorded by all who admire true heroism. The *Intrépide* was the last ship that struck her colours.

The Spanish ship that had followed the *Intrépide* into action, the 80-gun *Neptuno*, had shortly before been forced to strike to the *Minotaur* and the *Spartiate*, another of the prizes of Aboukir Bay.

Before these last two surrenders completed the long list of captured ships, Nelson had passed away. The story of his death in the cockpit of the *Victory* is too well known to need repetition. Before he died the cheers of his crew and the messages brought to him had told him of capture after capture, and assured him that his triumph was complete. As the firing ceased, Collingwood took over the command of the fleet, and transferred his flag from his own shattered and dismasted ship, the *Royal Sovereign*, to Blackwood's smart frigate, the *Euryalus*.

When the *Intrépide* struck, seventeen ships of the allied fleet had been taken, one, the *Achille*, was in a blaze, and soon to blow up; four were in flight far away to the north-west, eleven were making for Cadiz, all bearing the marks of hard hitting during the fight. Some desultory firing at the nearest fugitives ended the battle. Crowds on the breakwater of Cadiz and the nearest beaches had watched all the afternoon the great bank of smoke on the horizon, and listened to the rumbling thunder of the cannonade. After sunset ship after ship came in, bringing news of disaster, and all the night wounded men were being conveyed to the hospitals.

More than half the allied fleet had been taken or destroyed. The four ships that escaped with Dumanoir were captured a few days later by a squadron under Sir Richard Strachan. The French ships that escaped into Cadiz were taken possession of by the Spanish insurgents, when Spain rose against the French, and Cadiz joined the revolt.

As the battle ended, the British fleet was, to use the expression of the *Neptune's* log, "in all directions." The sun was going down; the sky was overcast, and the rising swell and increasing wind told of the coming storm. Most of the prizes had been dismasted; many of them were leaking badly; some of the ships that had taken them were in almost as damaged a condition, and many of them were short-handed, with heavy losses in battle and detachments sent on board the captured vessels.

The crews were busy clearing the decks, getting up improvised jury masts, and repairing the badly cut-up rigging, where the masts still stood. Nelson's final order had been to anchor to ride out the expected gale. Collingwood doubted if this would be safer than trying to make Gibraltar, and he busied himself getting the scattered fleet and prizes together, and tacking to the south-westward.

The gale that swept all the coasts of Western Europe caught the disabled fleet with the hostile shore under its lee. Only four of the prizes, and those the poorest ships of the lot, ever saw Gibraltar. Ship after ship went down, others were abandoned and burnt, others drove ashore. In these last instances the British prize crews were rescued and kindly treated by the Spanish coast population. One ship, the *Algéciras*, was retaken by the French prisoners, and carried into Cadiz. Another, the big *Santa Ana,* was recaptured as she drifted helplessly off the port.

But though there were few trophies left after the great storm, Trafalgar had finally broken the naval power of Napoleon, freed England from all fear of invasion, and given her the undisputed empire of the sea. Yet there were only half-hearted rejoicings at home. The loss of Nelson seemed a dear price to pay even for such a victory.

Some 2500 men were killed and wounded in the victorious fleet. Of the losses of the Allies it is difficult to give an estimate. Every ship that was closely engaged suffered severely, and hundreds of wounded went down in several of those that sank in the storm. For weeks after search-parties, riding along the shores from Cadiz to Cape Trafalgar gathered every day a grim harvest of corpses drifted to land by the Atlantic tides. The allied loss was at least 7000 men, and may have been considerably greater.

The news came to England, just after something like a panic had been caused by the tidings of the surrender of a whole Austrian army at Ulm. It reached Napoleon in the midst of his triumphs, to warn him that his power was bounded by the seas that washed the shores of the Continent. Well did Meredith say that in his last great fight Nelson *drove the smoke of Trafalgar to darken the blaze of Austerlitz.*

CHAPTER 10

The Coming of Steam and Armoured Navies

THE FIGHT IN HAMPTON ROADS MARCH 1862

Trafalgar was the greatest fight of the sailing-ships. There were later engagements which were fought under sail, but no battle of such decisive import. It was a fitting close to a heroic era in the history of naval war, a period of not much more than four centuries, in thousands of years. Before it, came the long ages in which the fighting-ship depended more upon the oar than the sail, or on the oar exclusively. After it, came our present epoch of machine-propelled warships, bringing with it wide-sweeping changes in construction, armament, and naval tactics.

Inventive pioneers were busy with projects for the coming revolution in naval war while Nelson was still living. The Irish-American engineer, Fulton, had tried to persuade Napoleon to adopt steam propulsion, and had astonished the Parisians by showing them his little steamer making its way up the Seine with clumsy paddles churning up the waters and much sooty smoke pouring from its tall, thin funnel. The Emperor thought it was a scientific toy. Old admirals—most conservative of men—declared that a gunboat with a few long "sweeps" or oars would be a handier fighting-ship in a calm, and if there was any wind a spread of sail was better than all the American's tea-kettle devices. Fulton went back to America to run passenger steamers on the Hudson, and tell unbelieving commodores and captains that the future of the sea power lay with the "tea-kettle ships."

In the days of the long peace that followed Waterloo, and the great industrial development that came with it, the steam-engine and the paddle-steamer made their way into the commercial fleets of the world, slowly and timidly at first, for it was a long time before a steamship could be provided with enough efficient engine power to enable her to show the way to a smart clipper-built sailing-ship, and the early marine engines were fearfully uneconomical. Steam had obtained a recognized position in small ships for short voyages, ferry-boats, river steamers, and coasting craft, but on the open ocean the sailing-ship still held its own.

An eminent scientist proved to demonstration that no steamship would ever be able to cross the Atlantic under steam alone. He showed that to do so it would be necessary for her to carry a quantity of coal exceeding her entire tonnage capacity, and he expressed his readiness to eat the first steamer that made the voyage from Liverpool to New York. But he lived to regret his offer.

In 1838 the *Great Western* and the *Sirius* inaugurated the steam passenger service across the Atlantic, and the days of the liner began. By this time paddle-wheel gunboats were finding their way into the British navy, and other powers were beginning to follow the example of England. Steamships were first in action in 1840, when Sir Charles Napier employed them side by side with sailing-ships that had shared the triumphs of Nelson. This was in the attack on Acre, when England intervened to check the revolt of the *Pasha* of Egypt, Ibrahim, against his suzerain, the Sultan.

But still the steamship was regarded as an auxiliary. The great three-decker battleships, the smart sailing frigates, were the main strength of navies. The paddle-steamer was a defective type of warship, because her paddle-boxes and paddle-wheels, and her high-placed engines, presented a huge target singularly vulnerable. A couple of shots might disable in a minute her means of propulsion. True she had masts and sails, but if she could not use her engines, the paddles would prove a drag upon all her movements.

It was the invention of the screw-propeller that made steam propulsion for warships really practical. Brunel was one of the great advocates of the change. He was a man who was in many ways before his time, and he had to encounter a more than usual amount of official conservatist obstruction. For years the veteran officers who advised the Admiralty opposed and ridiculed the invention. When at last it was fitted to a gunboat, the *Rattler*, it was obvious that it provided the best means of applying steam propulsion to the purposes of naval war. The propeller was safe under water, and the engines could be placed low down in the ship.

By 1854, when the Crimean War began, both the British and French navies possessed a number of steam-propelled line-of-battle ships, frigates, and gunboats, fitted with the screw. They had also some old paddle-ships. But in the fleets dispatched to the Baltic and the Black Sea there were still a considerable number of sailing-ships, and a fleet still did most of its work under sail. Even the steamships had only what we should now describe as auxiliary engines. The most powerful line-of-battle ships in the British navy had engines of only 400 to 600 horsepower.[1] With such relatively small power they still had to depend chiefly on their sails. Tug-boats were attached to the fleets to tow the sailing-ships, when the steamships were using their engines.

Another change was taking place in the armament of warships and coast defences. The rifled cannon was still in the experimental stage, but explosive shells, which in Nelson's days were only fired from mortars at very short range, had now been adapted to guns mounted on the broadside and the coast battery. Solid shot were still largely used, but the coming of the shell meant that there would be terrible loss in action in the crowded gun-decks, and inventors were already proposing that ships should be armoured to keep these destructive missiles from penetrating their sides.

---

1. Compare this with 23,000 horse-power of the *Dreadnought's* turbine engines.

The attack on the sea front of Sebastopol by the allied fleets on 17 October, 1854, was the event that brought home to the minds of even the most conservative the necessity of a great change in warship construction. It rang the knell of the old wooden walls, and led to the introduction of armour-clad navies.

The idea of protecting ships from the fire of artillery and musketry by iron plating was an old one, and the wonder is that it did not much earlier receive practical application. The Dutch claim to have been the pioneers of ironclad building more than three hundred years ago. During the famous siege of Antwerp by the Spaniards in 1585 the people of the city built a huge flat-bottomed warship, armoured with heavy iron plates, which they named the *Finis Belli*, a boastful expression of the hope that she would end the war.

An old print of the *Finis Belli* shows a four-masted ship with a high poop and forecastle, but with a low freeboard amidships. On this lower deck, taking up half the length of the ship, is an armoured citadel, with port-holes for four heavy guns on each side. The roof of the citadel has a high bulwark, loopholed for musketry. On three of the masts there are also crow's-nests or round tops for musketeers.

Heavily weighted with her armour, the ship had a deep draught of water, and probably steered badly. In descending the Scheldt to attack the Spaniards she ran aground in a hopeless position under their batteries, and fell into the hands of the Spanish commander, the Duke of Parma. He kept the *Finis Belli* "as a curiosity" till the end of the siege, and then had her dismantled. If she had scored a success, armoured navies would no doubt have made their appearance in the seventeenth century.

Between the days of the *Finis Belli* and the coming of the first ironclads there were numerous projects of inventors. In 1805 a Scotchman, named Gillespie, proposed the mounting of guns and "ponderous mortars" in revolving armoured turrets, both in fortifications on shore and on floating batteries. Two years later Abraham Bloodgood, of New York, designed a floating battery with an armoured turret.

During the war between England and the United States in 1812 an American engineer, John Steevens, who was a man in advance of his time, proposed the construction of a steam-propelled warship, with a ram-bow, and with her guns protected by shields. He prepared a design, but failed to persuade the Navy Department that it was practicable. His son, Robert L. Steevens, improved the design, made experiments with guns, projectiles, and armour plates, and at last in 1842 obtained a vote of Congress for the building of the "Steevens battery," a low-freeboard ram, steam-propelled, and armed with eight heavy guns mounted on her centre-line, on turntables protected by armoured breastworks. The methods of the American navy were very dilatory, professional opinion was opposed to Steevens, whose project was regarded as that of a "crank," and the ship was left unfinished for years. She was still on the stocks when the Civil War began. Then other types came into fashion, and she was broken up on the ways.

The man who introduced the armour-clad ship into the world's navies was the Emperor Napoleon III, the same who introduced rifled field artillery into the armies of the world. Like other great revolutions, this epoch-making change in naval war began in a small way. What forced the question upon the Emperor's attention was the failure of the combined French and English fleets in the attack on the sea-forts of Sebastopol on 17 October, 1854. The most powerful ships in both navies had engaged the sea-forts, and suffered such loss and injury that it was obvious that if the attack had been continued the results would have been disastrous.

Some means must be found of keeping explosive shells out of a ship's gun-decks, if they were ever to engage land batteries on anything like equal terms. Under the Emperor's directions the French naval architects designed four ships of a new type, which were rapidly constructed in the Imperial dockyards. They were "floating batteries," not intended to take part in fleet actions, but only to be used against fortifications. Their broad beam, heavy lines, rounded bows, and engines of only 225 horsepower, condemned them to slow speed, just sufficient to place them in firing position. They were armoured with 4-inch iron and armed with eighteen 50-pounder guns. The port-holes had heavy iron ports, which were closed while the guns were reloading.

Three of these floating batteries, the *Dévastation, Lave,* and *Tonnant*, came into action against the shore batteries at Kinburn on 17 October, 1855 (the anniversary of the attack on the Sebastopol sea-forts). There was some difficulty in getting into position, as they could just crawl along, and steered abominably. But when they opened fire at 800 yards at 9 a.m. they silenced and wrecked the Russian batteries in eighty-five minutes, themselves suffering only trifling damage, and not losing a dozen men.

It was the first and last fight of the floating batteries. But while in England men were still discussing the problem of the sea-going ironclad, the French constructors were solving it. They had to look not to parliamentary and departmental committees, but to the initiative and support of an intelligent autocrat. So events went quicker in France. In 1858 the keels of the first three French sea-going armour-clads were laid down at Toulon, and next year the armoured frigate *Gloire*, the first of European ironclads, was launched, and every dockyard in France was busy constructing armour-clads or rebuilding and armouring existing ships.

France had gained a start in the building of the new type of warship. When the *Dreadnought* was launched, it was said somewhat boastfully that single-handed she could destroy the whole North Sea fleet of Germany. It might be more truly said of the *Gloire* that she could have met single-handed and destroyed the British Channel or Mediterranean Fleet of the day. It was the moment when tension with France over the Orsini conspiracy had caused a widespread anticipation of war between that country and England, and had called the Volunteer force into existence to repel invasion.

But the true defence must be in the command of the sea, and

the first English ironclad, the old *Warrior*, was laid down at the Thames Ironworks. Work was begun in June, 1859, and the ship was launched in December, 1860. She was modelled on the old steam frigates, for the special types of modern battleships and armoured cruisers were still in the future. She was built of iron, with unarmoured ends and 4 ¼-inch iron plating on a backing of 18 inches of teak over 200 feet amidships of her total length of 380 feet.

There was a race of ironclad building between France and England, in which the latter won easily, and it was only for a very short time that our sea supremacy was endangered by the French Emperor's naval enterprise. But when the English and French fleets entered the Gulf of Mexico in 1861, our ships were all wooden walls, while the French admiral's flag flew on the ironclad Normandie, the first armoured ship that ever crossed the Atlantic.

Notwithstanding this fact, American writers are fond of saying, and many Englishmen believe, that the introduction of armoured navies was the outcome of the American Civil War of the early 'sixties. All that is true is that the War of Secession gave the world the spectacle of the first fight between armour-clad ships, and the experiences of that war greatly influenced the direction taken in the general policy of designers of ironclad warships.

Towards the close of the Crimean War a Swedish engineer settled in the United States, John Ericsson, had sent to the Emperor Napoleon a design for a small armoured turret-ship of what was afterwards known as the Monitor type. He wrote to the Emperor that he asked for no reward or profit, for he was only anxious to help France in her warfare with Russia, the hereditary foe of Sweden. The war was drawing to a close, and for his future projects the Emperor wanted large sea-going ships, not light-draught vessels for work in the shallows of the Baltic. So Ericsson received a complimentary letter of thanks and a medal, and kept his design for later use. His opportunity came in the first months of the Civil War.

H.M.S. *Warrior* the first British Ironclad

In the fifty years between the war of 1812 and the outbreak of the struggle between North and South, the American navy had been greatly neglected. It was a favourite theory in the United States that a navy could be improvised, and that the great thing would be, in case of war, to send out swarms of privateers to prey upon the enemy's commerce. Very little money was spent on the navy or the dockyards. On the navy list there were a number of old ships, some of which had fought against England in 1812. There were a number of small craft for revenue purposes, a lot of sailing-ships, and a few fairly modern steam frigates and smaller steam vessels depending largely on sail-power, and known as "sloops-of-war"—really small frigates.

While the dockyards of Europe had long been busy with the construction of the new armoured navies, the United States had not a single ironclad. Both parties to the quarrel had to improvise up-to-date ships.

Sea power was destined to play a great part in the conflict. As soon as the Washington Government realized that it was going to be a serious and prolonged war, not an affair of a few weeks, a general plan of operations was devised, of which the essential feature was the isolation of the Southern Confederacy. When the crisis came in 1861 the United States had done little to open up and occupy the vast territories between the Rocky Mountains and the Mississippi Valley. The population of the States was chiefly to be found between the Mississippi and the Atlantic, and in that region lay the states of the Confederacy.

They were mainly agricultural communities, with hardly any factories. For arms, munitions of war, and supplies of many kinds they would have to depend on importation from beyond their frontiers. It was therefore decided that while the United States armies operated on the northern or land frontier of the Confederacy, its sea frontiers on the Atlantic and the Gulf of Mexico should be closely blockaded, and its river frontier, the line of the Mississippi, should be seized and held by a mixed naval and military force. For these last operations troops on the banks and gunboats on the river had to combine. It was said at the time, that on the Mississippi army and navy were like the two blades of a pair of shears, useless apart, but very effective when working together.

Strange to say, it was not the industrial North, but the agricultural South, that put the first ironclad into commission as a weapon against the coast blockade. When the Secessionist forces seized the Navy Yard at Norfolk, in Virginia, a fine steam frigate, the *Merrimac* (built in 1855), was under repair there. The guard of the dockyard set her on fire before surrendering, but the flames were extinguished, and the *Merrimac*, with her upper works badly damaged, was in possession of the Southerners. A Northern squadron of frigates and gunboats, steam and sailing ships, anchored in Hampton Roads, the landlocked sheet of water into which runs not only the Elizabeth River, which gives access to Norfolk, but also the James River, the waterway to Richmond, then the Confederate capital. The northern shores of Hampton Roads were held by Federal troops, the southern by the Confederates. Presently spies brought to Washington the news that the Rebels were preparing a terrible new kind of warship at Norfolk to destroy the squadron in Hampton Roads and raise the blockade.

The news was true. The Confederates had cut down the *Merrimac* nearly to the water's edge and built a solid deck over her at this level. Then on the deck they erected a huge deck-house, with sloping sides pierced with port-holes for ten heavy smooth-bore guns. The funnel passed up through the roof of the deck-house. There were no masts, only a flagstaff. The flat deck space, fore and aft, and the sloping sides of the deck-house were to be armoured with four inches of iron, but there were no armour plates available. Railway iron was collected and rolled into long narrow strips, and these were bolted on the structure in two layers, laid crosswise in different directions.

An armoured conning-tower, low and three-sided, was built on the front of the deck-house roof. The bow was armed with a mass of iron, in order to revive the ancient method of attack by ramming. Thus equipped the *Merrimac* was commissioned, under the command of Commodore Buchanan, and renamed the "Confederate States' ironclad steam-ram *Virginia*," but the ship was always generally known by her former name.

At noon on Saturday, 8 March, 1862, the *Merrimac* started on her voyage down the Elizabeth River. It was to be at once her trial trip and her first fighting expedition. She was to attack and destroy the Federal blockading fleet in Hampton Roads. Up to the last moment the ship was crowded with working men. They were cleared out of her as she cast off from the quay. As the *Merrimac* went down the river the officers were telling off the men to their stations. Not one of her guns had ever been fired. There had been a few hurried drills. Everything was improvised.

The first disappointment was to find that with the engines doing their best she could only make five knots. She steered badly, answering her helm slowly and turning on a wide circle. As one of her officers put it, "she was as unmanageable as a water-logged vessel." She drew 22 feet of water, so that she had to keep to the narrow channel in the middle of the river, and the risk of getting hopelessly aground was serious.

The Confederate troops crowded the batteries on either bank, and cheered the *Merrimac* as she went slowly down. It was a fine day, with bright sunshine and absolutely no wind, and the broad stretch of water in Hampton Roads was like a pond. At the same time a small squadron of Confederate gunboats came down the James River to co-operate in the attack. These ships were the *Yorktown* (12 guns), the *Jamestown* (2 guns), and the *Teaser* (1 gun). Two other gunboats, the *Beaufort* and the *Raleigh*, followed the *Merrimac*. But the chief hope of the attack was placed upon the ironclad.

The nine vessels of the blockading fleet lay along the north side of Hampton Roads, from the point at Newport News to Old Point Comfort, where the Roads open on Chesapeake Bay. They were strung out over a distance of about eight miles. The shore on that side was held by the Federals, and the point at Newport News bristled with batteries. Near the point were anchored the sailing frigate *Congress*, of 50 guns, and the sloop

Cumberland, a full-rigged three-master, armed with 30 guns. On board the Federal ships there was not the remotest expectation of attack. Clothes were drying in the rigging. A crowd of boats lay alongside. It was known that the Confederates had been busy converting the old *Merrimac* into an armoured ram at Norfolk Navy Yard, but it was not believed that she was yet ready for action.

The men had just eaten their dinners, and were having a pipe, when the first alarm was raised. By the wharf at Newport News lay a tug-boat, the *Zouave*, which had been armed with a 30-pounder gun, and was rated as a gunboat and tender to the fleet. Her captain noticed the smoke of steamers coming down the Elizabeth River, and cast off from the wharf and went alongside the Cumberland. The officer of the watch told him to run across to the river mouth and find out what was coming down from Norfolk.

"It did not take us long to find out," he says, "for we had not gone over two miles when we saw what to all appearances looked like the roof of a very big barn belching forth smoke as from a chimney. We were all divided in opinion as to what was coming. The boatswain's mate was the first to make out the Confederate flag, and then we all guessed it was the *Merrimac* come at last."

The little *Zouave* fired half a dozen shots, which fell short. The *Merrimac* took no notice of this demonstration, but steadily held her way. Then the *Cumberland* signalled to the *Zouave* to come back, and she ran past the anchored warships and under shelter of the batteries. These were now opening fire on the Confederate gunboats issuing from the James River. The *Congress* and *Cumberland* had cleared for action and weighed anchor. Other ships of the fleet had taken the alarm, and were coming up into the Roads to help their consorts. The *Confederate* batteries at Sewell's Point opened fire at long range against these ships as they stood into the Roads.

he *Merrimac* was steering straight for the *Cumberland*, in grim silence, her unarmoured consorts keeping well astern. When the

HAMPTON ROADS (1ST DAY)
MERRIMAC COMES OUT. SINKS *CUMBERLAND* AND BURNS *CONGRESS*

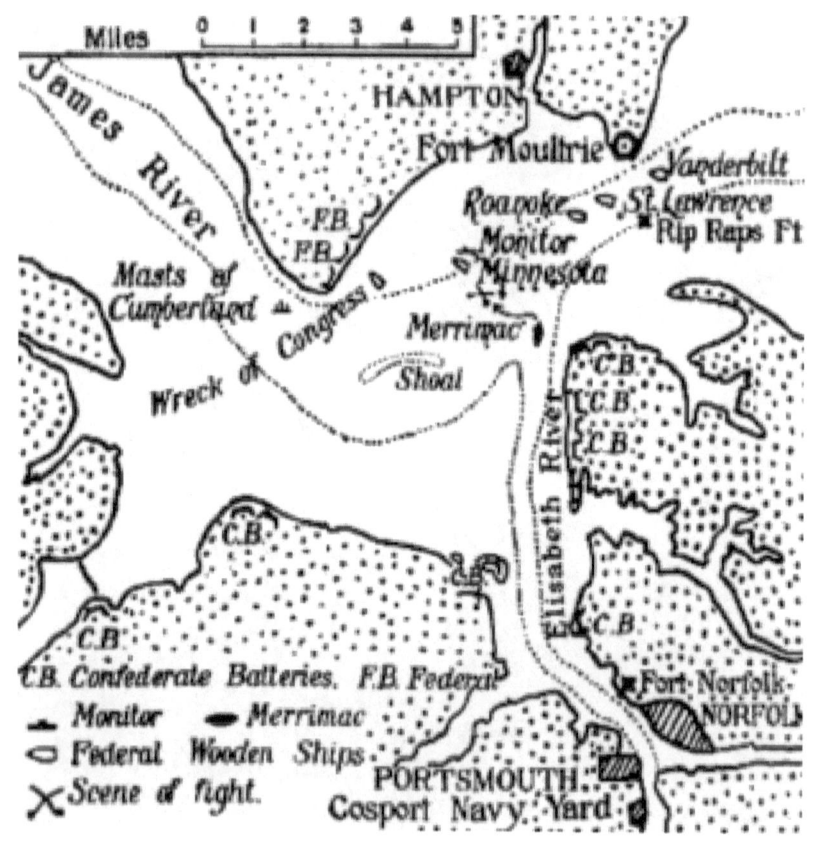

HAMPTON ROADS (2ND DAY)
DUEL BETWEEN *MONITOR* AND *MERRIMAC*

range was about three-quarters of a mile the two Federal ships opened fire with the heavy guns mounted on pivots on their upper decks, and the shore batteries also brought some guns to bear. A heavy cannonade from sea and shore was now echoing over the landlocked waters, but the *Merrimac* fired not a gun in reply. A few cannon-shot struck her sloping armoured sides, and rebounded with a ringing clang. The rest ricocheted harmlessly over the water, throwing up sparkling geysers of foam in the bright sunlight.

At last, when the range was only some 500 yards, the bow-gun of the *Merrimac* was fired at the *Cumberland*, with an aim so true that it killed or wounded most of the men at one of her big pivot-guns. A moment after the ram was abeam of the *Congress*, and fired her starboard battery of four guns into her at deadly close range. With the projectiles from 25 guns of the *Congress* and 15 of the *Cumberland* rattling on her armour, riddling her funnel, and destroying davits, rails, and deck-fittings, the *Merrimac* steamed straight for the *Cumberland*, which made an ineffectual attempt to avoid the coming collision.

At the last moment some men were killed and wounded in the gun-deck of the ram by shots entering a port-hole. Then came a grinding crash as the iron ram of the *Merrimac* struck the *Cumberland* almost at right angles on the starboard side under her fore-rigging. On board the Confederate ship the shock was hardly felt. But the *Cumberland* heeled over with the blow, and righted herself again as the *Merrimac* reversed her engines and cleared her, leaving a huge breach in the side of her enemy. The ram had crushed in several of her frames and made a hole in her side "big enough to drive a coach and horses through." The water was pouring into her like a mill-race.

From the *Merrimac*, lying close alongside with silent guns, came a hail and a summons to surrender. From the deck of the *Cumberland* her commander, Morris, replied with a curt refusal. The firing began again; the *Cumberland's* men, driven from the gun-deck by the inrush of rising water, took refuge on the upper deck. Some jumped overboard and began swimming ashore.

Others kept her two pivot-guns in action for a few minutes. Then with a lurch she went down. Boats from the shore saved a few of her people. Those who watched from the batteries could hardly believe their eyes as they saw the masts of the warship sticking out of the water where a few minutes ago the *Cumberland* had waited in confidence for the attack of the improvised "rebel" ironclad.

As her adversary went down, the *Merrimac* turned slowly to menace the *Congress* with the same swift destruction. She took no notice of the harmless cannonade from the shore. Lieutenant Smith, who commanded the *Congress*, had realized that collision with the enemy meant destruction, rapid and inevitable, and decided that his best chance was to get into shoal water under the batteries. He had slipped his cable, shaken out some of his sails, and signalled to the tug-boat *Zouave* to come to his help. The *Zouave* made fast to the *Congress* on the land side, but she had not moved far when the ship grounded within easy range of the *Merrimac's* guns. These were already in action against her.

The leading ship of the seaward Federal squadron, the frigate *Minnesota*, had come in within long range, and opened on the *Merrimac* and the gunboats. But she had only fired a few shots when she also ran aground on the edge of the main channel, but in such a position that some of her guns could still be brought to bear. Taking no notice of this more distant foe, the *Merrimac* devoted all her attention to the *Congress*. She sent a broadside into the stranded frigate, and then passing under her stern, raked her fore and aft and set her on fire.

Lieutenant Smith, of the *Congress*, was badly wounded. Lieutenant Prendergast, who succeeded to the command, decided that with his ship aground and the enemy able quietly to cannonade her without coming under fire of most of her guns, to prolong the fight would be to waste life uselessly. After consulting his wounded chief he dipped his colours and displayed a white flag. The little *Zouave* cast off from the frigate, and as she cleared her, fired a single shot from her one gun at the *Merrimac*, and then ran down to the *Minnesota*. This shot led afterwards to a false report that the *Congress* had reopened fire treacherously after surrendering.

Civil war has often been described as fratricidal. In this action between the *Congress* and the *Merrimac* two brothers were opposed to each other. Commodore Buchanan, who commanded the *Merrimac*, knew, when he attacked the *Congress*, that a younger brother of his was a junior officer of the frigate. The younger man escaped unscathed, but the commodore was slightly wounded during the fight. When the *Congress* struck her colours, Buchanan ordered two of the gunboats to take off her crew. Her flag was secured to be sent to Richmond as a trophy.

While the gunboats *Raleigh* and *Beaufort* were taking off the Federal wounded, there came from the batteries on shore a heavy fire of guns and rifles. Several of the wounded and two officers of the *Raleigh* were killed, and the gunboats drew off, leaving most of the crew of the *Congress* still on board. They escaped to the shore in boats and by swimming. Meanwhile the *Merrimac* fired a number of red-hot shot into her, and she was soon ablaze fore and aft. Then the ironclad turned and fired at the *Minnesota*.

The sun was going down and the tide was running out rapidly. The deep draught of the *Merrimac* made the risk of grounding, if she closely engaged the *Minnesota*, a serious matter. So Buchanan signalled to the gunboats to cease fire, and, accompanied by them, steamed over to the south side of the Roads, where he anchored for the night under the Confederate batteries, intending to complete the destruction of the Federal fleet next morning.

The first day's fight was over. It had been a battle between the old and the new—between a steam-propelled armoured ram and wooden sailing-ships. The *Cumberland* had been sunk, the *Congress* forced to surrender and set on fire, and the *Minnesota* was hopelessly aground and marked down as the first victim for next day. The Federals had lost some two hundred men. The Confederates only twenty-one. Buchanan was wounded, not severely, but seriously enough for the command of the *Merrimac* to be transferred to Lieutenant Jones.

As night came on the moon rose, but the wide expanse of water was lighted up, not by her beams only, but also by the red glare from the burning *Congress*. The flames ran up her tarred rigging like rocket trails, masts and spars were defined in flickers of flame. At last, with a deafening roar that was heard for many a mile, she blew up, strewing the Roads with scattered wreckage.

At ten o'clock that evening, while the *Congress* was still burning, a strange craft had steamed into the Roads from the sea, all unnoticed by the Confederates. She anchored in the shallow water between the *Minnesota* and the shore. Her light draught enabled her to go into waters where less powerful fighting-ships would have grounded. To use the words of one who first saw her as the sun rose next day, she looked like a plank afloat with a can on top of it. She was Ericsson's ironclad turret-ship, the *Monitor*.

In the first weeks of the war inventors had besieged the United States Navy Department with proposals for the construction of ironclad warships. The Department was still leisurely debating as to what policy should be adopted, when news came that the *Merrimac*, half-burnt at Norfolk Yard, was being reconstructed as an armoured ram, and it became urgent to provide an adversary to meet her on something like equal terms. It was at this moment that John Ericsson came forward with his offer to construct an armoured light-draught turret-ship, which could be very rapidly built and put in commission.

This last point was of cardinal importance, for report said that work on the *Merrimac* was far advanced, and no ship could be built on ordinary lines, of sufficient power to meet her, in the time now available. The vessel must be of light draught to work in the shallow coast waters, creeks, and river mouths of the Southern States. She might have to fight in narrow channels, where there would not be room for manœuvring to bring broadside guns to bear. Ericsson, therefore, proposed that her armament should be a pair of heavy guns mounted in a turret, which could be revolved so as to point them in any direction, independently of the position of the ship herself.

The hull was to be formed of two portions, a kind of barge-like structure or lower hull, built of iron, and mostly under water when the ship was afloat, and fixed over this the upper hull, a raft-like structure, wider and longer, and with overhanging armoured sides and lighter deck-armour. The dimensions were—

- Upper part of hull, length 172 feet, beam 41 feet.
- Lower hull, length 122 feet, beam 34 feet.
- Depth, underside of deck to keel-plate, 11 feet 2 inches.
- Draught of water, 10 feet.

Engines and boilers were aft, and the long overhang of the armoured deck astern protected the under-water rudder and screw propeller. In the overhang at the bow there was a well, in which the anchor hung under water. Forward, near the bow, there was a small armoured pilot-house, or, as we now call it, "conning-tower." Amidships, in an armoured turret, were mounted two heavy smooth-bore guns, of large calibre, and throwing a round, solid shot.

The conning-tower was built of solid iron blocks, nine inches thick. The sight-holes were narrow, elongated slits. This was the helmsman's station.

The committee to which Ericsson's plans were referred was at first hostile; some of the members declared that the ship would not float, that her deck would be under water, and she would be swamped at once. Further objections were that no crew could live in the under-water part of the hull. But at length all objections were met, and the Swedish engineer was told that his plans were accepted, and that a regular contract would be drawn up for his signature. Ericsson knew the value of time, and before the contract was ready the keel plates of his turret-ship had been rolled and a dozen firms had started work on her various parts. While the ship was being built, he proposed she should be named the *Monitor*, and the name became a general term for low-freeboard turret-ships.

The keel of the ship was laid at Greenpoint Yard, Brooklyn, in October, 1861. She was launched on 30 January, 1862. The

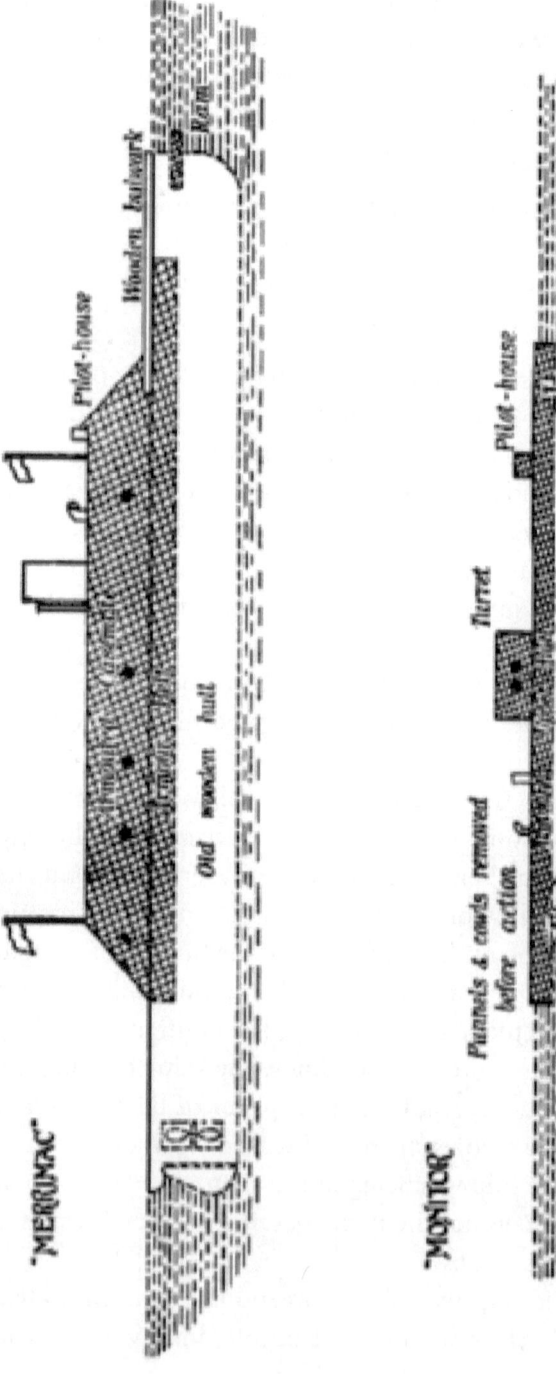

The *Merrimac* and *Monitor* drawn to the same scale

work of completing and fitting was carried on day and night, and she was commissioned for service on 25 February, 1862. But even when her crew were on board there were a number of details to be completed. Workmen were busy on her almost up to the moment of her departure from New York harbour nine days later, so there was no chance of drilling the men and testing the guns and turret.

Lieutenant Worden, United States Navy, was promoted to the rank of captain and given command. He formed a crew of volunteers for what was considered a novel and exceptionally dangerous service. Officers and men numbered fifty-eight in all.

On the morning of Thursday, 6 March (two days before the *Merrimac's* attack on the *Cumberland*), the *Monitor* left New York in tow of the tug *Seth Low*, bound for Hampton Roads. The two days' voyage southwards along the coast was an anxious and trying time, and though the weather was not really bad, the *Monitor* narrowly escaped foundering at sea.

At 4 p.m. on the Saturday she was off Cape Henry, and the sound of a far-off cannonade was heard in the direction of Hampton Roads. The officers rightly guessed that the *Merrimac* was in action. It was after dark that the turret-ship steamed up the still water of the landlocked bay, amid the red glare from the burning *Congress*. She anchored beside the United States warship *Roanoke*. On board the fleet which eagerly watched her arrival there were general disappointment and depression at seeing how small she was.

Worden shifted his anchorage in the night, and taking advantage of the *Monitor's* light draught steamed up the Roads, and anchored his ship in the shallow water to landward of the stranded *Minnesota*.

There was not much sleep on board the *Monitor* that night, tired as the men were. At 2 a.m. the *Congress* blew up in a series of explosions. After that the men tried to settle down to rest, but before dawn all hands were roused to prepare for the coming fight. A little after 7 a.m. the *Merrimac* was seen steaming slowly across the bay, escorted by her flotilla of gunboats. She was coming to complete the destruction of the United States squadron, and had marked down the *Minnesota* as her first victim, in blissful ignorance of the arrival of the *Monitor*. Worden realized that if he allowed the fight to take place near the stranded ship, the *Merrimac* might engage him with one of her broadsides, and use the other to destroy the *Minnesota*. He therefore steamed boldly out into the open water, challenging the Confederate ram to a duel. As he approached the wooden gunboats prudently turned back and ran under the shelter of the Confederate batteries on the south shore, leaving the *Merrimac* to meet the *Monitor* in single combat.

So that Sunday morning, 9 March, 1862, saw the first battle between ironclad ships, with North and South, soldiers, sailors, and civilians anxiously watching the combat from the ships in the Roads and the batteries on either shore.

Worden was in the pilot-house with a quartermaster at the wheel, and a local pilot to assist him. His first lieutenant, Dana Greene, commanded the two 11-inch guns in the turret. The *Merrimac* was the first to open fire. Worden waited to reply till she was at close quarters, then stopped his engines, let his ship drift, and sent the order by speaking-tube to the turret, "Commence firing!" The *Monitor's* turret swung round, and her two guns roared out, enveloping both ships in a fog of powder smoke as the huge cannon-balls crashed on the sloping armour of the *Merrimac*. They did not penetrate it, but the theory of the Northern artillerists was that the hammering of heavy round shot on an enemy's armour would start the plates, shear bolt and rivet heads, and crush in the wooden backing, and so gradually succeed in making a breach in the armour somewhere. But throughout this fight at close quarters the *Merrimac's cuirass* remained intact.

The Southern ship was replying with a much more rapid fire from her broadside guns. Hit after hit thundered on the *Monitor's* turret, but its plating held good, though the sensation of being thus pummelled was anything but pleasant to the men inside. At an early stage of the fight a quartermaster was disabled in a star-

The Battle of Hampton Roads.
The *Merrimac* and *Monitor* engaged at close quarters

tling way. He was leaning against the inside of the turret, when a shot struck it just outside. The momentary yielding of the plating to the blow passed on the shock to the man's body, and he fell stunned and collapsed, and had to be carried below.

Although the speaking-tube from conning-tower to turret was inside the armoured deck, a similar action of a shot, that did not penetrate, smashed it up, and after this orders had to be passed with difficulty by a chain of men. And this was not the only trouble the crew of the *Monitor* had to contend with. But the *Monitor*, with all her defects, had the great advantage over the *Merrimac* of a slightly greater speed and of a much greater handiness. Her turning circle was much smaller than that of the larger ship, and she could choose her position, and evade with comparative ease any attempt of her clumsy adversary to ram and run her down. The *Merrimac*, with her damaged funnel and diminished draught on her furnaces, found it even more difficult than on the previous day to get up speed. At times she was barely moving. Her depth was also a drawback in the narrow channel. While the light-draught *Monitor* could go anywhere, the *Merrimac*, drawing 22 feet of water, was more than once aground, and was got afloat again after many anxious efforts.

The *Monitor* had a good supply of solid shot; the *Merrimac* very few, for she had been sent out, not to fight an armour-clad, but to destroy a wooden fleet. Finding that his shell-fire was making no impression on the *Monitor's* turret, and recognizing the difficulty of ramming his enemy, Commander Jones made up his mind to disregard the *Monitor* for a while, and attempt to complete the destruction of the *Minnesota*. He therefore ordered his pilot to steer across the Roads, and take up a position near the stranded frigate. The pilot afterwards confessed that he was more anxious about facing the rapid fire of the *Minnesota's* numerous guns than standing the more deliberate attack of the *Monitor's* slow fire. He could have brought the *Merrimac* within half a mile of the *Minnesota*, but he made a wide detour, and ran aground two miles from the Federal ship. When after great efforts the ironclad was floated again, the pilot declared he could not take her any nearer the *Minnesota* without grounding again, and Commander Jones reluctantly turned to renew the duel with the *Monitor*, which had been steaming slowly after him. The *Monitor's* officers thought the *Merrimac* was running away from them, and were surprised when she closed with their ship again.

Once more there was a fight at close quarters. Those who watched the battle could make out very little of what was happening, for the two ships were wrapped in clouds of powder smoke and blacker smoke from their furnaces. The *Merrimac's* funnel was down, and the smoke from her furnace-room was pouring low over her casemate. In the midst of the semi-darkness Jones tried to ram the turret-ship, and nearly succeeded. Worden, using the superior handiness of his little vessel, converted the direct attack into a glancing blow, but the Confederates thought that if they had not lost the iron wedge of their ram the day before in sinking the *Cumberland* they would have sunk the *Monitor*.

The turret-ship now kept a more respectful distance. For more than a quarter of an hour she did not fire a shot. The Confederates hoped they had permanently disabled her, but what had happened was that the *Monitor* had ceased fire in order to pass a supply of ammunition up into the turret, which could not be revolved while this was being done. Presently the *Monitor* began firing again. Jones of the *Merrimac* now changed his target. Despairing of seriously damaging the *Monitor's* turret, he concentrated his fire on her conning-tower, and before long this plan had an important result. Dana Greene gives a vivid description of the incident:—

> A shell struck the forward side of the pilot-house directly in the sight-hole or slit, and exploded, cracking the second iron log and partly lifting the top, leaving an opening. Worden was standing immediately behind this spot, and received in his face the force of the blow, which partly stunned him, and filling his eyes with powder, utterly blinded him. The injury was known only to those in the

pilot-house and its immediate vicinity. The flood of light rushing through the top of the pilot-house, now partly open, caused Worden, blind as he was, to believe that the pilot-house was seriously injured if not destroyed; he, therefore, gave orders to put the helm to starboard, and 'sheer off.' Thus the *Monitor* retired temporarily from the action, in order to ascertain the extent of the injuries she had received. At the same time Worden sent for me, and I went forward at once, and found him standing at the foot of the ladder leading to the pilot-house.

He was a ghastly sight, with his eyes closed and the blood apparently rushing from every pore in the upper part of his face. He told me that he was seriously wounded, and directed me to take command. I assisted in leading him to a sofa in his cabin, where he was tenderly cared for by Dr. Logue, and then I assumed command. Blind and suffering as he was, Worden's fortitude never forsook him; he frequently asked from his bed of pain of the progress of affairs, and when told that the *Minnesota* was saved, he said, 'Then I can die happy!'[2]

In the confusion that followed the disablement of her commander, the *Monitor* had drifted away from the *Merrimac*, but still in a position between her and the *Minnesota*. The Confederate ship fired at the temporarily disabled turret-ship a few shots, to which there was no reply. Commander Jones and his officers believed they had put their opponent out of action. But the *Merrimac* was not in a position to profit by her advantage. It was near 2 p.m. The tide was running out rapidly, and the risk of grounding was serious.

Ammunition was beginning to be scarce. The crew was exhausted, and the ship's pumps had to be kept going, for under the strain of the heavy firing, and the repeated groundings during the two days, the hull was leaking badly. Jones judged the

---

2. *Battles and Leaders of the Civil War*, vol. 1, pp. 726, 727. Worden recovered, and there was no permanent injury to his sight. He lived to be a distinguished admiral of the United States Navy.

time had come to break off the action, and the *Merrimac* turned slowly, and began to steam into the Elizabeth River, on her way back to Norfolk.

The *Monitor*, seeing her retiring, fired a few long-range shots after her. They splashed harmlessly into the water. So the famous fight ended.

On board both ships no life had been lost, and only a few men were wounded, Captain Worden's case being the most serious. In fact, there were fewer casualties than on the first day, when the loss of life in the wooden ships had been serious, and the *Merrimac*, despite her armour, had had twenty-one men killed and wounded by the lighter projectiles of the *Cumberland* and *Congress* finding their way into her casemate through the port-holes. Neither ship had suffered severe injury, though if the battle had continued, the damage done to the conning-tower of the *Monitor* might have had serious results.

When the *Merrimac* was docked at Gosport Yard, Norfolk, to be overhauled and repaired, it was found that she had ninety-seven indentations on her armour. Twenty of these were judged to be the marks of the *Monitor's* 11-inch balls. In these places the outer layer of armour-plating was cracked and badly damaged. The under layer and the wood backing were uninjured. The other seventy-seven marks were mere surface dents made by the lighter artillery of the wooden ships. The *Monitor* had used reduced charges of 15 pounds of gunpowder, and it was believed that if the full charge of 30 pounds had been used, the results might have been more serious, but the Navy Department had ordered the reduced charge, as it was feared that with full charges the strain on the gun-mountings and turret-gear would be too severe. The *Merrimac's* funnel was riddled, and all outside fittings shot away. Two of her guns had been made unserviceable on the first day by shots striking their muzzles.

Both sides claimed the victory in the Sunday's battle. The Confederates claimed to have driven off the *Monitor*, and stated that Jones had waited for some time for her to renew the fight, before he turned back to Norfolk. The Federals argued that the object of the *Merrimac* was to destroy the *Minnesota*, and the *Monitor* had prevented this, and was therefore the victor. The frigate was successfully floated next tide. Sometimes the fight is described as a drawn battle, but most writers on the subject accept the Federal contention, and give the honours of the day to the little turret-ship.

The battle of Hampton Roads was notable, however, not so much for its immediate results, as for its effect on naval opinion and policy. It finally closed the era of unarmoured ships; it led to a perhaps exaggerated importance being attached to the ram as a weapon of attack; and it led to a very general adoption of the armoured turret, and for a while to the building of low-freeboard turret-ships in various navies. It was not till long after that the story of the *Monitor's* perilous voyage from New York was told, and thus even in America it was not realized that the *Monitor* type was fit only for smooth waters, and was ill adapted for sea-going ships.

On the Federal side there was a kind of enthusiasm for the *Monitor*. Numbers of low-freeboard turret-ships of somewhat larger size, and with improved details, were built for the United States, and even the failure of Admiral Dupont's *Monitor* fleet in the attack on the Charleston batteries did not convince the Navy Department that the type was defective. Ericsson's building of the *Monitor* to meet the emergency of 1862 was a stroke of genius, but its success had for a long time a misleading effect on the development of naval construction in the United States.

The *Merrimac* was abandoned and burned by the Confederates a few weeks later when they evacuated Norfolk and the neighbourhood. At the end of the year the *Monitor* was ordered to Charleston. She started in tow of a powerful tug, but the fate she had so narrowly escaped on her first voyage overtook her. She was caught in a gale off Cape Hatteras on the evening of 31 December, 1862. The tow-ropes had to be cut, and shortly after midnight the *Monitor* sank ten miles off the Cape. Several of her officers and men went down with her. The rest were rescued by the tug, with great difficulty.

Had the wind blown a little harder during the *Monitor's* first voyage from New York, or had the tow-rope to which she hung parted, there is no doubt she would have gone down in the same way. In that case the course of history would have been different, for the *Merrimac* would have been undisputed master of the Atlantic coast, and have driven off or destroyed every ship of the blockading squadrons. The fates of nations sometimes depend on trifles. That of the American Union depended for some hours on the soundness of the hawser by which the *Monitor* hung on to the tug-boat *Seth Low* of New York.

CHAPTER 11

Lissa 1866

In the American Civil War there had been no battle between ironclad fleets. *Monitors* had engaged batteries. The *Merrimac* had had her duel with the first of the little turret-ships. But experts were still wondering what would happen when fleets of armoured ships, built in first-class dockyards, met in battle on the sea.

The war between Austria and Italy in 1866 gave the first answer. The experiment was not a completely satisfactory one, and some of its lessons were misread. Others were soon made obsolete by new developments in naval armaments.

Still, Lissa will always count among the famous sea-fights of the world, for it was the first conflict in which the armoured sea-going ship took a leading part. But there is another reason: it proved in the most startling way—though neither for the first time nor the last—that men count for more than machines, that courage and enterprise can reverse in the actual fight the conditions that beforehand would seem to make defeat inevitable. "Give me plenty of iron in the men, and I don't mind so much about iron in the ships," was a pithy saying of the American Admiral Farragut. There was iron enough in the Austrian sailors, Tegethoff and Petz, to outweigh all the iron in the guns and armour of the Italian admirals, Persano and Albini, and the "iron in the men" gave victory to the fleet that on paper was doomed to destruction.

At the present time, when in our morning papers and in the

monthly reviews we find such frequent comparisons between the fleets of the Powers, comparisons almost invariably based only on questions of ships, armour, guns, and horse-power, and leaving the all-important human factor out of account, it will be interesting to compare the relative strength—on paper—of the Austrian and Italian fleets in 1866, before telling the story of Lissa.

Austria had only seven ironclads. All were of the earlier type of armour-clad ships, modelled on the lines of the old steam frigates, built of wood, and plated with thin armour. The two largest—ships of 5000 tons and 800 horse-power—mounted a battery of eighteen 48-pounder smooth bores. They had not a single rifled gun in their weak broadsides. These were the *Ferdinand Max* and the *Hapsburg*. The *Kaiser Max,* the *Prinz Eugen,* and *Don Juan de Austria* were smaller ships of 3500 tons and 650 horse-power, but they had a slightly better armament, sixteen smooth-bore muzzle-loading 48-pounders, and fourteen rifled guns, light breech-loading 24-pounders.

The *Salamander* and the *Drache* were ships of 3000 tons and 500 horse-power. They mounted sixteen rifled 24-pounders and ten smooth-bore 48-pounders. These five smaller ironclads were the only ships under the Austrian flag at all up to date. There were an old wooden screw line-of-battle ship and four wooden frigates, but these had neither rifled guns nor armour, and the naval critics of the day would doubtless refuse to take them into account. Then there were some wooden unarmoured gunboats and dispatch vessels.

Now turning to the Italian Navy List, we find that these six ironclads, two of them without a single rifled gun, would have to face no less than twelve armoured ships, every one of them carrying rifled guns. One of them was a thoroughly up-to-date vessel, just commissioned from Armstrong's yard at Elswick, the armoured turret-ram *Affondatore* (i.e. *The Sinker*). A correspondent of *The Times* saw her when she put into Cherbourg on the way down Channel. He reported that she looked formidable enough to sink the whole Austrian ironclad fleet single-handed.

She was a ship of 4000 tons and 750 horse-power, iron-built, heavily armoured, and with a spur-bow for ramming. She carried in her turret two 10-inch rifled Armstrong guns, throwing an armour-piercing shell of 295 pounds—say 300-pounders, and let us remember the heaviest rifled gun in the Austrian fleet was the little 24-pounder.

Then there were two wooden ironclads of 5700 tons and 800 horse-power, the *Re d'Italia* and the *Re di Portogallo*. The *Re di Portogallo* carried 28 rifled guns, two 300-pounders, twelve 100-pounders, and fourteen 74-pounders. The *Re d'Italia* mounted thirty-two rifled guns, two 150-pounders, sixteen 100-pounders, fourteen 74-pounders, and besides these four smooth-bore 50-pounders. On paper these three ships, the two *Kings*[1] and the *Affondatore*, ought to have blown the Austrian ironclads out of the sea or sent them to the bottom. Let us compare the number of rifled guns and the weight of metal. There is no need to count the smooth-bores, for the *Merrimac-Monitor* fight had proved how little they could do even against weak armour. Here is the balance-sheet:—

AUSTRIANS.

Ships.	Rifled Guns.	Projectile. lbs.
Ferdinand Max	none	—
Hapsburg	none	—
Kaiser Max	14	24
Prinz Eugen	14	24
Don Juan	14	24
Drache	16	24
Salamander	16	24
Total	74 guns throwing 1776 lbs. of metal.	

---

1. *Re d'Italia* (King of Italy); *Re di Portogallo* (King of Portugal).

ITALIANS.

Ships.	Rifled Guns.	Projectile. lbs.
Affondatore	02	300
Re d'Italia	02	150
	16	100
	14	074
Re di Portogallo	02	300
	12	100
	14	074
Total	62 guns	

throwing 6372 lbs. of metal.

Even the *Affondatore* was supposed to be what the *Dreadnought* is to older ships in these paper estimates. What would she be with the two *Kings* helping her? But this was not all; the Italians could place in line nine more ironclads. Here is this further list:—

Ship	Tonnage.	Horse-power.	Rifled Guns.	Weight of Broadside. lbs.
Ancona	4250	700	02 100-pders 01 074-pder	2274
Maria Pia	4250	700	18 100-pders 04 074-pders	2096
Castelfidardo	4250	700	22 100-pders 01 074-pder	2274
San Martino	4250	700	16 100-pders 06 074-pders	2044
Principe di Carignano[2]	4000	700	12 100-pders 06 074-pders	1644
Terribile	2700	400	10 100-pders 06 074-pders	1444
Formidabile	2700	400	10 100-pders 06 074-pders	1444

---

2. The *Principe di Carignano* was wooden built; all the rest iron.

Ship	Tonnage.	Horse-power.	Rifled Guns.	Weight of Broadside. lbs.
Palestro	2000	300	02 150-pders	0300
Varese	2000	300	02 100-pders	
			02 150-pders	050

Total 9 ships carrying 146 rifled guns throwing 14,020 lbs. metal

What could the seven Austrian ironclads with their 74 little guns throwing 1776 pounds of metal do against these nine ships with double the number of guns and nearly ten times the weight of metal in their broadsides? But add in the three capital ships before noted on the Italian side, and we have:—

- 12 ironclads against 7.
- 208 rifled guns against 74.
- 20,392 pounds of metal in the broadsides against only 1776.

Clearly it would be mad folly for the Austrian fleet to challenge a conflict! It would be swept from the Adriatic at the first encounter!

Here, then, are our calculations as to the command of the Adriatic at the outset of the war of 1866. They leave out of account only one element—the men, and the spirit of the men. Let us see how the grim realities of war can give the lie to paper estimates.

Wilhelm von Tegethoff, who commanded the Austrian fleet with the rank of rear-admiral, was one of the world's great sailors, and the man for the emergency. He had as a young officer taken part in the blockade of Venice during the revolution of 1848 and 1849; he had seen something of the naval operations in the Black Sea during the Crimean War, as the commander of a small Austrian steamer, and during the war of 1864 he had commanded the wooden steam frigate *Schwarzenberg* in the fight with the Danes off Heligoland. Besides these war services he had taken part in an exploring expedition in the Red Sea and Somaliland, and he had made more than one voyage as staff-captain to the Archduke Maximilian, whose favourite officer and close friend he had been for years. When the Archduke, an enthusiastic sailor, resigned his command of the Austrian fleet to embark for Mexico, where a short-lived reign as Emperor and a tragic death awaited him, he told his brother, the Emperor Francis Joseph, that Tegethoff was the hope of the Austrian navy.

The young admiral (he was not yet forty years of age) had concentrated his fleet at Pola, the Austrian naval port near Trieste. He had got together every available ship, not only the seven ironclads, but the old line-of-battle ship and the wooden frigates and gunboats. The Admiralty at Vienna had suggested that he should take only the ironclads to sea, but he had replied: "Give me every ship you have. You may depend on my finding some good use for them."

He believed in his officers and men, and relied on them to make a good fight on board anything that would float, whether the naval experts considered it was out of date or not. Among his officers he had plenty of men who were worthy of their chief and inspired with his own dauntless spirit, and the crews were largely composed of excellent material, men from the wilderness of creek and island that extends along the Illyrian and Dalmatian shores, fishermen and coasting sailors, many of them so lately joined that instead of uniform they still wore their picturesque native costume. The crew looked a motley lot, but, to use Farragut's phrase, *there was iron in the men.*

Twenty-seven ships in all, small and large, were moored in four lines in the roadstead of Fasana, near Pola. But they did not remain idly at their anchors. Every day some of them ran out to sea, to fire at moving targets or to practise rapid turning and ramming floating rafts. The bows were strengthened by cross timbers in all the larger ships, and in the target work the crews were taught to concentrate the fire of several guns on one spot. But Tegethoff knew he had not a single gun in his fleet that could pierce the armour of the Italian vessels. He told his officers that for decisive results they must trust to the ram. He had painted his ships a dead black. The Italian colour was grey.

"When we get into the fight," said Tegethoff, "you must ram away at anything you see painted grey."

War was declared on 20 June. Tegethoff had been training his fleet since 9 May, and was ready for action. He at once sent out the *Stadion* (a passenger steamer of the Austrian Lloyd line, employed as a scout and armed with two 12-pounders) to reconnoitre the Italian coast of the Adriatic. The *Stadion* returned on the 23rd with news that though war had been expected for weeks the Italian fleet was not yet concentrated. A few of the ships were at Ancona, but the greater part of it was reported to be at Taranto, with Admiral Count Persano, the commander-in-chief, who from the first displayed the strangest irresolution.

Tegethoff was anxious to attempt to engage the division at Ancona before it was joined by the main body from Taranto, but he was held back by orders from his Government directing him to remain in the Northern Adriatic covering Venice. It was not till 26 June that he obtained a free hand within limits defined by an order not to go further south than the fortified island of Lissa.

He left Pola that evening with six ironclads, the wooden frigate *Schwarzenberg*, five gunboats, and the scouting steamer Stadion. He had hoisted his rear-admiral's flag on the *Erzherzog Ferdinand Max*.[3] He made for Ancona, and was off the port at dawn next day. The first shots of the naval war were fired in the grey of the morning, when three of the Austrian gunboats chased the Italian dispatch vessel *Esploratore* into the port, outside of which she had been on the look-out. The Austrians were able clearly to see and count the warships under the batteries in the harbour. Besides other craft, there were eleven of Persano's twelve ironclads, the squadron from Taranto having reached Ancona the day before. Only the much-vaunted *Affondatore* had not yet joined.

Tegethoff cleared for action, and steamed up and down for

---

3. This was one of his least powerfully-armed ironclads, but Tegethoff seems to have selected her as his flagship because she was named after his old friend and chief, the Archduke Ferdinand Maximilian, who was at that time Emperor of Mexico, and involved in the final stage of the struggle that ended in his capture and execution by the Republican Juarez.

some hours, just beyond the range of the coast batteries. It was a challenge to the Italians to come out and fight. But Persano did not accept it. He afterwards made excuses to his Government, saying he had not yet completed the final fitting out of his ships. The moral effect on both fleets was important. The Austrians felt an increased confidence in their daring leader and a growing contempt for their adversaries. On the 24th the Austrian army, under the Archduke Albert, had beaten the Italians at Custozza, and the Austrian navy looked forward to the same good fortune. The Italians were depressed both by the news of Custozza and the hesitation of their admiral to risk anything.

Early in the day Tegethoff started on his return voyage to Fasana, where he arrived in the evening, and found the ironclad *Hapsburg* waiting to join his flag, after having been refitted in the dockyard of Pola. As there were now persistent rumours that the Italians were going to attempt an attack on Venice, Tegethoff remained in the Fasana roadstead, continuing the training of his fleet. On 6 July he again took it to sea, practised fleet manœuvres under steam, and showed himself in sight of Ancona. But the Italian fleet was still lying idly in the harbour, and Tegethoff once more returned to Fasana in the hope that Persano would attempt some enterprise, during which he would be able to fall upon him in the open.

The Italian admiral was meanwhile wasting time in lengthy correspondence with his Government, and sending it letters which revealed his irresolution and incompetence so plainly that they ought to have led to his immediate supersession. He complained he had not definite orders, though he had been directed to destroy the Austrian fleet, if it put to sea, or blockade it, if it remained in harbour. He explained now that he was mounting better guns in some of his ships, now that he was waiting for the Affondatore to join.

Once he actually wrote saying that some new ironclads ought to be purchased from other powers to reinforce him. At last he was plainly told that if he did not at once do something for the honour of the Italian navy he would be relieved of his command. With the Austrians victorious in Northern Italy, a raid on Venice would have been too serious an operation, but he proposed as an alternative that a small land force should be embarked for a descent on the fortified island of Lissa, on the Dalmatian coast. His fleet would escort it, and co-operate by bombarding the island batteries. The plan was accepted, and he proceeded to execute it.

It was about as bad a scheme as could be imagined. It is a recognized principle of war that over-sea expeditions should only be undertaken when the enemy's fleet has been either rendered helpless by a crushing defeat or blockaded in its ports. Before sending the transports to Lissa Persano should have steamed across to Pola and blockaded Tegethoff, fighting him if he came out. But Persano had a delusive hope that he could perhaps score a victory without encountering the Austrian fleet by swooping down on Lissa, crushing the batteries with a heavy bombardment, landing the troops, hoisting the Italian flag, and getting back to his safe anchorage at Ancona before Tegethoff could receive news of what was happening, and come out and force on a battle.

Lissa was defended by a garrison of 1800 men, under Colonel Urs de Margina. This small body of troops held a number of forts and batteries mounting eighty-eight guns, none of them of large calibre. The works were old, and had been hurriedly repaired. Most of them dated from the time of the English occupation of the island during the Napoleonic wars.[4] Persano expected that Lissa would be a very easy nut to crack.

On 16 July the Italian fleet sailed from Ancona. Even now Persano carried out his operations with leisurely deliberation. On the 17th he reconnoitred Lissa, approaching in his flagship under French colours. Early on the 18th the fleet closed in upon the island, flying French colours, till it was in position before the batteries.

The commandant had cable communication with Pola by a

---

4. Some of the forts were still known by English names, such as Wellington Tower, Bentinck Tower, and Robertson Tower.

line running by Lesina to the mainland. He reported to Tegethoff the appearance of the disguised fleet, and then the opening of the attack on his batteries. At first the Austrian admiral could hardly believe that the Italians had committed themselves to such an ill-judged enterprise, and thought that the attack on Lissa might be only a feint meant to draw his fleet away from the Northern Adriatic, and leave an opening for a dash at Pola, Trieste, or Venice itself.

But cablegrams describing the progress of the attack convinced him it was meant to be pressed home, and he telegraphed to Colonel de Margina, telling him to hold out to the last extremity, and promising to come to his relief with all the fleet. This message did not reach the colonel, for just before it was dispatched an Italian ship had cut the cable between Lissa and Lesina, and seized the telegraph office of the latter island. Tegethoff's message thus fell into Persano's hands. He persuaded himself that it was mere bluff, intended to encourage the commandant of Lissa to hold out as long as possible. He thought Tegethoff would remain in the Northern Adriatic to protect or to overawe Venice.

The attempt to reduce the batteries of Lissa by bombardment during the 18th proved a failure. In the evening Persano was in a very anxious state of mind. He had made no arrangements for colliers to supply his fleet, and his coal was getting low. It was just possible that Tegethoff might come out and force him to fight, and he thought of returning to Ancona. But if he did he would be dismissed from his command. At last he made up his mind to land the troops next morning, and try to carry the forts by an assault combined with an attack from the sea. His second in command, Admiral Albini, with the squadron of wooden ships and gunboats that accompanied the ironclads, was directed to superintend and assist in the landing of the troops. They were to be embarked in all available boats, and to land at 9 a.m. During the night the ram *Affondatore* joined the fleet, and Persano had all his twelve ironclads before Lissa.

On the morning of the 18th the sea was smooth, and covered with a hot haze that limited the view. The soldiers were being got into the boats, and the ships were steaming to their stations for the attack, when about eight o'clock the *Esploratore*, which had been sent off to scout to the north-westward, appeared steaming fast out of a bank of haze with a signal flying, which was presently read, "Suspicious-looking ships in sight." Tegethoff was coming.

He had left Fasana late on the afternoon of the 18th, with every available ship, large and small, new and old, wooden wall and ironclad. He would find work for all of them. All night he had steamed for Lissa, anxious at the sudden cessation of the cable messages, but still hoping that he would see the Austrian flag flying on its forts, or if not, that he would at least find the enemy's fleet still in its waters.

He had organized his fleet in three divisions. The first under his own personal command was formed of the seven ironclads. The second division, under Commodore von Petz, was composed of wooden unarmoured ships. The commodore's flag flew on the old steam line-of-battle ship *Kaiser*, a three-decker with ninety-two guns on her broadsides, all smooth-bores except a couple of rifled 24-pounders. With the *Kaiser* were five old wooden ships (*Novara, Schwarzenberg, Donau, Adria,* and *Radetzky*) and a screw corvette, the *Erzherzog Friedrich*. The third division, under Commandant Eberle, was composed of ten gunboats. A dispatch-boat was attached to each of the leading divisions, and the scout *Stadion*, the swiftest vessel in the fleet, was at the immediate disposal of the admiral, and was sent on in advance.

The fleet steamed during the night in the order of battle that Tegethoff had chosen. The divisions followed each other in succession, each in a wedge formation, the flagship of the division in the centre with the rest of the ships to port and starboard, not in line abreast, but each a little behind the other. The formation will be understood from the annexed diagram.

It was an anxious night for the Austrian admiral. For some hours there was bad weather. Driving showers of fine rain from

LISSA. BATTLE FORMATION OF THE AUSTRIAN FLEET

a cloudy sky made it difficult at times to see the lights of the ships, and it was no easy matter for them to keep their stations. The sea was for a while so rough that the ironclads had to close their ports, and there was a danger that if the weather did not improve and the sea become smoother they would not be able to fight most of their guns. But Tegethoff held steadily on his course for Lissa. On sea, as on land, there are times in the crisis of a war when the highest prudence is to throw all ordinary rules of prudence aside, and take all risks.

The admiral had resolved from the outset that, whatever might be the result, the Austrian fleet should not lie in safety under the protection of shore batteries, leaving the Italian command of the Adriatic unchallenged. He felt that it would be better to sink in the open sea, in a hopeless fight against desperate odds, rather than ingloriously to survive the war, without making an effort to carry his flag to victory. So he steamed through the night, followed by his strange array of ships that another leader might well have considered as little better than useless encumbrances, and in front the handful of inferior ironclads that might well be regarded as equally doomed to destruction when they met the more numerous and more heavily armed ships of the enemy.

But he had put away all thoughts of safety. He was staking every ship and every man and his own life against the faint chance of success. The coming day might see his fleet destroyed, but such a failure would be no disgrace. On the contrary, it would only be less honourable than a well-won victory, and would be an inspiration to the men of a future fleet that would carry the banner of the Hapsburgs in later days. So he rejoiced greatly when, as the day came, the weather began to clear, and the *Stadion* signalled back that Lissa was still holding out and the enemy's fleet lay under its shores.

As soon as he read the *Esploratore's* signal, Persano had no doubt that Tegethoff was upon him. He countermanded the attack on Lissa, ordered Albini to re-embark the troops, and proceeded to form his ironclads in line of battle, intending to engage the enemy with these only. The ironclads were standing in to attack the batteries of San Giorgio at the north-east end of the island. Persano formed nine of them in three divisions, which were to follow each other in line ahead, the ram Affondatore being out of the line and to starboard of the second division. The formation was as follows:—

First Division.

Rear-Admiral Vacca
Principe di Carignano.
Castelfidardo.
Ancona.

Second Division.

Rear-Admiral Faa di Bruno
Re d'Italia.
Palestro.
San Martino.
Affondatore. (to starboard of the line).

Third Division.

Rear-Admiral Ribotti
Re di Portogallo.
Maria Pia.
Varese.

The two other Italian ironclads, the *Formidabile* and the *Varese*, were not in the line, and took no part in the coming battle. The *Formidabile* had suffered heavily in the attack on the shore batteries, numerous shells entering her port-holes and making a slaughterhouse of her gun-deck. She had been ordered to Ancona, and had left Lissa in the early morning. The *Varese* had been detached to assist in operations on the other side of the island, and joined Albini's squadron of wooden ships while the fight was in progress. Persano's battle line first steered west along the north side of Lissa. About ten o'clock the driving mist on the sea cleared, and the Austrian fleet was then seen approaching on a S.S.E. course. Persano altered his own course, and, led by Vacca in the *Principe di Carignano*, the Italian ironclads turned in succession on a N.N.E. course. Thus as the Austrians closed on them the fleet in a sinuous line was steering across the bows of the attacking ships.

It was at this moment that Persano changed his flag from the *Re d' Italia* to the *Affondatore*, the former ship slowing down to enable the admiral to leave her, and thus producing a wide gap between Vacca's and Faa di Bruno's divisions. The result of this sudden change of flagship was confusing, as most of the Italian ships were unaware of it, and still looked to the *Re d' Italia* for guidance, and did not notice signals made by the Affondatore.

Tegethoff had given the successive signals as the mist dispersed, "Clear for action—Close order—Look-out ships return to their stations—Full speed ahead." As the last of the fog disappeared and the sun shone out, he saw to his delight the Austrian flag still flying on the hill-side batteries of Lissa, and close in front between him and the island shores the enemy's fleet crossing his bows. Out fluttered his battle signal, "Ironclads will ram and sink the enemy!"

A final signal was being prepared, "*Muss Sieg von Lissa werden!*" ("There must be a victory of Lissa!"), but the close encounter had begun, and the ships were wrapped in clouds of powder-smoke before it could be hoisted.

While Persano was passing from the *Re d' Italia* to the ram Affondatore, Vacca had begun the fight by firing his broadside at the advancing Austrians. The *Castelfidardo* and the *Ancona* followed his example. But Tegethoff held his fire, waiting for close quarters. One of these first shots killed Captain Moll of the *Drache* on the bridge of his ship. A young lieutenant took command of her. He was Weiprecht, who in later years became famous as the commander of the Austrian exploring ship *Tegethoff* in the Arctic regions.

As the fleets closed the Austrians opened fire, aiming, not at the armoured sides of the enemy, which no gun of theirs could penetrate, but at their port-holes and bridges. Tegethoff in his flagship the *Ferdinand Max* was looking for something to ram, but in the dense mass of smoke he passed through the wide gap

BATTLE OF LISSA
THE AUSTRIAN ATTACK AT THE BEGINNING OF THE BATTLE

between Vacca's division and the *Re d'Italia,* then finding no enemy in his front, he turned and went back into the battle fog of the Italian centre. The three ironclads on his left (*Hapsburg, Salamander,* and *Kaiser Max*) were engaged with Vacca's division, the van of the Italian fleet.

The three others, *Don Juan, Drache,* and *Prinz Eugen,* had flung themselves on Faa di Bruno's ships in the centre. Von Petz coming up with the wooden ships gallantly attacked Ribotti's rearward division, any one of which should in theory have been able to dispose of his entire force. The gunboats hung on the margin of the fight, which had now become a confused *mêlée.* And while the Austrian wooden ships were thus risking themselves in close action, Albini's Italian division of wooden ships looked on from a safe distance.

One can only tell some of the striking incidents of the battle, without being able even to fix the precise order of time in which they occurred. When the *Merrimac* sank the *Cumberland* with one blow of her ram in Hampton Roads, the Federal ship was at anchor. But even in the confusion and semi-darkness of the *mêlée* at Lissa it was found that it was not such an easy matter to ram a ship under way. The blow was generally eluded by a turn of the helm. Von Petz's flagship, the old three-decker *Kaiser,* towering amid the battle-smoke, attracted the attention of Persano in the *Affondatore,* and seemed an easy victim for his ram.

But the big ironclad was unhandy, and took eight minutes to turn a full circle, and twice Petz eluded her attack. The two 300-pounders of the *Affondatore* did much damage on board the *Kaiser,* but the wooden ship's broadside swept the upper works of the ram as the two vessels passed each other, and strewed her deck with wreckage. The fire of the heavy rifled guns on the Italian ironclads did severe execution on the Austrian wooden ships. The captain of the *Novara* was killed; the *Erzherzog Friedrich* and the *Schwarzenberg* were badly hulled, and leaked so that they were only kept afloat by their steam pumps. The *Adria* was three times on fire. But Petz and the wooden division did good service by keeping the rearward Italian ships fully occupied.

Meanwhile Tegethoff, standing on the bridge of the *Ferdinand Max*, all reckless of the storm of fire that roared around him had dashed into the Italian centre. He rammed first the *Re d'Italia*, then the *Palestro*, but both ships evaded the full force of the blow, and the Austrian flagship scraped along their sides, bringing down a lot of gear. The mizzen-topmast and gaff of the *Palestro* came down with the shock, and the gaff fell across the Austrian's deck, with the Italian tricolour flying from it.

Before the ships could clear an Austrian sailor secured the flag. It would seem that the glancing blow given to the *Re d'Italia* had disorganized her steering gear, and for a while she was not under control. Two other ships joined the flagship in attacking her, all believing she was still Persano's flagship. The *Palestro*, fighting beside her, was set on fire by shells passing through her unarmoured stern. The fire made such rapid progress that she drew out of the fight, her crew trying to save their ship.

Von Sterneck, the captain of the *Ferdinand Max,* had gone half-way up the mizzen-rigging, to look out over the smoke; he reported that the *Re d'Italia* was not under full control, and Tegethoff once more dashed at his enemy. The bow of the *Ferdinand* Max this time struck the *Re d'Italia* full amidships, and simply forced in her side, making an enormous gap, crushing and smashing plates and frames. As the *Ferdinand Max* reversed her engines and drew her bows out of her adversary's side, the *Re d'Italia* heeled over and sank instantly, carrying hundreds to the bottom and strewing the surface with wreckage and struggling men.

The Austrians, after a moment of astonished horror at their own success, cheered wildly. The *Ferdinand Max* tried to save some of the drowning men, and was lowering her only boat that remained unshattered by the fire, when the Italian ironclad *Ancona* tried to ram her. The Austrian flagship evaded the blow, and the *Ancona*, as she slid past her, almost touching her gun-muzzles, fired a broadside into her. The powder-smoke from the Italian guns poured into the port-holes of the *Ferdinand Max*, and for a few moments smothered her gun-deck in fog, but it was a harmless broadside. In their undisciplined haste to fire the Italians had loaded only with the cartridge, there was not a shot in the guns. This tells something of the confusion on board.

Another Austrian ironclad and two of the gunboats made plucky efforts to save some of the survivors of the *Re d'Italia*, but they, too, were driven off by the fierce attacks of Italian ships.

Meanwhile Petz with his wooden ships had fought his way through the Italian rear. With his old three-decker he boldly rammed the *Re di Portogallo*. The Italian ship evaded the full force of the blow, but the tall wooden vessel scraped along her side, starting several of her armour plates, carrying away porthole covers and davits, dragging two anchors from her bows, smashing gun-muzzles and jerking four light guns into the sea. But the *Kaiser* herself suffered from the close fire of the *Re di Portogallo's* heavy guns and the shock of collision. Her stem and bowsprit were carried away, the gilded crown of her figure-head falling on her enemy's deck. Her foremast came crashing down on her funnel, and wrecked it, and the mass of fallen spars, sails, and rigging was set on fire by sparks and flame from the damaged funnel, the collapse of which nearly stopped the draught of the furnaces and dangerously reduced the pressure on the boilers and the speed of the engines.

The *Re di Portogallo* sheered off, but her consort, the *Maria Pia*, came rushing down on the disabled *Kaiser*. Petz avoided her ram, and engaged her at close quarters, but the shells of the *Maria Pia* burst one of the *Kaiser's* steam-pipes, temporarily disabled her steering gear, and did terrible execution in her stern battery. Petz himself was slightly wounded. With great difficulty he extricated his ship from the *mêlée*, and cutting away the wreckage, and fighting the fire that was raging forward, he steered for San Giorgio, the port of Lissa, to seek shelter under its batteries. His wooden frigates gallantly protected his retreat and escorted him to safety, then turned back to join once more in the fight. This was the moment when Albini with the Italian wooden squadron might easily have destroyed Petz's division, but during the day all he did was to fire a few shots at a range so distant that they were harmless.

Persano, in the *Affondatore*, had for a moment threatened to attack the *Kaiser*, as she struggled out of the *mêlée*. He steamed towards her, and then suddenly turned away. He afterwards explained that, seeing the plight of Petz's flagship, he thought she was already doomed to destruction, and looked upon it as useless cruelty to sink her with her crew.

The fleets were now separating, and the fire was slackening. In this last stage of the *mêlée* the *Maria Pia* and the *San Martino* collided amid the smoke, and the latter received serious injuries. As the fleets worked away from each other there was still a desultory fire kept up, but after having lasted for about an hour and a half the battle was nearly over.

Tegethoff, having got between the Italians and Lissa, reformed his fleet in three lines of divisions, each in line ahead, the ironclads to seaward nearest the enemy; the wooden frigates next; and the gunboats nearest the land. Every ship except the *Kaiser* (which lay in the entrance of the port) was still ready for action. Some of them were leaking badly, including his flagship, which had started several plates in the bow when she rammed and sank the *Re d'Italia*. The fleet steamed slowly out from the land on a north-easterly course, the ironclads firing a few long-ranging shots at the Italians.

Persano was also reforming his fleet in line, and was flying a signal to continue the action, but he showed no determined wish to close with Tegethoff again. On the contrary, while reforming the line he kept it on a northwesterly course, and thus the distance between the fleets was increasing every minute, as they were moving on divergent lines. Gradually the firing died away and the battle was over. Albini, with the wooden squadron, and the ironclad *Terribile*, which had remained with him, and taken no part in the fight, ran out and joined the main fleet.

Persano afterwards explained that he was waiting for Tegethoff to come out and attack him. But the Austrian admiral had attained his object, by forcing his way through the Italian line, and placing himself in a position to co-operate with the batteries of Lissa, in repelling any further attempt upon the island. There was no reason why, with his numerically inferior fleet, he should come out again to fight a second battle.

But though the action was ended, there was yet another disaster for the Italians. The *Palestro* had been for two hours fighting the fire lighted on board of her by the Austrian shells. Smoke was rising from hatchways and port-holes, but as she rejoined the fleet she signalled that the fire was being got under and the magazines had been drowned. Two of the smaller ships, the *Governolo* and the *Independenza*, came to her help and took off her wounded. To a suggestion that he should abandon his ship, her commander, Capellini, replied: "Those who wish may go, but I shall stay," and his officers and men remained with him, and continued working to put out the fire. But the attempt to drown the magazines had been a failure, for suddenly a deafening explosion thundered over the sea, the spars of the *Palestro* were seen flying skyward in a volcano of flame. As the smoke of the explosion cleared, the heaving water strewn with debris showed where the ship had been.

The Austrian fleet was steaming into San Giorgio, amid the cheers of the garrison and the people, when the explosion of the *Palestro* took place. Persano drew off with his fleet into the channel between Lissa and the island of Busi, and when the sun went down the Italian ships were still in sight from the look-out stations on the hills of Lissa.

The Austrians worked all night repairing damages, and preparing for a possible renewal of the fight in the morning. But at sunrise the look-outs reported that there was not an Italian ship in sight. Persano had steered for Ancona after dark, and arrived there on the 21st.

He was so unwise as to report that he had won a great naval victory in a general engagement with the Austrians in the waters of Lissa. Italy, already smarting under the defeat of Custozza, went wild with rejoicing. Cities were illuminated, salutes were fired, there was a call for high honours for the victorious admiral. But within forty-eight hours the truth was known. It was impossible to conceal the fact that Lissa had been unsuccessfully attacked for two days, and that on the third it had been relieved by Tegethoff dashing through the Italian fleet, and destroying the *Re d'Italia* and the *Palestro*, without himself losing a single ship. There were riots in Florence, and the cry was now that Admiral Persano was a coward and a traitor. To add to the gloom of the moment the ram *Affondatore*, which had been injured in the battle, sank at her anchors when a sudden gale swept the roadstead of Ancona.

Three of the twelve Italian ironclads had thus been lost. Three more were unavailable while their damages were being slowly repaired. Peace was concluded shortly after, and the Italian navy had no opportunity of showing what it could do under a better commander.

In the sinking of the *Re d'Italia* some 450 men had been drowned. More than 200 lost their lives in the explosion of the *Palestra*, but the other losses of the Italians in the Battle of Lissa were slight, only five killed and 39 wounded. The Austrians lost 38 killed (including two captains) and 138 wounded. These losses were not severe, considering that several wooden ships had been exposed to heavy shell-fire at close quarters, and one must conclude that the gunnery of the Italian crews was wretched. The heaviest loss fell on Petz's flagship, the *Kaiser*, which had 99 killed and wounded. Some of the gunboats, among which were some old paddle-ships, though they took part in the fighting, had not a single casualty.

Persano was tried by court-martial and deprived of his rank and dismissed from the navy. Tegethoff became the hero of Austria. His successful attack on a fleet that in theory should have been able to destroy every one of his ships in an hour, will remain for all time an honour to the Austrian navy, and a proof that skill and courage can hope to reverse the most desperate disadvantages.

CHAPTER 12

The Battle of the Yalu 1894

One result of the victory won by Tegethoff at Lissa was that an exaggerated importance was for many years to come attached to the ram as a weapon of attack. In every navy in the world ships were built with bows specially designed for ramming. The sinking of the *Re d'Italia* had made such an impression on the public mind, that it was in vain for a minority among naval critics to urge that the ram was being overrated, and to point out that even at Lissa for one successful attempt to sink an enemy by running her down there had been an untold number of failures. It was very gradually that the majority was brought to realize that a ship under full control could generally avoid a ramming attack, and that it could only be employed under exceptional circumstances, and against an already disabled enemy.

Then the progress of invention and armaments introduced features into naval warfare that made it extremely difficult and dangerous for a large ship to come to such close quarters as an attempt to ram implies. First the introduction of the Whitehead torpedo as part of the auxiliary armament of battleships and cruisers gave the ship attacked a means of sinking the aggressor as she approached, and the increase in the power of guns led naval tacticians to accept as a principle that fleet actions must be fought at ranges which were regarded as too distant for any effective action in earlier days.

But for nearly thirty years after Lissa there were no fleet actions. Ships, armour, guns, were all improved, and the great naval

Powers built on a larger and larger scale. Steel took the place of iron as the material for shipbuilding and armour. Naval gunnery became a precise science. Torpedoes were introduced, and with them such new types of ships as the swift torpedo boat and the "destroyer." But there was very little fighting on the sea, though in the same period there were colossal conflicts on land.

Hundreds of armour-clads were built that became obsolete, and were turned over to the shipbreaker, without ever having fired a shot in action. Theories of tactics for fleet actions were worked out on paper, and tested to some extent at naval manœuvres, but the supreme test of battle was wanting. In the Franco-German War of 1870 the French navy had such a decided superiority that the few German warships of the day were kept in their harbours protected by batteries and sunken mines. The only naval action of the war was an indecisive duel between two gunboats. In the second stage of the war the officers and men of the French navy fought as soldiers in the defence of France. Guns were taken from the ships to be mounted on land fortifications. Admirals commanded divisions, formed largely of naval officers and bluejackets.

Again in the war of 1878 between Russia and Turkey the Russians had only a few light craft in the Black Sea, and the Turkish fleet under Hobart Pasha, weak as it was, held the undisputed command of these waters, and had only to fear some isolated torpedo attacks. In South American civil wars and international conflicts there were duels between individual ships, and some dashing enterprises by torpedo boats, but nothing that could be described as a fleet action between ironclads. The only time a British armoured fleet was in action was against the batteries of Alexandria on the occasion of the bombardment in July, 1882.

The forts, badly armed and constructed, and inefficiently defended, were silenced, but a careful examination of them convinced experts that if they had been held by a better-trained garrison, the victory would not have been such an easy matter. This and subsequent experiences have led to the general acceptance of the view that it will be seldom advisable to risk such valuable fighting machines as first-class battleships and armoured cruisers in close action against well-constructed and powerfully armed shore defences.

It was not till the summer of 1894 that at last there was another pitched battle between fleets that included a large proportion of armoured vessels. That action off the mouth of the Yalu River will be always remembered as the event that heralded the coming of a new naval power.

A long rivalry between China and Japan for the control of Korea had resulted in an outbreak of war between the two empires of the Far East. For an island state like Japan the command of the sea was a necessary condition for successful operations on the mainland of Asia, and for some years she had been building up a powerful fleet, the ships being constructed in foreign yards, as the Japanese yards were not yet in a position to turn out large warships.

In the memory of living men the Japanese fleets had been made up of primitive-looking war-junks. After failures to build ships in Japan on the European model, the Government had in the middle of the nineteenth century purchased some small steamships abroad, but it was not till 1876 that the first Japanese armour-clad, the *Fuso*, was constructed in England from designs by the late Sir Edward Reed. Naval progress was at first very slow, but solid foundations were laid. Young naval officers were attached to the British and other navies for professional training, and on their return to Japan became the educators of their fellow-countrymen in naval matters.

A serious obstacle to the acquisition of a numerous and powerful fleet was the financial question. Japan is not a rich country. At first, therefore, the Japanese did not venture to order battleships, but contented themselves with protected cruisers. They thought that these would be sufficient for the impending conflict with China, which possessed only a fleet of weak, protected cruisers of various types and a couple of small coast defence ironclads, that might be counted as inferior battleships.

When war broke out between China and Japan in 1894, the fleet of the latter consisted of older ships of miscellaneous types, and a number of new protected cruisers, some of them armed with quick-firing guns, a type of weapon only lately introduced into the world's navies. Of these modern cruisers most had been built and armed in French yards, but the best and swiftest ship was a fine cruiser delivered not long before from Armstrong's yard at Elswick.

The following lists give some details of the Japanese and Chinese fleets, only the ships engaged at the Yalu battle being included. But these ships represented almost the entire strength of the two rival navies, and no really effective ship was absent on either side, while to make up the two squadrons ships were sent to sea that in a European navy would have been considered obsolete and left in harbour (see tables following).

A comparison of these two lists brings out some interesting points. The advantage in gun power was clearly on the side of the Japanese. Of the heavier class of guns they had seventy to fifty-five, and there were no weapons in the Chinese squadron equal to the long 12½-inch rifled breech-loaders of French make, carried by four of the Japanese cruisers. But there was a further gain in gun power for the Japanese in the possession of 128 quick-firers, some of them of fairly heavy calibre. The quick-firing gun was then a new weapon.

It is really a quick loader, a gun fitted with a breech action that can be opened and closed by a rapid movement, and so mounted that the recoil is taken up by mechanism in the carriage which at once automatically runs the gun back into firing position, while the process of loading is further accelerated (for the smaller calibre guns) by making up the ammunition like that of a rifle, with projectile and charge in a big brass-cased cartridge, so that the gun can be loaded up by one movement, and the cartridge contains its own means of ignition, and is fired by pulling off a trigger.

The lighter quick-firers are further mounted on pivots, so that they can be easily moved through an arc of a circle by one man, who keeps his eyes on a moving target and his finger on the trigger ready to fire. The storm of shells that poured from the Japanese quick-firers was even more terrible for the Chinese than the slower fire of the heavy guns, and of these new quick-firing guns the Chinese only had three on the little Kwang-ping.

JAPANESE FLEET

Ships.	Tonnage.	Heavy Guns	Quick-firers	Mach. Guns
New protected cruisers				
Yoshino	4150	—	44	—

(Swiftest ship in either fleet: speed 23 knots; 2-inch steel protective deck. Built by Armstrong)

Matsushima	4277	12	16	06
Ikitsushima		12	16	06
Hashidate		12	16	15

(2-inch steel protective deck. Barbette forward covered with 12-inch armour, and armed with a long Canet 12½-inch gun.)

Takachico	3650	08	—	12
Naniwa Kan		08	—	12

(3-inch steel protective deck. Speed 18 knots.)

Akitsushima	3150	01	12	10

(2½-inch steel protective deck. One long 12½-inch Canet gun.)

Chiyoda	2450	—	24	13

(Small partly armoured cruiser; 4½-inch armoured belt over two-thirds of length; 1-inch steel protective deck.)

Old ironclads launched 1877–8.				
Fuso	3718	06	—	08

(4½-in. armour belt amidships.)

Hiyei	2200	09	—	—

(7-in. armour belt. 9-in. armour on battery.)

Akagi	0615	02	—	02

(Gunboat.)

Saikio Maru	0600	—	(?)	—

(Armed merchant steamer carrying only a few small quick-firers.)

		70	128	84

Chinese Fleet

Ships.	Tonnage.	Heavy Guns	Quick-firers	Mach. Guns
Armoured.				
Chen-yuen	7430	06	—	12
Ting-yuen		06	—	12

(Coast-defence battleships, 14-inch armour belt. Four 12-inch guns on each ship, mounted in pairs in turrets with 12-inch armour.)

Lai-yuen	2850	04	—	08
King-yuen		04	—	08

(Armoured cruisers, 9½-inch armour belt. 8-inch armour on barbettes forward.)

Ping-yuen	2850	03	—	08

(Armoured cruiser, 8-inch armour belt; 5 inches on barbette.)

Unarmoured.				
Tsi-yuen	2355	03	—	10
Ching-yuen	2300	05	—	16
Chi-yuen		05	—	16

(Quickest ships in the fleet: speed 18 knots.)

Yang-wei	1350	06	—	07
Chao-yung		06	—	07
Kwang-chia	1300	07	—	08
Kwang-ping	1030	—	03	08

4 torpedo-boats and 3 small gunboats.

		55	03	120

The Chinese fleet had more armour protection. The two coast-defence battleships were heavily armoured, and there were three other less completely protected ironclads, although seven other ships had no armour whatever. In the Japanese fleet the only armoured vessels were the two old ironclads, belonging to an obsolete type, and the armour-belted *Chiyoda*. The real fighting force of the fleet was made up of the seven new protected cruisers.

Some of these had armour on the barbettes in which their long bow-guns were mounted, but their "protection" consisted in a deck plated with steel covering the "vitals" of the ship, boilers, engines, and magazines, all placed as low as possible in the hull. There was some further protection afforded by the coal-bunkers placed along the water-line amidships. The theory of the protected cruiser was that everything below the water-line was safeguarded by this armoured deck, and as the over-water portion of the ship was further divided by bulk-heads into numerous water-tight compartments, the danger of the ship being sunk was remote. The protected cruiser is no longer regarded as having a place in the main fighting-line. But the Japanese cruisers gave such good results in the Yalu battle that for a while an exaggerated value was attached to it.

But in one point, and the most important of all, the Japanese had an overwhelming advantage. The Chinese officers and men were mostly brave enough, but almost entirely unskilled. The only really efficient officers and engineers they had were a few Englishmen and Americans and two Germans. The Japanese, from Admiral Count Ito, who commanded, down to the youngest of the bluejackets, were not only brave with the inherited recklessness of death and suffering, which is characteristic of their race, but were also highly trained in every branch of their profession, first-rate sailors, excellent gunners.

And the fleet had for years been exercised in manœuvres, so that the ships could work together as an organized whole. The spirit which animated it was that of "No surrender—Victory at any cost." It is a standing order of the Japanese navy that if a ship should strike her colours, the first duty of her consorts is not to try to recapture her, but to endeavour to sink her and her crew.

The Mandarin Ting, who commanded the Chinese fleet, was more of a soldier than a sailor, but he had some sea experience, and was a thoroughly brave man. As soon as war was declared he was anxious to go in search of his enemy. He urged upon the Pekin Government that the first step to be taken was to use the Chinese fleet to attack the Japanese transports, which were conveying troops to Korea. This would, of course, lead to a battle with the enemy's fleet, but Ting was quite confident that he would defeat the Japanese if he met them. In giving this advice the Chinese admiral was reasoning on correct principles, even if his confidence in his own fighting power was not justified by facts. To keep the fleet idle at Port Arthur or Wei-hai-wei would be to concede the command of the sea to Japan, without an effort to dispute it.

But the mandarins at Pekin would not accept their admiral's view. In the first place they were alarmed at the fact that in a minor naval engagement off the Korean coast, at the very outset of the conflict, the weak Chinese force in action had fared very badly. The quarrel in Korea had begun without a regular declaration of war. On the coast there were the Chinese cruiser, *Tsi-yuen*, and a small gunboat, the *Kwang-yi*.

On 24 July the two ships had gone to sea to look for, and give their escort to, some transports that were expected with reinforcements from China. In the grey of the morning on the 25th they fell in with, and were attacked by, three of the swift protected cruisers of the Japanese fleet, the *Yoshino, Akitsushima*, and *Naniwa Kan*. The fight was soon over. The gunboat was sunk, and the little cruiser was attacked at close quarters by the *Naniwa Kan*, whose shells riddled her weak conning-tower, killing all within it. The *Tsing Yuen* fled, pursued by the *Naniwa*, whose commander, by the way, was Captain Togo, famous afterwards as the victorious admiral of the Russo-Japanese War. The *Tsing Yuen* made good her escape, only because the chase brought the *Naniwa Kan* on the track of the transport *Kowshing*, and Togo stopped to dispose of her by sending her to the bottom.

This incident made the Pekin Government nervous about the fighting qualities of their ships. And then they were afraid that if Ting went to sea with all his ships, the Japanese fleet would elude him, and appear with an expeditionary force at the mouth of the Pei-ho, capture the Taku forts, and land an army to march on Pekin. They therefore ordered Admiral Ting to collect his fleet at Port Arthur, and watch the sea-approach to the capital.

The Japanese were therefore able to land their troops in Korea without interruption, and soon overran the peninsula. When they were advancing to capture Ping-yang, the Chinese began to concentrate a second army to defend the crossing of the Yalu River, the entrance into Southern Manchuria. It was now evident even to the Pekin mandarins that the Japanese plans did not at this stage of the war include a raid on the Pei-ho and the Chinese capital, so Admiral Ting was at last allowed to go to sea, in order to protect the movement of transports along the western shores of the Korean Bay to the mouth of the Yalu.

On 14 September five large steamers crowded with troops left Taku under the convoy of six Chinese cruisers and four torpedo boats, bound for the mouth of the Yalu River. Next day, as they passed Talienwan Bay, near Port Arthur, they were joined by Ting with the rest of the fleet. On the second day they safely reached their destination, and the troops were disembarked. And early on the 17th Ting again put to sea with his fleet to return to Port Arthur.

He had expected to have to fight the Japanese on his outward voyage, and he knew that there was a still greater chance of meeting them on his way back down the bay. He had a few white officers with him. On board his flagship, the armour-clad *Ting-yuen* was a German artillery officer, Major von Hanneken. On the other battleship was Commander McGiffen, formerly of the United States navy, nominally second in command to the Chinese captain of the *Chen-yuen*, but practically acting as her commander. On some of the other ships there were a few British-born engineer or gunnery officers, and some of the latter had been petty officers in the English navy. By the advice of these non-Chinese officers Ting had done something to remedy the defects of his fleet.

A good deal of woodwork had been cut away and thrown overboard, though far too much of it still remained, and on several ships there was a dangerous quantity of carved ornamental wood on the upper works, much of it all the more inflammable because it was gilded and lacquered in bright colours which it was the practice to clean with oiled rags. The thin steel roofs of barbettes, and the shields of many of the guns, had been removed, as the *Tsi-yuen's* experiences in the fight with the *Naniwa Kan* had shown that such light steel did not keep out the shells of the Japanese quick-firers, but served only to ensure their bursting with deadly effect.

Sometimes a gun-shield had burst a shell, which if there had been no such attempt at protection would perhaps have passed harmlessly over the heads of the gunners. Round the barbettes of the ships sacks of coal were stacked as an emergency method of strengthening these defences. Of coal the fleet had an abundance, but it was woefully short of ammunition, and much of what was on board was old and defective. If Ting had had more professional knowledge and training, he would have been more anxious as to the probable result of a battle.

Where were Admiral Ito and the Japanese fleet? Early in August he had crossed the Yellow Sea with his cruiser squadron, and shown himself before Port Arthur and Wei-hai-Wei. He drew the fire of the seaward forts at long range, and replied with a few shots, but he made no attack. He was engaged only in a reconnaissance, and was quite satisfied when he ascertained that the Chinese ships were remaining in harbour. He then returned to the Korean side of the Yellow Sea, and till nearly the middle of September was employed in escorting the convoys of transports from Japan, and protecting the disembarkation of the reinforcements they were bringing to Korea.

On Friday, 14 September—the same day on which the Chinese convoy with the reinforcements for Manchuria left Taku—Ito had completed his work in connection with the transport of Japanese troops, having landed the last detachments at Chinampo in the estuary of the Ta-tung River. Higher up the river General Nodzu's army was attacking the Chinese walled town of Ping-yang. Ito sent his gunboats up the Ta-tung to co-operate with Nodzu, and leaving his torpedo boats at the river mouth, went to sea with his fleet. He steered for the mouth of the Yalu River, intending to reconnoitre the Chinese positions there, and obtain information as to the reported concentration of troops near the river mouth, but under the belief that the enemy's fleet was still at Port Arthur, Admiral Ting was just as ignorant of his enemy's position and movements.

Early on the morning of Monday, 17 September, he had expended some ammunition in practice at floating targets off the mouth of the Yalu. The fleet had then anchored, and the men were given a rest while the cooks got dinner ready. This was about 11 a.m. A little later there was unexpected news, that interrupted the cooking. The lookouts at the mastheads of the anchored fleet reported that the smoke of many steamers was rising above the horizon far away to the south-westward. It was a bright sunny day, with a perfectly smooth sea, clear air, and a blue sky, and the lookout men could easily make out that the smoke rising above the skyline came from a long line of funnels. Admiral Ting had no doubt it was the Japanese fleet, and he gave orders to weigh anchor and clear for action.

Early that morning Admiral Ito had heard from coasting craft that the Chinese fleet was at sea, and one trader retailed to him a rumour that the fleet was anchored behind Hai-Yang island, where there was a sheltered roadstead. But on reaching Hai-Yang he found only a few fishing-boats lying behind the island. He continued his voyage towards the Yalu, now anticipating a meeting with Ting, unless the Chinese admiral had already run down the other coast of the bay, and so passed him at a distance during the previous night.

Ito's fleet was steaming in line ahead, and was organized in two squadrons. The van squadron was led by his second in command, Admiral Tsuboi, who had hoisted his flag on the fast cruiser *Yoshino*. After her in succession came the cruisers *Takachico*, *Akitsushima*, and *Naniwa Kan*. Then there was a considerable interval between the van squadron and the leading ship of the main squadron, the cruiser *Matsushima*, flying Count Ito's flag. Next to her came the armoured cruiser *Chiyoda*; then the *Matsushima*'s two sister ships, the cruisers *Ikitsushima* and *Hashidate*. The four ships of the van squadron and the four leading ships of the main squadron represented the chief strength of Ito's fleet, his eight modern cruisers.

After them came the two old ironclads *Hiyei* and *Fuso*, the gunboat *Akagi*, and the small armed merchant steamer *Saikio Maru*. The long line of warships steaming swiftly through the sunlight must have looked more like a fleet arrayed for some festive occasion than squadrons prepared for imminent battle, for every ship was painted a brilliant white, with the gilded device of the chrysanthemum forming a broad golden shield on her bows, and the red-and-white sun flag of Japan flew from every masthead.

At half-past eleven, half an hour after the Chinese had perceived the approach of the Japanese fleet, the *Yoshino*, which was leading the advancing line of the van squadron, signalled that there was a dense mass of black smoke on the horizon inshore. This was the smoke produced by Ting's furnaces, as his ships hurriedly stoked their fires to get full pressure on the boilers. Then the Chinese fleet was seen coming out and forming in line of battle.

Admiral Ting formed his ships in line abreast, that is side by side with every bow towards the enemy. In the centre were the two little battleships, with the armoured cruisers, *Lai-yuen* and *King-yuen*, to right and left of them. On each flank of these four heavy ships there was a group of three unarmoured cruisers— the *Ching-yuen, Chao-yung,* and *Yang-wei*—on the right; and the *Chi-yuen, Kwang-chia,* and *Tsi-yuen,* on the left. These were the ten ships on which he relied to bear the brunt of the fighting. Away to the left flank and rear of the line, and nearer the shore, was the small, armour-clad *Ping-yuen*, the corvette *Kwang-ping,* and four torpedo boats.

The Chinese fleet was under easy steam. The ships were painted a dull black, but had a large amount of gilding and colour on their bows, upper works, and deck-houses, and they were all dressed with flags. The decks had been strewn with sand, to prevent accidents by men slipping, and flooded with water from the fire hose to minimize the danger of fire.

The fleets were now rapidly closing. McGiffen, the American officer of the *Chen-yuen*, was impressed with the "holiday

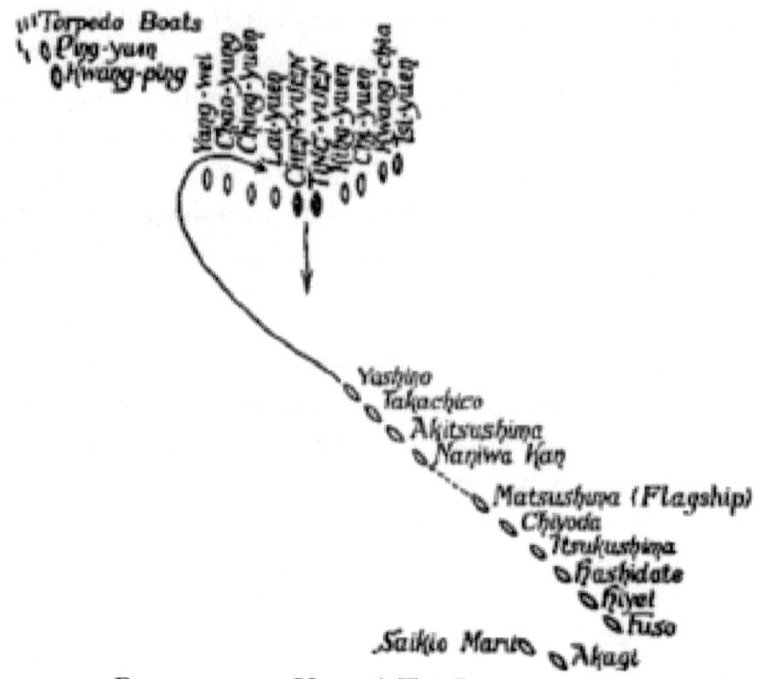

BATTLE OF THE YALU. 1. THE JAPANESE ATTACK

BATTLE OF THE YALU. 2. END OF THE FIGHT

aspect" of the scene. "The twenty-two ships," he wrote in an account of the battle, "trim and fresh in their paint and their bright new bunting, and gay with fluttering signal flags, presented such a holiday aspect, that one found a difficulty in realizing that they were not there simply for a friendly meeting."

When the range of the leading Japanese ship—the *Yoshino*—was just 5400 metres, or something less than 3½ miles, the Chinese admiral fired one of his heavy barbette guns at her from the *Ting-yuen*. The shot fell short, throwing up a great fountain of foaming water. The guns of the other Chinese ships roared out, and the line was wrapped in smoke, but the gunners had not the range in most cases, and their shooting was everywhere bad. Untouched by the hostile fire, the Japanese fleet came silently on.

At first the Japanese line had been heading directly for the Chinese centre. It now altered its course, ship after ship, the *Yoshino* leading the line so that it would pass obliquely across the right front of the enemy, and beyond the extreme right of his line, the wing of Ting's fleet that was furthest from the shore. At a range of about two miles, the *Yoshino* began replying to the Chinese fire with her bow guns and her starboard battery, and the other ships opened as they reached the same range. Thanks to McGiffen's narrative, we know what was the impression made on the few skilled observers in the Chinese fleet. The advancing line of hostile cruisers was wrapped in a dense cloud of smoke, out of which rose their tall masts.

Through the smoke came a continual flicker of the long red flashes of the Japanese quick-firers. To men used to the old guns the rapidity of the fire was something startling. But the Japanese had just missed getting the range. The showers of shells were falling ahead of the Chinese ships. The sea in front of their bows was a mass of spurting columns and fountains of foam, and some of these geysers of sea-water shot up so close ahead that they splashed over the Chinese ships, and numbers of men on their forward-decks were drenched to the skin.

But as the range shortened the rain of shells began to find its target, and fell crashing and exploding on the hulls and upper-works of the Chinese line. It had now lost something of its first formation. The centre had surged forward, the wings had hung back, and it had become slightly convex. Ito in his report stated that Admiral Ting had adopted a crescent formation, but this was only the result of his ships not keeping station correctly. His order had been to fight in "line abreast."

Presently the line became so irregular that some of the Chinese ships were masking each other's fire. The slow fire of the Chinese guns, ill directed as it was, did little damage to the Japanese cruisers. But the Chinese ships were already suffering from the shower of shells. The Japanese found themselves faced with an unexpected difficulty of detail. In the older type of guns the silk cartridge-case was burned when the shot was fired. But with the quick-firers the solid drawn brass case of the cartridge, a thing like a big metal can, is jerked out by an extractor as the breech-block is swung back after firing, and these brass cases began to accumulate in heaps at the gun positions. Extra men were sent to the batteries to throw them overboard.

The *Yoshino* was now on the extreme flank of Ting's right, about a mile away from the *Yang-wei*. Count Ito signalled from the *Matsushima* for the van squadron to circle round the enemy's fleet by changing its course to starboard. This would bring the weaker ships of the hostile squadron under a cross-fire from the van squadron, sweeping round astern of them, and the main squadron crossing their bows obliquely. At the same time the ships on the Chinese left had most of their guns masked by their consorts, and could only fire at relatively long range with their bow guns at the rearward ships of the Japanese main squadron. Ting was out-generalled, and was paying the penalty of a bad formation. His weak right wing was in imminent danger of being crushed by superior numbers and weight of fire.

The two ironclads in the Chinese centre had been made the target of the heaviest guns in Ito's fleet. Theoretically these guns should have been able to pierce even the heavily armoured plating of the barbettes, but no projectile penetrated the armour of the two ships, though shot after shot came thundering against them. Their unarmoured parts were pierced again and again, the shells bursting as they entered, and lighting several fires that were extinguished with difficulty.

But the unarmoured ships on the Chinese right were suffering terribly under the cross-fire of the enemy's van and main squadrons. The two outer ships on this flank were the *Chao Yung* and the *Yang-wei*. Each of these ships had a barbette armed with a 10-inch gun fore and aft. Amidships was a raised structure carrying machine guns on its roof, and having on each side of it a passage, off which opened a range of wooden cabins, oil-painted and varnished. Under the rain of bursting shells these masses of dry, inflammable woodwork were soon ablaze; the fire spreading rapidly made it impossible to bring up ammunition for the guns, and the two cruisers drifted helplessly out of the line, each wrapped in clouds of black smoke, through which long tongues of red flame shot up into the air.

On the other flank practically no damage had been done by the few shots fired by the Japanese in this direction. But here there was a miserable display of cowardice on the part of the Chinese. The ship on the extreme left was the *Tsi-yuen,* which still bore the marks of her encounter with the *Naniwa Kan,* in the first days of the war. The experiences of that adventure had evidently got on the nerves of Captain Fong, who commanded her. As the Japanese line swung round the other flank, he suddenly left his station and steamed at full speed away from his admiral, crossing astern of the Japanese, at what he thought a safe distance, and heading for Port Arthur.

The rearmost Japanese cruiser, the *Chiyoda,* sent a shell after him, that dismounted one of his guns, and added wings to his flight. The Kwang-chia, the next ship in the Chinese line, followed his bad example, and leaving the battle raging behind them, the two cruisers soon disappeared over the south-western horizon. Fong, with the *Tsi-yuen,* reached Port Arthur. He said he had been in the thick of the fight, and only left it when the day was lost. But the evidence of his own crew was against him. He was promptly tried by court-martial and beheaded. The other ship, the *Kwang-chia*, never reached Port Arthur. She was wrecked during the night after the battle, with much loss of life, on a reef outside Talienwan Bay.

There were some other instances of half-heartedness or worse among the Chinese as the fight developed, but on the whole they fought bravely, and many showed the most self-sacrificing courage.

While the large Japanese cruisers of the two squadrons kept perfect station and distance, and enveloped the Chinese right wing with as much precision as if they had been carrying out a fleet exercise in peace manœuvres, the older ships in their line, less speedy and handy, had dropped astern, and were under fire from Ting's two ironclads in the centre. The *Fuso* was at one time so close to them that one of the ironclads made an attempt to ram her, but the Japanese ship evaded it, and running along the broken front of the enemy, rejoined the main cruiser squadron. The other of the old Japanese ironclads, the *Hiyei*, boldly steamed between the Chinese battleships, amid a storm of fire. Two torpedoes were discharged at her, but both missed, and she joined the van squadron in the Chinese rear.

The little *Akagi* was for a while the target of many of the Chinese guns, and one of her masts went over the side. Ito had signalled to her, and to the armed merchantman, *Saikio Maru*, that they might keep out of the fight, but Japanese courage would not allow of this. The *Saikio Maru* had a narrow escape. As the two burning cruisers drifted away from the Chinese right, making for the Yalu, the *Saikio* pursued them, firing her light guns. Two Chinese gunboats opened upon her and four torpedo boats steamed out to attack her. But she turned her fire on them, and some of the Japanese cruisers helped her by accurate shooting at long range. The Chinese flotilla, which had expected an easy prey, turned back, and gunboats and torpedo boats disappeared in the Yalu estuary.

But in the brief encounter the *Saikio Maru* had received a good deal of damage from the light guns of the hostile flotilla.

Her funnel was riddled, and several steam-pipes cut through. She retired from the engagement. With her went the *Hiyei*, which had been seriously damaged in her dash through the Chinese centre. The *Akagi* also withdrew to clear her decks, which were encumbered with wreckage. The fall of her mast had killed her captain, Sakamoto, and her two lieutenants were badly wounded.

So far Ting had lost four of his unarmoured cruisers, and Ito had sent out of the fight three of his ships, the old ironclad *Hiyei*, the gunboat *Akagi*, and the armed steamer *Saikio Maru*. But none of these were fighting units of serious value. His two squadrons of protected cruisers were intact, and it was on these he counted for victory.

The second phase of the battle was a prolonged cannonade at a range of from one to two miles. Thanks to the superior speed of the Japanese fleet, Ito could choose position and distance, and the training of his officers and men enabled him to concentrate his fire now on one part, now on another, of the straggling Chinese line. His ships poured out a steady shower of shells, whose heavy bursting charges not only scattered hurtling fragments of steel among the Chinese crews, but also had a tendency to light a hot fire wherever they exploded. The Chinese had a very poor supply of inferior ammunition, most of it armour-piercing projectiles, that were practically solid shot. Their fire was slow and ill-directed, and even when it found its target the damage done was seldom serious.

Two more Chinese ships were soon disposed of. The cruiser *Chi-yuen* had been pluckily fought by her Chinese captain, Tang, and her English engineer, Purvis. She had received several shots between wind and water, and was leaking badly. Tang knew she could not be long kept afloat, and he made a desperate resolution to attempt to ram a Japanese ship before he went down. As the enemy's van squadron, headed by the *Yoshino*, came sweeping to closer range with the Chinese left the *Chi-yuen* made a dash for the leading cruiser. Even if she had not been half-sinking already, the Chinese ship had neither the speed nor handiness to ram the swiftest ship in the enemy's line.

As the *Chi-yuen* came on, the guns of the van squadron were concentrated on her. She was enveloped in a fierce storm of bursting shells, and suddenly her bows plunged in the sea, her twin screws whizzed for a moment in the air, and then all that was left to show where she had sunk was floating wreckage and drowning men. Purvis went down with his ship. Tang was seen swimming on an oar for a few minutes, with a big dog—a pet of his—paddling near him. Then the dog put its paws on his shoulders, and he was forced under and drowned.

Another Chinese cruiser, the *Lai-yuen*, which lay in the line to the right of the two armour-clads, was now seen to be burning fiercely. On board this ship the Chinese engine-room staff showed devoted courage. While the fire spread through the upper works, so that after the fight many of the iron deck beams were bare and twisted out of shape, not one of the brave men below quitted his post. Stokers, engineers, mechanics worked almost naked, in heat like that of a furnace. Some died, all were in the doctor's hands after the fight, but they kept the engines going, obeyed orders, and brought the half-burnt ship out of action.

More than half of the Chinese fleet had now been destroyed or beaten off, without any loss to the main fighting force of the Japanese. Disregarding the Chinese cruisers, which were now badly cut up and firing harmlessly at long range, Ito concentrated his attack on the two armour-clads. Though each ship was hit more than four hundred times, their armour was never pierced. Yet the Japanese had some guns that theoretically should have penetrated it. Battle results are, however, often very different from experimental work on the testing range.

Early in the fight a Japanese shell had cut down the foremast of the Chinese flagship, sending overboard and drowning seven men who manned the top—carrying away also the signal yards, so that no orders could for some time be conveyed to the fleet. But for more than an hour Admiral Ting was in no condition to give orders. Almost at the outset he had carelessly taken a position that brought him within the danger arc of the blast from his own big barbette guns. He was stunned, and for a while it was thought that he was dead.

The ship was fought by two European officers, Herr Albrecht, a German, and Mr. Nicholls, who had formerly been a petty officer in the British navy. Albrecht distinguished himself by more than once going to terribly exposed positions, and personally handling the hose with which he extinguished the fires lighted by the Japanese shells. Nicholls directed the barbette guns with a cool courage worthy of the service in which he had been trained, until he was killed by a bursting shell.

Two other white men, the German soldier, Captain von Hanneken, and the American commander, McGiffen, took a prominent part in the fighting on board the other armour-clad, the *Chen-yuen*. Both had more than one narrow escape. Von Hanneken was stunned for a while by an explosion, and slightly wounded while at the barbette guns. When the lacquered woodwork of the bow burst into flame and smoke, and none of the Chinese would go forward to extinguish it, McGiffen, who was in command of the ship, dragged the fire-hose to the danger point. Just as he had drowned the fire he was wounded in two places and stunned by a bursting shell. He had told the men in the barbette not to reopen fire till he rejoined them, but, to his horror, as he recovered from the shock he saw the guns swing round and point directly over the bow. He escaped being blown to pieces by dropping through an open hatchway. Altogether during the fight the *Chen-yuen* was on fire eight times.

Most of the Chinese crew fought pluckily, but there were some skulkers. McGiffen tells how once, when there was something wrong with the revolving gear of the barbette guns, and he went down into a recess under the barbette to clear it, he saw a group of frightened men huddled in the semi-darkness, and heard the voice of a Chinese officer saying: "You can't hide down here. There are too many of us already."

But he tells also of the courage of others. The captain of one of the guns was killed as he prepared to fire, the man's head being shattered by a shell, and his brains scattered over the gun. Another man dragged the corpse away, took the lanyard, looked along the sights, and fired without a moment's hesitation. Tsao-kai, the gunnery lieutenant, was badly wounded and taken below. He had brought his brother, a mere boy, on board for a holiday, and had him beside him in the barbette. The boy remained there to the end, helping to pass up ammunition, and apparently regarding the fight as an interesting game, though he was the only unwounded individual in the barbette when the battle ended.

McGiffen asserts that when the fight began the Chen-yuen had in her magazine, besides a quantity of armour-piercing (almost solid) shot, only three really effective shells for the 12-inch guns. Two of these were fired early in the day. In the afternoon, in handling the ammunition, a third was discovered. It was fired at the *Matsushima*, Ito's flagship, and did terrible execution. Ito, in his report, says that the incident occurred at 3.26 p.m., and that the shell came from the *Ting-yuen*, but this appears to have been a mistake. The shell dismounted a 5-inch gun, seriously damaged two more, and exploded a quantity of quick-firing ammunition that was lying ready near the guns. According to the Japanese official report, forty-six men were killed or badly wounded. Unofficial narratives make the loss even greater. One officer was simply blown to pieces. The flame of the explosion set the ship on fire, and she was for a while in imminent danger of destruction.

> "The crew," writes Mr. H. W. Wilson, "with unabated gallantry and courage, divided their attention between the fire and the enemy. The bandsmen went to the guns, and, though the position of the ship was critical, and her loss appalling, there was no panic. The fire was on the lower deck, just above the magazine. In charge of the magazine were a gunner's mate and a seaman. The shell had apparently dented the plating over the powder, and the red glow through the crevices showed the danger. But these brave men did not abandon their post. Stripping off their clothes, they crammed them into the cracks, and saved the

Matsushima' though nearly a third of the men above the waterline had been put out of action, the remnant got the fire under."

While the fire was still burning the *Matsushima* steamed out of the fight, and Ito transferred his flag to the cruiser *Hashidate*. This was really the second narrow escape the *Matsushima* had experienced during the battle. Early in the fight a 10-inch shell had passed through her side, killed four men in her torpedo-room, narrowly missed a loaded torpedo, smashed up an oil-tank, and then broke into pieces. Examination of the fragments showed there was no trace of a fuse, and a plug of cement filled the place where the bursting charge should have been. It was really a bad specimen of a solid shot. If it had been a live shell, it might well have destroyed the *Matsushima*. It was thanks to the wretched ammunition supplied by swindling contractors to the mandarins that the Japanese were able to fight the battle with such trifling loss.

After the transfer of Ito's flag to the *Hashidate* the battle became a cannonade at an increasing range. The Chinese ammunition was running low, and Ito, after having had his quick-firers in action for hours, had also his magazines nearly empty. The heavy fire of the afternoon had failed to destroy the two little "battleships" that represented the only remaining effective units of the Chinese fleet. Ito had accomplished enough in the destruction of the Chinese cruisers, and he had no intention of giving their torpedo boats a chance, by spending the night near the mouth of the Yalu River. At half-past five he broke off the engagement.

Shortness of ammunition supply and exhaustion of officers and men were probably his real reasons, for the explanation he gave in his official report is not very convincing.

"About 5.30 p.m.," he writes, "seeing that the *Chen-yuen* and the *Ting-yuen* had been joined by other ships, and that my van squadron was separated by a great distance from my main force, and considering that sunset was approaching, I discontinued the action, and recalled my main squadron by signal. As the enemy's vessels proceeded on a southerly course, I assumed that they were making for Wei-hai-wei; and having reassembled the fleet, I proceeded upon what I supposed to be a parallel course to that of the enemy, with the intention of renewing the engagement in the morning, for I judged that a night action might be disadvantageous, owing to the possibility of the ships becoming separated in the darkness, and to the fact that the enemy had torpedo boats in company. However, I lost sight of the Chinese, and at daylight there were no signs of the enemy."

There really were no ships of any importance available to join the Chinese ironclads, so one is puzzled to imagine what Ito saw. It was only when the firing died away that Admiral Ting sent orders to the *Kwang-ping*, the transports, gunboats, and torpedo craft to come out. Only the *Kwang-ping* and the torpedo boats obeyed. As the sun went down he formed line ahead, and steered for Port Arthur. First came the two ironclads; then the *Lai-yuen*, with her upper works still on fire in places; then the *Ching-yuen*, *Ping-yuen*, *Kwang-ping*, and the torpedo boats. Far astern the abandoned *Chao-yung* blazed like a bonfire in the twilight.

Ting honestly believed he had beaten off the Japanese fleet, and on his arrival at Port Arthur reported a victory. But though Japanese opinion was not quite satisfied, Ito had so damaged the Chinese fleet that henceforth he held command of the sea. He had won his success with comparatively small loss. Of all the units of his fleet his flagship, the *Matsushima*, had suffered most. She had two officers killed and three wounded, and 33 men killed and 71 wounded, a total of 109, and about a third of the losses in the entire fleet.

The *Hiyei* came next in the casualty list, with 56 killed and wounded. The losses of the other ships were trifling. The Ikitsushima had 31 killed and wounded; the *Akagi*, 28; the *Akitsushima*, 15; the *Fuso*, 14; and the *Yoshino* and *Saikio*, each 11. The

Takachico had an officer and two men wounded; the *Naniwa Kan* (Captain Togo's ship) one man wounded. The *Chiyoda*, which lay next to the *Matsushima*, in the main squadron, had not one single casualty. The official return of losses gave these totals:—

	Killed.	Wounded.	Totals.
Officers	10	016	026
Men	80	188	268
	90	204	294

There are no available returns of the Chinese loss. It was certainly much heavier, perhaps a thousand men. But, thanks to their armour, the two "battleships" suffered comparatively little loss, notwithstanding the terrible fire to which they were exposed for hours. The *Ting-yuen* had 14 killed and 20 wounded, the *Chen-yuen* 7 killed and 15 wounded. The two ships afterwards took part in the defence of Wei-hai-wei, where one was torpedoed and the other captured by the Japanese.

When the first reports of the Yalu battle reached Europe there was much exaggerated talk about the value of the protected cruiser. It was even said by amateur "naval experts" that this type and not the battleship would be the warship of the future. It is almost needless to say that the battle conveyed no such lesson. If anything, it rather proved the enormous resisting power of the armoured ship. If Ting, instead of his two antiquated coast-defence armour-clads, had had a couple of up-to-date battleships manned with trained crews, he would certainly have disposed of a good many of the Japanese cruisers. The Japanese quite realized this, and proceeded to build a heavily armoured fleet.

The most valuable lesson of the battle was the warning of the danger of fires lighted by exploding shells. This had an immediate influence on ship construction, and on the methods adopted by all navies in clearing for action.

But the most important point of all was that the conduct of the Japanese officers and men in the battle, and in the subsequent naval operations in the siege of Wei-hai-wei, made the world realize that a new naval power had arisen in the Far East.

CHAPTER 13

Santiago De Cuba 1898

The United States Navy had taken a decisive part in securing victory for the Union in the War of Secession. It had effectively blockaded the Atlantic and Gulf coasts of the Confederacy, captured New Orleans, given valuable help to the army, in seizing the line of the Mississippi, and by the combined effect of these operations isolated the Confederate States from the rest of the world, destroyed their trade, and cut off their supplies.

One would have expected that the importance of sea-power would have been fully appreciated in the United States after such experiences, and that steps would have been taken to form and maintain an effective fleet. But for some twenty years after the war the American Navy was hopelessly neglected. During this period the fleet consisted mainly of some of the miscellaneous collection of ships of various types built or purchased during the years of conflict.

Old monitors that had engaged the batteries of Charleston figured in the Navy List, beside sloops and steam frigates that were little better than armed merchantmen. The only good work that was done by the Navy Department was the training and maintenance of a corps of excellent officers, and to their influence it was due that at last a beginning was made of the building of a new navy.

The first ships built were of two classes. Public opinion was still clinging to the idea that the *Monitor* was a supremely effective type of warship, and accordingly considerable sums were expended on the building of coast-defence vessels of this type, low-freeboard turret-ships, carrying a couple of heavy guns in an armoured turret.

But ships were also required that could make ocean voyages, and show the flag in foreign waters, and for this purpose a number of protected cruisers were built, full-rigged, masted steamers, with their guns in broadside batteries.

Still, the United States possessed only a fourth or fifth-rate fleet, and could not have sent to sea a squadron that could rank with the fleets kept in commission regularly by several of the European powers. Advocates of the old American plan of "having no foreign policy" even maintained that the country had no need of an ocean-going fleet, and required only coast-defence ships and a few light cruisers.

It was not till the end of the 'eighties that American opinion was aroused to the danger of neglecting the sea-power of the States. The splendid American Navy of today is the creation of less than twenty years of systematic development. When the war broke out between the United States and Spain over the Cuban question several of the new cruisers and battleships were available, but many older ships were still in the service, and a number of armed liners and other makeshift auxiliaries were taken into the navy.

During the period of tension that immediately preceded the war two fleets were concentrated on the Atlantic coast. The North Atlantic Fleet, under Admiral Sampson, at Key West, Florida, and the reserve fleet, officially known as the "Flying Squadron," under Commodore Schley, at Hampton Roads. The Pacific Squadron, under Commodore Dewey, was at Hong Kong, waiting to sail for the Philippines as soon as war was declared.

In the following list of Sampson's and Schley's squadrons, besides the displacement of each ship, the date of her launch is noted, so as to distinguish between the older and the newer types of warships:—

North Atlantic Squadron.

	Displacement. Tons.	Date of Launch.	Speed. Knots.
Armoured cruiser (flagship)—			
New York	08,480	1891	21
Battleships—			
Iowa	11,296	1896	16
Indiana	10,231	1893	15½
Cruisers—			
Cincinnati	03,183	1892	19
Detroit	02,000	1892	19
Montgomery	02,000	1892	19
Marblehead	02,000	1892	19
Monitors—			
Puritan	06,060	1883	12
Terror	03,990	1883	12
Torpedo-boats—			
Cushing	00,105	1890	22½
Ericsson	00,120	1892	23
Rodgers	00,142	1896	25
Foote	00,142	1896	24½
Porter	00,185	1896	28½
Dupont	00,185	1896	27½
Winslow	00,142	1897	24½

(Besides gunboats and tenders.)

Flying Squadron.

	Displacement. Tons.	Date of Launch.	Speed. Knots.
Armoured cruiser (flagship)—			
Brooklyn	09,153	1895	17
Battleships—			
Texas	06,315	1892	21
Massachusetts	10,231	1893	16
Cruisers—			
Columbia	07,475	1892	23
Minneapolis	07,475	1893	23

These were the two fleets available for the blockade of Cuba, and the operations of attacking coast fortifications, covering the transportation of the army of invasion, and dealing with any naval force Spain might send to these waters.

Other units were subsequently added to the fleet after both squadrons had concentrated under Sampson's command.

In West Indian waters the Spaniards had only a few light craft and the old cruiser *Reina Mercedes* at Santiago, with her boilers and engines in such a state that she could not go to sea. For many years the Spanish Navy had been sadly neglected, but since 1890 some armoured cruisers had been built, and a flotilla of torpedo-boat destroyers added to the navy. A number of antiquated units figured on the Navy List, including useless "battleships" dating from the 'sixties, and small unarmoured cruisers little better than gunboats. There was one fairly modern battleship, the *Pelayo*, dating from 1887, but expert opinion was very divided about her value.

When the war broke out the Spanish Pacific Squadron, under Admiral Montojo, was at Manila. To use the words of an American naval officer, it was made up of "a number of old tubs not fit to be called warships." It was promptly destroyed by Commodore Dewey's squadron from Hong Kong (Battle of Manila Bay, Sunday, 1 May, 1898). It was the first American victory in the war, and in the national rejoicing there was much exaggeration as to Dewey's exploit, which was compared to Nelson's victories!

On the eve of the war a Spanish fleet, officially known as the Atlantic Squadron, had been concentrated, under the command of Admiral Cervera, in the Portuguese harbour of St. Vincent, in the Cape de Verde Islands, and the local authorities somewhat strained the laws of neutrality by allowing Cervera to use the port to complete his preparations for some time after the outbreak of the war.

The composition of the squadrons was as follows:—

	Displacement. Tons.	Date of Launch.	Speed. Knots.
Armoured cruisers—			
Infanta Maria Teresa (flagship)	6890	1891	20

Vizcaya	6890	1891	20
Almirante Oquendo	6890 1890	20	
Cristobal Colon	6480	1896	20

Torpedo-boat destroyers—

Terror	0400	1896–7	28
Furor	0400	1896–7	28
Pluton	0400	1896–7	28

Torpedo-boats—
Azor, Ariete, Rayo.

Auxiliary cruiser—
Ciudad de Cadiz (an armed liner acting as mother-ship to the torpedo-boats).

The armoured cruisers were all of the same type, ships with an armoured deck under water protecting the engines and magazines, a 6-inch armour belt, and an armoured barbette fore and aft, mounting a 9½-inch Hontoria gun. They had a secondary armament of ten 6-inch quick-firers, besides a number of lighter guns for defence against torpedo craft, and had maxims mounted in their fighting tops.

The *Cristobal Colon*, originally built for the Italian Navy as the *Giuseppe Garibaldi*, and purchased by Spain and renamed, had only the quick-firers, and had no guns in her barbettes. These had originally been armed with Armstrong guns. The heavy Armstrongs were taken out of her at Cadiz to be replaced by Hontorias, but these were not ready when the war came, and the *Cristobal Colon* sailed for St. Vincent without them. The torpedo-boat destroyers were of the best and latest type of their class, and recently built on the Clyde.

The war in the Atlantic began by Sampson's squadron leaving Key West, establishing the blockade of Western Cuba, reconnoitring the sea defences of Havana, and exchanging some shells with them at long range. Then, in order to satisfy popular feeling in America, Sampson bombarded the batteries of San Juan, in Puerto Rico, an operation that had no real effect on the fortunes of the war, and inflicted only trifling local loss on the

Spaniards.

An army had been assembled at Tampa, in Florida, and a huge fleet of transports was collected to ferry it over to Cuba. Its destination was supposed to be the western end of the island, where, in co-operation with the insurgents by land and the fleet by sea, it would besiege and capture Havana. But again and again the sailing of the fleet was delayed, and there was alarm in the cities of the Atlantic states, because the newspapers published wild reports of phantom armadas hovering off the coast. When news came that Cervera had sailed from St. Vincent, and for many days there was no trace of his movements, there was a quite unnecessary alarm as to what the Spanish squadron might do. A wise Press censorship would have been very useful to the United States, but there was little or no attempt to control the wild rumours published by the newspapers.

For some days after the declaration of war (23 April) Cervera's squadron lay at St. Vincent. All the ships were repainted a dead black, some coal was taken on board, and quantities of ammunition transferred from the holds of the "*Ciudad de Cadiz*" to the magazines of the cruisers. At last, on 29 April, Cervera sailed, leaving the torpedo-boats and the armed liner in port, and taking with him only his high-speed ships, the four armoured cruisers, and the three destroyers.

His course was westward, and it was conjectured that San Juan de Puerto Rico was his destination. The distance is about 2400 miles, and supposing that he would proceed at a cruising speed of ten knots, in order to economize his coal, it was calculated that he would be across the Atlantic in ten days, reaching the West Indies about 9 May. Two swift armed liners that had been attached to Schley's squadron were sent out to sweep the Western Atlantic, and it was expected that by the end of the first week in May they would bring back news of the enemy, but 7 May came and brought no news.

Ships arriving in ports on both sides of the ocean told of having seen the smoke of a squadron on the horizon in so many places that it seemed as if the Atlantic must be full of fleets.

Look-out stations as far north as the New England States told of glimpses of warships seen far off in the morning twilight, or vaguely distinguished through mist and rain. But definite news of Cervera there was none. It seemed as if his squadron had vanished into space.

Then there were theories started to account for his disappearance. It was suggested that he had altered his course and gone to the coast of South America, to intercept the battleship *Oregon*, which had come round from the Pacific to reinforce Sampson's fleet; or perhaps he was making for the Cape or the Horn, bound on a long voyage for Manila, to destroy Dewey's unarmoured cruisers and restore Spanish supremacy in the Philippines; or he was ranging the oceans to prey upon American commerce.

Then came a strange report, worth remembering as a caution against too easily accepting the rumours of wartime. From Cadiz came American Press dispatches, duly passed by the Spanish censor, stating that Cervera's squadron had steamed back into that port. The start westward from St. Vincent was said to be a mere feint. The Spaniards had hoped to draw some of the swifter American ships out into the Atlantic, and score a victory by fighting them in European waters. Naval experts gravely discussed Cervera's tactics. Correspondents described the position of his fleet in Cadiz harbour. Perhaps the Spanish censor helped the misleading rumours into circulation by letting Americans at Cadiz imagine that ships fitting out in the harbour were the missing fleet.

At last, on 12 May, came definite news of one unit of the squadron. The night before the destroyer Furor had paid a flying visit in the dark to the French port of St. Pierre, in Martinique, probably calling for cabled information and orders. On the 12th the Terror visited the same port in broad daylight. That evening, from the hills of Martinique, four large cruisers were seen far out at sea, steering northwards, under easy steam. The cable from Martinique by St. Lucia to the States was out of order, and it was not till the 15th that Admiral Sampson received the news. Several of his heavy ships were coaling at Key West. He hurried on the work, and sent his lighter ships to watch the Windward and Mona Passages. He sent off Schley with the Flying Squadron to the south of Cuba, with orders to sweep the island-fringed Caribbean sea and watch the Yucatan Channel with his cruisers. As soon as he had completed coaling he himself sailed for the waters north of Cuba.

Once more there was for a while no news of Cervera. After dark on 12 May he had altered his northern course and steered a little south of west, making for the Dutch island of Curaçao, where he expected to find some tramp steamers laden with coal and other supplies awaiting him. On Saturday, 14 May, the *Maria Teresa* and the *Vizcaya* entered the port, the two other cruisers, accompanied by two destroyers, remaining outside. The expected colliers had not arrived; the Dutch authorities insisted on Cervera leaving Curaçao within twenty-four hours, and he sailed on the Sunday without being able to fill up his bunkers. Once more the United States cruisers failed to sight him, as he steamed slowly across the Caribbean Sea, husbanding his coal and steering for Cuba.

On Wednesday, 18 May, three American warships were off Santiago de Cuba. They came so close in that the Morro battery at the entrance fired upon them. Before sundown they steamed away. They had missed Cervera by a few hours, for at sunrise next morning he brought his four cruisers and two destroyers into Santiago harbour.

Santiago is the oldest Spanish city in Cuba, and was its capital in the early days before Havana was founded.

The old city stands at the head of a landlocked arm of the sea, surrounded by forest-clad hills, and approached through narrow ravine-like straits. Cervera had come there to obtain coal and supplies. If he had made it only a temporary base, and had been able to coal immediately, and put to sea to attack the American cruisers scattered over the Caribbean waters, he might have scored successes for a while. But he waited at Santiago till he was hopelessly blockaded.

For some days the Washington Government, mindful of the Cadiz hoax, refused to believe reports that the Spanish fleet was hidden behind the headlands of Santiago harbour. It was not till 27 May that Admiral Schley obtained definite proof of the fact, and formed the blockade of Santiago with his squadron. Admiral Sampson then brought his fleet round, and took over the command.

Until he reached Santiago Cervera had shown no lack of energy, but now he was strangely devoid of enterprise. He allowed an American armed liner to capture, off the port, a steamer that was bringing him 3000 tons of much-needed coal, though he might have saved her by sending one of his cruisers outside the headlands. He allowed an inferior force to blockade the entrance for some days, without bringing out his cruisers by day to engage them, or sending out his destroyers by night to torpedo them. He waited until there was an overwhelming force assembled off the harbour.

Then came a month of deadlock. He was blockaded by a vastly superior force that watched the narrow pass through which, if he left the harbour, his fleet must come out one by one. But so long as he was within the headlands he was unassailable.

Admiral Sampson declined to risk his ships in an attempt to force the narrow entrance and destroy the Spanish squadron inside. An attempt to "bottle up" Cervera, by sinking a tramp steamer, the *Merrimac*, in the entrance, proved a failure. Long-ranging bombardments produced no effect on the Spaniards. All the plans formed at Washington for the Cuban campaign were disorganized. The blockade of the island had become the blockade of the one port of Santiago.

If the United States Government had known how short of supplies were the city and garrison of Santiago and Cervera's fleet, it might have trusted to the blockade by sea and the operations of the insurgents by land, with the help of a few regulars, to force the Spanish admiral either to surrender or come out and fight. But it was decided to abandon for the present the projected attack on Havana, and send the army, collected for this purpose at Tampa, to attack Santiago by land, and so deprive Cervera of his refuge in the harbour.

Santiago was defended by lines of entrenchments with some improvised outworks, and garrisoned by a division under General Linares. The American transports from Tampa began to arrive on 20 June, and the expeditionary force, under General Shafter, was disembarked during the following days some miles east of the city. There was then an advance over mere forest tracks through hilly country covered with dense bush. Cervera landed seamen gunners with machine-guns and light quick-firers to strengthen the defence, and anchored one of his cruisers so that her heavy artillery could enfilade an attack on the entrenchments nearest the harbour.

On 1 July Shafter made his attack. The Spaniards defended themselves with such obstinate energy that after fighting through a long summer day only two outposts had been taken by the Americans, and at the cost of heavy loss. Next day there was desultory fighting along the front, but no progress. It was difficult to bring up supplies along the forest tracks, now sodden with tropical rains. Sickness had broken out in the American lines. The resistance of the Spaniards showed a dogged determination that was a surprise to the invaders.

Shafter himself was ill. Late on Saturday, 2 July, he appealed to Admiral Sampson to help him by forcing the narrows at all costs, and in the early hours of Sunday, the 3rd, he sent off to his Government a dispatch which was a confession of failure.

This discouraging report was cabled to Washington early on the Sunday morning, and caused deep dismay at the White House, but before evening news arrived of events that had changed the whole situation.

The evening before (2 July) Mr. Ramsden, the British Consul at Santiago, had written in his diary:—

> It seems incredible that the Americans with their large force have not yet taken the place. The defence of the Spaniards has been really heroic, the more so when you consider that they are half-starved and sick. It was affirmed

today that the squadron would leave this evening, but they have not done so, though the pilots are on board. I will believe it when I see them get out, and I wish they would. If they do, they will fare badly outside.

During the Saturday Cervera had re-embarked the seamen landed for the defence of the city, and had got up steam. He was going out because the presence of his crews now only added to the difficulty of feeding the half-starved garrison and population of the place. He had a short supply of inferior coal, and the most he hoped for was that some of his ships would elude, or fight their way past, the blockading squadron, and reach Havana. It is impossible to understand why, having decided to go out, he did not make the attempt in the darkness of Saturday night, instead of waiting for broad daylight next day.

In one respect he was fortunate. His coming out was a complete surprise for the Americans, and found them quite unprepared, with some of their best ships far from the scene of action. Admiral Sampson had steamed off to the eastward in his flagship, the New York, intending to land at Siboney for his interview with General Shafter. The battleship *Massachusetts* had gone with two of the lighter cruisers to coal at Guantanamo. But there were quite enough ships left off the seaward opening of the narrows, where four battleships, an armoured cruiser, and two light craft were keeping up the blockade.

It was a bright summer day, with a light wind and a smooth sea. Due south of the harbour entrance, and about 5½ miles from it, lay the battleship *Iowa*. To the east of her lay the *Oregon*, with the *Indiana* between her and the land, and about two miles nearer in, west of the *Iowa*, was the battleship *Texas*, with the armoured cruiser *Brooklyn*, Commodore Schley's flagship, lying between her and the land, and still nearer in the small armed revenue cruiser *Vixen*, lying about three miles south-west of Morro Castle. On the other side of the entrance, close in to the land, was a small armed steamer, the *Gloucester*. She had been purchased by the Navy Department on the outbreak of the war from Mr. Pierpont Morgan, the banker, and renamed.

Before this she had been known as the steam yacht *Gloucester*. She was commanded by one of the best officers of the United States Navy, Captain Wainwright, who had been second in command of the Maine when she was blown up in Havana harbour. Wainwright was to show this day that even an armed steam yacht may do good service in a modern naval action. All the ships except the *Oregon* and the little *Gloucester* had let their fires burn low, and had hardly any steam pressure on their boilers.

At half-past nine the order was given for the crews to fall in for general inspection. A few minutes later an apprentice on board the Iowa called attention to a mass of black smoke rising over the headlands of the harbour mouth. And then between the cliffs of Morro and Socapa Points appeared the bows of Cervera's flagship. An alarm gun rang out from the *Iowa*, the signal, "Enemy escaping—clear for action," fluttered out from the halyards of the *Brooklyn*, and on every ship the bugles sounded, the men rushed to their battle stations, and the stokers worked madly to get steam on the boilers.

Admiral Cervera, guided by a local pilot, Miguel Lopez, had led his fleet down the harbour, the *Maria Teresa* being followed in succession by the cruisers *Vizcaya, Cristobal Colon,* and *Oquendo*, and the destroyers *Pluton* and *Furor*. As the flagship entered the ravine of the narrows Cervera signalled to his captains, "I wish you a speedy victory!" Miguel Lopez, who was with him in the conning-tower, remarked that the admiral gave his orders very deliberately, and showed no sign of anxiety or excitement. He had asked Lopez to tell him how soon he could turn to the westward.

On a sign from the pilot, he gave the order, "Starboard!" to the helmsman, put the engine-room indicator to "Full speed," and told his captain to open fire. As the guns roared out Cervera turned with a smile to Lopez and said, "You have done your part well, pilot; I hope you will come out of this safe and be well rewarded. You have deserved it."

The cruisers had run out with an interval of about 600 yards between the ships. There was a longer gap between the last of them and the destroyers, but the *Furor* was out within a quarter of an hour of the *Maria Teresa's* appearance between the headlands. That quarter of an hour had been a busy time for the Americans. The *Brooklyn* and the four battleships had at once headed for the opening of the harbour, the *Oregon* making the best speed till the steam pressure rose on the boilers of her consorts. They were no sooner moving than they opened fire with their forward guns, the Spanish cruisers and the batteries of Socapa and Morro replying with shots, every one of which fell short.

As Cervera turned westward the American ships also altered their course in the same direction. And now as the huge ships of the blockading squadron, each wrapped in a fog of smoke from her guns, converged upon the same course, there was a momentary danger of disastrous collision between them, a danger accentuated by an unexpected manœuvre of Commodore Schley's ship, the *Brooklyn*. The *Texas* and the *Iowa* just cleared each other in the smoke-cloud.

As they sheered off from each other, the *Oregon*, which had been following the *Iowa*, came rushing between the two ships, and the *Brooklyn* circled past their bows, suddenly crossing their course. Schley, in the first dash towards the Spaniards, had brought his great cruiser within 3000 yards of the *Maria Teresa*, then seeing the Spanish flagship turning, as if to ram, he swung round to starboard, bringing his broadside to bear on the enemy, but at the same time heading for his own battleships. He cleared them by completing a circle, coming back thus to the westward course, which had at the same time been resumed by the Spanish flagship. As the *Brooklyn* turned the battleships swept up between her and the enemy, masking her fire, the *Oregon* leading, but the speed of Schley's ship soon enabled him to secure a forward place in the chase near the *Oregon*.

While the giants were thus manœuvring the little *Gloucester* had come pluckily into action. Running in close under the Morro batteries, Commander Wainwright had fired some shots at the enemy's cruisers. Then realizing that his light guns could do them no vital harm, he almost stopped the way on his ship, and waited to engage the destroyers.

Out came the *Furor* and *Pluton*, turning eastward as they cleared the entrance, and dashing for the *Gloucester* with a mass of foam piling up over their bows. The *Indiana*, the rearmost of the battleships, fired some long-range shots at them, but it was a stream of small shells from the *Gloucester's* quick-firers that stopped their rush. The *Furor* was soon drifting towards the cliffs, enveloped in clouds of escaping steam. The *Gloucester's* fire had killed her helmsman, wrecked her steering gear, and cut up several of her steam-pipes, making her engine-room uninhabitable.

The *Pluton*, not so badly crippled, but with her hull penetrated in several places, was next turned back. The *New York*, hurrying up from the eastward at the sound of the firing, escorted by the torpedo-boat *Ericsson*, fired on her at long range. The *Pluton* kept her engines going just long enough to drive her ashore under the Socapa cliffs. The *Furor* sank before she could reach the land.

There was now a running fight, the four Spanish cruisers steaming westward close to the wooded shore, the American ships following them up and pouring in a deadly fire from every gun that could be brought to bear. It was soon evident that the Spaniards could not get up anything like their trial speed, and their gunnery was so defective that there was small chance of their stopping any of their pursuers by well-aimed fire, or even of inflicting any appreciable loss or damage on them. The *Maria Teresa* was the first to succumb. As she led the line out of the harbour she had received the converging fire of the American ships, but she had not suffered any serious injury. Until the American ships got up full steam the Spaniards had gained a little on them.

An Englishman, Mr. Mason, who watched the cruisers from a hill near Morro, till at ten o'clock the curve of the coast westward hid them from view, thought they were successfully escaping. So far as he could see they had not been badly hit, and none of the Americans were yet abreast of them. But soon after the

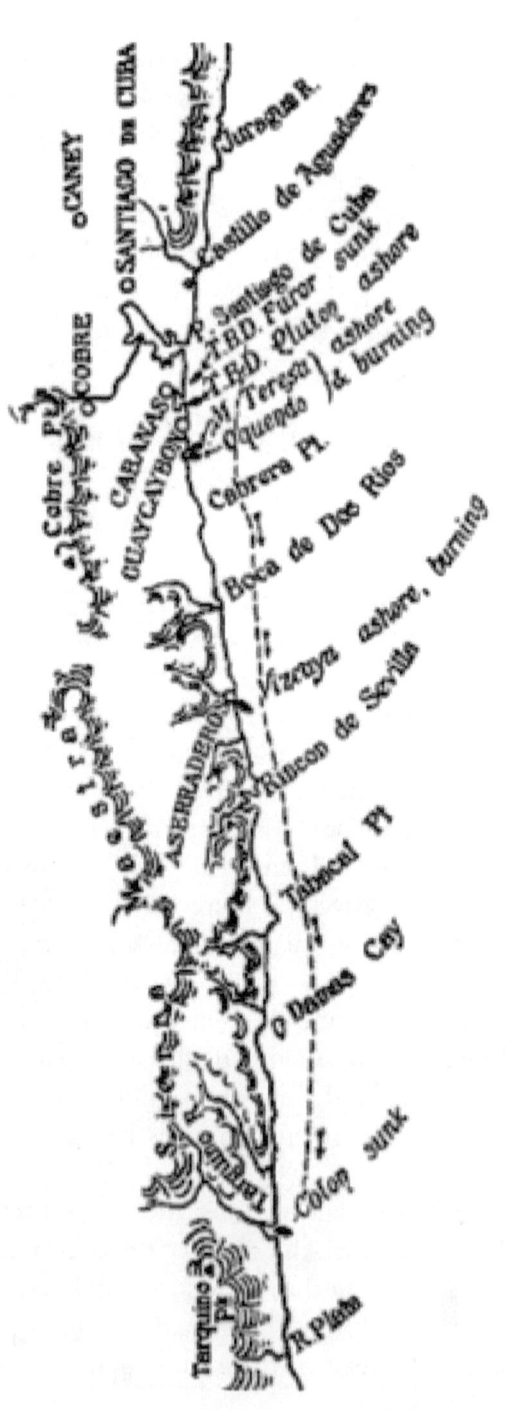

BATTLE OF SANTIAGO – SHOWING PLACES WHERE THE SPANISH SHIPS WERE DESTROYED & DOTTED LINE SHOWING GENERAL DIRECTION OF THE RUNNING FIGHT, THUS——

ships disappeared from the point of view near Morro, and when the *Maria Teresa* was only some six miles from the entrance, she suffered a series of injuries in rapid succession that put her out of action.

It was the secondary armament of the American ships, the guns of medium calibre, that proved most effective in the running fight. It appears that the big 13 and 12-inch barbette and turret guns only made two hits in the whole day. Two 12-inch shells fired simultaneously from a pair of guns struck the *Maria Teresa* just above the waterline on the port side, aft and below her stern turret. They burst in the torpedo-room, killing and wounding every one there, blowing a jagged hole in the starboard side, and setting the ship on fire. An 8-inch shell came into the after battery and exploded between decks, causing many casualties. A 5-inch shell burst in the coal-bunkers amidships, blew up the deck, and started a second fire. Another destructive hit was made by an 8-inch shell a few feet forward of the point where the pair of 12-inch shells had come in. The official report thus describes its course:—

> An 8-inch shell struck the gun-deck just under the after-barbette, passed through the side of the ship, and exploded, ranging aft. The damage done by this shell was very great. All the men in the locality must have been killed or badly wounded. The beams were torn and ripped. The fragments of the shell passed across the deck and cut through the starboard side. This shell also cut the fire main.

Shells from the lighter artillery of the American ships riddled the funnels, and cut up the deck-houses. One of these shells, bursting near the forward bridge, wounded Admiral Cervera slightly in the arm. He had come outside the conning-tower the better to watch the progress of his squadron. The armour belt had kept the water-line of the ship intact, and her barbettes and heavy guns were also protected efficiently by the local armour, but the enemy's shell fire had told on the unarmoured structure, inflicted heavy loss, and started two serious fires. All efforts to get these under failed. The blazing tropic heat had scorched the woodwork of the ship into tinder, the movement of the vessel produced a draught that made the burning bunkers and decks roaring masses of flame.

The men were driven by the heat from battery and engine-room. The *Maria Teresa*, with silent guns and masses of black smoke ascending to the sky, was headed for the land. At a quarter-past ten she drove ashore at Nimanima, 6½ miles west of Morro Castle. Some of the men swam ashore, others were taken off by the boats of the *Gloucester*, which came up just in time to help in saving life. Commander Wainwright had to land a party to drive off a mob of Cuban guerrillas, who came down to the shore, and were murdering the hapless Spaniards as they swam to the land. One of the *Gloucester's* boats took out of the water Admiral Cervera and his son, Lieutenant Cervera. They were brought on board the yacht, where Wainwright chivalrously greeted the unfortunate admiral with the words: "I congratulate you, sir, on having made as gallant a fight as was ever witnessed on the sea."

At half-past ten another of the Spanish cruisers was a helpless wreck only half a mile westward of the stranded and burning flagship. This was the *Almirante Oquendo*, whose station had been last in the line. This drew upon her a converging fire from the guns of the pursuing battleships and cruisers. The destruction was terrible. Two guns of the secondary battery were disabled. A shell came through the roof of the forward turret, killed and wounded all the gun crew, and put the gun permanently out of action. Ventilators and deck-fittings were swept away, the funnels cut up, and the unarmoured part of the sides repeatedly pierced by shells that started several fires amidships.

It was these that made further effort to keep up the fight hopeless. After her captain, Juan Lazaga, had been killed by a bursting shell, the *Oquendo*, now on fire in a dozen places, was driven ashore to save life. She blew up on the beach, the explosion of her magazines nearly cutting the wreck in two.

Of the Spanish squadron only the *Cristobal Colon* and the

Vizcaya still survived. The *Colon*, best and newest of the cruisers, was making good speed, and was furthest ahead. The *Vizcaya* lagged behind her, hard pressed by several American ships, led by the *Iowa*. The *Vizcaya* had suffered severely from the fire of the pursuit. Her coal-bunkers were ablaze on one side, and there was another fire making steady progress in the gun-deck. Schley, in the *Brooklyn*, urging his engines to the utmost, rushed past the *Iowa*, and attempted to head off the *Vizcaya*. Her gallant captain, Antonio Eulate, realized that the *Brooklyn* was the swiftest ship in the pursuit, and that her destruction would materially increase the chance of the *Colon* escaping.

So he made a last effort to ram or torpedo the *Brooklyn* before his own ship succumbed. He headed for Schley with a torpedo ready in his bow over-water tube. A shell from the *Brooklyn's* battery struck it fair, exploded the torpedo in the tube, and blew up and set fire to the forepart of the *Vizcaya*. Eulate then headed his ship for the land, and she struck the shore under the cliffs at Asseradores, fifteen miles west of Morro, at a quarter-past eleven. The *Brooklyn*, the *Iowa*, and the *Oregon* were pouring their fire into her as she ran aground.

Another explosion blew up part of her burning decks, and Eulate hauled down his flag. The Americans cheered as they saw the flag come down amid the clouds of smoke, but Captain Robley Evans, of the *Iowa*, called out from the bridge to stop the cheers of his men. "Don't cheer, boys. Those poor fellows are dying," he said. Evans, with the *Iowa*, stood by the burning ship to rescue the survivors.

The *Colon* alone remained. She had a lead of a good six miles, and many thought she would escape. The *Brooklyn* led the pursuit, followed closely by the battleships *Oregon* and *Texas*, and the small cruiser *Vixen*, with Sampson's flagship, the *New York*, far astern, too far off to have any real share in the action. On her trials the *Colon* had done 23 knots. If she could have done anything like this in the rush out of Santiago, she would have simply walked away from the Americans, but she never did more than fourteen.

For some time, even at this reduced speed, she was so far ahead that there was no firing. It was not until ten minutes past one that the *Brooklyn* and *Oregon* at last got within range and opened fire with their forward heavy guns. The *Colon*, with her empty barbettes, had nothing with which to reply at the long range. In the earlier stage of the fight she had been hit only by an 8-inch shell, which did no material damage. As the pursuers gained on her she opened with her secondary battery. Even now she received no serious injury, and she was never set on fire. But her captain, Moreu, realized that lack of speed had put him at the mercy of the enemy.

As they closed in upon him and opened fire with their heaviest guns, he turned his ship into the creek surrounded by towering heights amid which the little Tarquino River runs into the sea, forty-eight miles west of Morro Castle. He hauled down his flag as he entered the creek. Without his orders the engineers opened the Kingston valves in the engine-room, and when the Americans boarded the *Colon* she was rapidly sinking. She went down by the stern under the cliffs on the east side of the inlet, and lay with her bow above water and her after decks awash. It was twenty minutes past one when she surrendered.

The men of the *Iowa* and *Gloucester* had meanwhile rescued many of the survivors of the *Vizcaya*, not without serious risk to themselves, for there were numerous explosions, and the decks were red-hot in places. Some of the Spaniards swam ashore, made their way through the bush to Santiago, and joined the garrison. Captain Eulate was brought on board the *Iowa*, and received by a guard of marines, who presented arms as he stepped from the gangway. He offered his sword to Robley Evans, but the American captain refused to take it. "You have surrendered," he said, "to four ships, each heavier than your own. You did not surrender to the *Iowa* only, so her captain cannot take your sword."

Never in any naval action was there such complete destruction of a fleet. Of the six ships that steamed out of Santiago that summer morning, the *Furor* was sunk in deep water off the entrance; the *Pluton* was ashore under the Socapa cliff. At various points along the coast columns of black smoke rising a thousand feet into the sunlit sky showed where the burning wrecks of the *Maria Teresa*, the *Oquendo*, and the *Vizcaya* lay, and nearly fifty miles away the *Colon* was sunk at the mouth of the Tarquino River.

And never was success obtained with such a trifling loss to the victors. The Spanish gunnery had been wretchedly bad. The only ships hit were the *Brooklyn* and the *Iowa*, and neither received any serious damage. The only losses by the enemy's fire were on board the *Brooklyn*, where a signalman was killed and two seamen wounded. Nine men were more or less seriously injured by the concussion of their own guns.

It must be confessed that the gunnery of the Americans was not of a high order. Some 6500 shells were expended during the action. The Spanish wrecks were carefully examined, and all hits counted. Fires and explosions perhaps obliterated the traces of some of them, but so far as could be ascertained, the hits on the hulls and the upper works were comparatively few. And of hits by the heavy 13-inch and 12-inch guns, only two could be traced anywhere.

The Spanish squadron had 2300 officers and men on board when it left Santiago. Of these 1600 were prisoners after the action. It was estimated that in the fight 350 were killed and 150 wounded. This leaves some 200 to be accounted for. Nearly 150 rejoined the garrison of Santiago after swimming ashore. This leaves only fifty missing. They were probably drowned or killed by the Cuban guerrillas. The fact that three of the Spanish cruisers had been rendered helpless by fires lighted on board by the enemy's shells accentuated the lesson already learned from the battle of the Yalu as to the necessity of eliminating inflammable material in the construction and fittings of warships. The damage done to the *Vizcaya* by the explosion of one of her own torpedoes in her bow-tube proved the reality of a danger to which naval critics had already called attention. Henceforth the torpedo tubes of cruisers and battleships were all made to open below the water-line.

The result of the victory was a complete change in the situation at Santiago. The destruction of Cervera's fleet was the "beginning of the end" for the Spanish power in Cuba.

CHAPTER 15

Tsu-Shima 1905

When the war of 1894–5 between China and Japan was brought to a close by the Treaty of Shimonoseki (17 April, 1895), the Japanese were in possession of Korea and Southern Manchuria, Port Arthur and the Liao-tung Peninsula, Wei-hai-wei and the Pescadores Islands, and a joint naval and military expedition was ready to seize Formosa.

By the second article China ceded to Japan the fortress and dockyard of Port Arthur and the Liao-tung Peninsula. As soon as the terms of the treaty were published, Russia, which was the northern neighbour of China along the borders of Manchuria and Mongolia, and the neighbour of Japan by the possession of Vladivostock and Saghalien, protested against the cession of Port Arthur and its territory to the victors, arguing that the permanent occupation of Port Arthur by a foreign Power would be a standing menace to the Government at Pekin, and would put an end to the independence of China. Germany and France joined in the Russian protest, and the three Powers began to move their ships eastward. Their combined squadrons would have been more than a match for Admiral Ito's cruisers. England had a powerful squadron in the Eastern seas, but observed a strict neutrality in the diplomatic strife.

If England had joined her, Japan would undoubtedly have fought rather than yield up the fruit of her hard-won victories. But the Mikado's Ministers realized that single-handed they could not face a Triple Alliance of aggressive European Powers.

The treaty was revised, the cession of Port Arthur and its territory being struck out of it. They were to be restored to China.

But the statesmen of Japan, while they yielded the point, recognized in Russia their future rival for the empire of the East, and resolved to begin at once preparing for a struggle in years to come which would give them back more than they were now forced to abandon. They set to work to create a powerful navy, and at the same time added steadily to the fighting strength of their army, which for a while found useful war training in the subjugation of the hill tribes of Formosa.

The millions of the war indemnity and loans negotiated abroad were expended on a great scheme of armaments. A fleet of battleships, cruisers, and torpedo craft was built in foreign shipyards, and the personnel of the navy was increased to provide officers and crews. The Japanese Government went on for years patiently preparing, regardless of conduct on the part of Russia that might have tempted a less self-possessed Power to premature action.

The Russian Government had hardly forced Japan to abandon so large a part of her conquests when it took advantage of the weakness of China to obtain from the Pekin Government the right to make a railway through Manchuria to the treaty port of Niu-chwang, and to place garrisons along the new line for its protection, and further the right to garrison Port Arthur, use it as a naval station, and occupy the adjacent territory. When the first rumours of the Russo-Chinese Treaty reached Europe they were treated with incredulity.

It was said that it was impossible that Russia could cynically claim a position which she had just declared was incompatible with the independence of China, and which she had argued the nations of Europe could not permit to Japan or any other Power. But presently the treaty was published, and acted upon, Russia making Port Arthur her chief naval station in the East, announcing a project for a great commercial port at Talienwan Bay, and, further, occupying the treaty port of Niu-chwang. There was a brief period of tension, during which there was a talk of various

Powers resisting this barefaced aggression, but European statesmen thought that an easier course was open to them. Instead of resisting the aggressor, they embarked in a policy of aggression themselves, on the plea of securing compensations and guarantees. The weakness of China made her the ready victim of this policy.

Foreign aggression from so many quarters called forth a patriotic movement in China, which in 1900 culminated in the "Boxer" revolt. For a while Japan and the European Powers, including Russia, became allies, to save their embassies and repress the rising about Pekin. In the campaign the Japanese forces proved themselves the most efficient of all, and their chiefs returned home with an absolute confidence that they could successfully meet European soldiers in the field.

Japan had made the most unsparing use of its rights in Korea, acquired by the Treaty of Shimonoseki, all but absolutely annexing the country. After the Boxer revolt Admiral Alexieff, who was governor of the Russian possessions in the Far East, embarked on a dangerous policy of provocation towards Japan. He had an ill-informed contempt for the hardy islanders. He underrated their power of resistance, and felt sure that the mere fact that the Russian fleet outnumbered theirs would secure the command of the sea for Russia, and have a decisive effect in the event of a conflict. He believed that the sooner it came the better.

The Russian fleet in the East was steadily reinforced, unit by unit. The Japanese people began to see in these proceedings, and in the work done at Port Arthur, a threat of early hostilities, and there was a general call on the Government to anticipate the blow, when relations became strained between the two countries in 1903. The Tokio Government was anxious not to precipitate the war, for the organization of the army required some months for completion, but the feeling in the navy, army, and civil population forced its hand.

After a brief delay of negotiations, during which both parties worked with feverish energy to secure additional armaments, diplomatic relations were broken off at the beginning of February, 1904, and then, without waiting for any formal declaration of war, the Japanese torpedo flotilla swooped down on the Russian fleet lying in the roads outside the narrow entrance of Port Arthur, found them utterly unprepared to meet this sudden attack, and crippled several of the ships. A second blow was the destruction of the first-class armoured cruiser *Variag*, the Russian guardship at Chemulpo, by a Japanese squadron.

Most of the best ships in the Russian navy were in the East at the outbreak of the war. Alexieff had, however, made the initial mistake of dividing the force at his disposal. Away north at Vladivostock was a squadron of three large armoured cruisers, the *Gromoboi*, *Rossia*, and *Rurik*, and the protected cruiser *Bogatyr*. The Variag was isolated at Chemulpo, the port of Seoul, doing duty that might have been left to a gunboat.

At Port Arthur, under Admiral Stark, there was a strong fleet, including seven battleships, the *Petropavlosk, Poltava, Peresviet, Pobieda, Retsivan, Sebastopol*, and *Tsarevitch*, the cruisers *Askold, Boyarin, Bayan, Pallada, Diana*, and *Novik*, and a flotilla of torpedo craft and the mine-laying steamer *Yenessei*. In the torpedo attack on the evening of 8 February the *Retsivan, Tsarevitch*, and *Pallada* were badly damaged. The *Variag* was destroyed next day, and a few days later the *Yenessei* accidentally blew herself up while laying mines.

This series of disasters seemed for a while to have almost destroyed the morale of the fleet. Stark set to work to repair his damaged ships, made no attempt to meet the Japanese at sea, or interfere with the transport of their armies to the mainland of Asia, and, subordinating his fleet to the defence of Port Arthur, even landed guns and men to strengthen the landward works. The Japanese blockaded the port, insulted it with long-range bombardments, and tried to block the narrow entrance by sinking old steamers across it.

In March the arrival of the best officer in the Russian Navy, Admiral Makharoff, for a while inspired new energy into the Port Arthur fleet. The repairs of the injured ships were completed, and on 13 April the admiral steamed out to challenge Togo and the main Japanese fleet to battle. Notwithstanding precautions taken against the known danger of floating mines, the fleet entered a tract of water where several were afloat, and the flagship *Petropavlosk* was destroyed with fearful suddenness by the explosion of one of them. There was great loss of life, but the most serious blow to Russia was the death of the admiral.

After the fleet returned to the harbour there came another period of irresolute inactivity. It was not till August, when several ships had been injured at their anchors by the bombardment from the land batteries of the Japanese attack, and it was evident that the port would soon be a dangerous place for the ships, that Admiral Witjeft proceeded to sea, announcing that he was going to Vladivostock, the cruiser squadron from that port having been warned to come out and reinforce him on his way.

The sea-fight, known as the battle of the Tenth of August, took place a few miles to seaward of the port. Witjeft led the fleet in his flagship the *Tsarevitch*, followed by the battleships *Retsivan*, *Sebastopol*, *Pobieda Poltava*, and *Peresviet* (carrying the flag of the second in command, Rear-Admiral Prince Ukhtomsky), and the cruiser division made up of the *Askold* (carrying the flag of Rear-Admiral Reitzenstein), *Pallada*, *Diana*, and *Novik*, besides eight destroyers. The cruiser *Bayan* had been so damaged that she was left in port. Witjeft had a marked superiority in battleships. Togo had had six new first-rate ships of the class under his command at the outset of the war, but on 15 May he had lost two of them, one-third of his battleship fleet, by a disaster like that of the Petropavlosk.

On that May morning, while cruising off Port Arthur, he ran into a field of drift mines, and in a few minutes the battleships *Hatsuse* and *Yashima*, and the cruiser *Yoshino*, were destroyed. The Japanese managed till the end of the war to conceal the fact that the *Yashima* had been lost, and the Russians up to the battle of Tsu-shima believed Togo had five of his big battleships intact. In the battle of 10 August he put in his main fighting-line the two powerful armoured cruisers *Nisshin* and *Kasuga*, purchased from the Argentine Government on the eve of the war.

The battle began with long-range firing at 1 p.m., and continued till after seven in the evening. It was decided by the superior gunnery of the Japanese, and the damage done by their high explosive shells. The *Tsarevitch*, badly cut up and set on fire, was driven out of the line. Witjeft was killed by a shell. His last word was to reiterate his order to push for Vladivostock. As darkness came on Ukhtomsky lost heart, and led the fleet back to Port Arthur. If he had held on he might have got through the Japanese fleet, for their ammunition was almost exhausted when the firing ceased.

Reitzenstein, with the cruisers, tried to execute Witjeft's last order. The *Pallada*, however, left him and followed the battleships. The rest of the cruiser squadron and the destroyers that accompanied it were forced to part company, and only the *Novik* got through to the northwards. The *Diana* fled southwards to the French port of Saigon; the *Askold*, with a destroyer, reached Shanghai. The battered *Tsarevitch*, with three destroyers, took refuge at Kiao-chau. All these ships were disarmed by the French, German, and Chinese authorities, and detained till the end of the war, when they were restored to the Russian Government.

The *Novik* failed to get into Vladivostock, but reached a Russian port in Saghalien, where a few days later she was tracked down and destroyed by Japanese cruisers. The Vladivostock squadron had come out to meet the unfortunate Witjeft. The *Boyarin* was left behind, damaged by accidentally grounding, so the squadron was made up of the three big armoured cruisers *Gromoboi*, *Rossia*, and *Rurik*. They were approaching the straits of Tsu-shima, and were as far south as Fusan, when they were discovered and attacked by Admiral Kamimura's cruiser squadron, on 14 August.

Once more good gunnery against poor shooting decided the fight. The *Rurik* was sunk, and the *Gromoboi* and *Rossia* returned to Vladivostock, bearing marks of very hard hitting—riddled funnels, and sides hastily patched with plates of iron, told of the straight shooting of the Japanese cruisers. In both the action with the Port Arthur battleship fleet and the Vladivostock cruiser squadron the losses of the Japanese had been very slight.

On paper the Russians had had a distinct superiority over the Japanese in sea-power at the outset, so far as it can be measured by balancing off battleships, cruisers, and minor craft in parallel columns. In the months before the war there was ample material for the enterprising journalist to work up a navy scare at Tokio. But once more it was shown that not the number of ships but the temper and training of the men are the true measure of power on the sea. From the first Togo had asserted his superiority, and by asserting secured it. After the naval engagements of 10 and 14 August the Russian Navy in the Far East accepted a position of helpless inaction. Ukhtomsky kept what was left of the fine fleet, that had been originally assembled at Port Arthur, anchored in the land-locked harbour till the ships were sunk by fire of the besieging batteries.

While the Far Eastern fleet was still in being, and Port Arthur was holding out, the Russian Government had announced its intention of sending a second fleet from Europe to the seat of war. It had two fleets in European waters, those of the Black Sea and the Baltic. The Black Sea fleet was not available. International treaties barred its exit from the Dardanelles. Only the Baltic dockyards could supply the new armada.

As soon as the news of the first torpedo attack on Port Arthur arrived, in February, 1904, there was talk of the new fleet for the East, and unofficially the end of June was spoken of as the time when it would be ready to sail. From the first it was obvious that this was an over-sanguine estimate, unless the fleet was to be made up entirely of old and weak ships. The best units that could be made available, and without some at least of which the fleet could hardly be sent out, were five powerful battleships that were being completed in the Neva yards and at Cronstadt. Two had been launched in 1901, two in 1902, and the fifth in 1903, but even on the 1901 ships there was a large amount of work to be done.

Naval experts declared that the fleet would not be ready for a year, and that even then the difficulty of coaling would make its voyage to the other side of the world in war time a hopeless task for the admiral in command.

By hard work the fleet was made ready for sea by the middle of September. The coaling difficulty was overcome by taking colliers with the fleet, contracting with a German firm to send large coal-laden steamers to various points on the route selected, and straining to the utmost the benevolent neutrality of France, and using her colonial ports as halting places on the way. There was some difficulty in recruiting a sufficient number of engineer officers, and of stokers who could manage the novel tubular boilers of the new battleships, and the fleet was undoubtedly handicapped by the inexperience of its engine-room and stoke-hold staff.

Admiral Rojdestvensky, the officer chosen for the supreme command, had an excellent record. He was fifty-six years of age, and had served in the navy since 1865. In the Russo-Turkish War he had distinguished himself by brilliant attacks on Turkish ships of war with a small torpedo gunboat, the *Vesta*. He had been naval attaché in London, and had filled important technical and official positions at St. Petersburg, being for a while chief of the general Naval Staff. Finally he had personal knowledge of the Eastern seas and of the Japanese navy, for he had commanded the Russian squadron in the Far East during the war between China and Japan.

On 14 August—just after the news of the disastrous sortie of the Port Arthur fleet had reached Europe, and on the very day that Kamimura defeated the Vladivostock squadron and sank the *Rurik*—Admiral Rojdestvensky hoisted his flag on board his flagship, the *Knias Suvaroff*, at Cronstadt. But there was still much work to be done, and recent mishaps to some of the ships' machinery to be made good, so the fleet did not sail till 25 August. Even then it was only for a few days' training cruise in the Baltic.

On the 30th the fleet was back again at Cronstadt. Engineers and mechanics worked night and day, setting right defects in the ships, and on 11 September there was another start, this time for the port of Libau.

The fleet consisted of seven battleships, two armoured cruisers, and some protected cruisers and torpedo-boat destroyers. It was to be joined at Libau by a miscellaneous collection of craft—some small cruisers and a number of merchantmen to be used as auxiliary cruisers, store, hospital, and repair ships.

Of the five new battleships in the Neva yards four had been got ready for sea. These were the *Borodino, Orel, Imperator Alexander III,* and *Knias Suvaroff.* They were powerful ships of 13,000 to 13,500 tons displacement, with engines of nominal 16,000 horse-power, and their official speed, which they never realized, was eighteen knots.

Their heaviest armour was nine inches, and they carried two pair of 12-inch guns fore and aft in armoured turrets, with an auxiliary armament of twelve 6-inch quick-firers besides lighter guns. The three other battleships, the *Ossliabya, Navarin,* and *Sissoi Veliki* were older ships. The newest of them, the *Ossliabya,* launched in 1898, was on her way to the East when the war broke out, and had turned back. She was of 12,600 tons displacement, and claimed a speed of eighteen knots. She carried four 10-inch and eleven 6-inch guns. The other two ships were rated as having sixteen knots speed, but probably could not much exceed twelve. Their displacement and principal armament were:—

Navarin, 10,000 tons, four 12-inch guns, eight 6-inch Q.F.

Sissoi Veliki, 8880 tons, four 12-inch guns, six 6-inch Q.F.

The two armoured cruisers were old ships:—

Admiral Nakhimoff, 8500 tons, eight 8-inch, ten 6-inch guns.

Dimitri Donskoi, 7796 tons, six 6-inch, ten 4.7 inch guns.

Two of the protected cruisers, the *Aurora* and *Oleg*, were ships of about 7000 tons, carrying for their main armament the former eight and the latter twelve 6-inch guns. The other cruisers were four smaller ships, but some of them were comparatively new vessels with good speed—useful as scouts.

Well manned with competent engineers and trained gunners the fleet would have been formidable enough, notwithstanding its weaker units. But here again it was the men that counted.

In the first week of October the fleet was taken to Revel. The Tsar arrived there on the 9th and inspected it next day. On the 11th it sailed. But it stopped again at Libau, until October 15, when at last it started for the East.

There had been wild rumours that the Japanese had sent emissaries to Europe, obtained some light craft, and fitted them as improvised torpedo-boats for the purpose of attacking the fleet on its voyage through the narrow waters that form the exit from the Baltic or during the crossing of the North Sea. The Russian police attached such importance to these canards that Rojdestvensky was warned to take precaution against attack until he was out on the open ocean. He passed the Danish straits with his ships partly cleared for action, fired on a Swedish merchantman and a German fishing-boat, and, avoiding the usual course from the Skaw to the Channel, ran by the Dogger Bank, and in a panic of false alarm opened fire on the steam trawling fleet, sinking a boat and killing and wounding several men.

The result was an outburst of indignation in England, a partial mobilization of the British fleet, and some days of extreme tension, when it seemed likely that England would be drawn into the war, with the probability that France would then, under the terms of her alliance with Russia, have also to enter into the conflict. An agreement was arranged under which there was to be an international inquiry into the Dogger Bank incident, and Russia promised to make full reparation.

Meanwhile the Baltic fleet had run down Channel and across the Bay of Biscay, and southwards to Tangier, where it was concentrated on 3 November, watched by Lord Charles Beresford and the Channel Fleet, for the period of sharp tension was not over. At Tangier Rojdestvensky divided his force. He went southward along the African coast with the first division, and sent the second division under Admiral Fölkersham into the Mediterranean to go eastwards by the Suez Canal route. A third division had been formed at Libau to reinforce the fleet. It was composed of the armoured cruisers *Izumrud* and *Oleg*, three auxiliary cruisers (armed liners of the volunteer fleet), the *Terek*, *Rion*, and *Dnieper*, a flotilla of destroyers, and a number of storeships. It sailed from Libau on 7 November.

Rojdestvensky put into various African ports, mostly in the French colonies, and coaled his ships from his colliers. He was at Dakar, in West Africa, on 13 November; at Gaboon on the 26th; in Great Fish Bay on 6 December; and at Angra Pequeña on the 11th. He passed Cape Town on 19 December. Rounding the Cape, he steered for Madagascar, and on 1 January, 1905, he anchored in the Bay of Ste. Marie, near Tamatave.

On that same New Year's Day General Stoessel sent a flag of truce out to General Nogi, to inform him that he was anxious to arrange the immediate surrender of Port Arthur. The capitulation was signed next day. Thus at the very moment that Rojdestvensky and the main fighting force of the Baltic fleet established itself in the Indian Ocean, its nearest possible base in the Eastern seas passed into Japanese hands, and the problem the Russian admiral had to solve became more difficult.

Fölkersham, with the second division, rejoined Rojdestvensky's division in the waters of Madagascar.

From Ste. Marie the fleet moved to the roadstead of Nossi-Bé, at the north end of Madagascar, where it was joined in February by the reinforcements for Libau. Rojdestvensky had now under his command an armada of some forty ships of all kinds, including storeships and colliers. Now that Port Arthur had fallen he seemed in no hurry to proceed eastwards.

There had been an agitation in Russia for a further reinforcement of the fleet, and though the addition of a few more old and weak ships could add no real strength to Rojdestvensky's armada, the Government yielded to the clamour, and on February 15 dispatched from Libau a fourth division, under the command of Admiral Nebogatoff. The flagship was an armoured turret-ship, the *Imperator Nikolai I*, of 9700 tons, dating from 1889, and classed in the Navy List as a battleship; with her went three small armoured "coast-defence battleships," the General Admiral Apraxin, the Admiral Ushakoff, and the Admiral Senyavin, all of about 4000 tons, and the cruiser *Vladimir Monomach*, of a little over 5500 tons.

Rojdestvensky seemed inclined to wait at Nossi-Bé for Nebogatoff's arrival, but the Japanese addressed strong protests to Paris against Madagascar being made a base of operations for a huge expedition against them; the French Government sent pressing remonstrances to their friends at St. Petersburg, and the admiral was ordered by cable to move on.

Sailing from Nossi-Bé on 25 March, Rojdestvensky steered first for the Chagos Archipelago, and then for the Straits of Malacca. In the afternoon of 8 April the fleet passed Singapore, keeping well out to sea. The ships were burning soft coal, and an enormous cloud of black smoke trailed from the forest of funnels. Steamers ran out from the port to see the splendid sight of the great crowd of ships moving four abreast into the China Sea. Before the fleet sailed many critics of naval matters had prophesied that as Russia had no coaling stations the coaling difficulty would make it impossible for Rojdestvensky ever to carry his fleet so far. The successful entry into the Eastern seas was therefore regarded as something of an exploit. It was a revelation of the far-reaching power that would belong to better-equipped fleets in future wars.

While the Baltic fleet was on its way the Japanese Government, patriotically supported by the Press and the people, kept a strict silence on all naval matters. There were wild conjectures that under this veil of secrecy Togo had moved southwards, that he would fall on his enemy during the voyage across the Indian Ocean, or wait for him in the China Sea. But the Japanese admiral had no reason for embarking in such adventures. He knew that if he kept his fleet near the shores of Japan his enemy must come sooner or later within effective striking distance.

Rojdestvensky might attempt a raid on the coasts of Japan, or make a dash for Niu-chwang to seize that port, now the nearest base of supply of the Japanese field army. Far-seeing precautions were taken against this eventuality by accumulating enormous stores of supplies in the immediate rear of the army. But it was far more likely that the Russian admiral would try to reach Vladivostock, either with or without a battle. To do so he would have ultimately to pass through one of three channels into the Sea of Japan. He must choose between the Korean or Tsu-shima straits between Japan and Korea, or the Tsugaru channel between Nippon and Yozo, or the La Pérouse Straits (known to the Japanese as the Soya channel) still further north. Whatever course he chose, the best position for the Japanese fleet was near the Tsu-shima straits, with the arsenal and dockyard of Shimonoseki close by on the Japanese shore. This the Russians themselves foresaw would be the most likely position for Togo to select.

He made Masampho Bay on the Korean side of the straits, and inside them (the Douglas Bay of our Admiralty Charts), the station for his fleet. Freed from all harassing blockading and cruising work, he devoted the period between the retirement and destruction of the Port Arthur fleet in the late summer of 1904, and the approach of the Russians in May, 1905, to repairing his ships very thoroughly, substituting new guns for those they had mounted at the beginning of the war, which had had their rifling worn down.

Continual target practice and manœuvre exercises kept every ship and every man up to the mark. Charts of the sea around Japan were ruled off into small numbered squares, so as to facilitate the reporting of the enemy's position and movements from the moment he would be first sighted. An elaborate system of scouting by light cruisers was organized; signal stations were established on islands and headlands, and wireless installations erected at central and outlying points. If Rojdestvensky made for the Tsu-shima channels, Togo was there to meet him. If he went for either of the more northern straits, the Japanese admiral counted on having news of his movements in sufficient time to enable him to steam at full speed by a shorter route, and still interpose between the Baltic armada and Vladivostock.

After passing Singapore, on 25 March, there was another delay before the final advance of the Russian fleet. Rojdestvensky was anxious to give time to Nebogatoff to join him. This last reinforcement was coming by the Mediterranean route. The Russian commander-in-chief again strained French neutrality to the utmost. In April and May he passed week after week in the ports of French Cochin China, first at Kamranh and then at Van Fong or Honkohe. Here, early in May, he was at last joined by Nebogatoff's squadron.

Again Japan protested against the use of French harbours by her enemy. The diplomatic tension became acute, and at one moment it seemed as if the Russian admiral were anxious to produce complications that would force France into the war. But at last, to the general relief, on 14 May he sailed from Honkohe Bay. He passed through the Bashi Strait between Formosa and the Philippines, and then steered for Shanghai. Here, on 25 May, the fighting portion of the fleet lay out at sea, while a crowd of auxiliary steamers, colliers, store-ships, and armed merchantmen were sent into the Wusung River, the mouth of the Yang-tse, and anchored there.

Their appearance without the fleet to which they belonged led to many conjectures. The Japanese at once grasped its real meaning. To quote the message cabled by the Tokio correspondent of *The Times*:—

> They read it as a plain intimation that Rojdestvensky intended to put his fate to the test at Tsu-shima, since, had it been his purpose to make for Tsugaru or Soya, he must have retained the services of these auxiliary ships during several days longer. It is apparent, indeed, that the Russian admiral here made his first cardinal mistake; he should have kept his non-combatant vessels out of sight as long as possible. Their absence from the arena would have been a mysterious element, whereas their apparition, especially as a segregated squadron in the Yang-tse River, furnished an unerring clue to expert observers.

With the fleet the admiral retained only the hospital and repairing ships and those laden with naval stores for the Vladivostock dockyard. On the evening of the 25th the fleet stood out to sea heading for Tsu-shima. The weather was bad, with a probability that it would be worse. There was a rising wind and sea with cold rain that made a blinding haze, but the Russian staff officers were rather pleased than depressed at such unpleasant conditions. Thick weather would baffle the Japanese scouts and lookout stations, and rough seas would keep their torpedo flotillas at anchor.

Out ahead were the fast cruisers of the scouting division, the *Svietlana*, *Almaz*, and *Ural*. After these came the main body of the fleet in line ahead in two columns, the heavy armour-clads on the starboard (right side), the rest of the armoured ships and four cruisers in the port line. Abreast of the leading ships each flank was guarded by a cruiser and two torpedo destroyers. After the fighting lines and between their foaming wakes steamed four store-ships and two repairing ships. Last of all were the two steamers fitted as hospital ships. The arrangement is best shown by a rough diagram:—

		SVIETLANA.		
	Almaz	(Cruisers.)	*Ural*	
		PORT LINE.	STARBOARD LINE.	
(Cruiser)				(Cruiser)
Jemschug		*Imperator Nikolai*	*Knias Suvaroff*	*Izumrud*
2 torpedo				2 torpedo
		Admiral Senyavin	*Imperator Alexander*	
destroyers		*Admiral Apraxin*	*Borodino*	destroyers.
		Admiral Ushakoff	*Orel*	
Cruisers.		*Oleg*	*Ossliabya.*	
		Aurora	*Sissoi Veliki*	
		Dimitri Donskoi	*Navarin*	
		Alexander Monomach	*Admiral Nakhimoff*	

5 torpedo destroyers.

Store-ships. *Anadir, Irtish, Korea, Kamschatka*

Repairing ships and tugs *Russ, Svir.*
Hospital ships *Orel, Kostroma.*

In this order the great fleet steamed slowly through the rain and darkness. On board the great battleships there was much grumbling at "Nebogatoff's old tubs," though they themselves could not do much better, for poor coal, inefficient stoking, and weed-grown bottom-plates handicapped even the newest of them. The next day, 26 May, was the eve of the greatest naval battle in all history. "The clouds began to break and the sun shone fitfully," says Captain Semenoff,[1] "but although a fairly fresh south-westerly wind had sprung up, a thick mist still lay upon the water." Rojdestvensky meant to pass the perilous straits in daylight, and he calculated that by noon next day the fleet would be in the narrows of Tsu-shima.

Behind that portal of the Sea of Japan Togo was waiting confidently for his enemy, who, he knew, must now be near at hand. Never before had two such powerful fleets met in battle, and the fate of the East hung upon the result of their encounter.

That result must depend mainly upon the heavy armoured ships. In these and in the number of guns of the largest calibre, the Russians had an advantage so far as mere figures went, as the following tables show:—

ARMOURED SHIPS

Class.	Japan.	Russia.
Battleships	04	08
Coast-defence armour-clad	—	03
Armoured cruisers	08	03
Total	12	14

---

[1] Semenoff had served with the Port Arthur fleet on board one of the cruisers which were disarmed in a neutral port after the battle of August 10th, 1904. He then returned to Europe, was attached to the staff of the Baltic fleet, and went out to the East on board the flagship. His remarkable narrative, *The Battle of Tsu-shima*, is a vivid detailed account of the Suvaroff's fortunes during the fight. He died in 1910.

Heavy Guns

	Guns.	12-inch.	10-inch.	9-inch.	8-inch.	Quick-firers. 6-inch.	4.7-inch.
Japan		16	01	—	30	160	—
Russia		26	15	04	08	102	30[2]

The annexed tables give some details of Russian and Japanese armoured ships.

With regard to the armour it must be kept in mind for purposes of comparison that the armoured belts of the newer ships, nine inches at the thickest part, were of Harveyized or Krupp steel, and could resist penetration better than the thicker belts of the older ships. It will be noticed that the Japanese carried fewer of the heavier types of guns, but had more 6-inch quick-firers than the Russians. This is a point to bear in mind in following the story of the battle. It was the steady rain of 100-pounder shells from the quick-firers that paralysed the fighting power of the Russian ships.

Far more important than the mere number of guns was the fact that the Japanese shot straighter and had a more effective projectile. There was such a marked difference between the effect of the Japanese shells at Tsu-shima and in the naval battle of 10 August, 1904, that Captain Semenoff, who was present at both battles, thought that in the interval the Japanese must have adopted a more powerful kind of high explosive for their bursting charges. This was not the case. Throughout the war the Japanese used for their bursting charges the famous Chimose powder. But perhaps between 10 August, 1904, and the following May they had improved their fuses, so as to detonate the charge more certainly and thoroughly.

The first five battleships on the Russian list were up-to-date modern vessels. The *Navarin* was fairly fit to lie in line with them. The rest were, to use a familiar expression, "a scratch lot,"

---

2. These tables are from Sir George Sydenham Clarke's preface to Captain Lindsay's translation of Semenoff's *Tsu-shima*, p. 11.

coast-defence ships of small speed and old craft quite out of date. The decks of the larger ships were encumbered with an extra supply of coal, and this must have seriously diminished their margin of stability, with, as we shall see, disastrous results.

Admiral Togo could oppose to them only four modern battleships. But his two heavy cruisers, the *Nisshin* and *Kasuga* (the ships bought from Argentina on the eve of the war), might almost have been classed as smaller battleships, and certainly would have been given that rank a few years earlier. His fine fleet of armoured cruisers were at least a match for the Russian coast-defence ships and the older battleships.

RUSSIA

Class.	Displacement. Tons.	Thickest Armour. Inches.	Principal Armament. Guns.	Men.
Battleships:	13,516	09	4 12-inch 12 6-inch	740

Knias Suvaroff (Flagship of Admiral Rojdestvensky.)
Imperator Alexander III
Borodino
Orel
These four ships were all completed in 1904.

Ossliabya	12,674	09.0	4 10-inch 11 6-inch	732

Flagship of Rear-Admiral Fölkersham. Completed 1901.

Sissoi Veliki	08,880	15.7	4 12-inch 6 6-inch	550

Completed 1894.

Navarin	10,206	16.0	4 12-inch 8 6-inch	550

Completed 1895.

Imperator Nikolai I	09,672	14.0	4 9-inch 8 6-inch	604

Completed 1892. Flagship of Rear-Admiral Nebogatoff.

Coast-defence Armour-clads:

Gen. Adm Apraxin	04,162	10.0	3 10-inch 4 6-inch	400

Completed 1898.

Admiral Senyavin & Admiral Ushakoff	04,684	10.0	4 9-inch 4 6-inch	400

Completed 1895.

Armoured Cruisers:

Admiral Nakhimoff	08,524	10.0	8 8-inch 10 6-inch	567

Completed 1898. Reconstructed 1895.

Dimitri Donskoi	06,200	07.0	6 6-inch 10 4.7-inch	510

Completed 1885. Reconstructed 1896.

Vladimir Monomach	05,593	10.0	5 8-inch 12 6-inch	550

Completed 1885. Rearmed 1898.

JAPAN

Class. [3]	Displacement. Tons.	Thickest Armour. Inches.	Principal Armament. Guns.	Men.
Battleships:				
Mikasa	15,200	09	4 12-inch 14 6-inch	795

Completed 1902. Flagship of Admiral Togo.

Skikishima	14,850	09	4 12-inch 14 6-inch	810

Completed 1899.

Asahi Fuji	12,320	14	4 12-inch 10 6-inch	600

Completed 1897.

Armoured Cruisers:

Nisshin, Kasuga	07,294	06	4 8-inch 14 6-inch	500

Completed 1904. Nisshin was flagship of Vice-Admiral Misu.

Idzumo, Iwate	09,750	07	4 8-inch 14 6-inch	500

Completed 1901. Idzumo—flagship of Vice-Admiral Kamimura.

Adzumo	09,436	07	4 8-inch	

---

[3]. The old turret-ship Chin-yen—captured from the Chinese (formerly the Chen-yuen) (4 12-inch and 4 6-inch guns)—was with the fleet, but is not included in a list of effective armour-clads.

			12 6-inch	500
Completed 1901.				
Asama, Tokiwa	09,700	07	4 8-inch	
			14 6-inch	500
Completed 1899.				
Yakumo	09,850	07	4 8-inch	
			12 6-inch	498
Completed 1901.				

Besides his armoured ships, Admiral Rojdestvensky had a squadron of six protected cruisers under Rear-Admiral Enquist, whose flag flew in the *Oleg*, a vessel of 6750 tons launched in 1903, and completed next year. She had for her principal armament twelve six-inch quick-firers. The other cruisers were the *Aurora*, of a little over 6000 tons, the *Svietlana*, of nearly 4000, the *Jemschug*, and *Izumrud*, of 3000 tons (these two armed with 47 quick-firing guns), and the *Almaz*, of 3285, a "scout" of good speed, carrying nothing heavier than 12-pounders. There was one auxiliary cruiser, the *Ural*,[4] a flotilla of nine destroyers, four transports, two repairing ships, and two hospital steamers.

Awaiting the battle in sight of his own shores, Togo had concentrated as auxiliary squadrons to his armoured fleet a considerable number of protected cruisers and a whole swarm of torpedo craft. At this stage of her naval development, and on the eve of a life-and-death struggle, Japan had no idea of "scrapping" even the older ships. Anything that could carry a few good guns, and brave men to fight them, might be useful, so even the old Chinese ironclad which had carried Ting's flag at the Yalu battle, a ship dating from 1882, was under steam in one of the auxiliary squadrons, with four new 12-inch guns in her barbettes.

There were three of these auxiliary squadrons, commanded by Rear-Admiral Dewa, Rear-Admiral Uriu, and Rear-Admiral Kataoka, the last having as a subordinate commander Rear-Admiral Togo, a relative of the commander-in-chief. Dewa's flag

---

4. A German Atlantic liner purchased at the beginning of the war—formerly known as the *Königin Maria Theresa*—"roomy and luxurious, but as a warship useless," says the Naval Constructor Politovsky, Chief Engineer of the Baltic Fleet.

flew in the *Kasagi*, a fine cruiser of nearly 5000 tons, built in America, and he had with him her sister ships, the *Chitose* and *Taka-sago*. Uriu's flag flew in the *Naniwa*, Togo's ship when he was a captain in the Chinese war. Several of the fine cruisers which Ito had then led to victory were present, many of them remodelled, and all provided with new guns. Then there were a number of small protected cruisers, built in Japanese dockyards since the Chinese war, the heralds of the later time when the Japanese navy would all be home-built. Battleships, armoured cruisers, and protected cruisers were all swifter than the Russian ships. The fleet as a whole could manœuvre at fully fifty per cent greater speed than the enemy, and this meant that it could choose its own position in battle.

The five torpedo squadrons included two or three torpedo-gunboats, twenty-one fine destroyers, and some eighty torpedo-boats. Togo's plans had the simplicity which is a necessity in the rough game of war, where elaborate schemes are likely to go wrong. Some of the swift protected cruisers were scouting south of the straits. The fleet was anchored in a body in Masampho Bay, and in wireless communication with its scouts. The armoured fleet was to make the main attack on the head of the Russian advance. The protected cruiser squadrons were to sweep round the enemy's flanks, fall upon his rear, and destroy his transports and auxiliaries. The torpedo flotilla was to be ready to dash in and complete the defeat of the enemy when his fleet was crippled by the fight with the heavy ships.

Most of the officers and men of the Russian fleet had the dogged courage that could carry them through even a hopeless fight, but they looked forward to the immediate future with forebodings of disaster. Even among the officers on board the great Suvaroff there was a feeling that the most that could be hoped for was that a few ships would struggle through to Vladivostock, if there was a battle, and that the best thing that could happen would be for the thick weather and rough seas to enable them to avoid anything like a close fight with the Japanese.

During the last day before the fight Rojdestvensky, who did

not want to hurry forward, but was timing his advance so as to pass the straits in the middle of the next day, spent some time in manœuvres. Captain Semenoff's notes on the proceedings convey a useful lesson.

> "Once again" (he says), "and for the last time, we were forcibly reminded of the old truism that a 'fleet' is created by long practice at sea in time of peace (cruising, not remaining in port), and that a collection of ships of various types hastily collected, which have only learned to sail together on the way to the theatre of operations, is no fleet, but a chance concourse of vessels."[5]

Wireless telegraphy had come into use since the last naval war, and a fleet could now try to overhear the aerial messages of an enemy. In the Russian fleet the order had been given that no wireless messages were to be sent. In other words, the operators were to keep silence, and listen by watching their apparatus. In the morning of the 26th they thought they detected messages passing. In the evening these were more frequent—"short messages of a word or two" was the interpretation that the experts in the signal cabins put upon the unintelligible flickerings of the indicator, and they suggested that they were mere negative code-signals from the Japanese scouts to their main fleet, repeating an indication that they were on the alert, and had seen nothing.

This was mere guesswork, however, and Politovsky's diary of the voyage[6] shows that near the Cape, at Madagascar, and out in the midst of the Indian Ocean, Rojdestvensky's wireless operators had thought that they detected Japanese aerial signalling, simply because the receivers gave indications they could not understand. Possibly these were merely the effect of electric storms on the apparatus.

Once or twice, on 26 May, they thought they could read fragments of sentences, such as—"Last night—nothing—eleven

---

5. *Tsu-shima*, p. 10.
6. *From Libau to Tsu-shima*. By the late Eugene S. Politovsky. Translated by Major F. R. Godvey, R.M.L.I. 1906.

lights—not in line." The short messages in the evening came at fixed times. This showed that prearranged signalling was really going on. It gave the impression that perhaps the fleet was being watched by unseen enemies.

As the sun went down the ships closed up, and half the officers were detailed for duty at the guns during the hours of darkness. The rest lay down fully dressed, ready to turn out at a moment's notice. Many slept on the decks. No lights were shown. Semenoff's description of that night of anxious expectation is worth quoting. He was on board the flagship, the *Suvaroff*:—

> The night came on dark. The mist seemed to grow denser, and through it but few stars could be seen. On the dark deck there prevailed a strained stillness, broken at times only by the sighs of the sleepers, the steps of an officer, or by an order given in an undertone. Near the guns the motionless figures of their crews seemed like dead, but all were wide awake, gazing keenly into the darkness. Was not that the dark shadow of a torpedo-boat? They listened attentively. Surely the throb of her engines and the noise of steam would betray an invisible foe. Stepping carefully, so as not to disturb the sleepers, I went round the bridges and decks, and then proceeded to the engine-room. For a moment the bright light blinded me. Here life and movement were visible on all sides. Men were nimbly running up and down the ladders; there was a tinkling of bells and a buzzing of voices. Orders were being transmitted loudly, but on looking more intently, the tension and anxiety—that same peculiar frame of mind so noticeable on deck—could also be observed.[7]

At daybreak the Japanese scouts were in touch. As the day came in grey light over the misty broken sea, one of their scouts, the auxiliary cruiser *Siano Maru* (an armed passenger liner), sweeping round through the haze, almost collided with the hospital ships, and then dashed off and disappeared in the twilight.

---
7. *Tsu-shima*, pp. 27, 28.

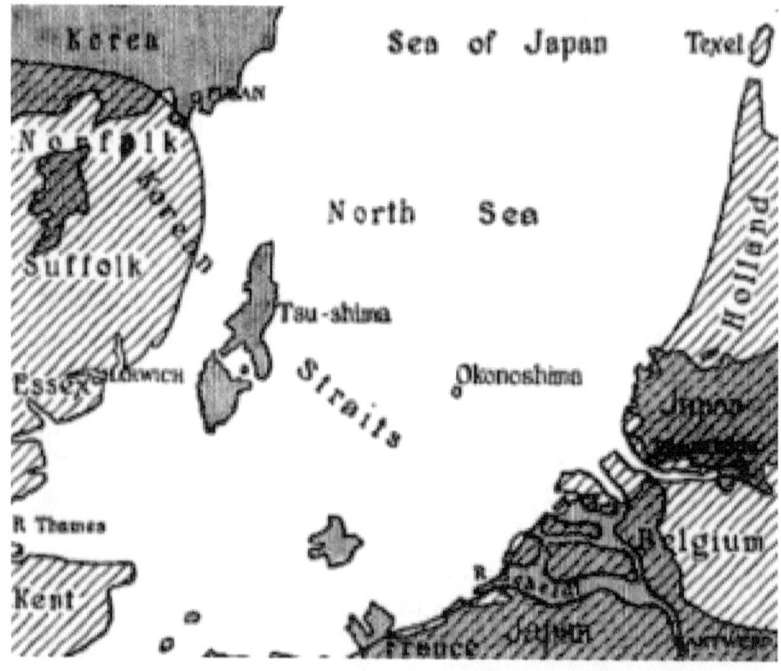

BATTLE OF TSU-SHIMA

Sketch map to show the extent of the waters in which the first part of the fight took place. the main features of the Korean (or Tsu-shima)

In former wars she would have had to run back to the fleet with her news. Now from her wireless apparatus the information was sent through the air to the receivers of the *Mikasa* in Masampho Bay, and in a few minutes Togo knew that "the enemy's fleet was in square No. 203 of the chart, apparently steering for the eastern passage," *i.e.* the strait between Tsu-shima Island and Japan.

In the straits and outside Masampho Bay a heavy sea was running, and though the wind blew strongly from the southwest, the weather was still hazy at sunrise, with patches of fog here and there. The main body of the Japanese fleet began to get up anchors and slip from its moorings.[8]

At dawn Rojdestvensky had called in the Almaz, leaving the *Jemschug* and *Izumrud* steaming in advance of his two divisions. The six auxiliary ships had closed up, so that the leading ship, the transport *Anadir*, was abreast of the centre of the two lines. The *Almaz*, *Svietlana*, and *Ural*, steamed at the rear of this central line of transports, to protect them in that direction. The two hospital ships, flying the Red Cross flag and trusting to it for safety, were well astern. About 6 a.m. the huge *Ural* came running up between the lines, and semaphored to the flagship that four ships in line ahead were passing across the rear of the fleet, but could not be clearly made out in the mist.

They could only be some of Togo's cruisers "shepherding" the fleet. Just before seven a fine cruiser was seen some five miles away on the starboard beam of the *Suvaroff*. She closed up to three miles, and was soon identified as the *Idzumo*. The big turret-guns were swung round to bear on her, but the Japanese cruiser, having seen what she wanted, increased her distance, but could be seen still keeping the fleet in sight. Togo's report notes that at 7 a.m. the *Idzumo* sent by wireless the second definite report of the enemy, stating that he was twenty-five miles

---

8. English people have so seldom occasion or opportunity of consulting large-scale maps of Japan, that there is an impression that the battle of Tsu-shima was fought in narrow waters, where there was no chance of the Russians eluding Togo and little room for manœuvring. The strait in which the battle took place is really about as wide as the North Sea between Harwich and the Hook of Holland. (See accompanying sketch map.)

north-west of Ukushima, steering north-east. This would make the Russian position about thirty miles south of the Tsu-shima Islands, heading for the channel to the east of them. An hour later, about 8 a.m., some Japanese ships showed themselves the other side of the fleet. Semenoff notes how:—

> The *Chin-yen, Matsushima, Itsukushima,* and *Hashidate,* appeared out of the mist, steaming on an almost parallel course. Ahead of them was a small, light cruiser, apparently the *Akitsushu,* which hurriedly drew off to the north as soon as we were able to see her well (and equally she us), and the whole squadron began slowly to increase their distance and gradually to disappear from sight.

This was Vice-Admiral Takeomi's division, composed of three of the cruisers that had fought at the Yalu battle, eleven years before, and the *Chin-yen,* which had fought against them as the *Ting-yuen.* The ship that ran out ahead was the only quick or modern ship in the squadron, the small Clyde-built armoured cruiser *Chiyoda.* If Rojdestvensky had had any speedy cruisers available, he might have severely punished this slow squadron of old ships. Takeomi showed he knew his enemy by thus boldly approaching in the mist.

The Russians now realized that they had watchful enemies all round them, and rightly conjectured that they would find the enemy's heavy ships in the straits ready for battle.

At 10 a.m. another cruiser squadron appeared on the port beam. This was Dewa's division, made up of the American-built sister ships *Kasagi* and *Chitose,* of nearly 5000 tons, and two smaller protected cruisers, the *Niitaka* and *Otowa,* lately turned out by Japanese yards. They seemed to invite attack. At a signal from the admiral, the eight armour-clads of the starboard line steamed ahead of the port line, turned together to port, and then, turning again, formed line ahead, leading the whole fleet. At the same time the transports moved out to Starboard, guarded by the *Vladimir Monomach* (detached from the port division), the *Svietlana, Almaz,* and *Ural.*

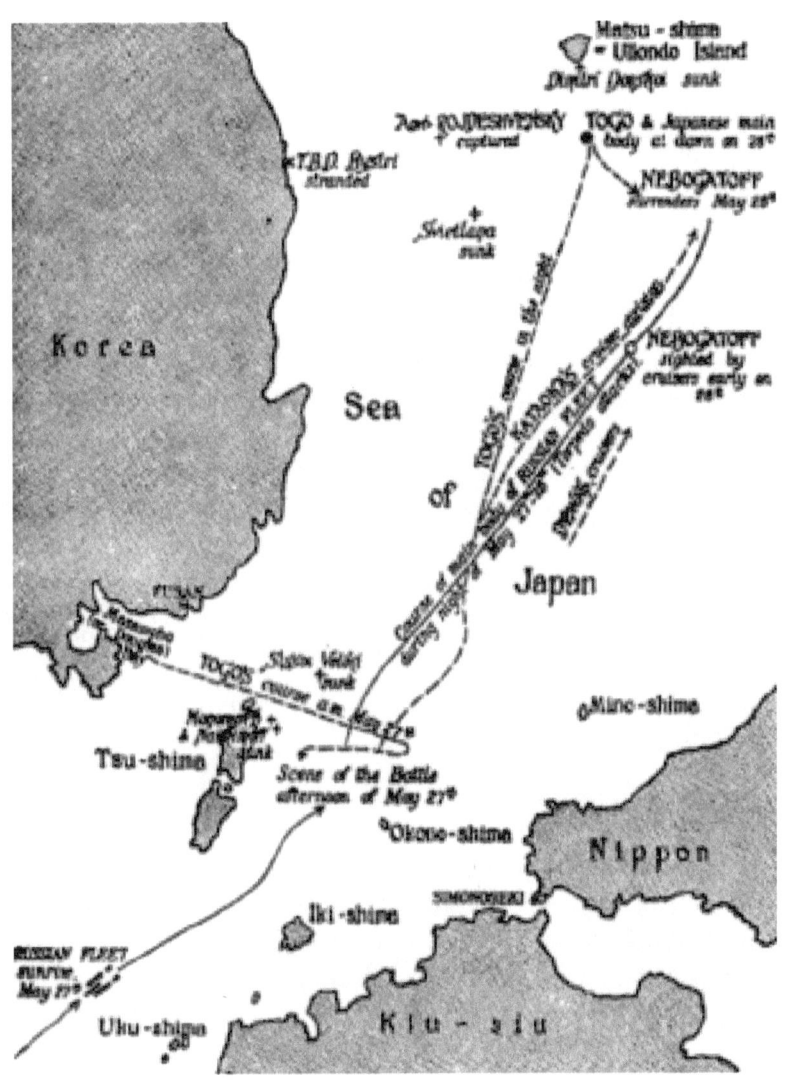

BATTLE OF TSU-SHIMA—GENERAL MAP

Dewa's cruisers held a parallel course with the Russian battleships for more than an hour, still apparently unsupported. The range was about five miles. At 11.20 the Russians opened fire on them. Semenoff says that it was the result of a mistake:

> The *Orel* fired an accidental shot (which she immediately reported by semaphore). Unable, with smokeless powder, to tell by which of the leading ships it had been fired, the fleet took it as a signal from the Suvaroff and opened fire. Of the whole fleet the fire of the 3rd Squadron was the heaviest.

This squadron was made up of Nebogatoff's "old tubs." Their heavy fire was probably the result of undisciplined excitement. The Japanese fired a few shots in reply, but no harm was done on either side. Rojdestvensky, who had kept the guns of his flagship silent, signalled "Ammunition not to be wasted," and the firing ceased in five minutes, just as the Japanese turned slowly and increased their distance.

Orders were now signalled for the men of the Russian fleet to have their dinners, and the officers lunched in turn. The harmless skirmish encouraged some of the Russian crews with the idea that they had been in action and were none the worse, and had driven the Japanese away. At noon the fleet was due south of Tsu-shima, which towered like a mountain out of the sea a few miles ahead. The signal was hoisted, "Change course N.23°E. for Vladivostock." It was the anniversary of the Tsar's coronation. Round the wardroom tables in his doomed fleet the officers stood up and drank with enthusiasm to the Emperor, the Empress, and "victory for Russia!"

The cheering had hardly died down when the bugles sounded the alarm. Every one hurried to his post. The enemy's cruisers had again shown themselves, this time accompanied by a flotilla of destroyers, that came rolling through the rough sea with the waves foaming over their bows. On a signal from the admiral the four leading battleships turned to starboard and stood towards the enemy, then re-formed line ahead on a course parallel to the rest of the fleet, and slightly in advance of it. The Japanese on the threat of attack had turned also and went off at high speed to the northwards.

At 1.20 p.m. the admiral signalled to the four next ships of the fleet to join the line of battleships, forming astern of them. The Russian armada was now well into the wide eastern strait of Tsu-shima, and far ahead through the mist a crowd of ships could be dimly seen. The crisis was near at hand.

On receiving the first wireless message from the *Shinano Maru* at daybreak, Togo had weighed anchor and come out of Masampho Bay, with his main fleet steering east, so as to pass just to the north of Tsu-shima. He had with him his twelve armoured ships, and Rear-Admiral Uriu's division of protected cruisers (*Naniwa, Takachico, Tsushima,* and *Akashi*), and a strong flotilla of destroyers. The smaller torpedo-boats, more than sixty in number, had been already sent to shelter in Miura Bay in the island of Tsu-shima, on account of the heavy seas.

During the morning Togo received a succession of wireless messages from his cruisers, and every mile of the enemy's progress, every change in his formation was quickly signalled to him. Shortly after noon he was able to note that the Russians were entering the straits, steaming at about 12 knots on a northeasterly course; that they were formed in two columns in line ahead, the starboard column being the stronger, and that they had their transports astern between the columns. He decided to attack them on the weaker side at 2 p.m., when he calculated that they would be near Okinoshima, a small island in the middle of the eastern strait, about half-way between Tsu-shima and the south-western headlands of Nippon.

At half-past one he was joined by Dewa's division of cruisers, and a few minutes later the divisions of Kataoka and the younger Togo rejoined. They had till now hung on the flanks of the Russian advance. At a quarter to two the enemy's fleet came in sight away to the south-westward of Okinoshima. Flags fluttered up to the signal yards of the *Mikasa*, and the fleet read with enthusiasm Togo's inspiring message:—

The rise or fall of the Empire depends upon today's battle. Let every man do his utmost.

He had been about ten miles north of Okinoshima at noon (by which time he had steamed some 90 miles from Douglas Bay since 5 a.m.), thence he turned back slowly, going west and a little south, till he sighted the Russians. He crossed their line of advance diagonally at about 9500 yards distance. His light cruiser divisions had received orders to steam southwards and attack the Russian rear, and were already well on their way.

The heavy Japanese ships, circling on the left front of the enemy's advance, put on speed, and were evidently intending to recross the bows of the battleship division, bringing a converging fire to bear on the leading ships—the manœuvre known as "crossing the T." As the *Mikasa* led the Japanese line on its turning movement Rojdestvensky swung round to starboard and opened fire at 8500 yards. Togo waited till the distance had shortened to 6500, and then the guns of the *Mikasa* flashed out.

At that moment only three other of his ships had made the turn. They also opened fire, and ship after ship as she came round into line joined in the cannonade. The Russians turned more slowly, and it was some time before the whole of their line was in action. Meanwhile a storm of fire had burst upon the leading ships of Rojdestvensky's lines, the *Suvaroff* and the *Ossliabya* at the head of the starboard and port divisions being each made a target by several of the enemy.

The Japanese gunners were firing with a rapidity that surprised even those who had been in the action of 10 August, and with much more terrible effect. In Captain Semenoff's narrative of the fate of the *Suvaroff* we have a remarkably detailed description of the execution done by the Japanese shells in this first stage of the battle. The opening shots went high. They flew over the *Suvaroff*, some of the big 12-inch projectiles turning over and over longitudinally in their flight. But at once Semenoff remarked that the enemy were using a more sensitive fuse than on 10 August. Every shell as it touched the water exploded in a geyser of smoke and spray.

As the Japanese corrected the range shells began to explode on board or immediately over the deck, and again there was proof of the improved fusing. The slightest obstacle—the guy of a funnel, the lift of a boat derrick—was enough to burst the shell.

The first fair hit was on the side, abreast of the forward funnel. It sent up a "gigantic column of smoke, water, and flame." Then several men were killed and wounded near the fore-bridge, and then there was a crash beside one of the quick-firers, and, the shell bursting as it penetrated the deck, set the ship on fire. In the battle of 10 August the flagship *Tsarevitch*, which had borne the brunt of the Japanese fire, had been hit just nineteen times, but now that the *Mikasa* and her consorts had got the range hit followed hit on the leading Russian ships.

"It seemed impossible," says Semenoff, "even to count the number of projectiles striking us. I had not only never witnessed such a fire before, but I had never imagined anything like it. Shells seemed to be pouring upon us incessantly one after another.... The steel plates and superstructure on the upper deck were torn to pieces, and the splinters caused many casualties. Iron ladders were crumpled up into rings, and guns were literally hurled from their mountings. Such havoc would never be caused by the simple impact of a shell, still less by that of its splinters. It could only be caused by the force of the explosion.... In addition to this there was the unusually high temperature and liquid flame of the explosion, which seemed to spread over everything. I actually watched a steel plate catch fire from a burst. Of course, the steel did not burn, but the paint on it did. Such almost incombustible materials as hammocks and rows of boxes, drenched with water, flared up in a moment. At times it was almost impossible to see anything with glasses, owing to everything being so distorted with the quivering, heated air. No! It was different to the 10th of August!"

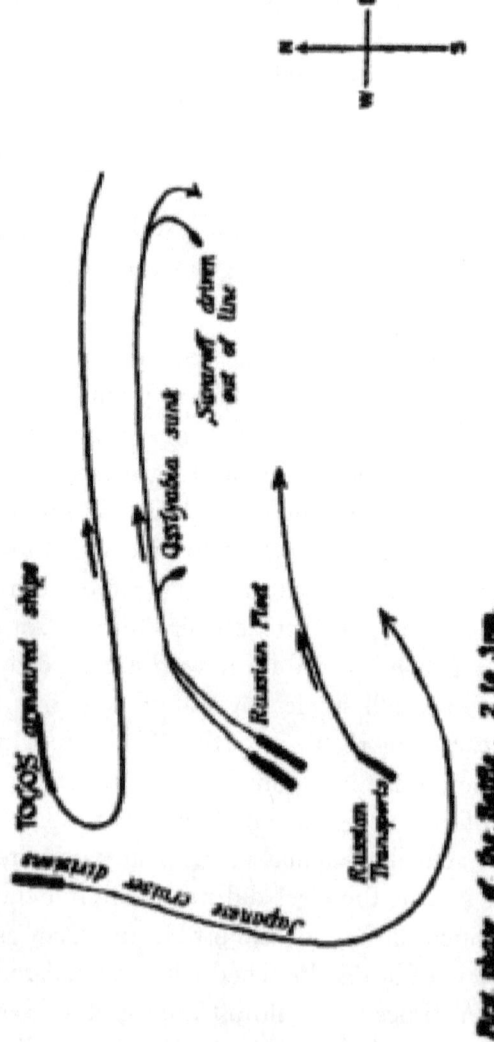

Battle Of Tsu-Shima – Diagrams of Movements during the fighting of May 27th
First Phase

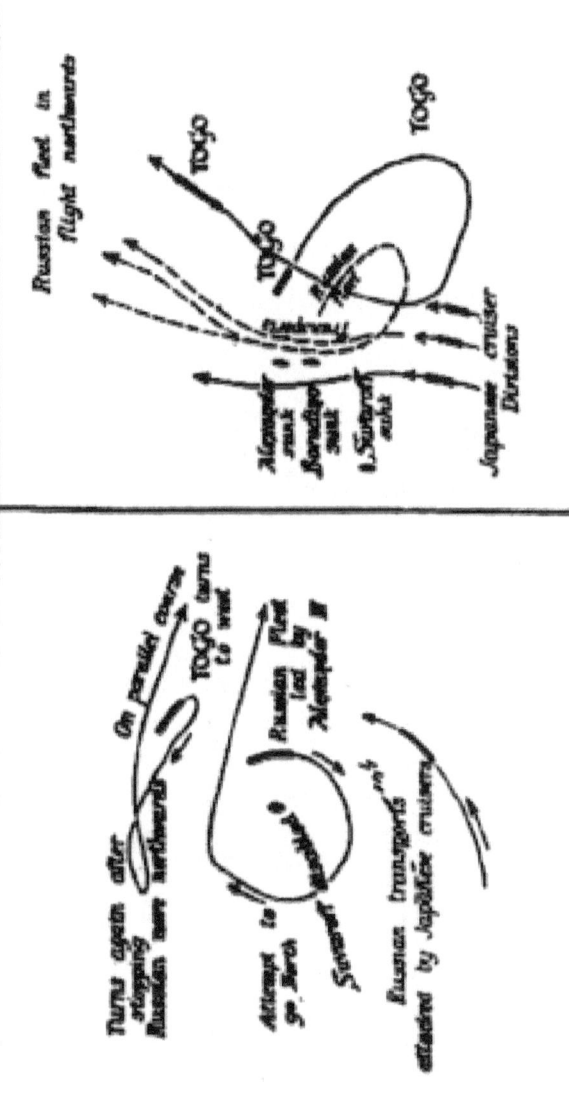

SECOND AND THIRD PHASES

In this storm of fire there was heavy loss of life. A shell-burst killed and wounded most of the signallers as they stood together at their station. An explosion against the opening of the conning-tower killed two officers beside Rojdestvensky, and slightly wounded the admiral. The fight had not lasted more than twenty minutes, and the *Suvaroff*, the *Alexander*, and *Borodino*, the three leading Russian ships, were all wrapped in black smoke from the fires lighted on board of them by the Chimose shells.

How was the Japanese line faring? I talked over his battle experiences with a Japanese officer not long after the day of Tsushima. He told me his impression was that at first the Russians shot fairly well, causing some loss of life at the more exposed stations on board the leading Japanese ships. "But," he added, "after the first twenty minutes they seemed suddenly to go all to pieces, and their shooting became wild and almost harmless." No wonder that under such a tornado of explosions, death and destruction, and with their ships ablaze, and range-finding and fire-controlling stations wrecked, the gunnery of the Russians broke down. One of the pithy sayings of the American Admiral Farragut was: "The best protection against the enemy's fire is the steady fire of your own guns." Tsu-shima gave startling proof of it.

Semenoff hoped that the Japanese were also suffering from the stress of battle. From the fore-bridge of the *Suvaroff* he scanned their line with his glasses. In the sea-fights of other wars both fleets were wrapped in a dense fog of powder smoke, but now with the new powder there was no smoke except that of bursting shells and burning material. So he could distinguish everything plainly.

> The enemy had finished turning. His twelve ships were in perfect order at close intervals, steaming parallel to us, but gradually forging ahead. No disorder was noticeable. It seemed to me that with my Zeiss glasses (the distance was a little more than two miles) I could distinguish the mantlets of hammocks on the bridges and the groups of men. But with us? I looked round. What havoc! Burning

bridges, smouldering débris on the decks, piles of dead bodies. Signalling and judging distance stations, gun-directing positions, all were destroyed. And astern of us the *Alexander* and the *Borodino* were also wrapped in smoke.

Men were killed in the turrets by shell splinters flying through the narrow gun openings. The fire hose was repeatedly cut to ribbons, and the men fighting the fire killed. The injuries caused by near explosions were terrible. Men were literally blown to atoms, or limbs were torn off. Eleven wooden boats piled up on the spar-deck were a mass of roaring flame. Gun after gun was disabled. And all the while a glance at the Japanese fleet showed them steaming and firing as if at peace manœuvres, without even one of their numerous flagstaffs and signal yards shot away. The battle had not lasted an hour, and it was already evident that it could have only one ending.

In the smoke and confusion Semenoff could only see what was happening in the front of the line, but the other ships were exposed to a heavy fire, and had less resisting power. The *Ossliabya*, the fifth of the battleships, and Fölkersham's flagship during the voyage,[9] was the first to succumb. The firing had hardly begun when a 12-inch projectile penetrated her forward above the water-line. In fine weather the effect would not have been very serious, but the heavy sea flooded her two bow compartments.

Then another shell started an armour plate on the water-line amidships, flooded the bunkers on the port side, and gave her a heavy list in that direction. Unsuccessful attempts were made to right her by opening valves and admitting water on the other side. Then a shell burst in the fore-turret and put all the crews of the two guns out of action. She was now settling down by the head and heeling over more and more to port. Suddenly the sea reached her lower gun-ports and poured into her. Then, like the unfortunate *Victoria*, she "turned turtle," and sank. It was at 2.25 that she disappeared thus suddenly, the first battleship ever sunk by gun-fire. Three of the destroyers picked up some of the crew

---

9. Admiral Fölkersham had a paralytic stroke while at Honkohe Bay, and died at sea two days before the battle.

who had jumped overboard.

As she sank, the three other ships of her division (*Sissoi*, *Navarin*, and *Nakhimoff*), under the stress of the Japanese fire, sheered for a while out of the line with their upper works ablaze in several places. The four stately battleships at the head of the line had then to face the concentrated attack of the enemy. The *Orel* was suffering like her consorts. Though her armour was nowhere penetrated, the shells burst their way into her unarmoured superstructure, and reduced everything on her upper decks to tangled wreckage.

Five minutes after the *Ossliabya* sank a shell wrecked the after-turret of the *Suvaroff*, tearing the after-bridge to pieces with the flying fragments. Her steering gear was temporarily disabled, and she drifted from her station at the head of the line. One by one in quick succession the heavy steel masts and two huge funnels crashed down. The upper deck was impassable from end to end. In the midst of the confused wreckage handfuls of brave men fought the fires with buckets as they broke out now here now there. Most of the guns were silent. "She no longer looked like a ship," says a Japanese account.

When the *Suvaroff* swerved out of the line at a few minutes before three o'clock her steering gear had been disabled, and probably for a few minutes before the crisis she had not been answering her helm. The course of the fleet, while she led it during the fight with the Japanese armoured fleet, had been due east, but, as she lost her direction, it turned slightly to the south. When she drifted away from the line the *Imperator Alexander III* became the leading ship. Captain Buchvostoff, who commanded her, led the fleet in a circle round the disabled *Suvaroff*, first running southwards, increasing the distance from the enemy, and then sweeping round as if trying to break through to the northward.

Togo followed on a parallel course until the Russian fleet seemed to be going due south, then he signalled an order, and, as accurately as if they were performing a practice evolution at manœuvres, his twelve ships turned simultaneously through half a circle, thus reversing the direction and changing the order of the fleet so that the last ship in the line became the leader. As the Russians swept round to the north Togo was thus ready to cross their bows, and the *Alexander* received the concentrated fire of several ships.

She turned eastwards, followed by her consorts in a straggling line, and then drifted out of her place at the head of it, leaking badly, and with her upper works ablaze. On a smoother sea the *Tsarevitch* had been hit once below the armour belt on 10 August.

The *Borodino* now had the dangerous post at the head of the line. It steamed eastwards for nearly an hour, followed by Togo on a parallel course, the Japanese fire only slackening when fog and smoke obscured its targets, and the fire of the Russians dwindling minute by minute, as gun position after position became untenable or guns were disabled and dismounted.

Long before this the divisions of protected cruisers under Admiral Dewa and his colleagues had worked round to the southward of the Russians. Dewa and Uriu, with their swift ships, were in action by a quarter to three. The slower ships of Takeomi and the younger Togo's squadrons, united under the command of Rear-Admiral Kataoka, came into the fight a little later. In the heavy sea that was running the light cruisers afforded a less steady platform for the guns than the big armoured ships, and their fire was not so terribly destructive.

But it was effective enough, and that of the Russian rear ships was hopelessly bad. The Japanese cruisers drove the transports and their escort, in a huddled crowd, north-eastwards towards the main Russian fleet. The great wall sides of the German liner, now the auxiliary cruiser *Ural*, were riddled, and the giant began to settle down in the water. The cruiser *Svietlana*, hit badly in the forepart, was dangerously down by the head. The transports *Kamschatka* and *Irtish* were both set on fire, and the latter was also pierced along the water-line. She sank at four o'clock. The *Oleg* and *Aurora* were both badly damaged.

But the Japanese unarmoured cruisers did not escape scath-

THE RUSSIAN BATTLESHIP *OREL*
TAKEN AFTER THE BATTLE OF TSU-SHIMA, SHOWING EFFECTS
OF JAPANESE SHELL FIRE

less. Dewa's fine cruiser, the *Kasagi*, was badly hit below the waterline, and was in such danger of sinking that he handed the command of his squadron over to Uriu and, escorted by the *Chitose*, steamed out of the fight, steering for the Japanese coast. Togo's old ship, the famous *Naniwa Kan*, was also hit below the water-line, and had to cease firing and devote all the energy of the crew to saving the ship.

At five o'clock the Russian fleet, battleships, cruisers, and transports, were huddled together in a confused crowd, attacked from the eastward by Togo and Kamimura with the heavy squadrons, while from the south the line of light cruisers under Uriu and Kataoka poured a cross-fire into them. Away to the westward lay the disabled and burning *Suvaroff* with the Russian naval flag, the blue cross of St. Andrew on a white ground, still flying from a flagstaff in the smoke. The admiral had been twice wounded, the second blow slightly fracturing his skull, and making it difficult for him to speak. Her captain, Ignazius, had been simply blown to pieces by a Japanese shell while, after being already twice wounded, he was directing a desperate effort to master the conflagration on board.

The decks were strewn with dead, the mess-deck full of helpless wounded men. Most of the guns were out of action, but a 6-inch quick-firer and a few lighter guns were kept in action, and drove off the first attempt of the Japanese destroyers to dash in and sink her. Still there was no thought of surrender. The few survivors of her crew fought with dogged Russian courage to the last. A torpedo destroyer, the *Buiny*, taking terrible risks, came up to her, hung on for a few moments to her shattered side, and succeeded in getting off the wounded admiral and a few officers and men. Rojdestvensky sent a last message to Nebogatoff, telling him to take over the command and try to get through with some part of the fleet to Vladivostock.

About half-past five some of the Russian ships struggled out of the press, led by the burning *Borodino*, with the *Orel* next to her. In the straggling line battleships and cruisers, armoured and unarmoured, were mingled together. The *Alexander* had succeeded in stopping some of her leaks and had rejoined the line. She was near the end of it. The *Ural*, deserted by her crew, was drifting, till one of Togo's battleships sank her with a few shots.

The Russians were now steering northwards, and for the moment there was no large ship in front of them. The Japanese could have easily headed them off, but Togo now regarded them as a huntsman regards a herd of deer that he is driving before him. The Japanese squadron steamed after them at reduced speed, just keeping at convenient range, the heavy ships on their right, the light squadrons behind them.

At first the armoured ships concentrated their fire on the Alexander. Shells were bursting all over her, and throwing up geysers of water about her bows. Then the merciless fire was turned on the *Borodino*. A few minutes after seven the *Alexander* was seen to capsize and disappear. A quarter of an hour later there was an explosion on board of the *Borodino*. Next moment a patch of foam on the waves showed where she had been. About the same time a division of torpedo-boats came upon the unfortunate *Suvaroff*, torpedoed her, and saved some of the crew, who were found floating on the water after she sank.

As the sun went down, and the twilight darkened into night, the firing died away. What was left of the Russian fleet was steaming slowly into the Sea of Japan, some of the ships isolated, others holding together in improvised divisions, all bearing terrible marks of the fight, some of them still on fire, others leaking badly.

Togo had been hit during the fight, but it was only a slight bruise. The losses of his fleet had been trifling. Of the armoured ships the only one that had been badly hit was the *Asama*. She was struck by three shells aft near the water-line, her rudder was disabled, and she was leaking badly. She left the fighting-line for a while, but was able temporarily to repair damages, and rejoined later in the day.

At sunset Togo ordered his squadrons to steam north-eastward during the night, and unite at sunrise at a point south of Matsu-shima or Ullondo Island. They were to keep away from the Russian ships in the darkness. The victorious admiral was about to let loose his torpedo flotillas, to complete the destruction of the flying enemy, and meant that his torpedo officers should have no anxiety about hitting friends in the dark.

He had with the main fleet twenty-one destroyers organized in five squadrons. In the bays of Tsu-shima nearly eighty torpedo-boats had been sheltering all day. The destroyers had been directed to pursue and attack the beaten enemy during the night. No orders had been given to the torpedo-boats. The sea was going down, but it was still rough, and Togo had doubts about risking the smaller craft. But without orders, sixteen groups of four boats each, sixty-four in all, got up steam and sallied out into the darkness.

It was an awful night for the Russians. After dark they had extinguished the fires lighted by the enemy's shells, and in some cases got collision mats over the leaks. The dead were committed to the sea, the wounded collected and cared for. For more than an hour they were allowed to hold their course uninterrupted, and the lights of the Japanese fleet were disappearing far astern. After all, Vladivostock might be reached. But just after eight o'clock the throb of engines, the hurtling beat of propellers, came sounding through the night from all sides.

On the sea black, low objects were rushing along with foaming phosphorescent wakes trailing behind them. Bugles ran out the alarm; crews rushed to quarters; searchlights blazed out, and the small quick-firers that were still serviceable mingled their sharp ringing reports with the crackle of machine-gun fire. The sea seemed to be swarming with torpedo craft. They appeared and disappeared in the beams of the searchlights, and the surface of the water was marked with the long white ripples raised by the rush of discharged torpedoes.

Loud explosions, now here now there, told that some of them had found their target, though in the confusion and the rough sea there were more misses than hits. The *Sissoi Veliki,* which had been on fire in the action, and pierced below the waterline, had a new and more serious leak torn open in her stern, the rudder was damaged and two propeller blades torn off. But she floated till next day. Several ships received minor injuries, but kept afloat with one or more compartments flooded. But the effect of the attack was to disperse the fugitive Russians in all directions.

When it began Nebogatoff was at the head of a line of ships in the old battleship *Imperator Nikolai I*. In the confusion only three of the line kept up with him, the much-battered *Orel* and the *Admiral Apraxin* and *Admiral Senyavin*. The *Orel* had no searchlight left intact. The *Nikolai* and the two others did not switch on their searchlights, and kept all other lights shaded. The remarkable result was that as they moved northwards through the darkness they were never attacked, though more than once between 8 p.m. and midnight they saw the enemy's torpedo craft rushing past them. The ships with searchlights drew all the attacks.

Admiral Enquist, with his flag in the *Oleg*, and followed by the *Aurora* and *Jemschug*, had run in amongst the remains of the transport flotilla at the first alarm, narrowly escaping collision with them. Then he turned south, in the hope of shaking the enemy off, but came upon another flotilla arriving from that direction. He had some narrow escapes. The lookouts of the *Oleg* counted seventeen torpedoes that just missed the ship. Having got away, he tried more than once to turn back to the northward, but each time he ran in among hostile torpedo-boats, and saw that beyond them were ships with searchlights working and guns in action, so he steered again south.

At last he gave up the attempt and headed for the Tsu-shima Straits. He got safely through them, because the main Japanese fleet was miles away, steaming steadily north, with tired men sleeping by the guns. Next day he was in the open sea with no enemy in sight, and set his course for Shanghai.

At midnight the defeated Russians thought they had at last shaken off the pursuit of the sea-wolves. But at 2 a.m. the attacks began again. The *Navarin* and the *Admiral Nakhimoff*, among the rearmost ships, were attacked by Commander Suzuki's squadron of destroyers. The *Navarin* was sunk after being hit by two torpedoes. The *Nakhimoff* was severely damaged. About the same time the *Vladimir Monomach* and the *Dimitri Donskoi* were torpedoed, but managed to keep afloat. The attacking force had a good many casualties. Torpedo-boats Nos. 35 and 65 were sunk by the Russian fire. Their crews were rescued by their consorts. Four destroyers (the *Harusami, Akatsuki, Izazuchi,* and *Yugiri*) and two torpedo-boats (Nos. 31 and 68) were so seriously damaged by hostile fire, or by collision in the darkness, that they were put out of action. As the dawn began to whiten the eastern sky the torpedo flotillas drew off.

At sunrise the Russian fleet was scattered far over the Sea of Japan. Some of the ships for a while steamed alone with neither consort nor enemy in sight within the circle of the horizon. But new dangers came with the day. Togo's fleet was at hand, flinging out a wide net of which the meshes were squadrons and detached cruisers to sweep the sea northwards, and gather up the remnants of the defeated enemy. The weather was clearing up, and it was a fine, bright day—just the day for the work the Japanese had to do.

Steaming steadily through the night, Togo, with the main body of the Japanese fleet, had passed to eastward of the scattered Russians, and was about twenty miles south of Ullondo. The distances covered in this battle of Tsu-shima were beyond any that had ever been known in naval war. The running fight during the night had passed over more than 150 miles of sea. At 5.20 a.m. the admiral on board the *Mikasa* received a wireless message from Kataoka's cruisers, reporting that they were sixty miles away to the southward of him, and that they could see several columns of black smoke on the horizon to the eastward. Shortly after Kataoka sent another wireless message—"Four of the enemy's battleships and two cruisers are in sight, steering north-west." Togo at once signalled to his own ships to head off this detachment of the enemy, and sent wireless orders to Kataoka and Uriu to close in on their rear. It was probably the main fighting division left to the Russians, and would soon be surrounded by an overwhelming Japanese force.

The ships sighted by the cruisers were those that Admiral Nebogatoff had led through the night, and was trying to take to Vladivostock. He had with him the battleships *Nikolai I* and *Orel*, the coast-defence armour-clads *Admiral Apraxin* and *Admiral Senyavin*, and the cruisers *Izumrud* and *Svietlana*. This last ship was leaking badly and down by the bows. She could not keep up with the others, and at daylight fell far astern and lost sight of them. At 7 a.m. Uriu's division in chase of *Nebogatoff* came up with her, and the cruisers *Niitaka* and *Otowa* were detached to capture her.

The Russian captain, Schein, had held a council with his officers. He had only a hundred shells left in the magazines, and the *Svietlana* was being kept afloat by her steam pumps. Under the regulations he could have honourably surrendered to a superior force, but it was unanimously resolved to fight to the last shot, and then sink with colours flying. The fight lasted an hour. There were heavy losses. The Japanese fire riddled the ship, and first the starboard, then the port engine was disabled. As the hundredth shot rang out from the *Svietlana's* guns, Captain Schein stopped the pumps and opened the sea-cocks, and the ship settled down rapidly in the water. The Japanese cruisers went off to join the fleet as the *Svietlana* disappeared, but an armed Japanese liner, the *America Maru*, stood by and picked up about a hundred men.

At 10.30 a.m. Nebogatoff was completely surrounded eighteen miles south of the island of Takeshima. The *Izumrud* had used her superior speed to get away to the south-west. The four battered ships that remained with him saw more than twenty enemies appear from all points of the compass, including Togo's battleships and heavy armoured cruisers, all as fit for work as when the first fighting began. They opened fire at long range with their heavy guns.

The situation was desperate. Nebogatoff consulted his officers, and all those on board the *Nikolai* agreed that he must surrender. In a memorandum he subsequently wrote he pointed out that, though some ammunition was left, the Japanese were using their superior speed to keep a distance at which he could not reply effectively to their overwhelming fire; neither the shore nor other ships were within reach; most of the boats had been shattered, the rest could not be lowered; even the life-belts had been burned or used to improvise defences in the ships; continued resistance or the act of sinking the ships would only mean the useless sacrifice of some 2000 men. After the ships had been only a short time in action, during which time they received further severe damage, he hauled down his colours. Togo allowed the Russian officers to retain their swords, as a proof of his opinion that they had acted as befitted brave and honourable men.

While the brief action with Nebogatoff's squadron was in progress, the third of the Russian coast-defence battleships, the *Admiral Ushakoff*, hove in sight. She turned off to the westward pursued by the armoured cruisers *Iwate* and *Yakumo*. They soon overhauled her, and signalled a summons to surrender, adding that Nebogatoff had already done so. The *Ushakoff* replied with her 9-inch guns. The cruisers sank her in an hour, and then rescued some three-fourths of her crew of 400 men.

The *Sissoi Veliki*, badly injured in the action of the day before, and torpedoed during the night, was in a sinking condition when the sun rose on 28 May. No ships were in sight, all the boats had been destroyed, and while the pumps were still kept going the crew was set to work to construct rafts. While this was being done with very scanty materials, the *Vladimir Monomach* hove in sight, accompanied by the destroyer *Iromki*. In reply to a signal for help, the *Monomach* answered that she could do nothing, as she was herself expecting to sink soon. The *Iromki* offered to take a few men, but the captain of the *Sissoi* generously refused to deprive the *Monomach* of her help. The two ships then steamed away. An hour later the *Sissoi* was just settling down in the water, when three Japanese armed merchant steamers appeared and took off her crew. At half-past ten the *Sissoi* heeled over to starboard and sank.

Soon after she lost sight of the *Sissoi*, the *Monomach* came upon the armoured cruiser *Admiral Nakhimoff*, which also signalled that she was in a sinking condition. Presently there was smoke on the horizon, and then the armed steamer *Sadu Maru* and the Japanese destroyer *Shiranui* appeared. In such conditions the enemy proved a friend. The crews of the two unfortunate ships were transferred to the *Sadu*, which stood by till, about ten o'clock, both the *Nakhimoff* and the *Monomach* went to the bottom.

The *Navarin* was comparatively little injured in the battle, but was torpedoed during the night. Leaking badly, she struggled northward at a slow rate till two in the afternoon of the 28th, when she was found and attacked by a Japanese destroyer flotilla. She still made a fight with her lighter guns, and was hit by two torpedoes. The crew were all at their battle stations when she began suddenly to sink. The order, "All hands on deck," came too late, and very few lives were saved.

The armoured cruiser *Dimitri Donskoi*, last survivor of Rojdestvensky's fourteen battleships and armoured cruisers, escaped the torpedo attacks in the night, and eluded pursuit all through the morning of the 28th. At 4 p.m., when she was near the island of Ullondo, she sighted some Japanese ships in the distance, Uriu's cruiser division and some destroyers. They closed slowly on her, and it was not till six o'clock that she was attacked by the cruisers *Niitaka* and *Otowa*, and three destroyers. The *Donskoi* made a gallant fight for two hours, beating off the torpedo-boats, losing sixty killed and twice as many wounded, and finally disengaging herself in the darkness about eight o'clock.

The water-line armour was intact, but one boiler was penetrated and ammunition was nearly exhausted. In the night, the captain, who was himself slightly wounded, decided to land his men on Ullondo Island and sink the ship. All the boats had been shattered and the cutter that was left had to be hastily repaired before it could be lowered. With the one boat the disembarkation went on slowly during the night. At dawn the enemy's torpedo-boats were sighted. The rest of the crew jumped overboard and swam ashore, leaving a few men with the second-in-command on the ship. They ran the *Donskoi* out into a hundred fathoms of water, opened the sea-cocks, embarked in their one boat, and saw their ship go down as they pulled ashore. The Japanese sent a couple of steamers to take the crew off the island.

The torpedo destroyer that conveyed the wounded Admiral Rojdestvensky, Captain Semenoff, and a few other officers and men away from the fight was found and captured by a Japanese flotilla during the afternoon of the 28th.

The cruiser *Izumrud*, one of the few fast ships the Russians had with them, escaped the torpedo attacks in the night. In the morning she was chased by several of the enemy's cruisers. She kept up a good speed, and one by one they abandoned the chase, the *Chitose* being the last to give it up. By 2 p.m. all pursuit was left behind, and she reduced speed. In the battle and the chase she had burned so much coal that she had not enough left to make for Vladivostock, so she steered for Vladimir Bay, in the Russian Coast Province of Siberia, north of Korea. She was off the entrance of the Bay at midnight with only ten tons of coal left in her bunkers.

Unfortunately, in trying to go in in the dark on the flood-tide she drove hard on a reef. Next day unsuccessful efforts were made to get his ship off and in the afternoon, as her captain expected the enemy's ships might arrive to secure the Izumrud and refloat her, he landed his crew on Russian ground, destroyed his guns one by one with blasting charges, and then blew up the ship.

The destroyer *Groki* was chased and captured by the Japanese destroyer *Shiranui* and a torpedo-boat, and after a sharp fight close to Tsu-shima Island surrendered at 11.30 a.m. She was so injured that she sank within an hour of her capture. Admiral Enquist, with the three protected cruisers *Oleg, Aurora*, and *Jemschug*, had, after turning south for the last time during the night of torpedo attacks, got through the Tsu-shima Straits in the darkness. Next day no enemy was in sight, and he steered for Shanghai under easy steam, repairing damages on the way. He intended to lie off the port, bring a couple of colliers out of the

Woosung River, fill his bunkers at sea, and try to reach Vladivostock by the Pacific and the La Pérouse Straits.

On the morning of the 29th he was overtaken by the repairing ship and tug *Svir*, and from her learned the full extent of the disaster. Fearing that if he approached Shanghai he would be driven into the port and blockaded by the enemy, he changed his course for Manila, where he arrived on 3 June. The *Svir*, after communicating with him, had gone on to the Woosung River. She was joined on her way there by the transport *Anadir*, which had got successfully south through the Tsu-shima Straits. The transport Korea, which had escaped in the same way, and had a cargo of coal, did not go to Woosung, but crossed the Indian Ocean and appeared unexpectedly in the French port of Diego Suarez in Madagascar. Of the nine torpedo destroyers with the Russian fleet seven were hunted down and sunk or taken by the Japanese.

The only ships of all the Russian armada that finally reached Vladivostock were the two destroyers *Brawy* and *Gresny*, and the small swift cruiser *Almaz*. She had been with Enquist's cruiser division in the first hours of the night after the battle. During the torpedo attacks she had become separated from her consorts. Escaping from the destroyers, she headed at full speed first towards the coast of Japan, then northward. At sunrise on the 28th she was well on her way and many miles north-east of Togo's fleet. Next day she reached Vladivostock with 160 tons of coal still on board.

A hundred years after Trafalgar Togo had won a victory as complete and as decisive. The Russian power had been swept from the Eastern Seas, and the grey-haired admiral who had secured this triumph for his native land—"Father Togo," as the Japanese affectionately call him—had lived through the whole evolution of the Imperial Navy, had shared in its first successes, and for years had been training it for the great struggle that was to decide who was to be master in the seas of the Far East.

The war was followed by an immediate expansion of the Japanese Navy. Numbers of captured Russian ships were repaired, re-armed, and placed in the Navy List under Japanese names. No longer dependent on foreign builders, the Japanese yards were kept busy turning out yet a new navy of every class, from the battleship to the torpedo-boat. The laying down of the gigantic *Aki* and *Satsuma*, battleships of over 20,000 tons, opened a new period in naval construction, and nations began to count their sea-power by the number of *Dreadnoughts* afloat or on the slips.

The great maritime powers are now engaged in a race of construction, and the next naval war will see forces in action far surpassing even the armadas that met at Tsu-shima. And maritime war, hitherto confined to the surface of the sea, will have strange auxiliaries in the submarine stealing beneath it, and the airship and aeroplane scouting in the upper air. But still, whatever new appliances, whatever means of mutual destruction science supplies, the lesson taught by the story of all naval war will remain true. Victory will depend not on elaborate mechanical structures and appliances, but on the men, and will be the reward of long training, iron discipline, calm, enduring courage, and the leadership that can inspire confidence, command self-sacrificing obedience, divine an enemy's plans, and decide swiftly and resolutely on the way in which they are to be frustrated.

ALSO FROM LEONAUR
AVAILABLE IN SOFTCOVER OR HARDCOVER WITH DUST JACKET

DOING OUR 'BIT' by *Ian Hay*—Two Classic Accounts of the Men of Kitchener's 'New Army' During the Great War including *The First 100,000* & *All In It*.

AN EYE IN THE STORM by *Arthur Ruhl*—An American War Correspondent's Experiences of the First World War from the Western Front to Gallipoli and Beyond.

STAND & FALL by *Joe Cassells*—A Soldier's Recollections of the 'Contemptible Little Army' and the Retreat from Mons to the Marne, 1914.

RIFLEMAN MACGILL'S WAR by *Patrick MacGill*—A Soldier of the London Irish During the Great War in Europe including *The Amateur Army, The Red Horizon* & *The Great Push*.

WITH THE GUNS by *C. A. Rose & Hugh Dalton*—Two First Hand Accounts of British Gunners at War in Europe During World War 1- Three Years in France with the Guns and With the British Guns in Italy.

EAGLES OVER THE TRENCHES by *James R. McConnell & William B. Perry*—Two First Hand Accounts of the American Escadrille at War in the Air During World War 1-Flying For France: With the American Escadrille at Verdun and Our Pilots in the Air.

THE BUSH WAR DOCTOR by *Robert V. Dolbey*—The Experiences of a British Army Doctor During the East African Campaign of the First World War.

THE 9TH—THE KING'S (LIVERPOOL REGIMENT) IN THE GREAT WAR 1914 - 1918 by *Enos H. G. Roberts*—Like many large cities, Liverpool raised a number of battalions in the Great War. Notable among them were the Pals, the Liverpool Irish and Scottish, but this book concerns the wartime history of the 9th Battalion – The Kings.

THE GAMBARDIER by *Mark Severn*—The experiences of a battery of Heavy artillery on the Western Front during the First World War.

FROM MESSINES TO THIRD YPRES by *Thomas Floyd*—A personal account of the First World War on the Western front by a 2/5th Lancashire Fusilier.

THE IRISH GUARDS IN THE GREAT WAR - VOLUME 1 by *Rudyard Kipling*—Edited and Compiled from Their Diaries and Papers Volume 1 The First Battalion.

THE IRISH GUARDS IN THE GREAT WAR - VOLUME 2 by *Rudyard Kipling*—Edited and Compiled from Their Diaries and Papers Volume 2 The Second Battalion.

AVAILABLE ONLINE AT **www.leonaur.com**
AND OTHER GOOD BOOK STORES

ALSO FROM LEONAUR
AVAILABLE IN SOFTCOVER OR HARDCOVER WITH DUST JACKET

ARMOURED CARS IN EDEN by *K. Roosevelt*—An American President's son serving in Rolls Royce armoured cars with the British in Mesopotamia & with the American Artillery in France during the First World War.

CHASSEUR OF 1914 by *Marcel Dupont*—Experiences of the twilight of the French Light Cavalry by a young officer during the early battles of the great war in Europe.

TROOP HORSE & TRENCH by *R.A. Lloyd*—The experiences of a British Lifeguardsman of the household cavalry fighting on the western front during the First World War 1914-18.

THE LONG PATROL by *George Berrie*—A Novel of Light Horsemen from Gallipoli to the Palestine campaign of the First World War.

THE EAST AFRICAN MOUNTED RIFLES by *C.J. Wilson*—Experiences of the campaign in the East African bush during the First World War

THE FIGHTING CAMELIERS by *Frank Reid*—The exploits of the Imperial Camel Corps in the desert and Palestine campaigns of the First World War.

WITH THE IMPERIAL CAMEL CORPS IN THE GREAT WAR by *Geoffrey Inchbald*—The story of a serving officer with the British 2nd battalion against the Senussi and during the Palestine campaign.

STEEL CHARIOTS IN THE DESERT by *S.C. Rolls*—The first world war experiences of a Rolls Royce armoured car driver with the Duke of Westminster in Libya and in Arabia with T.E. Lawrence.

INFANTRY BRIGADE: 1914 by *Edward Gleichen*—The Diary of a Commander of the 15th Infantry Brigade, 5th Division, British Army, During the Retreat from Mons

HEARTS & DRAGONS by *Charles R. M. F. Crutwell*—The 4th Royal Berkshire Regiment in France and Italy During the Great War, 1914-1918.

TIGERS ALONG THE TIGRIS by *E. J. Thompson*—The Leicestershire Regiment in Mesopotamia During the First World War.

DESPATCH RIDER by *W. H. L. Watson*—The Experiences of a British Army Motorcycle Despatch Rider During the Opening Battles of the Great War in Europe.

ALSO FROM LEONAUR
AVAILABLE IN SOFTCOVER OR HARDCOVER WITH DUST JACKET

A JOURNAL OF THE SECOND SIKH WAR by *Daniel A. Sandford*—The Experiences of an Ensign of the 2nd Bengal European Regiment During the Campaign in the Punjab, India, 1848-49.

LAKE'S CAMPAIGNS IN INDIA by *Hugh Pearse*—The Second Anglo Maratha War, 1803-1807. Often neglected by historians and students alike, Lake's Indian campaign was fought against a resourceful and ruthless enemy-almost always superior in numbers to his own forces.

BRITAIN IN AFGHANISTAN 1: THE FIRST AFGHAN WAR 1839-42 by *Archibald Forbes*—Following over a century of the gradual assumption of sovereignty of the Indian Sub-Continent, the British Empire, in the form of the Honourable East India Company, supported by troops of the new Queen Victoria's army, found itself inevitably at the natural boundaries that surround Afghanistan. There it set in motion a series of disastrous events-the first of which was to march into the country at all.

BRITAIN IN AFGHANISTAN 2: THE SECOND AFGHAN WAR 1878-80 by *Archibald Forbes*—This the history of the Second Afghan War-another episode of British military history typified by savagery, massacre, siege and battles.

UP AMONG THE PANDIES by *Vivian Dering Majendie*—An outstanding account of the campaign for the fall of Lucknow. This is a vital book of war as fought by the British Army of the mid-nineteenth century, but in truth it is also an essential book of war that will enthral.

BLOW THE BUGLE, DRAW THE SWORD by *W. H. G. Kingston*—The Wars, Campaigns, Regiments and Soldiers of the British & Indian Armies During the Victorian Era, 1839-1898.

INDIAN MUTINY 150th ANNIVERSARY: A LEONAUR ORIGINAL

MUTINY: 1857 by *James Humphries*—It is now 150 years since the 'Indian Mutiny' burst like an engulfing flame on the British soldiers, their families and the civilians of the Empire in North East India. The Bengal Native army arose in violent rebellion, and the once peaceful countryside became a battleground as Native sepoys and elements of the Indian population massacred their British masters and defeated them in open battle. As the tide turned, a vengeful army of British and loyal Indian troops repressed the insurgency with a savagery that knew no mercy. It was a time of fear and slaughter. James Humphries has drawn together the voices of those dreadful days for this commemorative book.

AVAILABLE ONLINE AT
www.leonaur.com
AND OTHER GOOD BOOK STORES

www.ingramcontent.com/pod-product-compliance
Lightning Source LLC
Chambersburg PA
CBHW030217170426
43201CB00006B/116